At Home Entertaining

The Art of Hosting a Party
with Style and Panache

Jorj Morgan

CUMBERLAND HOUSE
NASHVILLE, TENNESSEE

Published by

CUMBERLAND HOUSE PUBLISHING, INC.
431 Harding Industrial Drive
Nashville, Tennessee 37211
www.cumberlandhouse.com

Cover design by Karen Phillips
Text design by Julie Pitkin

Library of Congress Cataloging-in-Publication Data has been applied for.

ISBN 1-58182-306-1

Printed in Canada

1 2 3 4 5 6 7 8 9 10—05 04 03 02

At Home Entertaining

To Morgo, twenty-five years and it just keeps getting better. I love you.
To Trey, Chris, and Jon—you make me so incredibly proud.

In loving memory of my mother, Re Re Magner, who taught me everything there was to learn
about being a wife and a mom... I will always miss her.

Contents

Foreword

I have always loved to party. In fact, when I was first introduced to my soon-to-be-father-in-law, he was a little concerned that I was too much of a party girl. Twenty-five years later, he and I have bonded over many a celebration, everything from a great football win, to a milestone birthday, to a summer cookout and to all of our holiday get togethers. Whatever the occasion, I can count on my father-in-law to be part of the good times and he can count on the fact that I will have as much fun as he does.

The secret to throwing a great party is to be a relaxed host or hostess. Your guests want to be with you—not your fondue. You set the tone for your party and ultimately it's your style, smile and panache that guarantee that your guests will enjoy themselves.

Your style shows through whether you are hosting a casual backyard patio party or a sit-down, fussy affair. The setting you choose, your attention to detail, the menu you create is all evidence of your style. For example, you can host a cook-out in your backyard by simply setting a picnic table with a plastic cloth, some paper plates, disposable utensils and a potted plant for decorations. Or you can host a backyard party and design individual picnic baskets for each guest. You can throw blankets on the lawn and organize a scavenger hunt for entertainment. Both of these parties are held in the backyard and are an easy way to entertain—but which one of these party plans shows off your style?

The idea for a backyard party featuring individual picnic baskets was born out of an Easter celebration that I hosted for my family that included eight adults and eight children from ages two to twelve. I wanted to organize the food so that both the children and the adults could enjoy their afternoon. Toddlers munched on chicken fingers packed in colorful straw baskets with side dishes of applesauce and Jell-O. Bigger kids unpacked salads with their fried chicken and adults discovered spicy muffins and veggie slaw in their baskets. There was something for everyone—including either a chocolate bunny or a sweet lemon tart. After the baskets were emptied, we turned them into containers to collect plastic eggs that had been hidden in the bushes. The eggs were filled with jelly beans, pennies and stickers. Everyone had a blast, and after awhile no one minded that the Easter outfits definitely needed to be dry-cleaned.

My love of throwing parties soon led to a partnership with my two great friends when we formed our party planning and catering business. We drew on our entire home entertaining experience to create fun events for special customers. We used the individual basket theme when we created a sunset picnic supper for a corporate client. The party givers wanted a formal affair in an informal setting. We decided to erect a white tent on a beautiful lawn and line the perimeter with potted shrubs, creating a fragrant and aesthetic outdoor atmosphere. Smaller shrubs were used to section off a portion of the tent for cocktails and passed hors d'oeuvres that we served at 5 o'clock in the afternoon. As the sun began to fall, the guests moved further into the tent. We set tables for ten with floral printed cloths. At each place setting we set a green painted basket. Inside the baskets, guests discovered china plates, silver utensils, a crystal wine glass, coordinating cloth napkins and individual vases, which held a single floral stem. We stationed a server/helper at each table whose first task was to unpack the baskets. The vases and emptied baskets became the table centerpieces. The menu was created so that each table was served family style with platters of seconds passed around by the helpers. The style of the party was formal and informal at the same time. We had created an outdoor sunset picnic supper that was a huge success.

When you design your party, remember that style is as uncomplicated as throwing a weekday supper for pals and serving all of the food from pots cooking on the stove. Style is hosting a bridal shower that you craft as a tea party. Style is serving breakfast after dark and throwing an everyday celebration just for the two of you. Style is asking the gang back to your place for dinner when the game is rained out or hosting a paella party to celebrate Cinco de Mayo.

Spontaneous parties can be as much—and even more fun than those that are planned out weeks in advance. During a visit to my son in Washington, D.C., we hosted a party for my cousins who live in the area, but who we hadn't seen in years. Trey also took this opportunity to invite several of his friends. We ended up having over 30 people in his two-bedroom apartment. We moved the furniture against the wall, and Trey and I moved into the kitchen. We created the fillings for quesadilla. With only two burners, we could only prepare one or two at a time. His tiny oven would not hold the overflow—so our continuous quesadilla party was born. Much like an omelet station, we cooked quesadilla to order and offered fresh guacamole and salsa for condiments. Everyone had a great time—including Trey and I—a great short order tag team!

A host's smile is the greatest weapon against the party pitfalls that can occur to even the most experienced party-giver. I remember throwing a dinner party for friends that we met at our children's school. My hubby and I invited several couples that we had only barely met. These were cool parents—you know the ones that bring their totally trained golden retriever to pet day while you are scrambling to find a lizard from the yard to put in a shoebox. This is the mother at the science fair who stands next to her son's paper mache volcano watching the suds erupt on cue, while you are running around the back of the grocery store looking for moldy bread because you couldn't grow it to save your life. This is the father of the star pitcher who plays catch for hours every evening while you search the house for your child's glove. These were the totally cool parents.

I planned a sit down affair using my best china and silver. The flowers were perfect, the music was just loud enough, the conversation was sparkling and the kids were asleep. Things were going along quite well. Until dessert. In honor of the fall season, I prepared—from scratch—Indian pudding, a rich concoction of molasses and corn meal that bakes for hours and hours and gives off a heavenly aroma. I served spoonfuls of the warm, brown pudding in individual Val Saint-Lambert crystal bowls placed on top of matching dessert plates to each guest. After I was seated, I noticed that everyone was looking at the dessert, quizzically. A bold dad, Ed, even poked around at it a bit. Before I could explain the ingredients and origins of the pudding, Ed looked at me in all sincerity and asked, "What is this? It looks like Great Dane dog do." Seven pairs of wide eyes looked at me waiting for a reply. I smiled my brightest smile and replied, "Of course it's not Great Dane dog do. Only the best for you guys—it's domestic—American dog do." I immediately plunged my spoon into the pudding, took a huge mouthful and smiled yummily. Our guests took my cue, dug into the dish, and had a huge laugh. These pals still turn up at my parties—and are still kidding me on my "Great Dane Doggie Doo Dessert."

The first boat party that we catered had an interesting complication. We had designed a menu for fifty guests and presented it to the clients—who loved all of our ideas. On the day of the party, we arrived at the dock, several hours before the event with cartons and cartons of food and libations. As we started to move the provisions onto the boat, we discovered that the galley was a closet-size, windowless room that could hold only one of us at a time. We scouted around, trying to figure out how we were going to cook all of the food that we had brought along. This was the precise moment that I discovered that even though the boat was securely tied to the dock and even though the seas were calm, that once I stepped onto the deck—I was seasick! Smiling our way through all of the tasks was the only way that we got through that party. But my partners never allowed me near a boat again!

Your smile gets you through the rough spots, such as spilled red wine on your snow white tablecloth, a leaky diaper on a dining room chair, burned marinara sauce, undercooked lamb, forgetting to place forks on the dessert table or spoons by the coffee. Whatever the snag, your smile is the trick that lets everyone know things are okay. After all, red wine comes out of a tablecloth with a little salt, a well placed pillow covers chair stains, a little added sugar removes the burned taste from sauce and just a reach into a drawer solves a utensil problem. Solutions are made easy with a great big smile, and your guests will smile back as they pitch in to lend a hand.

Panache is that little part of you that thumbs your nose at traditions. That part of you that wears white shoes after Labor Day, serves baked ham for Thanksgiving dinner or uses real butter (in place of the politically correct fat-free substitutes) in your cooking. Panache takes style to the next level. It dares you to be different, to create an atmosphere that is unique, a menu that is distinctive and a party that will leave them smiling for days afterwards.

A host with panache throws a blanket by the fireplace in the winter and invites a special someone to dinner for two. A hostess with panache places over sized pillows around a coffee table and serves fondue to guests sitting on the floor. Panache compels you to host lunch at the beach when the weather turns warm and to create tapas by the ton for an informal cocktail party. Panache forces you to get the gang together to say goodbye to good friends or to howl at the moon for no reason at all. Panache comes from that tiny voice inside you that wants you to be slightly daring in your party planning. And, with good reason—being a little daring can be a whole bunch of fun.

I threw a surprise birthday party for my husband and invited one hundred guests from class mates, to college pals, to business group associates, to relatives, to golfing buddies. I themed it a "baby-boomer" party and invited everyone to dress in their preppiest attire—circle pins on girls, Izod golf shirts, loafers, khakis and madras shorts in every shade of pink, blue and lime green. The invitation was a recreation of the front page of the local paper announcing that my baby boomer was approaching a milestone birthday. I had a sixties rock group for cocktails and a five piece band playing "Shout" throughout the evening. The entertainment consisted of a roast where the guests took turns toasting and bashing my blushing boomer. It was a great party! I prepared all of the food in advance, stashing it at neighbor's homes so that I could gather it just before the guests arrived and set everything out on buffet tables. I hired plenty of helpers and worked with each one so that they knew exactly what to do. It was a great success, and people enjoyed themselves so much, that we re-create this party every five years.

My baby-boomer celebration is just one example of panache. Taking a theme to the next level, adding over-the-top entertainment, terrific music, decorations and atmosphere, is the epitome of entertaining and really a fun way to partee.

Whether your style is sly and shy or over-the-top circus-like crazy, hosting a party is a terrific way to share yourself with friends and family. Working together with others to throw a party can be totally rewarding. Simply inviting friends for dinner or lunch is one of the best ways to reach out and bond friendships.

The party plans in this book are meant to spark your imagination and creativity. Take from them what you want. I encourage you to add your own special touches. Whatever your choice, know that you have my support. Email me with your party stories, tips and pitfall challenges. We'll smile together through problems, share war stories and I'll do my best to answer your questions at www.Jorj.com. Most importantly, you will be constantly reminded to have fun at your party. Isn't that really what celebrating is all about?

Happy Cooking and Happy Party!
Jorj Morgan

Party Basics

WHAT EVERY HOST SHOULD KNOW

You have weaned yourself from frozen foods, driven past the drive-through restaurant and discovered that room in the center of your home that houses pots and pans, what's next? Admit it, you are enjoying cooking great meals. Its kind of fun experimenting with fresh herbs and flavored oils. Experience has led to creativity and you have learned to treat recipes as guidelines, substituting with what you have on hand—or what is most available in the market. You have opened the door to your own creativity in the kitchen and you like it. You are comfortable—at home in the kitchen!

Now it's time to share your talents with your pals, family and coworkers. It's time for you to throw a PARTY.

There are a few things to keep in mind to insure that your party is a blast not a bust. Certain questions pop to mind. What are the secrets that separate great hosts and hostesses from everyday cooks? What little touches, special treats, organizational skills and talents do these people possess that you don't? The answer is simple—every outstanding host starts with an outstanding Party Plan.

The goal of a relaxed hostess is to enjoy her guests, effortlessly attending to their needs, while creating a warm, inviting atmosphere and a lasting impression. Sound stressful? Armed with a great party plan—a written record of all of the elements that you want to include in your party—stress never enters the picture.

Who do you want to invite? Do you want to incorporate a theme? What do you want to serve and where should you serve it? What should the invitations say—do you need to have favors? These are just some of the details that you should plan before you invite your first guest and some of the items covered in a well-thought-out party plan.

Think of yourself as the producer of a stage play. Your job is to create, direct, hire, orchestrate, costume and imagine the scenes of your party production. Your play can be as elaborate as a Broadway musical or as simple as a one-act puppet show. Regardless of the magnitude, thinking through the details will assure you as a hostess thus relax and welcome your guests to a wonderful experience.

Begin at the beginning—with the party motivation. Why do you want to host this party? Do you want to share an intimate evening with someone special? Do you want to get to know the new neighbors who just moved in across the street? Perhaps bonding with coworkers is just what the office needs to meet next month's goals—or maybe it's time to impress the boss. Whatever the reason for a celebratory get-together, motivation takes an important role in shaping the party. For example, the two of you will fast enjoy a candlelit supper suitable for soft conversation when set by a warm fire. An unstuffy, relaxed menu best serves a getting-to-know-each-other gathering while when impressing a boss or soon-to-be-mother in law, a little style and flare goes a long way.

The invitation is the part of the party plan that imparts your motivation—your reason to partee. The invitation can be as casual as a telephone conversation or email and as formal as a waxed-sealed engraved note delivered by a tuxedoed messenger, presented on a silver tray. The manner in which you invite your guests states your motivation, thus acting like the overture of the play.

The party backdrop sets the mood for your well-orchestrated affair. Four great pals, chatting into the wee hours, are perfectly arranged on oversized pillows sitting around a low coffee table while nibbling on four variations of fondue. A gaggle of chattering teens move easily from room to room sampling the allure of your home-based spa and snacking on spa-like food. A polished dining table is perfect for a multi course New Year's Eve dinner especially if the fare is as formal as the place setting.

Set the party mood further by creating your specific tone. Use props like candles for an intimate setting, fresh potted plants for an al fresco gathering, blankets with sports logos as table clothes when hosting a big game party, and a highly polished silver tea service for an afternoon bridal shower. Use picnic baskets for an Easter luncheon and thermal coolers for perfectly packed antipasti.

Your party scenes begin and end with the menu courses that your offer to your guests. Introduce the evening with an appetizer that will build to a sumptuous main course. Enhance the main attraction with an array of accompanying dishes. Prepare for a standing ovation as you present a huge splash of a dessert.

Your party menu is as simple or as complicated as you want it to be—a one-act monologue or a large cast extravaganza. Regardless of the size, the attention to detail is just as important with the former as it is with the latter.

The party strategy determines the plot of the production. When do you shop for groceries? How far in advance do you cook and clean? How do you breakdown a seven-course menu for twelve people into three evenings of preparation? Is it possible to host a backyard wedding for fifty and still catch the bouquet? The answer of course is yes! With a great party plan, your event will be a well-organized, stress free occasion that you will enjoys as much as your guests do.

What makes your event a little more special? How do you impart the special affection, warmth and congeniality that you want to convey to each of the guests that you have invited?

The denouement—the surprise, is that over-the top dish, favor or theme that you have taken the time to create. A well-constructed party plan allows you to carve out a little time to do a something special for your partygoers guaranteeing a happy guest.

Let's not forget the tricks of the trade. Those secret tidbits that professional party planners, caterers and experienced hosts and hostesses have learned by throwing tens of hundreds—even thousands of parties. Purchasing pre-made crepes, packages of gourmet lettuce or carrots that are already shredded, save time in the kitchen without impacting the quality of the dish. Using cake gel to decorate the inside of beverage glasses or choosing just the right music to croon through the sound system adds to the mystique of the evening. Details make the party and good planning allows you to remember the details.

All of the parties in this book come with a well-thought-out Party Plan. As with a critically acclaimed play, each plan includes all of the aspects that you will need to host the perfect party. Begin with the Party Motivation, the reason for throwing your special party and the method in which you invite your guests. Included in the plan is the Party Backdrop, suggesting where to set the party, how to present the food, tableware and product suggestions. The Party Menu offers well-tested, terrific tasting dishes that blend to create a wonderful meal. Also included are beverage suggestions, shortcuts for the busy party host, and over-the-top suggestions that make your party just that much more special. Party Strategy provides a timeline to help you organize and breakdown the tasks that you want to accomplish so that you will have met every detail allowing you to enjoy your party with your guests. Tucked into all of the fun, you will find some party tidbits, words of wisdom from experienced party professionals and celebrated hosts. Each one generously shares his or her secrets with you, thus giving you the confidence needed to become a gracious party giver yourself.

At Home Entertaining puts everything in place for your party production. Now is the time for you to jump into the fray. Grab the megaphone and yell as loud as you can: Lights, Camera, Action!

It's time to PARTEE!

SHAPING YOUR PARTY

How do you decide whether your party should be set as a buffet or as a sit-down occasion? Do you need a formal invitation or is word of mouth okay? When is a party theme taken way too far? These are all questions that you must answer in order to guarantee a great party plan, thus insuring a great party.

Informal parties are just that, casual affairs that are unfussy and easy-going. A weekday invite to coworkers to come over for dinner is a casual affair. So is the gang coming over to watch the game on television, or an indoor "cook-in". Invite guests to an informal party by telephone, email or a shout across the desk. Expect that your guests will attend in the same manner that they are invited, casually. Make them feel at home by serving them, casually. This is not the occasion for formal china and florist-delivered centerpieces. Keep the decorations to a minimum, restrain from using place cards and save the jazz band for next week.

For an informal party, choose a relaxed setting, stack tables near an open fire, pillows around a coffee table, a kitchen table with extra chairs. Set up a bar area that allows guests to serve themselves. Choose a menu that is easy to prepare and encourages pals to assist in the kitchen. The place setting is relaxed with stacked dishes and utensils that encourage a hands-on affair.

A formal party is an occasion to celebrate milestone events, a son's engagement, a daughter's shower, a friend's wedding, New Year's eve. For a formal affair, written invitations are a must. Decorations and music should be well thought out. This is the time to bring out Grandma's china and borrow Aunt Lily's crystal. Proper place settings are fun and have their roots in function.

A formal place setting begins with a service plate or charger. The food never touches this plate. Instead it holds a smaller salad, soup or first course dish. When the first course is removed, the service plate is also removed. Customarily, four glasses are used at a formal place setting. Placed from left to right, these include the water goblet, champagne glass, white or red wine glass, and the dessert wine glass. Forks are set to the left of the service plate and are set in the order they are to be used from left to right. The outermost fork is used for the first course. Next in line is the salad fork, then the dinner fork. From the outside right-hand side begin with a shellfish fork, soupspoon, meat knife and dinner knife. A butter knife sits on a butter plate that is set above the forks. Dessert utensils sit above the service plate. The napkin is folded and placed on the top of the service plate or to the left of the forks.

Formal affairs are enhanced by special flower arrangements and tapered candles. Place cards aid each guest in finding their seats and printed menus take the party way over the top.

Both informal and formal parties can be shaped by the time frame, and the choice of menu. Choose a cocktail party to serve guests over a two or three hour time frame ending early enough for guests to move on to another party. When planning the amount of food to prepare for a cocktail party, allow four to five tastes per guest per hour. For example, if you hare hosting twenty guests from six o'clock until eight o'clock you want to have at least two hundred items of food. This sounds like a lot, but it really isn't. One cup of yummy dip yields eight to ten bites, while a pound of medium size cooked shrimp yields about two-dozen pieces. If you have a hungry crowd, plan more food. In fact, my rule of thumb is to always plan to have left-overs after a party. This way, you can be sure that you won't run out of food and you won't have to cook for the next week!

A buffet party is a terrific way to serve a crowd, and again can be shaped into either a formal or informal party.

A buffet party is a style of entertaining that permits the guests to serve themselves. Create a buffet in whatever party space you have to work with, on a kitchen island or counter top, a dining room sideboard or a family room bar, an outside barbecue grill area or a living room coffee table. Take a look at all of your surroundings as you envision your party. There are two tips that make any section of your home a great place to set a buffet. First, make the buffet accessible so that your guests aren't stumbling over each other. Secondly, begin at the beginning. Build the meal with each dish.

A relaxed hostess is attentive to the needs of her guests, thus making her buffet table easily maneuverable. Place all of the utensils, dishes, and napkins at the beginning of the food platters. Wrap utensils in the napkins so they can be held easily. Place them in a large basket at the front of the buffet for easy identification. Place the platters in succession as you would serve the meal. For a supper buffet table, the first course is the first platter. Soup or salad leads the way. Serve fresh crisp salad greens in a chilled bowl. Salad dressings are placed next to the bowl so that every guest is able to view each available selection. Place a pepper mill nearby. Next in line is the bread or rolls. Rolls that are to be used for sandwiches with a meat entrée such as turkey breast or tenderloin are pre-sliced and kept covered in a basket or large bowl.

Following the bread basket is the entrée platter. You want your guests to know that they have hit the crescendo of the meal. The entrée platter should be lavish and well garnished in its presentation. Place sauce or gravy next to the entrée and not at the end of the buffet. Condiments are placed after the meat dish and may be served in interesting containers like mayonnaise from a candy dish or ketchup from a small pitcher. Set all of the side dishes after the main course. Scatter pairs of salt and pepper shakers at several points on the table.

A brunch buffet begins with pitchers of juice served in juice glasses, bowls of fresh fruit served in fruit dishes followed by dinner plates for the egg casserole or French toast. End the buffet with miniature muffins and pastries in napkin lined baskets. Set the coffee service in a separate location to avoid confusion.

A dessert buffet, is not only a great ending to every party, but also an excuse for a party in itself! Place each dessert in a separate area surrounded by everything required to serve. A serving utensil, eating utensils, napkins, plates and any garnish or accompaniment, surrounds each yummy desserts. Balance the table by offering several desserts.

When space is limited, or to accommodate a large crowd, utilize buffet stations for a party. An aperitif station offers a specialty cocktail and includes chilled opened wine bottles and cold beer arranged in large ice-filled buckets at the center of a table. Place appetizer platters onto decorative napkins or fabric squares on the table with stacks of cocktail napkins readily available. As soon as most of the guests have arrived and the tidbits on the platters diminish, it is time to set the second station for the salad course. A low coffee table is the perfect place for a mini salad bar. Drape a small cloth or fabric square over part of the table. Set a chilled bowl of greens on top. Offer crocks of cheese, croutons and pitchers filled with various dressings. Small salad dishes, salad forks and more napkins are a must.

The kitchen makes an excellent place for the entrée station. Piping hot baking dishes sit on a clean counter top with crinkled fabric surrounding each one. The same fabric is used for dinner napkins and bread basket liners. The dining room table is perfect for the desserts. Light candles and lay fresh flowers among the platters.

Offer coffee and after dinner cordials on a sideboard. To ensure that the buffet stations are well-manned by every guests, be sure that each dish offers bite size pieces that are easy to eat. (The triple threat of a knife, fork and lap held plate definitely invite disaster).

Whatever your choice of party, formal, informal, cocktail party, buffet party, attention to details is the secret to making your event a fun party that both you and your guests will enjoy.

HOW TO PARTEE AT YOUR PARTY

I find that the absolute best way to entertain is the casually fussy approach, a blend of formal traditions with a twang of contemporary approaches, a validation that if you host a party – the guests will come. A casually fussy approach to a dinner party invites you to use good china when serving homemade pizza to your jean clad guests, or to serve elegant lobster bisque from a ceramic mug. The idea is to make your family, friends or guests totally comfortable so that they can enjoy wonderfully prepared and delightfully presented food.

An important component is an inviting table. Pick up treasures from thrift stores and garage sales to blend with what you have in your china cabinet. Mix and match the place settings to create interest. There are several ways to accomplish this. One suggestion is to set a different china pattern at each seat. For example, use a gold embossed place setting at the host's place, and a colorful, patterned place setting for a guest. Continue setting the table with full place settings that include a dinner plate, cup and saucer, salad plate, and butter dish. Each place is set exactly like the next, except the china is mixed rather than matched. This is a great way to utilize that thrift shop bargain.

A second suggestion for a fun table is to alternate between two or more sets of china with the various table setting pieces. For example, on a table for six, place the same dinner plates, and contrast with a different pattern for the salad bowls. Continue with six butter plates from a third china pattern. Make sure that the china colors blend well together and with the rest of your table decorations.

The secret to setting a beautiful and irresistible table is in your well though out creativity. There should be a pattern to each place setting that works on the table as a whole. If you are using cups and saucers, don't insert a mug. If you are using salad plates, then only use plates - no bowls. Get the idea? There is a definite order to the table, but you set the tone with the mixing and matching of patterns.

A casually fussy style of entertaining is a constant invitation to be creative. Explore new ways to serve food. Serve hot soup in a coffee cup or cold soup in a large balloon wine glass. Serve a saucy entrée in a shallow pasta dish. Use oversized coffee cups for a chilled chopped salad and offer your guests a drizzle of dressing from a cream pitcher. A tall glass vase makes an interesting presentation for bread sticks. Experiment with various dishes, bowls and containers while choosing the menu. Your guests will be delighted with your innovative presentation.

Although bundles of fresh flowers are the favorite objects to work with when creating centerpieces, many things can create interest on your table. A centerpiece does not have to be in the center of the table and it can even be two or more objects. As long as the pattern is balanced, the centerpiece can even wander all over the table, by using porcelain figurines with lace, ribbon or fabric to tie it all together. An array of Victorian doll statues, placed decoratively on top of crushed velvet fabric, serves as a romantic centerpiece.

Piles of fresh fruit and vegetables in baskets work very well as centerpieces. Or, stack them on platters, place them on fabric, paint them with spray paint or dust them with sugar. There is no end to the effects that you can achieve.

Place cards are white folded cards, written with your absolute best penmanship, that tell your guests where they are to sit. However, when thinking in a casually fussy party approach to table setting, the place card becomes a part of the table decor, and is seldom just a folded card. For example, names painted onto miniature pots filled with fresh herbs, are an easy place card for a summer party. For sports themed parties, "autograph" a ball with your guest's name on it at his or her place. Miniature picture frames, with the guests name printed where the picture should be, make fun place cards. So do napkins that have been tied with strands of wide ribbon, on which the guest's name is written with a calligraphy pen.

When you think of tablecloths and napkins, think also of fabrics and ribbons, and use them interchangeably. Doing so, especially when working within a budget, can change the entire appearance of the table. Spruce up a plain white tablecloth by tying the corners with beautiful ribbon. Or, take that same white table cloth and throw a colorful piece of fabric on top. Bunch it up, lay some flowers around, and you have a very interesting table.

A lace square placed below the dinner plate adds a romantic flavor to the place setting. If that same square is fiesta striped, a Mexican celebration is on the way. Flowered sheets work well as table cloths for a garden party. Lace napkins, tied with rich red ribbon are fabulous for a tea party. Even a faux fur pelt can be draped over a buffet table when you are serving wild game.

Again, the idea is to let your imagination and creativity shine.

Both flowers and candles are an absolute must on most party tables. When entertaining with a casually fussy flair, flowers don't have to be in vases. For example, tulips are wonderful in a pottery pitcher, and fragrant flowers like gardenias can float in small custard cups. Vary the heights of both candles and flowers to lend interest to your table. Votive candles and floating flowers can sit alternately on inverted bowls draped with fabric or on pedestal plates. Large candles can sit on mirrored trays to double the brightness of the flames. Although not technically flowers, fresh herb sprigs stuffed in bud vases are fragrant, and can serve equally well amid floating flowers, or around the base of candles.

Casually fussy entertaining requires absolutely delicious food, the right blend of fun guests, and a relaxed host or hostess. By incorporating a few simple tips, stress-free hosting is easy to do. First, plan a straightforward menu with dishes that you prepare in advance. Arrange food and libations so that your guests assist you by serving themselves. Ask a pal or neighborhood teen to be your party helper during the evening.

Start with the libations. Choose among sodas, punch, liquor with mixers, beer and chilled wine. To make sure that your guests flow easily through your home remember it's all about location, location, location! Strategically place the bar table at the far end of your party space. This will encourage guests to walk through the room to grab a cocktail. Arrange the table so that everything is within your guest's fingertips. Place ice in a large container with tongs nearby. Glasses, lemon slices, stir sticks and cocktail napkins are all within easy reach. Choose a large tub or porcelain container to hold chilled cans of soda, beer and open bottles of wine.

Make a list of everything that you will need. A well stocked bar includes bar towels, glasses, joggers for pouring, a blender with an extra canister for a large crowd, a cocktail shaker with a coiled strainer, a long handled spoon for both stirring and cracking ice, a pitcher, an ice bucket with scoop or tongs, a lemon zestier, cork screw, bottle opener, measuring spoons, stir sticks, sharp knife and cutting board, olive and onion fork, cocktail napkins and coasters. Bar condiments include grenadine syrup, superfine sugar, simple syrup, bitters, hot sauce, Worcestershire sauce, margarita salt, green olives and cocktail onions. Citrus fruit slices, peel and wedges from lemons, limes and oranges are standard, but sliced strawberries or pineapple can also be included. Mint sprigs, celery stalks, prepared horseradish and even whipping cream are included in a well stocked bar. Customize your bar based on the tastes of your guests. Make things even simpler by offering one or two specialty drinks.

Choose a doable menu. Take on only those dishes that you can make in advance and that are sure to please your crowd. For food that is best served warm, prepare it in the serving dish, bake at the last minute and place the hot dish directly onto the table. If oven space is at a premium, make sure that you blend plenty of chilled or room temperature entrees that can be brought directly from the refrigerator to the table.

Arrange for helpers. A best pal, neighborhood college teen or a culinary art school student are all good choices. Make sure that you spend time with you helper before the party so that you can direct them to be attentive to any last minute tasks. He or she can pick up discarded glasses and plates and keep an eye on the buffet to refill platters and stack fresh napkins. While you are greeting guests, your assistant will light candles and make sure the ice bucket is filled.

A perfect casually fussy party scenario has your guests entering your home and immediately crossing the room to locate the libations at your totally complete self-serve bar. (That's you at the front door, warmly welcoming each friend!) On the way to the bar, the guests get a sugarplum preview as they pass by the brilliantly laid out dessert buffet. When most of the fun people have arrived, you and your assisting pal easily arrange the scrumptious food with only a few last minute details. (No one even realizes that you have momentarily left the room.) When your guests take notice of the completed buffet, or preset first course, they ooh and ahh at the scrumptious presentation. As tummies get full, you turns up the music and guests begin to sing and dance. Your helper is picking up the used plates and cups and stacking them in the laundry room to clean later on. You are relaxed, having a great time and really enjoying yourself. (It looks like you have just learned to partee at your own party.)

The casually fussy style of entertaining relies on all of the rules of the past, yet opens the door for today's host and hostess to work creatively within their budget and time frame. When fashioning an event to share with friends and family, you build on the freedom and inventiveness that this concept allows. Before you realize it, you will develop a passion for entertaining.

Just The Two of Us

(PARTIES FOR TWO VERY CLOSE FRIENDS)

Two Cooks in the Kitchen
Breakfast After Dark
Supper by the Fire
Intimate Valentine's Day Dinner
Table for Two

"Hosting a party is not about the 'art' of entertaining, it does not need to be elevated to an art form because the main objective is to have fun, and the novice host is likely to be intimidated by such an aesthetic concept. Instead, plan your party with the idea of comfort in mind, and your experience will be relaxing and enjoyable. For example, be sure to plan your party in advance. You want to allow enough time to be able to make your preparations at a leisurely pace to avoid burnout and stress. Create a menu that you can easily prepare. Shop and cook before the day of the party and freeze what you can. Accept help wherever you find it. Enlist the help of a friend to serve food, cut the cake and whisk away dirty plates. Keep the music low to allow for conversation. Most important, relax and have a good time."

Laura Brody
Author of
The Entertaining Survival Guide: A Handbook for the Hesitant Host
Boston, MA
www.diynet.com

Two Cooks in the Kitchen Party Plan

Party Motivation

He's stayed too long at the office. She's had three business trips in two weeks. Your schedules surprisingly overlap on a weekday evening and you want to enjoy a long conversation together.

Party Menu

Stuffed Artichokes with Warm Balsamic Sauce
Creamy Asparagus and Mushroom Risotto
Grilled Herb Flatbread
Steamed Mussels in Ginger Broth
Individual Chocolate Soufflés **

**** Over-the-Top Suggestion**

Celebrate being together with the two best words in dessert—chocolate and soufflé. While you prepare the dish, your pal whips up a great sauce. Prepare a warm mocha sauce by melting 2 ounces of semisweet chocolate and 1 ounce of bittersweet chocolate in the top of a double boiler until melted. Whisk in 3 tablespoons brewed coffee and 2 tablespoons corn syrup until the sauce is smooth and shiny.

Serve the soufflés with a dusting of confectioners' sugar and cocoa powder. Use a spoon to cut a cross in the top of the soufflé. Pour the warm chocolate sauce into the center.

Party Strategy

You want to spend time together so we'll build this menu with foods that you can cook while working together in the kitchen. In place of courses, bring everything to the table at once and sample each dish as you savor your conversation.

Make sure that you both plan to leave work at the same time!

In the morning before you leave for work: Place the ingredients for the flatbread into the bread machine and set the timer so that the dough is ready when you get home.

Two hours before: Prepare the artichokes and the ingredients for the pungent sauce. Set the table and implement the voice mail option on your phone.

One hour before: Chop the veggies for the risotto.

Before you sit for dinner: Prepare the individual soufflés for baking.

Shortcuts

In place of the warm balsamic sauce, melt butter to accompany the steamed artichokes. Purchase flatbread from a bakery and warm it in the oven. Prepared chocolate sauce will warm nicely for the soufflés.

Party Backdrop

The mood is upbeat and intimate. It's you and your partner against the world. Avoid distractions. Turn the television off. Dim the lights. Throw out the newspaper. A little soft jazz is all you need to set an inviting atmosphere. Set the table with your best tablecloth. Arrange a bunch of candles on the table and around the room. Locate your long forgotten linen napkins (look in the back of the drawer). Chill a good bottle of wine.

The Table Setting

It is always nice to have a dish that is intended solely for a particular food. (Of course it's also great to use that dish for something totally unrelated—but that's another fun idea.) For this party, I suggest using an artichoke plate. This dish has a place for everything from the indentation in the center to place the whole artichoke, to the outer indentation to place leaves, to the smaller indentation to place warm sauce or butter.

Use a large pasta bowl to serve the risotto. Choose one that is dishwasher safe to save on clean-up time. Garnish with curls of shaved Parmesan cheese for garnish.

Use a second large bowl to hold the mussels and fragrant sauce.

Serve the flatbread from a napkin-lined basket with a small pitcher of olive oil for dipping.

Individual soufflés are served directly from the oven in the ramekins they have been baked in. Pour the warm sauce from a decorative pitcher. Sprinkle with confectioners' sugar for a sweet garnish.

STUFFED ARTICHOKES with WARM BALSAMIC SAUCE

Choose medium-sized artichokes that are firm with the leaves unopened. Or, if you are in the mood to share—one large artichoke will do just fine.

2   medium artichokes

1   cup breadcrumbs
¼   small red onion, diced (about 2 table-
     spoons)
2   medium cloves garlic, minced (about 1
     teaspoon)
4   tablespoons olive oil

¼   small red onion, diced (about 2 table-
     spoons)
1   medium clove garlic, minced (about ½
     teaspoon)
1   tablespoon olive oil
¼   cup balsamic vinegar
2   tablespoons chicken stock
1   tablespoon chopped fresh oregano
     leaves
¼   teaspoon dry mustard
     Salt and freshly ground pepper

1.   Prepare the artichokes by cutting off the tip
     about ⅓ down. Cut the stem, leaving about
     1 inch. Use a vegetable peeler to scrape of
     the outer edge of the stem. Remove the
     tough outer leaves at the base of the stem.
     Use kitchen scissors to cut the thorny tips
     from the remaining leaves. Steam the arti-
     chokes in a covered pan on the stove top or
     in a microwave oven until a fork inserted
     into the bottom heart of the artichoke slides
     in easily, about 20 minutes for medium arti-
     chokes.

2.   Gently open the top of the artichoke and
     remove the thorny center.
3.   Prepare the filling by placing the bread-
     crumbs, 2 tablespoons of the red onion, and
     2 teaspoons of the garlic in a bowl. Use a
     fork to blend with 2 tablespoons of the olive
     oil.

Preheat the oven to 350°.
4.   Place the steamed artichokes into a baking
     dish. Spoon the stuffing into the center and
     in between the outer leaves. Drizzle with 2
     more tablespoons of the olive oil and place
     into a 300° oven to keep warm while you
     prepare the vinaigrette.
5.   Prepare the vinaigrette by cooking 2 table-
     spoons diced red onion and 1 teaspoon
     minced garlic in 1 tablespoon olive oil over
     medium high heat until soft about 2 min-
     utes.
6.   Stir in the balsamic vinegar, chicken stock,
     oregano, and dry mustard. Cook for 1 to 2
     minutes. Season with salt and pepper.
7.   Remove the artichokes from the oven. Place
     a stuffed artichoke onto an artichoke plate
     with a spoonful of sauce poured into the
     well of the plate. Tear off the leaves and dip
     into the vinaigrette for a "hands-on" eating
     experience. Don't forget the heart and the
     stem, that's the best part.

Serves 2
Preparation Time: 20 minutes plus steaming

---

*If you are unfamiliar with artichokes and have difficulty removing the fuzzy choke try this idea.
After the artichokes are steamed, cut each one in half from stem to tip. Now you can easily
remove the choke with a teaspoon. Stuff the cavities and outer leaves with the breadcrumb
mixture. Drizzle some additional olive oil on top of the artichokes and keep warm
while you complete the sauce.*

CREAMY ASPARAGUS and MUSHROOM RISOTTO

The secret to a creamy risotto is Arborio rice. Adding warm liquid brings out a creamy consistency that is not found in other varieties of rice.

1	tablespoon olive oil
2	green onions, thinly sliced (about 2 tablespoons)
1	4-ounce package shiitake mushrooms, finely diced (about 1½ cups)
6	to 8 medium asparagus spears, tough stems removed, cut into 1 inch pieces (about 1 cup)
1	teaspoon cumin
¾	cup Arborio rice
2	cups chicken stock, heated
	Salt and freshly ground pepper
¼	cup grated Parmesan cheese
2	tablespoons heavy cream

1. Heat the olive oil in a deep skillet or saucepan over medium high heat.
2. Add the green onions, mushrooms, and asparagus pieces. Cook until just soft (about 3 minutes).
3. Add the cumin and stir.
4. Add the rice and stir. Cook for 2 minutes.
5. Reduce the heat to medium. Add enough warm stock to just cover the rice vegetable mixture. Stir until most of the liquid is absorbed. Then pour in another ladle of stock. Repeat this process until all of the stock is absorbed into the rice, about 20 minutes. The rice will maintain a soft but crunchy texture.
6. Remove the risotto from the heat. Season with salt and pepper.
7. Gently stir in the Parmesan cheese and cream.

Serves 2
Preparation Time: 30 minutes

Use this helpful tip to prepare risotto in advance. Cook the rice and veggies using half of the liquid. Cover and remove from the heat for up to 2 hours. When you are ready to serve, warm the stock and begin the cooking process again. Add a little extra cream and cheese to guarantee a smooth result.

GRILLED HERB FLATBREAD

Get a head start on this recipe by preparing the bread dough in a bread machine. Save extras for terrific croutons or savory bread crumbs.

4   cups all-purpose flour
1½   cups water
2   tablespoons olive oil
½   teaspoons salt
1   tablespoon chopped fresh rosemary
1   tablespoon chopped fresh thyme leaves
½   teaspoon yeast

1. Place the flour, water, olive oil, salt ,and fresh herbs into the bucket of a bread machine.
2. Place the yeast into the yeast compartment.
3. Set the machine for the dough cycle and start.
4. Remove the dough from the machine and onto a lightly floured surface. Divide into 4 balls.
5. Place the balls into a bowl that has been sprayed with a vegetable oil spray. Cover the bowl with a clean towel and let rise for 30 minutes.
6. Roll out each ball to a disk about ½-inch thick.
7. Heat an outdoor or indoor grill or a grill pan to medium high heat.
8. Brush both sides of the disks with additional olive oil.
9. Place the disks onto the grill. Cook until brown. Turn over and continue cooking until brown.
10. Serve the flatbread with olive oil for dipping, spread with hummus or tapenade, or plain with a pat of butter.

Yield: 4 individual flatbreads
Preparation Time: 45 minutes plus dough cycle

The bread machine is a great tool to use when incorporating fresh baked bread into your weekly menu plan. Feel free to experiment by adding all sorts of your favorite herbs and spices to flavor your favorite loaf.

STEAMED MUSSELS in GINGER BROTH

Talk about fast food! This dish comes together faster than you can get in the car.

1   **tablespoon olive oil**
2   **medium cloves garlic, thinly sliced (about 1 teaspoon)**
1   **large shallot, minced (about 1 table-spoon)**
1   **½-inch piece ginger, grated (about 1 tea-spoon)**
2   **plum tomatoes, diced (about 1 cup)**
1   **cup white wine**
    Juice of 1 lemon (about 2 tablespoons)
2   **pounds mussels, cleaned**
½   **teaspoon red pepper flakes**

1. Heat the olive oil in a deep skillet over medium high heat.

2. Add the garlic, shallot, and ginger. Cook until soft (about 2 minutes) being careful not to burn.

3. Add the tomatoes, white wine, and lemon juice to the pot and simmer.

4. Place the mussels in the pot.

5. Season with red pepper flakes.

6. Cover the pan and cook until the mussels are open, about 3 to 5 minutes.

7. Serve the mussels in shallow bowls covered in extra sauce for dipping.

Serves 2
Preparation Time: 15 minutes

Most of the mussels that are available are cultivated. Buy fresh mussels from a reputable fish monger. Make sure the shells are closed. Discard those with open shells.
Have the fishmonger remove the beards and scrub the mussels.
Frozen mussels are very acceptable and are an affordable choice.

Individual Chocolate Soufflés

You can make this yummy dessert in advance and bake just as you are sitting down to supper.

⅔ **cup cream**
¼ **cup confectioners' sugar**
2 **tablespoons cocoa powder**
1 **teaspoon all-purpose flour**
1 **egg yolk**
½ **teaspoon vanilla extract**
1 **egg white**
⅛ **teaspoon cream of tartar**
1 **tablespoon granulated sugar**

Preheat the oven to 350°.

1. Prepare 2 individual soufflé (8-ounce) ramekins by coating the inside with butter and sprinkling with granulated sugar. Shake off excess.
2. Combine the cream, confectioners' sugar, cocoa powder, flour, and egg yolk in the top of a double boiler.
3. Simmer over hot water, stirring constantly until the mixture thickens, about 10 minutes. Remove from heat.
4. Stir in the vanilla extract.
5. Beat the egg whites with the cream of tartar using an electric mixer until stiff peaks form. Add the granulated sugar.
6. Gently fold the egg whites into the chocolate mixture.
7. Spoon the mixture into the ramekins. Bake for 20 minutes or until the soufflés rise.

Serves 2
Preparation Time: 20 minutes plus baking

The secret to a great soufflé is to whip the egg whites well and then gently fold them into the custard. Over-stirring will break down all the air that you have whipped into the mixture.

Breakfast After Dark Party Plan

Party Motivation

Remember when you were a kid and your mom would scramble up some eggs or fry up some bologna for dinner? Or, perhaps a bowl of corn flakes and milk was your supper of choice during exam week in college. Have you ever visited a diner at midnight for a couple of eggs prepared "sunny side up" on your way home from a rollicking evening? Then you know what I am talking about. There is something that is sort of "anti-establishment" about eating breakfast foods at night. That is why Breakfast After Dark is a great way to party.

Party Menu

Huevos Rancheros Mexicalli **
Country Ham Steaks with Red Eye Gravy
Cheddar Scones
Fresh Berries with Cointreau Crème

** Over-the-Top Suggestion

Take a terrific egg dish to the next level by adding your own special salsa made as spicy as you can handle then tempered with naturally sweet fruit. Prepare a simple fresh salsa by combining diced onion, diced and seeded tomato, diced jalapeño pepper, fresh cilantro, lime juice and olive oil. For more flavor, you can toss in diced mango or pineapple chunks. Season with salt and freshly ground pepper.

Party Strategy

Bake the scones and prepare the crème sauce for the dessert in advance. The ham steaks and gravy can be kept warm while you prepare the eggs, which are best served immediately

The evening before: Cut up the berries and prepare the crème sauce. Refrigerate both separately.

Several hours before: Bake scones. Warm them before serving in a warming drawer or low heated oven.

30 Minutes before: Prepare the ham steak and gravy, keep warm.

Immediately before: Prepare eggs and serve.

Shortcuts

Purchase scones from your favorite bakery. A scoop of vanilla ice cream is a nice addition to the berries in place of Cointreau Crème.

Party Backdrop

Slightly mischievous and somewhat festive, breakfast after dark takes on even higher expectations when you add the flavors of spicy Latin fare. Find a recording of a Spanish acoustical guitarist for background music. Pull out your most colorful shirt and drape a scarf over the lampshade. Throw a colorful tablecloth over a low coffee table and place pillows on the floor. Several pillar candles are all the lighting that is required. A basket of peppers and onions is the perfect centerpiece. Place a bottle of hot sauce nearby as this is a spicy event.

The Table Setting

Use rainbow-colored china like deep blue Fiesta Ware to create a spicy looking table. For a unique presentation, serve huevos rancheros in individual tortilla dishes. The rustic ones that are made from pottery, copper colored and have a lid to keep several tortillas warm will work well.

Use silver toned baking/serving dishes to hold the ham steaks and spicy gravy. Keep warm in a low oven and dust the top with fresh chopped herbs immediately before serving.

Pile the scones in a basket that is lined with one or two primary colored cloth napkins.

Mound the berries into a large balloon goblet and serve the crème from individual four-inch, Mexican-inspired rooster pitchers.

HUEVOS RANCHEROS MEXICALI

This basic recipe is easily adapted to an on-the-run breakfast burrito. Prepare the recipe through step 4. Scramble the eggs in place of frying. Roll the filled tortilla into a cylinder. Wrap each one in aluminum foil and off you go!

1	8-ounce can refried beans
	Canola oil for frying
2	8-inch corn tortillas
1	tablespoon butter
4	large eggs
	Salt and freshly ground pepper
½	cups grated extra sharp Cheddar cheese
2	to 3 plum tomatoes, seeded and diced (about ½ cup)
1	medium jalapeño pepper, seeded and diced (about 2 tablespoons)
2	green onions, thinly sliced (about 2 tablespoons)

Sour cream
Salsa

1. Warm the refried beans in a pot over medium high heat until cooked through.
2. Heat a small amount of oil in a skillet over medium high heat.
3. Cook the tortillas one at a time in the hot oil until soft (about 30 seconds each).
4. Remove the tortillas, drain on paper towels. Lay each tortilla on a baking sheet and spread the warm beans on top. Keep warm.
5. Remove the excess oil from the skillet. Add the butter and coat the bottom of the skillet.
6. Fry the eggs in the skillet over medium high heat for 2 minutes for soft centers or up to 4 minutes for firmly set centers.
7. Season the eggs with salt and pepper. Remove the eggs from the heat and top with grated cheese.
8. Place 1 tortilla on a plate. Top the beans with 2 eggs. Top each tortilla, beans, eggs, and cheese with chopped tomatoes, jalapeños, and a sprinkling of sliced green onion. Top with a dollop of sour cream and a spoonful of salsa.

Serves 2
Preparation Time: 15 minutes

Eggs are best stored in the carton that they are sold in. Fancy egg holders on refrigerator doors are standard—but won't keep the egg fresh as long. Eggs that are stored properly will last up to 5 weeks after the "sell by" date.

COUNTRY HAM STEAK with RED EYE GRAVY

Brewed coffee is the beginning of the terrific sauce for the dish. It also may serve as the reason that the dish has its interesting name. Many a "red-eye" has been opened with strong coffee.

2	tablespoons butter
1	8-ounce thick ham steak
1	small white onion, finely diced (about 2 tablespoons)
1	tablespoon all-purpose flour
½	cup brewed strong coffee
½	cup chicken stock
2	green onions, thinly sliced (about 2 tablespoons)
2	tablespoons heavy cream
	Salt and freshly ground pepper

1. Heat 1 tablespoon of butter in a skillet over medium high heat.
2. Add the ham steak to the skillet and cook, turning once, for about 4 to 5 minutes. Remove the steak to a platter and keep warm.
3. Melt 1 tablespoon of butter in the skillet.
4. Cook the diced onion in the butter until just soft.
5. Stir the flour into the butter mixture until bubbling.
6. Add the coffee and chicken stock to the pan. Stir until thickened about 5 minutes.
7. Add the green onions and cream. Season with salt and pepper.
8. Pour the gravy over the ham steak.

Serves 2
Preparation Time: 15 minutes

Cooking together flour and butter forms a roux and is used to flavor and thicken sauce or gravy. The secret to a great roux is to make sure that you cook out the flour taste. The roux will darken the longer that you cook it also coloring the sauce from white to caramel to golden brown.

CHEDDAR SCONES

Savory scones are just as good as the sweet ones. Feel free to toss some fresh herbs into the dough for a fragrant and cheesy treat.

2   cups self-rising flour
½   cup butter, chilled and diced (1 stick)
¼   cup extra sharp Cheddar cheese, grated
Zest of ½ medium orange (about 1 table-
spoons)
⅓   cup buttermilk

1   large egg, beaten

Preheat the oven to 400°.

1. Place the flour and the butter into the bowl of a food processor. Pulse until the mixture resembles course crumbs.
2. Add the cheese and orange zest and pulse just to combine.
3. Pour just enough of the buttermilk through the feed tube so that a dough forms around the blade.
4. Remove the dough to a floured board and knead lightly.
5. Roll out the dough. Use a biscuit cutter dipped in flour to cut out scones. (Or roll the dough into a thick circle and cut into triangular, pie-shaped pieces).
6. Place the scones on a Silpat lined baking sheet.
7. Brush the tops with beaten egg.
8. Bake for 12 to 15 minutes depending on size. The scones should be golden brown on the top.
9. Cool on a wire rack.

Yield: 10 to 12 scones
Preparation Time: 10 minutes plus baking

For terrific scones, try not to overwork the dough. It should be light and sticky. You should be able to see the small pieces of butter in the dough. Roll out the dough and cut as many scones as you can. Gather extra dough together with your hands and pat out to cut more shapes. Rolling out the dough more than once will produce tough scones.

FRESH BERRIES with COINTREAU CRÈME

The sauce for this simple dessert is kin to a butterscotch sauce. Watch the sugar carefully to prevent burning.

1	tablespoon butter
¼	cup brown sugar
2⅓	cups cream
1	tablespoon granulated sugar
1	tablespoon cornstarch
1	large egg yolk
1	tablespoon Cointreau liquor
2	cups assorted fresh berries such as strawberries, blueberries and raspberries

1. Melt the butter in a saucepan over medium heat.
2. Stir in the brown sugar and the cream. Bring to a boil stirring constantly. Remove from heat.
3. Whisk together the granulated sugar, cornstarch and egg yolk in a small bowl. Pour a tablespoon of the warm cream mixture into the egg yolk mixture and whisk to combine. Pour the egg mixture into the pan with the cream and cook over medium-low heat, stirring constantly, until it thickens (about 2 to 4 minutes).
4. Stir in the Cointreau liquor.
5. Remove the pan from the heat. Pour the sauce into a bowl, cover and chill.
6. Place the berries in a bowl, drizzle the sauce over top. Garnish with a slice of orange and a fresh mint leaf.

Serves 2
Preparation Time: 15 minutes

Tempering is the technique used to prepare egg yolks for a sauce without cooking them first. Pour a small amount of the warm liquid into the egg yolk and stir well. This warms the yolk. The yolk mixture is then heated slowly with the other sauce components producing a smooth, velvety outcome.

Supper By The Fire Party Plan

Party Motivation

As autumn breezes blow a cool wind, we scramble inside to hearth and home. For this intimate bash, we'll pull two chairs right up next to the hearth and stoke the season's first fire's flames with a scrumptious supper that is a perfect celebration of the season.

Party Menu

Tossed Green Salad with Creamy Buttermilk Dressing
Grilled Pork Chops with Port Wine Reduction
Braised Fennel and Leeks
Scottish-Style Shortbread **

** Over-the-Top Suggestion

Turn a traditional Scottish treat into your favorite chocolate fix by dipping each wedge into warm chocolate. Melt 8 ounces of semisweet chocolate in the top of a double boiler. Remove from the heat. Whisk in ¼ cup of butter cut into small pieces. Pour in a tablespoon of heavy cream and stir until shiny. Dip the shortbread into the chocolate. Lay onto a rack to cool.

Party Strategy

Browse local thrift shops and antique stores to find vintage tray tables, serving tins, placemats, plaid blankets or table cloths to give a Scottish flair to the evening.

The day before: Bake shortbread and dip in chocolate.

The evening before: Prepare the salad greens and dressing. Prepare the leeks and fennel. Refrigerate.

Several hours before: Marinate pork. Assemble the ingredients for the sauce.

30 Minutes before: Braise the vegetables. Grill the pork chops and keep warm. Prepare the port wine reduction.

Shortcuts

Purchase a bag of exotic salad greens to class up an everyday salad. In place of a double boiler, you can melt chocolate using a microwave oven. Microwave on low heat checking frequently to prevent burning the chocolate.

Party Backdrop

Stackable TV tables were all the rage in the early 50's as families left the dinner table to join their favorite black and white television hosts and game shows that were taking up residence in the living room. Let the TV table return for this intimate supper by the fire. In place of the aluminum tray top on wobbly legs of yesteryear, today's television table offers several classic wood styles that are sure to add interest to even the smallest space.

The fire is a must—but let it die down a touch so that there is plenty of warmth and atmosphere and not a fiery blaze. Think paneled den and oversized leather sofa for this party. If you are using a wooden tray table, line it with a heavy cork-backed placemat perhaps depicting horses or Scottish dogs. Or scoot an ottoman near the fire, throw a plaid, fringed blanket on top and set an oversized wooden tray as a tabletop. No tray table or ottoman—not to worry, throw a wool blanket on the floor and aim for an indoor picnic.

The Table Setting

Serve the tossed salad from a chilled, clear glass bowl using oversized tongs. Keep the bowl secure using plaid napkins for a base.

An ovenproof platter holds both the grilled pork chops and the braised veggies. Drizzle some of the braising liquid over top and use an oversized serving spoon to capture the juices. Use a gravy boat or sauce dish to hold the port wine sauce.

Pile the shortbread wedges (chocolate tips pointing up) into a tin that has been lined with plaid fabric.

Tossed Green Salad with Creamy Buttermilk Dressing

The fresh buttermilk dressing enhances this simple salad. Feel free to add cherry tomatoes, diced cucumber and a handful of sprouts to give it even more oomph.

½ **cup sour cream**
½ **cup buttermilk**
2 **teaspoons cider vinegar**
1 **tablespoon sugar**
1 **medium clove garlic, minced (about ½ teaspoon)**
1 **tablespoons snipped fresh garlic chives**
1 **tablespoons chopped fresh dill**
  Salt and freshly ground pepper

2 **cups fresh salad greens**

1. Whisk together the sour cream, buttermilk, cider vinegar and sugar.
2. Stir in the garlic and fresh herbs.
3. Season with salt and pepper.
4. Pour the dressing over the mixed greens and toss.

Yield: about 1 cup
Preparation Time: 5 minutes

Buttermilk is a cultured product made by adding bacteria to skim milk. Originally buttermilk was the liquid left behind when cream was turned into butter. Today's product is thick and tangy—a perfect ingredient for a sharp salad dressing and easily balanced with the addition of sugar.

Grilled Pork Chops with Port Wine Reduction

Thick chops are seasoned and grilled to perfection while a sweet and simple wine sauce reduces for a mouth-watering result.

2   6- to 8-ounce 1-inch thick pork chops
1   tablespoon Worcestershire sauce
Salt and freshly ground pepper

½   cup Port wine
¾   cup Merlot wine
2   teaspoons honey
¼   cup olive oil
Juice of 1 fresh lime (about 2 table-spoons)
2   tablespoons chopped fresh sage leaves

1. Season both sides of the pork chops with salt, pepper and a drizzle of Worcestershire sauce.

2. In a saucepan over medium high heat combine the Port wine, Merlot and honey. Bring to a boil and cook until the liquid is reduced to about ½ cup about 10 minutes.
3. Reduce the heat to low.
4. Slowly whisk in the olive oil.
5. Season the sauce with lime juice, salt and pepper. Stir in the chopped sage. Keep warm.
6. Grill the pork chops over medium high heat until done, about 8 minutes per side. Serve immediately with a drizzle of sauce over top.

Serves 2
Preparation Time: 20 minutes

You may grill the pork chops using and outdoor or indoor grill or use a grill pan on top of the stove. Check for doneness using the tip of your finger. When the meat springs back, the chops should be medium rare. When the meat shows greater resistance, he pork chops will be more well-done.

BRAISED FENNEL and LEEKS

Braising is a terrific cooking technique to use for fibrous vegetables like the aromatic fennel bulb and the multi-layered leek. The flavorful cooking liquid imparts great taste with very little effort on your part.

1   **tablespoon olive oil**
2   **heads fennel quartered**
2   **leeks, white part only, cut into quarters**
½   **cup white wine**
1   **cup chicken stock**
    Salt and freshly ground pepper

1. Heat the olive oil in a saucepan over medium high heat.

2. Add the fennel and leeks and brown gently on all sides.
3. Add the white wine and chicken stock. Cover the pan, reduce the heat and cook until the vegetables are soft about 10 to 15 minutes.
4. Season with salt and freshly ground pepper.

Serves 4
Preparation Time: 20 minutes

The fennel plant's leaves and stem have an anise-like flavor and aroma. Anise is a plant that belongs to the parsley family and produces a seed that has a licorice taste. Your grocer may label a fennel bulb as "anise", but don't be confused. You are looking for a plant that has a white bulb with dill like looking stems on top.

Scottish-Style Shortbread

This recipe makes more than enough shortbread for an intimate dinner by the fire. Store extras in an airtight container for next week's date.

1½ cups all-purpose flour
⅔ cup confectioners' sugar
¼ cup cornstarch
Zest of 1 medium lemon (about 1 table-spoons)
½ teaspoon salt
¾ cup butter (1½ stick), chilled, cut into pieces

Preheat the oven to 300°.

1. Place the flour, sugar, cornstarch, lemon zest and salt into the bowl of a food processor. Pulse to combine.
2. Add the butter and pulse until the mixture forms a dough.
3. Pour out the dough onto a lightly floured surface and form into two disks.
4. Press each circle into the bottom of an 8-inch round cake pan. Pierce the dough with a fork.
5. Bake for 40 minutes or until the shortbread is just beginning to color.
6. Cool the pans on racks for 5 minutes. Cut warm shortbread into triangle shaped pieces. Use a spatula to remove the wedges.

Yield: 16 to 24 wedges
Preparation Time: 20 minutes plus baking

Shortbread comes out perfectly, every time, if you remember not to overwork the dough. Use short on and off motions to quickly pulse the chilled butter into the flour.

For a extra treat dip the tips of the shortbread into warm chocolate and allow to cool. Heat 8 ounces of semisweet chocolate in the top of a double boiler. Remove from the heat and whisk in ½ stick of butter cut into small pieces. Whisk in a tablespoon of heavy cream and stir until smooth and shiny.

Intimate Valentine's Day Dinner Party Plan

Party Motivation

Love is in the air and you've carved out a special evening together. Leisurely enjoy a multi course meal that can be prepared in advance and cooked at your convenience. Leave room for the decadent chocolate dessert. After all, it is Valentine's Day!

Party Menu

Roasted Portobello Mushrooms Stuffed with Sautéed Spinach and Fontina Cheese
Nut-Crusted Rack of Lamb **
Braised Carrots with Tarragon
Soft Center Chocolate Cakes

** Over-the-Top Suggestion

Serve these yummy lamb chops on top of a mound of roasted garlic mashed potatoes. Place peeled and cut potatoes into a pot of boiling, salted water. Slice off the top of a whole head of garlic. Place it on a sheet of aluminum foil. Drizzle the garlic with olive oil, dried oregano, salt and pepper. Close the top of the foil over the garlic and roast until soft about 20 to 30 minutes at 375°. Once the garlic is roasted, squeeze the soft garlic from the peel and place it in a bowl with the cooked potatoes. Whip the potatoes and garlic together with some butter and cream. The potatoes will stay warm in the oven for an hour or more—so feel free to make them in advance.

Party Strategy

The menu for this party allows the dishes to be assembled in advance and then quickly cooked. This is one party that you don't want to rush through. The appetizer is completed in minutes. Luxuriate over the flavor combinations while you enjoy your favorite aperitif. When you are ready, proceed to the next course. The lamb chops roast in less than 15 minutes and the carrots braise in even less time. Enjoy your favorite cabernet with the entrée. The individual desserts bake in 10 to 15 minutes. That's just enough time to choose some romantic music for later.

The evening before: Prepare the cakes and pre bake or refrigerate for last-minute baking.

Several hours before: Stuff the mushrooms, prepare the lamb for roasting, and peel the carrots

Thirty minutes before: Roast the mushrooms, braise the carrots, bake the cakes and roast the lamb.

Shortcuts

If you are throwing this menu together on the spur of the moment, you can defrost frozen spinach in butter sauce and use this to stuff the mushrooms. Sprinkle your favorite cheese over top.

Party Backdrop

Black tie not required, but upscale table dressing is definitely in order. Set a fine table with your best crystal and china. Use blood red clothes and napkins, accented with the most delicate lace. For a striking centerpiece, place a bowl of fresh roses on top of a circle of lace on top of a damask cloth. Sprinkle the table with glittery mini hearts and use paper hearts for place cards. A single rose placed on top of the dinner plate signals a tender evening party for two.

The mood is elegant but comfortable. The menu is fussy, but you are relaxed. Dine on a small table and place two chairs across from each other so you can look directly into your pal's eyes. Dim the lights, fire up two tapered candles and slowly enjoy the stylish fare.

The Table Setting

Use chargers on the tablecloth to set an inviting table. An ebony charger on a red cloth is striking—especially when topped with a single red rose.

Use a china salad plate to serve the appetizer. Set it on top of the charger. Garnish the dish with a handful of fresh arugula and spinach leaves that have been lightly tossed with terrific olive oil, a dash of champagne vinegar and a grinding of fresh black pepper. Remove the charger when you have finished the first course.

Place two to three lamb chops onto a matching china dinner plate with the braised carrots and a spoonful of the liquid. Sprinkle the rim of the plate with fresh, chopped parsley.

Dust a dessert plate with cocoa powder. Invert the ramekin onto the plate. Dust the cake with confectioners' sugar. Garnish with a sprig of mint and a drizzle of red raspberry sauce.

ROASTED PORTOBELLO MUSHROOMS
stuffed with SAUTÉED SPINACH and FONTINA CHEESE

This dish is a giant step forward from the stuffed mushroom caps of yesteryear. With a little imagination—this mushroom becomes a whole meal.

2   **large portobello mushrooms**

2   **tablespoons olive oil**
    Salt and freshly ground pepper
6   **ounces fresh spinach leaves, torn (about 2 cups)**
2   **green onions, thinly sliced (about 2 tablespoons)**
1   **7-ounce jar sun-dried tomatoes in oil, drained and diced**
½   **cup shredded Fontina cheese**

Preheat the oven to 375°.
1.   Remove the stems from the mushrooms, brush each side with a small amount of olive oil, and season with salt and pepper.

2.   Place the mushrooms onto a baking sheet and roast for 5 minutes, turning once.
3.   Heat the remaining olive oil in a skillet over medium high heat.
4.   Add the spinach leaves and cook until just wilted. Season with salt and pepper.
5.   Remove the pan from the heat. Add the onions and sun-dried tomatoes. Toss to combine.
6.   Stuff the underside of each mushroom with half of the spinach mixture. Sprinkle cheese on top.
7.   Bake the stuffed mushrooms for 5 to 10 minutes, or until the cheese begins to melt.

Serves 2
Preparation Time: 10 minutes

Use a small amount of hot oil to quickly cook the spinach. This will only take a few moments.
A huge handful of spinach will cook down to just a few tablespoons.
If the oil is not hot enough, the spinach will taste greasy.

NUT-CRUSTED RACK OF LAMB

Choose a rack of lamb that is generous enough to serve two or think decadently and roast two racks. Since it is just the two of you—it's okay to lick your fingers!

1 rack of lamb, frenched
¼ cup Dijon mustard
4 ounces pistachio nuts, shelled (about 1 cup)
½ cup breadcrumbs
1 tablespoon chopped fresh parsley leaves
1 tablespoon olive oil

Preheat the oven to 425°.

1. Brush the lamb with the mustard coating all sides of the meat, but not the bones.
2. Place the nuts in the bowl of a processor and pulse until the nuts are coarsely ground.
3. In a bowl mix together the ground nuts, breadcrumbs, parsley, and olive oil.
4. Dredge the lamb into the nut mixture until well coated.
5. Place the lamb on a rack in a baking pan with the bone side up. Cover the bones with aluminum foil to prevent burning.
6. Roast for 12 to 15 minutes or until a meat thermometer inserted into the thickest part reaches 125 to 130° for medium rare.

Serves 2
Preparation Time: 10 minutes plus roasting

"Frenching" a rack of lamb is a term used to describe the process of cutting away the fat and meat in between the bones. This allows for a clean bone that can be dressed with tiny white frilled "hats" just before serving. Covering the bones will prevent discoloring and even burning in a hot oven.

BRAISED CARROTS with TARRAGON

Use whole, baby carrots with green tops for a dramatic presentation of this really simple recipe.

1	tablespoon olive oil
1	small red onion, thinly sliced (about ½ cup)
6	to 8 whole baby carrots with tops, about 1 pound
¾	cup chicken broth
2	tablespoons fresh tarragon leaves

1. Heat the olive oil in a skillet over medium high heat.
2. Place the onion slices into the pan and cook until soft and just beginning to brown, about 5 minutes.
3. Place the carrots in the pan and cook turning once.
4. Pour the chicken broth into the pan. Reduce heat to medium.
5. Sprinkle the tarragon leaves into the pan.
6. Cover the pan and simmer until the carrots are soft, about 10 minutes.
7. Serve the carrots on a dish and spoon the juices over top.

Serves 2 to 4
Preparation Time: 15 minutes

Did you know that the carrot is a member of the parsley family? Perhaps that is why their leafy tops are so enticing when shopping for fresh produce.

SOFT CENTER CHOCOLATE CAKES

Individual cakes may be prepared as much as a day in advance and baked just before serving. Remember to add a couple of minutes to the cooking time when baking chilled batter. A scoop of vanilla ice cream is the perfect accompaniment.

2   ounces semi-sweet chocolate
3   tablespoons unsalted butter
1   large egg
1   egg yolk
½   cup confectioners' sugar
3   tablespoons all-purpose flour

Preheat the oven to 450°.
1. Prepare 2 individual 8-ounce soufflé ramekins by coating the inside with butter.
2. Stir together the chocolate and butter in a saucepan over medium high heat. Remove from heat and cool.
3. Whisk the egg and egg yolk together in a bowl.
4. Whisk in the sugar, the melted chocolate mixture, and flour.
5. Pour the batter into the ramekins about ¾ full.
6. Bake the cakes until the sides are set and the center wiggles when shaken about 8 to 10 minutes.
7. Serve the cakes by running a sharp knife around the center and inverting the ramekins onto a dessert plate. Garnish with a scoop of ice cream, a sprinkling of cocoa powder, and a fresh mint sprig.

Serves 2
Preparation Time: 20 minutes plus baking

As with many inventions, this dish was created by accident. The chef under-baked the cake so that the center turned out to be soft and runny. The result—a dessert that became an overnight sensation and can be found on many restaurant menus.

Table for Two Party Plan

Party Motivation

This party for two is fabulous for an unexpected celebration—a raise, a promotion, a pat on the back for a job well done. Any of these is a great reason to serve a fussy supper. A little preparation is in order to enjoy all of the fun treats. Expect a giggle or two when you unveil the surprising dessert.

Party Menu

Mesclun Salad with Champagne Shallot Vinaigrette
Gnocchi with Golden Garlic Cream Sauce
Sole Cooked in Lemon Butter Wine Sauce **
Sugared Dessert Doughnuts

** Over-the-Top Suggestion

For a challenge, try preparing a whole sole that has been skinned and gutted. The cooking process is the same but allow for some additional cooking time, as the fish will be thicker. Serve the whole fish on a platter and garnish with additional sauce.

Party Strategy

Begin with the dessert. The doughnut dough needs to rest for several hours in the refrigerator before frying so combine the ingredients as soon as you can—or the day before. Choose the freshest greens and whisk together the vinaigrette, which will stay fresh for quite awhile. Dust the sole with flour immediately before cooking—or your results will be sticky instead of golden.

The evening before: Prepare the doughnut dough and refrigerate.

Several hours before: Prepare the gnocchi and make the vinaigrette. Cook the garlic in olive oil. Fry the doughnuts and let cool before sugaring.

Thirty minutes before: Make the golden garlic cream sauce for the gnocchi. Put the water on to boil. Boil the gnocchi while you prepare the sole.

Shortcuts

Purchase a bag of gourmet greens instead of collecting fresh mesclun greens and purchase fresh gnocchi from an Italian market.

Party Backdrop

A vase filled with tulips and a matching pair of candlesticks is all that is need for this fun meal. Celebrate successes with a toss of confetti as you present the dessert.

The tone is fussy yet casual. You have a reason to celebrate in a relaxed atmosphere. Enjoy this not-so-everyday fare on any day that you want to partee.

The Table Setting

Serve the salad from a wooden salad bowl to allow the assorted leaves to show their distinctive shapes.

Prepare the dinner plates in the kitchen. Because both of the main dish foods are white, use your favorite brightly-colored, over-sized buffet plates. Carefully transfer the fillets to the plates and garnish with extra sauce and chopped parsley.

Pile the doughnuts onto a pedestal cake plate and sprinkle with confectioners' sugar.

MESCLUN SALAD with CHAMPAGNE SHALLOT VINAIGRETTE

Make this vinaigrette in moments. Be careful to only use enough to lightly coat the greens. Too much will overwhelm their delicate flavor.

2   cups assorted mesclun greens

1   large shallot, minced (about 1 table-spoon)
1   teaspoon Dijon mustard
1   tablespoon champagne vinegar
¼   cup olive oil
Salt and freshly ground pepper

1. Place the greens in a bowl.

2. In a small bowl whisk together the shallot, mustard, and vinegar.
3. Slowly whisk in the olive oil. Season with salt and pepper.
4. Pour enough of the salad dressing over the greens to lightly coat them. Toss and serve.

Serves 2
Preparation Time: 15 minutes

The term mesclun *originates from the Nice area of France and has its roots in the word* mesclu-mo *meaning "a mixture." It refers to a mixture of young, slightly bitter leaves and young shoots of wild plants such as chicory, arugula, curly endive, dandelion, and chervil to name a few. You can also add red oak leaf, frisee, and radicchio for a terrific blend.*

Gnocchi with Golden Garlic Cream Sauce

This is a wonderfully rich dish that comes together more quickly than you think. If time is short, you can prepare the gnocchi a day or two before you need them. After they cook in boiling water transfer immediately to a bowl of ice water. Drain and toss with a bit of olive oil. Store in an airtight container in the refrigerator for up to two days. To reheat drop the gnocchi into boiling water until they float to the surface.

3	medium russet potatoes
1	cup all-purpose flour
1	egg, beaten
4	to 6 large cloves garlic
¼	cup olive oil
¾	cup heavy cream
2	tablespoons grated Parmesan cheese
2	tablespoons chopped fresh parsley leaves
	Salt and freshly ground pepper

1. Peel the potatoes. Place them into a large saucepan and boil until soft, about 30 to 40 minutes. Drain in a colander to remove excess moisture.
2. While still warm pass the potatoes through a vegetable mill or ricer.
3. Make a well in the center of the potatoes. Sprinkle all of the flour over top.
4. Place the egg into the center of the well. Use a fork to begin combining the mixture from the center out.
5. Use your hands to bring the mixture into a ball. Knead for several minutes until the dough is not sticky. Divide the dough into 2 halves. Cover and refrigerate half for later use.
6. Roll the remaining half into a 1 inch diameter cylinder. Cut the cylinder into 1-inch pieces. Press and roll each piece off the back tines of a fork to create an indentation in the gnocchi.
7. Cook the garlic in the olive oil in a small saucepan over medium high heat until golden brown. Remove the garlic from the oil. Reserve oil for another use.
8. Smash the soft garlic into small pieces. Place into a saucepan over medium high heat.
9. Add the cream to the pan and bring to a boil. Simmer until the cream reduces and thickens slightly.
10. Add the cheese and parsley and stir. Season with salt and pepper.
11. Cook the gnocchi in a pot of salted boiling water until they begin to float to the surface, about 1 minute. Drain.
12. Toss the gnocchi with the sauce and garnish with additional Parmesan cheese and chopped parsley.

Serves 2
Preparation Time: 1 hour

Gnocchi is a dumpling. Russet potatoes are recommended as the potato of choice when making gnocchi because of their starchiness. The only way to get a really terrific gnocchi is to use a ricer or food mill. A food processor does not work nearly as well. The other secret is to get the dough to absorb as much flour as possible without overworking it. It takes a little practice—but even the mistakes taste super.

SOLE cooked in LEMON BUTTER WINE SAUCE

This delicate dish is the perfect "fast food" as it cooks in minutes and the preparation is nominal.

2   6- to 8-ounce white sole fillets
¼   cup all-purpose flour
**   Salt and freshly ground pepper**
¼   cup butter (½ stick)
½   cup white wine
**   Juice of 2 lemons (about ¼ cup)**
2   tablespoons chopped fresh parsley leaves

1. Dredge each fillet into the flour. Shake off excess and season with salt and pepper.
2. Heat butter in a large skillet over medium high heat until bubbling.
3. Lay the fillets into the butter and cook for 3 to 4 minutes or until golden brown.
4. Use a fish spatula to gently turn the fillets.
5. Cook on the other side until golden, about 2 minutes more.
6. Pour the white wine and lemon juice over the fillets.
7. Allow the fish to cook in the sauce for 5 minutes more, spooning the sauce over the fish as it cooks.
8. Transfer the fish to warm plates, spoon the sauce over top, and garnish with fresh parsley.

Serves 2
Preparation Time: 20 minutes

Sole is a delicate, lean, ocean flat-fish whose common varieties include Dover sole, lemon sole, petrale and rex. Because of its delicate nature, cook sole quickly and cautiously to prevent breaking. A fish spatula is an excellent kitchen gadget to use when turning this delicate fish.

SUGARED DESSERT DOUGHNUTS

These basic doughnuts are fun to make and even more fun to sugar. For alternative coatings try dredging warm doughnuts in granulated sugar or icing cool doughnuts with your favorite frosting.

¼ **cup vegetable shortening, melted**
1 **cup granulated sugar**
2 **large eggs**
1 **cup evaporated milk**
2 **teaspoons vanilla extract**
4 **cups all-purpose flour**
4 **teaspoons baking powder**
1½ **teaspoons ground nutmeg**
¼ **teaspoon ground mace**
1 **teaspoon salt**

1 **cup confectioners' sugar**
2 **tablespoons cocoa powder**

1. Use an electric mixer to beat the sugar and shortening together.
2. Add the eggs, one at a time, mixing well.
3. Mix in the milk and vanilla.
4. Mix in the flour, baking powder, nutmeg, mace, and salt, in three additions, until just combined. The dough will be sticky.
5. Turn out the dough onto a large piece of plastic wrap, cover, and refrigerate for 4 hours or overnight.
6. Place the dough onto a floured surface. Roll out the dough in a rectangle about ½ inch thick.
7. Use a doughnut cutter dipped in flour to cut out the doughnuts. Place the doughnuts (and the holes) on a baking sheet lined with a Silpat liner.
8. Pour vegetable oil into a deep pot filling about a third of the way to the top. Heat the oil to 375°.
9. Fry the doughnuts in the hot oil in batches (cooking no more than 4 doughnuts at a time). Cook until golden brown about 2 to 3 minutes. Use a slotted spoon to transfer the doughnuts to a rack lined with paper towels to drain.
10. Cool the doughnuts.
11. Sift together the confectioners' sugar and cocoa powder. Sprinkle over the doughnuts.

Yield: 1 dozen doughnuts
Preparation Time: 1 hour

When frying foods remember that as the oil gets hot in the pan it will expand. It will also expand when you add the food to be fried and it will bubble. Therefore, to be safe, always start with a pot that is ⅓ to ½ full. Maintain a consistent temperature in between frying. If the oil is too hot, the doughnuts will brown too quickly. If the oil is not hot enough, the doughnuts will be greasy. Use a hot-oil thermometer to make sure the oil is at the correct temperature.

Everyday Celebrations

(WEEKDAY PARTIES FOR FOUR)

Lunch Bunch
Wacky Wednesday Dinner with Pals
Fondue for Four on the Floor
High Rise High Jinks
Supper Italian Style

"Guarantee a stress-free home party by following these simple tips. First, make sure that you cover all of the bases. Spend time concentrating on details. Prepare grocery-shopping lists, take inventory of china, and plan a menu that works within your budget and time frame. Secondly, make sure that your house is clean—before the party. You do not want to be mopping the floor as your guests arrive. Third, buy as many freshly cut flowers as your budget will permit, place them in vases and set them everywhere in your house—on coffee tables, end tables and in the bathrooms. Filling your house with flowers decorates a party. Fourth, plan the menu in advance. If you are incorporating a new dish, one that you have never prepared, eliminate stress by practicing on family members first. When hosting a large party, hire helpers and work with them in advance so that everyone knows their job. Finally, if you have small children in the house hire a babysitter to play with them—so that you can play at your party."

Joy Wallace
Owner of A Joy Wallace Catering Production and Design Team, Miami, Florida
www.joycater.com

Lunch Bunch Party Plan

Party Motivation

At noontime is there a group of people hanging around the makeshift kitchen office waiting for his or her turn at the microwave oven? Perhaps you are looking to be a kinder and gentler employer and want to encourage your coworkers to spend quality time with each other—sort of a team building exercise. Maybe you are looking for some free time during the workday or a way to limit those fast food, high calorie lunches on the run. The idea of eating and not enjoying the taste of the food, or sharing that time socializing with others is a casualty of our fast paced society. But, there is an alternative experience. Start a Lunch Bunch—a terrific vehicle for pals coming together, eating well, and enjoying some moments of pampering during the workweek.

Party Menu

Easy Broccoli and Cheese Soup
Quick Chili with Lentils and Black Beans
Spicy Grilled Chicken Salad with Roasted Asparagus, Yellow Peppers,
and Creamy Basil Vinaigrette
Cobb Salad Wrap Arounds
Roasted Tomato and Ricotta Tart
Oatmeal Chocolate Chip Cookies

** Over-the-Top Suggestion

Pack the lunch of your choice in individual wicker baskets and deliver the basket to your coworker's desk when the clock strikes noon.

Party Strategy

Choose two or three of your coworkers to share this party plan. The members of a convenient Lunch Bunch should have the same workplace (in the same building, if not on the same floor), similar schedules (working in the office, not out on daily sales calls), and similar tastes in food (willing to experiment with wraps in place of turkey on rye every day).

The idea is that each member of the Lunch Bunch chooses a day to bring lunch for the other members—each week. One person prepares and delivers four lunches including himself, one day a week. Three days a week he receives lunch at his desk. The fifth day of the week is free to allow for lunch meetings and errands.

Shortcuts

These recipes are simple and easy to prepare in just minutes, but shortcut the effort even further, by incorporating upscale leftovers into your Lunch Bunch plan. Leftover grilled chicken works well in either the salad or the wrap. Leftover roasted veggies are super on a tart, and extra cookies baked on Saturday and stored well are perfect for Wednesday's lunch.

Party Backdrop

The office is the backdrop for your Lunch Bunch meal. Add a vase with a fresh cut flower, a party placemat and a cloth napkin for a festive setting. Don't forget disposable plates and utensils!

The Table Setting

Delivery is the key to making a lunch bunch a party—not a drudgery. Serve each meal in a Fun manner. Pack individual lunches in a flexible lunchbox, picnic basket or oversized brown bag. If you are eating together, remember a tablecloth and add a bowl of fresh fruit!

Easy Broccoli and Cheese Soup

Make this soup in less than 30 minutes, pour it into a thermos and off you go.

1	tablespoon olive oil
1	large yellow onion, diced (about 1 cup)
2	medium cloves garlic, minced (about 1 teaspoon)
1	teaspoon curry powder
½	teaspoon cumin
1	quart chicken stock
1	medium bunch broccoli florets, chopped
⅓	cup all-purpose flour
2	cups cream
2	cups grated extra sharp Cheddar cheese
	Salt and freshly ground pepper

1. Heat the olive oil in a pot over medium high heat.
2. Add the onions and cook until soft, about 5 minutes.
3. Add the garlic, curry powder and cumin. Cook for 2 minutes more.
4. Pour the stock into the pan. Add the broccoli. Reduce the heat to medium and cook until the broccoli is tender, about 10 minutes.
5. Whisk the flour into the cream until smooth. Pour this mixture into the pot. Cook until the soup begins to thicken, stirring constantly, about 5 minutes.
6. Add the cheese and stir until melted.
7. Pour half of the soup into a blender or food processor. Pulse until smooth. Add this mixture back to the soup. Season with salt and pepper.

Serves 4 to 6
Preparation Time: 25 minutes

Use this format to create your own favorite take-along soup.
Substitute with different cheese and veggies. Feel free to alter the spices with you favorites.
Make the soup a real favorite by substituting processed cheese in place of the real thing!

QUICK CHILI with LENTILS and BLACK BEANS

Prepare this easy-to-make chili the night before. Reheat it at the office and serve from over sized coffee mugs.

1   tablespoon olive oil
1   large yellow onion, diced (about 1 cup)
1   large red bell pepper, seeded and diced (about 1 cup)
4   medium cloves garlic, minced (about 2 teaspoons)
1   tablespoon chili powder
1   teaspoon ground cumin
1   teaspoon dried oregano
1   medium jalapeño pepper, seeded and diced (about 2 tablespoons)
1   cup dried lentils
1   cup chicken stock
1   16-ounce can black beans, drained
1   14.5-ounce can diced tomatoes
1   tablespoon chopped fresh cilantro leaves
1   tablespoon chopped fresh rosemary
    Salt and freshly ground pepper

Sour cream
Diced avocado
Blue corn chips

1. Heat the olive oil in a large pot over medium high heat.
2. Add the onion and pepper and cook until soft about 5 minutes.
3. Stir in the garlic, chili powder, cumin, oregano, and jalapeño pepper. Cook for 2 minutes.
4. Stir in the lentils, chicken stock, black beans and tomatoes. Reduce heat to medium, cover and simmer until the lentils are soft, about 20 to 30 minutes.
5. Stir in cilantro. Season with salt and pepper.
6. Serve with a dollop of sour cream, diced avocados and corn chips for dipping.

Serves 4 to 6
Preparation Time: 30 minutes

Dried spices are often cooked in hot oil to intensify their flavors. This process takes only moments and makes the kitchen smell soooo good.

Spicy Grilled Chicken Salad with Roasted Asparagus, Yellow Peppers, and Creamy Basil Vinaigrette

This easy to assemble salad has flavors that jump off the plate.

2	**6- to 8-ounce skinless boneless chicken breast halves**
2	**tablespoons olive oil**
2	**tablespoons Worcestershire sauce**
2	**medium cloves garlic, minced (about 1 teaspoon)**
1	**teaspoon paprika**
1	**teaspoon dried red pepper flakes**
2	**large yellow bell peppers**
8	**to 12 medium asparagus spears, stems peeled**
2	**tablespoons olive oil**
	Salt and freshly ground pepper
¼	**cup champagne vinegar**
	Juice of 2 lemons (about ¼ cup)
¼	**cup fresh basil leaves**
2	**tablespoons mayonnaise**
1	**tablespoon Dijon mustard**
½	**cup olive oil**
12	**Kalamata olives, pitted and chopped**
	Parmigiano Reggiano cheese, shaved

1. Marinate the chicken breasts in 2 tablespoons olive oil, Worcestershire sauce, garlic, paprika and pepper flakes for at least 20 minutes and up to overnight.

2. Heat a grill pan on medium high heat. Grill the breasts, turning once, about 5 minutes per side. Set aside.

Preheat the oven to the broil setting.

3. Roast the peppers turning until the skin is charred. Place into a bowl, cover and steam for 10 minutes. Peel the peppers and cut into thin strips.

Reduce oven temperature to 350°.

4. Place the asparagus onto a rack on a baking sheet. Drizzle with olive oil. Season with salt and pepper. Roast for 10 minutes.

5. Place the champagne vinegar, lemon juice, basil, mayonnaise, and mustard into a blender. Pulse to combine. With the machine running, slowly add the olive oil. Season with salt and pepper.

6. To assemble the salad, slice the chicken breasts into thin strips. Place the chicken strips, peppers and asparagus onto a serving plate. Drizzle with vinaigrette. Garnish with chopped olives and shaved cheese.

Serves 4 to 6
Preparation Time: 30 minutes

To take this salad along with you to the office, pack the chicken, peppers and asparagus into separate plastic bags. Pour the vinaigrette into an airtight disposable container. Chop olives and place into a plastic bag. Shave the cheese into long curls and place into a disposable bag. Arrange the salad onto 4 plates and deliver each one to your coworkers' desk!

COBB SALAD WRAP-AROUNDS

Eat your favorite salad without using a fork in this fun salad/sandwich twist.

8	**6-inch flour tortillas**
2	**6- to 8-ounce skinless boneless chicken breast halves, grilled and sliced into strips**
¼	**head iceberg lettuce, shredded (about 2 cups)**
½	**pound bacon, diced and cooked**
1	**large avocados, diced (about 1 cup)**
⅓	**cup sliced black olives**
3	**to 4 plum tomatoes, seeded and diced (about 1 cup)**
4	**ounces blue cheese, crumbled**
2	**tablespoons prepared vinaigrette dressing**
	Salt and freshly ground pepper

1. Divide the ingredients into 8 portions. Prepare wraps by stacking ⅛ of the ingredients onto the bottom third of 1 flour tortilla.
2. Layer chicken strips with shredded lettuce, bacon, avocados, black olives, tomatoes, and blue cheese. Drizzle a small amount of vinaigrette over top.
3. Roll up the tortilla around the filling. Wrap with parchment paper. Before serving, cut each wrap into half leaving the parchment paper in place. Serve 2 wraps per person.

Serves 4
Preparation Time: 20 minutes

Use this same wrap around technique with your other favorite salads like grilled chicken Caesar salad or my favorite, chopped chef salad. If you are really adventuresome, try using large iceberg, romaine or bibb lettuce leaves to wrap up your favorite sandwich fixin's like bacon, tomato and cheddar cheese or corn beef and Swiss cheese slices.

Roasted Tomato and Ricotta Tart

This simple tart can be made with your favorite roasted veggies like baby artichokes, asparagus and fennel.

3	medium red tomatoes, cut into wedges (about 2 cups)
1	tablespoon olive oil
4	medium cloves garlic, minced (about 2 teaspoons)
	Salt and Freshly ground pepper
½	cup ricotta cheese
1	large egg yolk
¼	cup sour cream
1	sheet (16-ounce) puff pastry sheet, thawed
	All-purpose flour
1	large egg
1	tablespoon water
1	bunch (6 to 8) green onions, sliced in half lengthwise
2	tablespoons chopped fresh basil leaves

Preheat the oven to 400°.

1. Place the tomato wedges on a baking sheet. Toss with olive oil, garlic, salt, and pepper. Roast until soft and caramelized, about 10 minutes.
2. Stir the ricotta, egg yolk and sour cream together. Season with salt and pepper.
3. Roll out the puff pastry, on a lightly floured board, to an 8 x 11-inch rectangle. Transfer to a baking sheet. Use the tip of a knife to score a 1-inch border into the pastry.
4. Make an egg wash by mixing together 1 egg with 1 tablespoon water. Brush the egg wash on the border of the puff pastry.
5. Spread the ricotta filling onto the pastry leaving the 1-inch border.
6. Arrange the roasted tomatoes on top of the ricotta. Arrange the sliced onions around the tomatoes.
7. Bake until the cheese is bubbly and the crust is golden, about 20 to 25 minutes.
8. Sprinkle with fresh basil. Serve at room temperature.

Serves 4 to 6
Preparation Time: 30 minutes plus baking.

The tart can be prepared in advance and refrigerated until the next day.
Bake as directed, allow to rest for several minutes and serve warm. If you are really industrious, you can prepare your own tart dough by placing 1¼ cups flour and 1 stick of chilled butter (cut into small pieces) into the bowl of a food processor. Pulse until the mixture resembles course crumbs. Beat 1 large egg yolk with 2 tablespoons of ice water. With the machine running add only enough of the egg mixture to hold the dough together. Place the dough onto a piece of plastic wrap and form into a rectangle. Wrap and chill for at least 1 hour.
Roll out the dough to ¼-inch thickness and continue with the recipe.

OATMEAL CHOCOLATE CHIP COOKIES

My grandmother's recipe that has been handed down is a favorite in *At Home in the Kitchen,* and the perfect cookie to share with co-workers' at lunch!

2½	**cups all purpose flour**
1	**teaspoon baking soda**
¾	**teaspoon salt**
½	**teaspoon cinnamon**
½	**cup margarine, room temperature (1 stick)**
½	**cup unsalted butter, room temperature (1 stick)**
1	**cup brown sugar**
½	**cup granulated sugar**
2	**large eggs**
1	**teaspoon vanilla extract**
¾	**cup old fashioned rolled oats**
6	**ounces semisweet chocolate chips**
6	**ounces white chocolate chips**

Preheat the oven to 350°.

1. Combine the flour, baking soda, salt and cinnamon in a small bowl.
2. Use an electric mixer to blend together the margarine and butter until creamy.
3. Stir in both sugars to the butter mixture and blend well.
4. Add the eggs one at a time.
5. Stir in the vanilla.
6. Add in the flour mixture in three parts, scraping down the bowl after each addition.
7. Stir in the oats and both the white and dark chocolate chips using the slow speed.
8. Drop the cookie batter by rounded teaspoons onto a Silpat-lined baking sheet. Bake for 10 minutes or until slightly browned and firm to the touch. Cool on baking racks for several minutes.

Yield: 5 dozen cookies
Preparation Time: 20 minutes

Make your own cookie tradition by substituting ingredients with your favorites. For example, you might substitute all-spice for cinnamon, peanut butter or mint chips for white chocolate or add ½ cup chopped walnuts or pecans for a nutty taste.

Wacky Wednesday Dinner for Pals Party Plan

Party Motivation

It's the middle of the week—you've made it through Mad Monday and Hectic Tuesday—why not invite a few pals from work to your place and cook up a quick and easy supper to share with all.

Party Menu

Sun-Dried Tomato Dip
Avocado and Curly Endive Salad with Citrus Vinaigrette
Grilled Red Snapper with Olives and Cilantro Relish
Roasted Garlic Smashed Potatoes with Truffle Oil **
Apple Blueberry Crisp with Pecan Topping

**** Over-the-Top Suggestion**

Mashed potatoes are yummy all of the time, but the addition of roasted garlic and a drizzle of truffle oil take this standard fare to new taste heights.

Party Strategy

Serve the dip to your pals while you boil the potatoes and toss the salad. You can bake the dessert while you enjoy the meal.

The night before: Prepare dip, cover and refrigerate.

On your way home: Make a quick stop to pick up the freshest fish fillets available. The fresher the fish—the better the dish.

One hour before: Prepare the olive relish. Boil the potatoes. Prepare the dessert.

As the guests arrive: Make the vinaigrette and toss the salad. Serve the appy and take off your tie!

Shortcut

You can bake a terrific fruit crisp by using canned pie fillings. Just watch the sugar content, as too much is not always such a good thing!

Party Backdrop

Let's aim for that big SIGH of relaxation that comes from your guests as they whip off their ties and kick of their heels. Place a large basket by the front door. Toss in your beeper, pager and cell phone. Invite your friends to do the same. An upbeat FM station on the stereo offers plenty of mood music—or you might try a couple of muted disks like Pure Moods I and II. Set out a bucket filled with ice and a pair of tongs and invite your pals to make like Tom Cruise in *Cocktail* offering mixers and sodas, cold beer and a chilled bottle of wine. Pass the corkscrew. Pile plates and utensils on the table. Add a stack of cloth napkins. Serve the meal family style passing platters and bowls.

The Table Setting

Serve the dip in a small bowl. Fill a cloth-lined basket with crackers, breadsticks, carrot slices and celery. Toss the salad in a large wooden bowl and drizzle the dressing from a pitcher. A pepper mill is the perfect salad companion. Place the golden snapper fillets on top of a mound of smashed potatoes in the center of a large platter. Check out pearl-colored earthenware platters for serving. Available in several different styles, the white platters highlight the food with just a tiny pearl detail on the edge of each piece. Surround the fish with spoonfuls of olive and cilantro relish and drizzle a dash of truffle oil around the outside rim of the dish.

SUN-DRIED TOMATO DIP

You can make this dip in a matter of moments with the ingredients that you have stored in your pantry. Use extras to smear on a bagel or layer on your turkey wrap.

1	6-ounce jar sun-dried tomatoes, drained
1	8-ounce package cream cheese, room temperature
½	cup sour cream
1	tablespoon chili sauce
½	teaspoon hot pepper sauce (or more)
4	green onions, thinly sliced (about ¼ cup)
2	tablespoons fresh cilantro
	Salt and freshly ground pepper

1. Place all of the ingredients into the bowl of a food processor.
2. Pulse to combine.

Yield: 2 cups
Preparation Time: 10 minutes

Be inventive when you prepare a spur-of-the-moment dip. Feel free to add favorite spicy ingredients like anchovies, red pepper flakes or roasted pine nuts! You can also be creative with the "dippers." Toasted pita chips, baby carrots, chunks of crusty bread, or slices of prosciutto rolled around thin breadsticks are just a start. Look around your kitchen and find your favorite dippers.

AVOCADO and CURLY ENDIVE SALAD
with CITRUS VINAIGRETTE

This simple salad comes together in moments and combines the distinctive tastes or fresh orange and blue cheese.

2   heads curly endive lettuce (about 4 cups)
2   large avocados, peeled and sliced (about 2 cups)
2   large oranges, peeled and sectioned (about 1 cup)
3   ounces blue cheese, crumbled (about ½ cup)

Juice of 1 medium orange (about ⅔ cup)
¼   cup cider vinegar
1   teaspoon chili powder
¼   teaspoon salt
⅓   cup peanut oil
Freshly ground pepper

1. Clean and dry the lettuce leaves. Tear into bite size pieces.
2. Toss the lettuce with the avocado slices, orange wedges and crumbled cheese.
3. In a medium bowl whisk together orange juice, vinegar, chili powder and salt until combined.
4. Slowly whish in the peanut oil.
5. Drizzle the dressing over the salad. Toss gently. Season with pepper.

Serves 4
Preparation Time: 20 minutes

Curly endive (sometimes called chicory) is native to the Mediterranean.
A terrific salad green it has dark, frilly leaves that are somewhat bitter.
If you like curly endive you might try preparing it as you would spinach—sautéed
with caramelized onions or dropped into simmering vegetable soup.

Grilled Red Snapper with Olives and Cilantro Relish

Fresh fish fillets are the ultimate "fast food." They cook in minutes and are terrific fare to serve for an impromptu party.

4	6-ounce red snapper fillets
1	tablespoon olive oil
½	teaspoon ground cumin
½	teaspoon ground coriander
	Salt and freshly ground pepper

1	2-ounce jar Spanish olives, chopped (about 20)
6	to 8 plum tomatoes, seeded and diced (about 2 cups)
1	16-ounce can pinto beans, drained
2	medium cloves garlic, minced (about 1 teaspoon)
2	green onions, thinly sliced (about 2 tablespoons)
	Juice of 1 fresh lime (about 2 tablespoons)

2	tablespoons olive oil
2	tablespoons chopped fresh cilantro leaves
½	teaspoon red pepper flakes

1. Brush both sides of the fillets with olive oil.
2. Sprinkle with cumin, coriander and season with salt and pepper.
3. Grill the fish turning once, about 4 to 5 minutes per side.
4. Prepare the relish by combining the chopped olives, tomatoes, pinto beans, garlic and onions in a small bowl.
5. Toss with lime juice and olive oil.
6. Stir in the cilantro and red pepper flakes.

Serves 4
Preparation Time: 20 minutes

Spanish olives are large and dense and have a terrific flavor that works well in relish, salsa and sauces. Usually a Spanish olive is found pitted and stuffed with pimentos, almonds or anchovies. Choose your favorite for this dish or substitute with Kalamata or Nicoise olives.

ROASTED GARLIC SMASHED POTATOES with TRUFFLE OIL

Truffle oil adds an upscale flavor burst to already savory roasted garlic. The combination of flavors is out of this world.

2   **to 3 large russet potatoes, peeled and cut into pieces (about 2 pounds)**
4   **to 6 cloves roasted garlic**
½   **cup whipping cream**
¼   **cup sour cream**
2   **tablespoons fresh chives**
    Salt and freshly ground pepper
1   **tablespoon truffle oil**

1. Place the potato pieces into boiling water. Cook until tender about 10 minutes.

2. Drain the potatoes into a colander. Place into a bowl.
3. Use a potato masher to mash the potatoes.
4. Add the roasted garlic cloves, cream, sour cream and chives. Season with salt and pepper.
5. Drizzle truffle oil over the top.

Serves 4
Preparation Time: 20 minutes

To roast garlic, cut the top ¼ from the bulb. Place the bulb, stem side down, on a sheet of aluminum foil. Drizzle olive oil over top of the garlic. Sprinkle with dried oregano, salt, and freshly ground pepper. Wrap foil around the garlic leaving a small opening at the top. Roast in the oven at 350° for about 30 minutes or until the cloves are soft and beginning to turn golden brown.

APPLE BLUEBERRY CRISP with PECAN TOPPING

The pecans add a special flavor to this simple dessert. Feel free to vary the fruit with your seasonal favorites like pear and strawberry or nectarine and blackberry.

3	medium apples, peeled and sliced (about 3 cups)
8	ounces fresh blueberries (about 1½ cups)
1	tablespoon granulated sugar
1	tablespoon all-purpose flour
1	teaspoon ground ginger
¾	cup brown sugar
¾	cup pecans
¼	cup all purpose flour
¼	cup butter (½ stick), chilled and cut into pieces
¼	cup rolled oats
½	teaspoon ground cinnamon
½	teaspoon ground nutmeg
¼	teaspoon salt

Preheat the oven to 350°.

1. Toss the apples and the blueberries with 1 tablespoon sugar, 1 tablespoon flour and the ginger.
2. Place the fruit in an 11 x 9 x 2-inch baking pan.
3. Place the brown sugar, pecans, flour, butter, oats, cinnamon, nutmeg and salt into the bowl of a food processor. Pulse until the mixture resembles course crumbs. Spread this mixture over the fruit.
4. Bake until brown and bubbling about 30 to 40 minutes.

Serves 6 or more
Preparation Time: 20 minutes plus baking

Blueberries are a wonderful addition to desserts. Handle them with care. Rinse the blueberries and remove any small stems. Gently stir the blueberries into the dessert to prevent breaking them apart.

Fondue for Four on the Floor Party Plan

Party Motivation

Getting to know new friends over a communal pot—or a perfect celebration that brings together old friends to share a bit of gossip. Tabletop dining represents a leisurely supper that allows conversation to become the dominant ingredient of the meal.

Party Menu

Lightly Battered Veggie Fondue
Swiss Cheese Fondue with Pesto Swirl **
Beef Fondue with Three Dipping Sauces
Warm Chocolate Fondue

**** Over-the-Top Suggestion**

Traditional cheese fondue is a must, but by adding a swirl of freshly made pesto, this fondue becomes an elegant dish.

Party Strategy

Cut up veggies, fruit and meat in advance. Make sauces the day before. This party cooks itself! Serve the Swiss cheese fondue as a first course. Chilled white wine is the perfect beverage to accompany the meal. Serve the beef and veggie fondue together. If you have two pots, use one for the battered veggies and reserve the other for the beef. Chocolate fondue does not need to be warm—however, it's so much more fun if it is.

The day before: Cut up veggies and beef. Store in separate containers and refrigerate until party time.

Make dipping sauces and refrigerate in an airtight containers until ready to serve.

Two hours before: Prepare chocolate fondue and keep warm. Prepare cheese fondue and keep warm.

One hour before: Set out fondue pots and check warmers. Measure out the amount of oil needed for each pot. Prepare to warm oil. (*Note:* Never leave hot oil unattended whether in a pan on the stove or in a heated fondue pot!)

Shortcuts

Purchased pesto, either basil or sun-dried tomato will easily garnish the cheese fondue. The veggies will cook quite nicely without the light batter and in the same pot with the beef. Substitute with a prepared sauce for dipping the veggies like ranch salad dressing. Simple chocolate syrup makes a suitable substitute for a chocolate dipping dessert.

Party Backdrop

Find the most comfortable spot in you house. For me it's sitting on oversized pillows around a low coffee table in the living room. A fondue pot is a must. Two fondue pots would be better. Three fondue pots will take you through dessert. Borrow from your pals.

Think casual and conversational. This is a relaxing way to entertain—a time to enjoy your guests. Use sturdy placemats under the fondue pots to collect drips.

The Table Setting

There are several great fondue pots on the market. I prefer a set with a stainless steel body and a separate glass insert that is perfect for cheese or chocolate fondue. Forks have cute domino heads so that everyone can easily remember which one belongs to them. Simple fondue plates are white, ceramic round dishes that have up to six separate compartments. That's plenty of places to take your party guest from a cheesy starter to a beef and veggie main course with room left for a chocolaty dessert.

LIGHTLY-BATTERED VEGGIE FONDUE

Feel free to use your favorite veggies in this lightly battered dish. Make sure that the oil stays very hot for the crispiest fondue.

Cauliflower florets
Broccoli florets
Baby portobello mushrooms
Zucchini slices
Baby carrots

1   **cup all-purpose flour**
½   **teaspoon salt**
1   **tablespoon olive oil**
⅔   **cup beer**
2   **egg whites, whipped to stiff peaks**

1. Prepare the veggies so that they are small and uniform in size.
2. Place the flour and salt in a bowl.
3. Whisk in the olive oil and beer until smooth.
4. Fold in the egg whites.
5. Heat the oil over medium high heat until it reaches 350°. Carefully transfer the oil to the fondue pot making sure that it is filled no more than halfway to the top.
6. Use a fondue fork to immerse the veggies first into the batter and then into the hot oil until cooked.
7. Serve the veggies with your favorite dipping sauce or simply serve with bottles of hot sauce, soy sauce, or chili sauce.

Serves 4
Preparation Time: 20 minutes

The smaller the veggie, the quicker it will cook in the hot oil. Prepare the vegetables so that they are small enough to cook quickly, but still retain their true nature. The beer adds a fun flavor and keeps the batter light, but you can easily substitute with water if you prefer.

Swiss Cheese Fondue with Pesto Swirl

The word fondue comes from the French word fonder meaning "to melt." Traditional cheese fondue is the blending of melted cheese seasoned with wine or sherry or both! The addition of pesto adds an elegant look to this terrific dish. You can make your cheese fondue your own by swirling in your favorite garnish like sun-dried tomato pesto, or caramelized onions, or perhaps fresh herbs. You choose!

1   **medium clove garlic**
½   **cup dry white wine**
    Juice of ½ lemon (about 1 tablespoon)
6   **ounces Emmanthal cheese, grated**
6   **ounces Gruyere cheese, grated**
1   **tablespoon all-purpose flour**
1   **tablespoons sherry**
¼   **teaspoon ground nutmeg**

1   **cup fresh basil leaves**
1   **cup fresh spinach leaves**
½   **cup grated Parmesan cheese**
½   **cup pine nuts, toasted**
4   **medium cloves garlic**
    Juice of ½ lemon (about 1 tablespoon)
½   **cup olive oil**

1. Heat the garlic clove, wine and lemon juice in a saucepan over medium high heat until bubbles form. Remove the garlic and discard. Reduce the heat to low.
2. Toss the grated cheese with the flour.
3. Add the cheese in small batches stirring constantly.
4. When the cheese is melted, stir in the sherry and season with nutmeg.
5. For the pesto sauce place the basil, spinach, cheese, pine nuts, garlic and lemon juice in the bowl of a food processor. Pulse.
6. With the feed tube running add the olive oil.
7. Transfer the cheese fondue to a fondue pot and keep warm over medium heat.
8. Swirl a tablespoon or more of the pesto on the top of the fondue. (Reserve extra pesto for another use.)
9. Serve with your favorite dippers like cubes of crusty bread, carrot sticks, broccoli flowerets, pearl onions, spears of endive, celery stalks, cooked shrimp, boiled red potatoes and cherry tomatoes.

Serves 4
Preparation Time: 30 minutes

Emmenthaler is a cheese made from cow's milk produced predominantly in Switzerland. It is know for its random holes that can be small or large. You can substitute with Jarlsberg or a good quality Swiss cheese. Gruyere is also a cow's milk cheese predominantly produced in France and Switzerland but readily available in your local grocery store.

Beef Fondue with Three Dipping Sauces

Fondue is an easy way to entertain. Simply prepare a few wonderful sauces, heat the oil and permit your guests to cook their own dinner.

2 **pounds tenderloin steak, trimmed of all fat**
2 **tablespoons olive oil**
2 **medium cloves garlic, minced (about 1 teaspoon)**
½ **cup dry white wine**
   Vegetable oil

CURRIED MAYONNAISE
1 **cup mayonnaise**
2 **tablespoons ketchup**
1 **medium clove garlic, minced (about ½ teaspoon)**
1 **teaspoon curry powder**
2 **tablespoons chopped fresh cilantro leaves**

MOCK BEARNAISE SAUCE
½ **cup mayonnaise**
½ **cup sour cream**
2 **tablespoons tarragon vinegar**
   Juice of 1 lemon (about 2 tablespoons)
2 **tablespoons chopped fresh tarragon leaves**

MUSTARD CAPER SAUCE
½ **cup mayonnaise**
½ **cup sour cream**
2 **tablespoons whipping cream**
1 **tablespoon Dijon style mustard**

1 **teaspoon capers, drained**
2 **tablespoons chopped fresh parsley**

1. Marinate the steak in olive oil, garlic and white wine for 1 hour or over night.
2. Cut the steak into ¾-inch pieces. Arrange the steak pieces on a platter lined with lettuce leaves.
3. Heat the oil over medium high heat until it reaches 350°. Carefully transfer the oil to the fondue pot making sure that it is filled no more than halfway to the top. Keep warm over medium high heat.
4. Use a fondue fork to immerse the meat into the hot oil until cooked. Dip the meat into the accompanying sauces.

FOR CURRIED MAYONNAISE:
1. Mix all of the ingredients together in a small bowl.

FOR MOCK BEARNAISE SAUCE:
1. Mix all of the ingredients together in a small bowl.

FOR MUSTARD CAPER SAUCE:
1. Mix all of the ingredients together in a small bowl.

Serves 4
Preparation Time: 30 minutes

Take your fondue over the top by using flavored oil as the base. The market place is full of new flavored oils that you can purchase with names like Lemon Dill oil for Fondue or Rosemary Garlic flavored oil. Better yet, make your own by infusing your favorite herbs or garnish into vegetable oil. Simmer the oil for several minutes. Turn off the heat and allow the oil to steep. Cover the pot and let stand for at least one hour. Remove the herbs and spices from the oil and reheat to use in the fondue pot.

WARM CHOCOLATE FONDUE

The fun of this dessert is in the drips of chocolate that run onto the plate, the table, and your cheek!

1   cup heavy whipping cream
1   pound semi-sweet chocolate, finely chopped
     Juice of 1 medium orange (about ⅔ cup)
     Zest of 1 medium orange (about 2 tablespoons)
1   tablespoon Cointreau

1. Heat the cream in a double boiler over medium high heat.
2. Add the chocolate stirring constantly until melted.
3. Stir in the orange juice, zest and Cointreau.
4. Transfer the chocolate fondue to a fondue pot and keep warm on medium to medium low heat.
5. Serve with your favorite dippers like chunks of pound cake, dried apricots, sliced bananas, marshmallows, strawberries and raspberries, biscotti and chunks of apple and pineapple.

Serves 4
Preparation Time: 20 minutes

Cointreau is orange flavored liquor with a distinctive taste.
If it is not your favorite, feel free to flavor your chocolate fondue with other tastes like mint, molasses, or brewed coffee for mocha fondue.

High Rise High Jinks Party Plan

Party Motivation

New neighbors move in down the hall and you want to get to know them. Invite them over for a fun dinner and perhaps a game of cards.

Party Menu

Roasted Veggie Salad with Warm Goat Cheese Garnish **
Pan-Sautéed Pork Medallions in Ginger Butter Sauce
Crisp Oven-Roasted Fingerling Potatoes
French Fried Onion Rings
Double Chip Bundt Cake

**** Over-the-Top Suggestion**

Warm veggie salad starts off this simply satisfying meal. The addition of sautéed goat cheese adds an upscale twist that your guests can't resist.

Party Strategy

Prepare the plates in the kitchen to avoid too many platters on the table. Serve the warm salad as the first course. While you clear the table and prepare the main course, have your buddy pour water and refresh wine glasses.

The evening before: Bake the Bundt cake and prepare the veggies for roasting including the potatoes. Store the veggies separately, covered in the refrigerator. Peeled potatoes can be store in a bowl of cold water also placed in the refrigerator.

Two hours before: Cut the onions into rings. Cut pork into medallions and refrigerate. 30 minutes before: Roast potatoes. Roast veggies for salad. Fry onion rings and sauté goat cheese.

As the guests arrive: Prepare the pork with the ginger butter sauce.

Shortcuts

For a little less ambitious menu, roast the vegetables for the salad and mix together with roasted potatoes as a veggie side dish in place of the elaborate salad.

Party Backdrop

Set the dining room table for four. Use you favorite placemats or most fun tablecloth. Water and wine glasses are a must. Fan the napkins in the wine glass to add height. Serve the dessert with coffee in the living room or on the balcony.

Easy does it! These are new friends and you want to show them that you are interested in getting to know them. This casually—yet slightly fussy dinner is a great way to break the ice.

The Table Setting

Shallow bowls are perfect for the salad. Buffet plates (over-sized dinner plates) are wonderful for serving your meal from the kitchen. An essential white buffet plate made of durable glazed porcelain and sized at eleven inches in diameter is a must for entertaining. Place the pork medallions on the plate. Drizzle with ginger sauce. Place a spoonful of roasted potatoes alongside the pork. Mound the onion rings on top of the pork. Garnish the plate with a curl of fresh ginger. Place dessert plates and matching coffee mugs on the table in the living room. Use a tray to bring coffee, cream and sugar and the cake to the table.

Roasted Veggie Salad with Warm Goat Cheese Garnish

The wonderful flavor of roasted vegetables is accented by tangy Arugula leaves in this simple warm salad.

1	medium zucchini, cut into 1-inch cubes (about 1½ cups)
2	medium yellow squash, cut into 1-inch cubes (about 1½ cups)
4	plum tomatoes, cut in half lengthwise (about 2 cups)
1	small red onion cut into 1-inch cubes (about ½ cup)
2	medium clove garlic, minced (about 1 teaspoon)
1	tablespoon olive oil
1	tablespoon balsamic vinegar
	Salt and freshly ground pepper
2	cups arugula leaves, washed and well dried
1	tablespoon chopped fresh cilantro leaves
8	ounces goat cheese
3	tablespoon olive oil
½	cup flour
1	egg beaten with 1 tablespoon water
½	cup breadcrumbs

Preheat the oven to 400°.

1. Place the zucchini, squash, tomatoes, onion and garlic into a shallow baking pan.
2. Sprinkle with olive oil and vinegar.
3. Season with salt and freshly ground pepper. Toss.
4. Bake for 10 minutes. Use a spatula to turn the veggies. Bake for another 5 minutes.
5. Place the Arugula leaves in a bowl. Just before serving, toss the warm vegetables with the leaves. Add the fresh cilantro and toss gently.
6. Form the goat cheese into 1 ounce cakes.
7. Heat the olive oil over medium high heat.
8. Dredge the cakes in flour. Dip the cakes in the egg wash, removing any excess. Dredge the cakes in the bread crumbs.
9. Sauté the cakes turning once until they are golden brown, about 2 minutes per side. Drain on a paper towel.
10. Serve the cakes as a garnish to the warm veggie salad. Top with additional olive oil and freshly ground pepper.

Serves 4
Preparation Time: 20 minutes plus roasting

Feel free to substitute with any veggies that are in season.
Pumpkin and butternut squash are perfect veggies for fall roasting.
Cauliflower and Brussels sprouts will add a new taste with wilted red leaf lettuce.

Pan-Sautéed Pork Medallions in Ginger Butter Sauce

Butter is the main flavor in this dish. Searing pork medallions in butter gives the meat a rich taste. By adding ginger and soy sauce to the pan, you can create a great sauce in just a matter of moments.

2 **tablespoons butter**
1 **16-ounce pork tenderloin, cut into 8 diagonal medallions**
1 **large shallot, minced (about 1 tablespoon)**
1 **1-inch piece ginger, grated (about 1 tablespoon)**
2 **tablespoons soy sauce**
   Juice of ½ medium orange (about ⅓ cup)
   Freshly ground pepper

1. Melt the butter in a large pan over medium high heat until just smoking. (Be careful not to burn the butter!)
2. Place the medallions in the hot butter and sear on both sides (about 2 minutes). Remove the medallions to a platter.
3. Reduce the heat to medium.
4. Add the shallot and ginger to the pan. Cook for 1 minute.
5. Add the soy sauce and orange juice to the pan and cook for 1 minute more. Season with black pepper.
6. Place the medallions back into the pan and finish cooking (about 4 to 5 minutes).
7. Add a tablespoon or more water to the pan if the sauce gets too dry.
8. Serve 2 medallions on a plate. Serve with a spoonful of sauce.

Serves 4
Preparation Time: 15 minutes

This is a quick cooking method that works equally well with swordfish steaks, tuna, shrimp, chicken breast and beef tenderloin. Feel free to experiment with various ingredients added to the butter. Try a tablespoon of prepared mustard with sherry wine vinegar, chopped green onions with capers, and chopped tomatoes with dried basil leaves.

To cut the tenderloin into elongated diagonal medallions, place it on a cutting surface. Instead of cutting from top to bottom to produce round slices, place your sharp knife at a 45 degree angle and cut from top to tip. Repeat with 1 inch slices.

CRISP OVEN-ROASTED FINGERLING POTATOES

This is a foolproof side dish that comes together in minutes, roasting while you finish the rest of the meal.

6 **to 8 small fingerling potatoes cut into long wedges (about 2 cups)**
2 **tablespoons olive oil**
1 **medium clove garlic, minced (about ½ teaspoon)**
Salt and freshly ground pepper

Preheat the oven to 400°.

1. Place the potato wedges on a shallow baking pan.

2. Sprinkle with olive oil and garlic.
3. Season with salt and freshly ground pepper. Toss.
4. Bake for 15 minutes. Use a spatula to turn the potatoes. Bake for another 5 to 10 minutes or until the potatoes are brown and crisp.

Serves 4
Preparation Time: 5 minutes plus roasting

This simple potato dish easily morphs into an upscale veggie with the addition of fresh herbs and spices sprinkled on the potatoes before baking. In addition to olive oil, garlic, and seasonings try fresh chopped rosemary and thyme, chili powder and cumin, or chopped jalapeño pepper, and fresh cilantro.

Fingerling potatoes are white potatoes also know as "wax" potatoes. Their thin, knobby shape identifies them. The smaller the size of the potato wedge, the faster your dish will cook. If you are attempting a quick cook meal, 1-inch wedges will cook in less than 20 minutes.

French Fried Onion Rings

The secret to these yummy friend onion rings is in the cooking. Hot oil will insure a crispy, crunchy treat. Oil that is not quite hot enough will yield a greasy onion ring. Check out the hint to see how to get the perfect result!

2 medium white onions, sliced into ½ inch rings (about 2 cups)
Salt and freshly ground pepper
Canola oil for frying
1 cup all-purpose flour
1½ cups beer
2 to 6 drops hot sauce

1. Season the onion rings with salt and pepper.
2. Heat the oil in a deep pan or fryer to about 375°.
3. In a small bowl mix together the flour and the beer. Season with as much hot sauce as you prefer.
4. Dip the onion rings into the batter. Coat the onion completely and allow the excess to drip off.
5. Fry the onion rings in batches making sure not to over crowd the pan. Cook until golden brown turning once about 1 to 2 minutes.
6. Transfer the rings to a baking sheet that has been lined with paper towelsl. Season with additional salt. Keep warm while all of the onions have been cooked.

Serves 4
Preparation Time: 30 minutes

Perfect fried foods are a function of how well you control the temperature of the oil. Food is immersed into oil that ranges from 350 to 375°. If the temperature of the oil goes above 400° you are flirting with disaster. The oil will cool as you add the food and then heat up in between batches. Use a frying thermometer to make sure that you are using the oil at it's optimum temperature. Remember that you should only fill the pan one-third to halfway to the top with oil. As it cooks it will expand and as you add food the oil will bubble up towards the top.

DOUBLE CHIP BUNDT CAKE

Here is an easy cake that works for a morning brunch or as the base for a chocolaty trifle.

2   cups all-purpose flour
1   tablespoon baking powder
¼   teaspoon salt
½   cup butter (1 stick), room temperature
4   ounces cream cheese, room temperature
1½   cups granulated sugar
3   eggs
⅔   cup milk
1   tablespoon vanilla extract
1   11-ounce package chocolate/peanut but-
**   ter chips**
**   Confectioners' sugar for dusting**

Preheat the oven to 375°.
1. Prepare a Bundt pan by spraying with vegetable oil spray and dusting with flour.

2. Sift together the flour, baking powder and salt and set aside.
3. Use an electric mixer to combine the butter, cream cheese and sugar until fluffy.
4. Add the eggs one at a time.
5. Add the dry ingredients alternating with the milk.
6. Stir in the vanilla and the chips.
7. Bake for 35 to 40 minutes or a toothpick inserted into the center comes out clean.
8. Use a knife to loosen the cake from the pan. Cool for 15 minutes in the pan and then invert onto a rack to cool completely. Dust the top with confectioners' sugar.

Serves a crowd
Preparation Time: 15 minutes plus baking

Use this recipe as a guideline to create your own favorite Bundt cake. In place of chips use dried fruit, cinnamon streusel, sugared nuts or a treat of your choice.

Supper Italian Style Party Plan

Party Motivation

You just have to satisfy your craving for upscale Italian food. Not to mention that the pot of basil that you purchased at the store is blooming like mad!

Party Menu

Garlic-Infused Caesar Salad
Stuffed Flank Steak in Tomato Basil Sauce
Sautéed Polenta **
Double Chocolate Walnut Biscotti

** Over-the-Top Suggestion

Polenta is a classic Italian staple. Sautéing the polenta takes classic to upscale. It's easier than it sounds—and fun to serve.

Party Strategy

Make the biscotti the night before. Stuff and roll the flank steak in the morning. Begin preparing the meal as soon as you come home from work or carpool so that the beef will have enough time to simmer in the sauce.

The evening before: Prepare and bake the double chocolate biscotti

The morning of: Stuff and roll the flank steak. Secure with string and toothpicks and refrigerate.

Two hours before: Brown and simmer the flank steak. Prepare the polenta and refrigerate until firm. Wash and dry the lettuce for salad.

Shortcuts

Stuffed flank steak is just as terrific served with pasta like penne or mostaccioli in place of polenta. Cook the pasta in salted water and toss with the sauce left in the pan after you have removed the beef.

Party Backdrop

If a rooftop table and solo violinist are not available—your kitchen table will do quite nicely.

Think checkered tablecloth, a dripping candle in an empty Chianti bottle and a bowl of freshly grated cheese on the table. A little Sinatra playing through the speakers reminds you of the corner Italian restaurant.

The Table Setting
White ceramic dishes will ably present the dish and look terrific on a red-checkered cloth. Decorated with an oversized check holding rosy red hearts, a cloth like this is definitely reminiscent of those found in European bistros and cafes—the perfect setting for our Italian-style supper. Serve the authentic salad from the wooden bowl in which you have prepared the dressing. Steaming cups of espresso are just the right dipping medium for crunchy biscotti.

Garlic-Infused Caesar Salad

Caesar salad is a staple in our house and on many of our party menus. This is my favorite—and easiest recipe.

1 tablespoon dark brown mustard
1 2-ounce tin anchovy fillets packed in oil
1 tablespoon Worcestershire sauce
Juice of 1 lemon (about 2 tablespoons)
¼ cup red wine viegar
¼ cup balsamic vinegar
½ cup garlic infused olive oil
6 cups Romaine lettuce leaves, washed, dried and torn into 1-inch pieces
Freshly ground pepper
½ cup grated Parmesan cheese
1 cup seasoned croutons

1. Place the mustard, anchovies and Worcestershire sauce in the bottom of a wooden salad bowl.

2. Use a wooden spoon to smash the anchovies, mustard and Worcestershire into a paste.
3. Stir in the lemon juice.
4. Whisk in the vinegars.
5. Whisk in the olive oil until the mixture is smooth.
6. Toss the lettuce into the dressing.
7. Season with pepper. Add the cheese and croutons and toss again.

Serves 4
Preparation Time: 10 minutes

To make garlic infused olive oil combine 8 to 10 peeled garlic cloves and 1 cup olive oil in a small saucepan. Simmer the oil over medium high heat until the garlic turns golden brown. Remove the garlic from the oil (use it in another recipe such as Gnocchi with Golden Garlic Cream Sauce). Bring the oil to room temperature, cover and store in an airtight container.
Try this technique to create other types of flavored oil.
Try lemon peel, rosemary or red pepper flakes for a fun treat!

STUFFED FLANK STEAK in TOMATO BASIL SAUCE

This dish gets better the longer you simmer the beef. The steak is tender and soaks up the Italian-style sauce.

1	12- to 16-ounce flank steak
1	tablespoon olive oil
	Salt and freshly ground pepper
¼	cup pine nuts, toasted
4	ounces Prosciutto ham, thinly sliced
½	cup grated mozzarella cheese
½	cup grated Romano cheese
2	tablespoons chopped fresh basil leaves
2	tablespoons olive oil
4	to 6 large garlic cloves, minced, about 2 tablespoons
2	28-ounce cans chopped tomatoes
1	tablespoon chopped fresh oregano leaves
2	tablespoons chopped fresh basil leaves

Preheat the oven to 325°.

1. Use a meat mallet to pound the flank steak to ¼ inch thickness.
2. Season both sides of the steak by brushing with olive oil and sprinkling with salt and pepper.
3. Sprinkle the pine nuts on top of the steak.
4. Lay the Prosciutto on top of the pine nuts. Top with both cheeses. Sprinkle the chopped basil on top of the cheese.
5. Pat down the filling onto the steak leaving about a ½-inch border.

6. Roll the steak from the wide end, jelly roll style making sure that the stuffing does not fall out. Secure the roll with toothpicks and butcher string.
7. Heat 2 tablespoons olive oil in a large skillet over medium high heat. Brown the rolled steak on all sides and remove it to a platter. Reduce the heat of the skillet to medium.
8. Add the minced garlic to the pan. Cook, stirring constantly to prevent burning. Add the chopped tomatoes, and fresh herbs to the pan. Stir.
9. Place the stuffed steak back into the pan. Spoon the sauce over top. Cover the pan and place it in the oven. Cook for about 2 hours, turning the flank steak after 1 hour.
10. Remove the pan from the oven. (Remember to use pot holders, as the handle will be very HOT!)
11. Remove the flank steak to a platter to rest for at least 10 minutes before carving. Remove toothpicks and string. Cut the steak into 1 inch slices.
12. Spoon the sauce in puddles onto a serving platter. Lay the flank steak slices on top. Garnish with chopped fresh basil.

Serves 4 to 6
Preparation Time: 20 minutes plus cooking

Toast pine nuts by placing on a baking sheet. Toast for 5 minutes at 350°.
The pine nuts should just begin to turn golden brown and exude a small amount of oil.

SAUTÉED POLENTA

A delicious side dish, polenta is a preferred food to absorb all the terrific flavors of accompanying sauces while adding the sweet taste of corn.

1   **cup milk**
1   **cup water**
1   **cup yellow cornmeal**
½   **cup grated Parmesan cheese**
1   **tablespoon butter**
     Salt and freshly ground pepper

3   **to 4 tablespoons olive oil**

1.   Bring water and milk to a boil over medium high heat.
2.   Reduce heat to medium. Slowly add the cornmeal, stirring constantly until thickened and bubbling about 5 minutes.
3.   Remove from heat and stir in the cheese and butter. Season with salt and pepper.

4.   Spread the polenta into an 8 x 8-inch glass baking dish, about ¼ inch thick. Cool until firm or refrigerate, covered overnight.
5.   Cut the polenta into 2 inch squares.
6.   Heat the olive oil, in a skillet, over medium high heat. The oil must be very hot or the polenta will stick to the pan.
7.   Sauté the polenta squares in the hot oil, turning once until golden brown on both sides.
8.   Use a slotted spoon to transfer the polenta to a paper towel to drain. Place the polenta on a platter and sprinkle with additional Parmesan cheese.

Serves 4
Preparation Time: 30 minutes

Polenta is cornmeal that is either white or yellow, coarsely ground or finely ground. Traditional Italian cooks choose evenly ground yellow cornmeal to serve with their best stews and sauces.

DOUBLE CHOCOLATE WALNUT BISCOTTI

You can make these Italian cookie treats days in advance and store in an airtight container until party time!

¾ **cup shortening, room temperature**
⅔ **cup dark brown sugar**
2 **large eggs**
½ **cup chocolate syrup**
2 **cups all-purpose flour**
2 **teaspoons baking powder**
½ **teaspoon salt**
1 **cup walnuts, chopped**
1 **6-ounce package semi-sweet chocolate chips, 1 cup**

Preheat the oven to 350°.

1. Use an electric mixer to beat together the shortening and brown sugar until well combined.
2. Add the eggs one at a time.
3. Stir in the flour, baking powder and salt.
4. Stir in the chopped nuts and chocolate chips.
5. Divide the dough in half and form two long loaves, about 2 inches in diameter.
6. Place the loves onto a cookie sheet lined with a Silpat liner or lightly greased pan. Flatten the loaves slightly.
7. Bake for 18 to 20 minutes or until firm. Let cool slightly.
8. Cut each loaf into ¾-inch slices. Place the cut side down onto the baking sheet.
9. Bake for an additional 10 minutes or until the biscotti are lightly browned.

Yield: about 2½ dozen
Preparation Time: 20 minutes plus baking

Biscotti is a dense cookie perfect for dipping into strong coffee.
Feel free to add your favorite ingredients. For example, add raisins in place of chocolate pieces
or pecans in place of walnuts.

Laid Back Gatherings
for a Few Good Friends

(WEEKEND PARTIES FOR SIX TO EIGHT)

Brunch with a Punch
Rained Out Rendezvous
Alfresco Lunch at the Beach
Paella Party

"I love to give and go to parties. I keep a combination diary/scrapbook with copies of invitations, guest lists, menus, recipes, shopping lists, photographs, and even details about what I wore! I'll make notes on place settings, decorations, centerpieces, and entertainment. I find that so much of the fun of entertaining is in the planning. I always make food that is labor intensive several days in advance so that I have very little kitchen work to complete once the guests arrive. I collect all the serving platters and utensils and set up everything the day before. Party planning allows me to enjoy being a hostess when the party gets going!"

Susan Ross
Rotary International
Chicago, Illinois

Brunch with a Punch Party Plan

Party Motivation

A three-day weekend or out-of-town visitors, both are good reasons to round up your pals and luxuriate over an often overlooked fun meal—brunch.

Party Menu

Brunch Rum Punch
Spinach and Caramelized Onion Frittata **
Sticky Bubble Bread
Chicken Livers with Sage and Sherry on Toast Points
Cheesy Baked Grits
Butterscotch Pudding with Toasted Almonds

** Over-the-Top Suggestion

Garnishing a dish with a unique twist pleases the eye and adds to the allure. A drizzle of truffle oil takes the frittata from rustic to chic. The same is true for the fried whole sage leaves in the chicken liver dish.

Party Strategy

Brunch really takes the place of two meals—breakfast and lunch. It deserves at least two meals worth of time to enjoy. Serve the frittata and bubble bread first—warm from the oven. After refilling Rum Punch cocktails, serve the chicken livers with the cheesy baked grits. Finish the meal with individual puddings lavishly garnished.

The day before: Set up the buffet table and create a cocktail area so that guests can serve themselves.

The evening before: Prepare the bread for baking, cook and chill the pudding, arrange sunflowers.

Two hours before: Prepare the toast points, cook almonds for pudding, and prepare the ingredients for frittata.

One hour before: Bake bread, cook chicken livers, and bake grits.

Thirty minutes before: Prepare punch ingredients.

As your guests arrive: Invite them to join you in assembling the frittata.

Shortcuts

If you do not have a bread machine, you can make Sticky Bubble Bread with frozen bread dough. Thaw the dough and proceed with the recipe.

Party Backdrop

Place platters of these great dishes on the kitchen table and invite your guests to serve themselves and return for seconds and thirds.

The party mood is slow and conversational. Current events and whispery gossip are the highlight of the meal. If the discussion gets too spirited, retreat to the kitchen and offer yet another dish.

The Table Setting

Spread a colorful cloth over the kitchen table. Set out a pile of oversized plates and a basket full of utensils and napkins. Plan for extras for your guests, thus encouraging them to sample everything. A pitcher full of fresh sunflowers on the table is sure to lighten the mood. The perfect cocktail deserves the perfect barware. Check out the contemporary fashion of square glasses. The rectangle styling boasts a great feel in the hand with thick walls and a heavy sham base. Double old fashion glasses retain plenty of punch and double as great umbrella holders—for those paper umbrellas of course.

BRUNCH RUM PUNCH

This great aperitif sets the stage for a terrific meal. For a crowd-size entertaining, combine both the rum mixture and the juice mixture into a large container and allow guests to refill on their own.

12	**ounces Mount Gay Rum (or any dark rum)**
2	**ounces Amaretto liquor**
1	**cup pineapple juice**
1	**cup orange juice**
½	**cup lime juice**
¼	**cup grenadine**
4	**dashes bitters**

Pineapple chunks
Orange wedges

1. Stir the rum and Amaretto in a pitcher.
2. Pour the juices, grenadine and bitters into a separate pitcher and stir together.
3. Pour 1 ounce of the rum mixture into a tall glass that has been filled with ice.
4. Pour the juice mixture to the top of the glass. Stir.
5. Garnish with skewers of pineapple chunks and orange wedges.

Yield: 10 to 12 cocktails
Preparation Time: 15 minutes

Bitters are a liquid made from aromatic herbs, roots and plants that are used to flavor cocktails.
Customarily they are thought to increase appetite and ease digestion.
A most popular brand is Angostura bitters, often called for in recipes.

SPINACH and CARAMELIZED ONION FRITTATA

A frittata is a simple dish that adds an upscale element to any brunch. Use the recipe below as a guideline to create your own favorite frittata by substituting with any fresh veggie or cheese preference.

2 tablespoons olive oil
1 large yellow onion, diced (about 1 cup)
2 tablespoons Balsamic Vinegar
1 10-ounce bag fresh spinach, chopped

8 large eggs
3 ounces Prosciutto, diced
1 cup grated fresh Parmesan cheese
   Salt and freshly ground pepper
1 tablespoon rich, flavorful oil such as truffle oil
2 tablespoons snipped fresh garlic chives

Preheat the oven to 375°.

1. Heat a skillet over medium high heat. Add 1 tablespoon olive oil to the hot pan.
2. Place the onion in the pan. Reduce the heat to medium. Cook the onion until they are quite brown, but not burned.
3. Add the Balsamic vinegar and continue stirring until the onion begins to look syrupy.
4. Add the spinach to the pan a cook until the leaves are just wilted. Transfer to a bowl.
5. Whisk the eggs in a medium bowl to blend. Season with salt and pepper.
6. Heat the same skillet over medium high heat. Add the remaining olive oil to the hot pan
7. Pour the eggs into the skillet.
8. Add the onion and spinach mixture to the eggs.
9. Stir in the prosciutto and Parmesan cheese. Cook until the mixture begins to set, about 5 minutes.
10. Bake the frittata in the oven until it is puffed and set, about 15 minutes more.
11. Loosen the edges and bottom of the frittata with a flexible spatula. Slide it onto a serving platter.
12. Drizzle the frittata with truffle oil and sprinkle with garlic chives.

Serves 6
Preparation Time: 30 minutes plus baking

Truffle oil is flavorful oil that is somewhat expensive and best used to season foods rather than to cook them. There are both white and black truffle oils and both are easily purchased in a gourmet food store. Truffle oil tends to loose its aroma over time. My suggestion is that you buy a small bottle and use it often! The frittata forms by using a spatula to fold the cooked portion of the mixture to the center while the uncooked portion comes to the side of the pan. This method helps it to set up before you place it in the oven.

STICKY BUBBLE BREAD

Nothing beats out-of-the-oven warm bread—unless of course you add sugar and cinnamon. Yummm!

1¼   **cups milk**
¼   **cup butter (½ stick), cut into small pieces**
¼   **cup granulated sugar**
1   **teaspoon salt**
4   **cups bread flour**
1   **large egg, beaten**
2½   **teaspoons yeast**

½   **cup butter (1 stick), melted**
1   **cup brown sugar**
1   **teaspoon cinnamon**

1. Combine the milk, ¼ cup butter pieces, granulated sugar, salt, bread flour, and egg in the bucket of a bread machine.
2. Pour the yeast into the yeast compartment (or follow the specific directions for your bread machine).
3. Complete the process for the dough cycle.
4. Remove the dough from the bucket and place it onto a floured surface. Knead the dough for 30 seconds. Cover and let rest for 15 minutes.
5. Divide the dough into 24 equal pieces. Roll each piece into a ball.
6. Dip each ball into melted butter and then into brown sugar mixed with cinnamon.
7. Place the balls into the bottom of a Bundt pan that has been sprayed with vegetable oil spray. Cover and let rise for 45 minutes.

Preheat the oven to 350°.
8. Bake for 25 to 30 minutes. Cool the bread in the pan for 10 minutes. Remove the bread from the pan onto a serving platter large enough to allow the melted sugar to drizzle down the sides of the bread.

Serves: 6 to 8
Preparation Time: 30 minutes plus dough cycle and baking

You can make the bread the evening before and warm it in the oven before serving. Or, you can make the bread through step 7. Cover and let the bread rise in the refrigerator overnight. Bake the bread just before your guests arrive.

CHICKEN LIVERS with SAGE and SHERRY on TOAST POINTS

This is a wonderful brunch dish—perfect with scrambled eggs or French toast. For a mealtime variation, add roasted potatoes and this dish morphs into a terrific midnight supper.

2	tablespoons olive oil
2	tablespoons butter
1	medium white onion, diced (about ⅔ cup)
2	medium cloves garlic, minced (about 1 teaspoon)
1½	pounds chicken livers, trimmed of fat
¼	cup dry sherry
2	tablespoon fresh sage leaves, thinly chopped
	Salt and freshly ground pepper
6	slices thin white bread, crusts removed

1. Melt the olive oil and butter in a sauté pan over medium high heat.
2. Cook the onions in the pan until golden brown.
3. Add the garlic and chicken livers to the pan.
4. Stir the sherry into the pan. Cook until the livers are no longer pink in the center.
5. Add the sage. Season with salt and pepper. Cook for 2 minutes more.
6. Toast the bread and cut into triangles.
7. Place the toast points onto a plate. Cover with a spoonful of sautéed chicken livers.

Serves 6
Preparation Time: 20 minutes

A terrific garnish for this dish is fried whole sage leaves. Heat olive oil in a pan over medium high heat to 350 degrees. Place several sage leaves into the hot oil. Cook for 1 to 2 minutes. Drain on a paper towel. Sprinkle with a touch of fresh pepper.

CHEESY BAKED GRITS

The addition of tumeric and Parmesano Regiano cheese to this traditional porridge style dish heightens both the color and the flavor. Feel free to experiment with your favorite cheese like sharp cheddar or maybe even Brie for a grit side dish that everyone will love.

4   **cups chicken broth**
3   **cups milk**
1   **tablespoon salt**
1¼ **cups grits (not instant)**
1   **cup grated Parmesano Regiano cheese**
¼   **cup butter (½ stick)**
¼   **teaspoon tumeric**
    Salt and freshly ground black pepper
3   **large eggs, beaten**
    Fresh parsley for garnish

Preheat the oven to 350 degrees

1. Heat the chicken broth and milk over medium high heat until it begins to boil.
2. Lower the heat to simmer. Slowly whisk in the grits.
3. Cook until thickened, stirring constantly about 30 seconds.
4. Stir in the cheese, butter, and tumeric. Season with salt and pepper. Cool to room temperature.
5. Stir the eggs into the grits.
6. Transfer this mixture to a baking pan that has been sprayed with vegetable oil spray.
7. Bake until the grits begin to turn golden brown and the center is just set about 1 hour.
8. Let the casserole sit for 10 minutes before serving. Garnish with fresh chopped parsley.

Servings: 6
Preparation Time: 20 minutes plus baking

Grits is a grain made from the ground meal of yellow or white hominy. This traditional Southern side dish appears on dishes designed for breakfast, lunch or dinner. For this recipe do not use instant grits, but feel free to choose from either coarsely ground or finely ground variety.

BUTTERSCOTCH PUDDING with TOASTED ALMONDS

The yummy rich color and flavor of this pudding is created by cooking the brown sugar and butter together for just a couple of minutes. Skip your workout—because your arm will get a whisking workout.

6	tablespoons unsalted butter, cut unto pieces
1¼	cups dark brown sugar
1	teaspoon vanilla extract
2	cups milk
1	cup heavy cream
2	tablespoons cornstarch
¼	teaspoon salt
3	egg yolks
1	tablespoon butter
1	teaspoon cinnamon
½	cup sliced almonds
	Whipped cream

1. Whisk together the butter, brown sugar and vanilla in a saucepan over medium high heat. Cook until the butter is melted, then cook for 5 minutes more whisking constantly. The mixture will be bubbly. Remove from heat.
2. Cook the milk and cream in a saucepan over medium high heat until it just begins to boil.
3. Pour the warm milk into the butter mixture. Return to medium high heat and whisk until smooth.
4. Place the cornstarch and salt in a small bowl. Pour about ¼ cup of the butterscotch mixture into the cornstarch and whisk until smooth.
5. Whisk the cornstarch back into warm milk. Bring to a boil and cook until the butterscotch thickens.
6. Place the egg yolks in a small bowl. Pour about ¼ cup of the butterscotch mixture into the eggs. Whisk this mixture back into the warm milk. Cook for several minutes, whisking constantly. The mixture will thicken as it cooks.
7. Strain the mixture through a sieve or colander to get rid of any lumps.
8. Pour into six ½-cup ramekins. Refrigerate for at least 1 hour.
9. Melt the butter in a small skillet over medium high heat.
10. Add the cinnamon and the almonds. Cook until the almonds begin to turn golden brown about 5 minutes.
11. Serve the chilled pudding with a sprinkle of toasted almonds and a dollop of whipped cream.

Servings: 6
Preparation Time: 30 minutes plus refrigeration

This recipe uses a process called tempering to add the eggs to the hot milk and cream. If you were to drop the eggs into the hot liquid, the eggs would cook and ruin the pudding. By first adding a little warm liquid to the eggs, you condition them, so that they easily blend into the milk creating the custard or pudding.

Rained Out Rendezvous Party Plan

Party Motivation

A rainy weekend, a soggy round of golf, or a canceled soft-ball game are all good reasons to gather your pals and invite them for supper - especially when this party plan comes together so easily.

Party Menu

Banana Coladas
Veggie Salad with Thousand Island Dressing
Dilled Crab Cakes with Arugula Sauce **
Spinach and Cheese Soufflé
Vanilla and Chocolate Marble Cake

** Over-the-Top Suggestion

The simple arugula sauce that accompanies the crab cakes is an elegant garnish. The light soufflé beats the everyday casserole—well, everyday!

Party Strategy

Greet your pals with festive cocktails as they come in the door. When the time is right, bring everyone to the table. Serve the salad on chilled plates and pass the yummy dressing. Offer other dishes family style. Save room for the simple dessert.

A change of plans brings an easy get together. You find yourself entertaining instead of being entertained. Share the fun. Bring out a deck of cards and make it an all-night occasion.

Four hours before: Prepare the crab cakes, chop the veggies for the salad and bake the cake.
Two hours before: Prepare the soufflé ingredients.
One hour before: Prepare the salad dressing.
Thirty minutes before: Relax—there's nothing to do!
As your guests arrive: Bake the soufflé and sauté the crab cakes.

Shortcuts

Feel free to use as many veggies (or as few) as you have on hand for the salad. If fresh crabmeat is hard to come by, substitute with imitation crab product, canned salmon or tuna.

Party Backdrop

Take an extra minute to set the dining room table. Use complimenting mix and match china so that the table looks put together but not fussy.

The Table Setting

Mix and match place settings are fun to work with. Basic white buffet plates double as chargers for the more traditional blue and white patterns. Fill in with cornflower blue ceramic dinner plates or highlight with bright yellow napkins. Accent with blue pitchers filled with fresh cut white and yellow tulips in the center of the table.

Banana Coladas

Using a blender will make this drink foamy and fun. A food processor or immersion blender is the next best tool for the job.

3   ripe bananas, peeled and sliced
3   cups pineapple juice
2   cups orange juice
1   cup coconut milk
4   ounces cup dark rum

1. Place bananas, pineapple juice and orange juice in a blender and pulse until smooth.

2. Add the coconut milk and rum. Fill the blender with ice cubes.
3. Pulse until frothy.
4. Garnish with orange slices and shredded coconut.

Yield: 4 to 6 cocktails
Preparation Time: 10 minutes

Veggie Salad with Thousand Island Dressing

This salad is at its best when served very cold right from the fridge. The veggies retain their crispness and are well enhanced with a spicy rich dressing.

2   medium celery ribs, thinly sliced (about 1 cup)
2   large carrots, thinly sliced (about ½ cup)
1   medium cucumber, cut into thin diagonal strips (about 2 cups)
2   green onions, thinly sliced (about 2 tablespoons)
1   large red bell pepper, diced (about 1 cup)
1   pint ripe cherry tomatoes, cut in half (about 2 cups)
1   head iceberg lettuce, chopped (about 4 cups)

1   cup mayonnaise
2   tablespoons sweet pickle relish
2   tablespoons chili sauce

2   tablespoons ketchup
1   tablespoon Dijon mustard
1   teaspoon capers, drained
    Salt and freshly ground pepper

1. Combine the vegetables and lettuce in a salad bowl. Chill.
2. Stir together the mayonnaise, relish, chili sauce, ketchup, mustard, and capers. Season with salt and pepper. (Note: For a thinner dressing you can add ¼ cup or more water.) Cover and chill.
3. Serve the salad with the dressing on the side.

Servings: 6
Preparation Time: 15 minutes

Feel free to add your favorite ingredients to this easy salad.
Some fun variations include chopped hard-boiled eggs, home baked parmesan croutons,
black olives, marinated artichoke hearts and sliced hearts of palm.

DILLED CRAB CAKES with ARUGULA SAUCE

The luscious green sauce is not only flavorful but really pretty on the plate. Serve the crab cakes with a swirl of sauce. Garnish with fresh arugula leaves.

3 cups fresh breadcrumbs
8 ounces fresh crabmeat
2 green onions, thinly sliced (about 2 tablespoons)
2 tablespoons chopped fresh dill
1 teaspoon Old Bay Seasoning
¼ cup mayonnaise
1 tablespoon prepared mustard
Juice of ½ fresh lime (about 1 tablespoon)
1 large egg, beaten
Salt and freshly ground pepper
2 tablespoons olive oil

2 cups arugula leaves, washed and well dried
1 medium clove garlic, minced (about ½ teaspoon)
Juice of ½ fresh lime (about 1 tablespoon)
2 tablespoons olive oil

FOR CRAB CAKES:
1. Mix together 2 cups of the fresh breadcrumbs, crabmeat, onion, dill and Old Bay seasoning until just combined.
2. Gently stir in the mayonnaise, mustard and lime juice.
3. Stir in the egg and season with salt and freshly ground pepper.
4. Form the mixture into 6 patties.
5. Place the remaining breadcrumbs in a shallow bowl. Dip each patty into the breadcrumbs, coating both sides.
6. Place the crab cakes on a baking sheet and refrigerate for at least 30 minutes or up to 4 hours.
7. Heat a skillet over medium high heat. Add 2 tablespoons of olive oil. Cook the crab cakes until they begin to brown, about 4 minutes per side.

FOR SAUCE:
1. Place the arugula leaves in a blender. Pulse to chop.
2. Add the garlic and lime juice. Pulse briefly.
3. With the machine running, slowly add the olive oil.

Serves 6
Preparation Time: 20 minutes plus refrigeration

The lightest crab cakes are made with the least effort. Stir the ingredients until they just come together. Prepare fresh bread crumbs by placing slices of crustless bread in the food processor and pulsing to produce fine crumbs.

Spinach and Cheese Soufflé

This is a wonderful vegetable side dish that is best served right from the oven while it is hot and puffy.

1	**10-ounce package frozen chopped spinach**
¼	**cup butter (½ stick)**
⅓	**cup all purpose flour**
1	**cup milk**
1	**cup grated Swiss cheese**
6	**large eggs, separated**
½	**teaspoon ground nutmeg**
¼	**teaspoon red pepper flakes**
	Salt and freshly ground pepper
¼	**teaspoon cream of tartar**
½	**cup breadcrumbs**

Preheat the oven to 350°.

1. Cook the spinach in a microwave oven according to the package directions. Drain the spinach through a colander. Press down with paper towels to get as much moisture out of the spinach as possible.
2. Melt the butter in a saucepan over medium high heat.
3. Whisk in the flour. Stir until the mixture begins to turn golden brown and bubbly about 2 minutes.
4. Pour in the milk and stir until the sauce thickens about 5 minutes.
5. Add the cheese and stir until the cheese melts and the sauce is smooth.
6. Use and electric mixer to beat the egg yolks until they are light and frothy.
7. Gradually add the warm cheese sauce to the egg yolks.
8. When all of the sauce has bee added, stir in the spinach, nutmeg and red pepper flakes. Season with salt and pepper. Set this mixture aside.
9. Use an electric mixer (with clean beaters and bowl) to whip the egg whites with cream of tartar until stiff.
10. Carefully fold the egg whites into the cheese mixture being careful to keep the mixture light and fluffy. Do not over mix.
11. Spray a 11 x 8 x 2-inch glass baking dish or 2-quart soufflé dish with vegetable oil spray and sprinkle the bottom with breadcrumbs. Pour the spinach mixture into the dish. Bake for 35 to 40 minutes or until the center of the soufflé is just set.

Servings: 6
Preparation Time: 30 minutes plus baking

The secret to a great soufflé is to not overwork the egg whites. Use an electric mixer to beat the egg whites until peaks form when you lift the beater from the whipped eggs. You want the egg whites to remain moist and not dry. Fold in egg whites by gently sliding the spatula across the bottom of the bowl and then upward, turning the bowl and repeating the movement until the mixture is just blended. This is done so that the air remains in the mixture and not released.

Vanilla and Chocolate Marble Cake

This is a super easy-to-bake cake that you can whip up in minutes for your guests.

½   teaspoon salt
½   teaspoon baking soda
1½   cups all-purpose flour
6   tablespoons unsalted butter, room temperature
1   cup granulated sugar
1   teaspoon vanilla extract
4   large eggs
¾   cup buttermilk
3   tablespoons cocoa powder
½   teaspoon black walnut flavoring

Preheat the oven to 350°.
1. Prepare a round cake pan by spraying with vegetable oil spray and dusting with flour.
2. Combine the salt, baking soda and flour in a small bowl. Set aside.
3. Use an electric mixer to combine the butter and sugar until light and fluffy.
4. Stir in the vanilla and the eggs adding one at a time.
5. Add the flour mixture and buttermilk in 3 additions, alternating ⅓ flour mixture with ⅓ buttermilk until just blended.
6. Spread half of the batter into the prepared cake pan.
7. Stir in the cocoa and black walnut flavoring into the remaining batter.
8. Place the remaining batter onto the vanilla batter in large spoonfuls. With the tip of a knife swirl the chocolate batter into the vanilla batter being careful not to overmix.
9. Bake for 30 to 35 minutes or until a toothpick inserted into the center comes out clean. Cool on a wire rack. Dust with confectioners' sugar before serving.

Servings: 6
Preparation Time: 20 minutes plus baking

For best results when baking a cake, set the oven rack in the center so that there is an even amount of heat on the top and the bottom. That old wives tale about not opening the oven door really does apply. If you open the door to check on the cake, you will vary the temperature of the oven jeopardizing the evenness of the cooking. Place the baked cake on a wire rack and cool for at least 10 minutes. Place a second rack on top of the cake. Invert the pan so that the cake comes onto the rack to continue cooling.

Alfresco Lunch at the Beach Party Plan

Party Motivation

Alfresco is the term that describes everything fresh. Alfresco dining combines garden-fresh bounty with the ease of outdoor dining—an experience that is meant to be shared with good friends. The food and libations are plentiful and served amid cool breezes. Greenery abounds and the senses go wild with fragrant herbs and spices. Sounds like a scene out of *Roman Holiday*.

Party Menu

Minted Lemonade
Chilled Gazpacho Soup
Dilled Chicken Salad Sandwiches
Curried Egg Salad Sandwiches
Tuna and White Bean Pitas
Raspberry Orange Cupcakes with Orange Cream Cheese Frosting

** Over-the-Top Suggestion

There are a great variety of sandwiches in this menu, everything from tuna to eggs to chicken. The recipes in this party plan allow for an ample amount of each so that everybody can taste one of everything. Serve the sandwiches in wax paper containers. Fold the wax paper into the shape of an envelope. Place a sandwich (or sandwich half) inside the envelope. Wrap each sandwich and envelope in a cloth napkin and stack into a large picnic basket.

Party Strategy

Serve the chilled soup from a thermos kept in a cooler on ice. Individual sandwiches wrapped in waxed paper envelopes are served from large baskets. The luscious dessert will hold well in a plastic container in a cooler on top of an ice shelf.

The day before: Assemble everything that you will need to move your portable feast. Picnic baskets and large tubs are great containers. Make sure that you have collected all of the greenery that you will need to enhance your outdoor party.

The evening before: Prepare the soup. Make all of the salads for the sandwiches.

That morning: Bake cupcakes, prepare lemonade. Pack up plates and utensils.

Four hours before: Assemble sandwiches and place them in individual folded wax paper envelopes. Keep the sandwiches chilled.

Two hours before: Frost the cupcakes and place into a covered container.

Thirty minutes before: Pour the soup into a thermos. Place into a cooler. Stack the sandwiches into a large basket. Pack up your alfresco feast.

Shortcuts

Get help with the transporting of this party by packing each guest his own personal picnic basket with a sampling of each sandwich, a container filled with soup and a plastic wrapped cupcake for desert.

Party Backdrop

A picnic table in the sand, an outdoor garden, backyard deck or screened porch is a perfect place for this party. But, don't stop there. An apartment rooftop, public garage, or corporate lobby can be transformed to simulate outdoor dining. The secret is to surround the dining table with lots of fresh greenery. Enhance your outdoor setting by bringing in several large, potted green plants. Many nurseries rent these items for a nominal fee. Incorporate small pots of flowering plants to give your dinner setting the feel of sitting in the midst of an intimate garden.

Take advantage of the freshest seasonal ingredients, served with effortless simplicity in your favorite natural setting. This very idea implies a relaxed atmosphere, carefree mingling of good friends, and a desire to return to the scene again and again.

The Table Setting

In place of an elaborate centerpiece, use a rustic bowl filled with whole fruit such as lemons and limes. Spread a tablecloth in a color that blends with your outdoor garden like pale green or mint. Experiment with sheer, white organdy cloths to create a gauzy atmosphere. Decorate the table with earthy, seasonal favorites like piles of bell peppers or stems of fresh cut flowers. Opt for making use of china and crystal when setting each place rather than the more casual paper products utilized at barbecues. Place a pitcher of Minted Lemonade with lemon slices next to a chilled bottle of Pinot Grigio. Create a fresh, green atmosphere that takes advantage of everything the outdoors have to offer.

Minted Lemonade

This thirst quencher is easy to make and even easier to adapt to your favorite flavors.

12 large lemons, thinly sliced, about 4 cups
2 cups fresh mint leaves
2 cups sugar
Juice of 3 lemons (about ½ cup)
4 cups water
Ice cubes

1. Place sliced lemons, mint, 1½ cups of the sugar and the lemon juice in the bowl of a food processor. Pulse briefly until the mixture is juicy.

2. Strain this mixture into a pitcher extracting as much juice as possible.
3. Add 4 cups of water to the pitcher.
4. Stir in the remaining ½ cup of sugar.
5. Place ice cubes in chilled glasses. Pour the lemonade over the ice cubes.
6. Garnish with a sugared lemon slice on the side of the glass.

Serves 6 to 8
Preparation Time: 10 minutes

Fresh mint adds a wonderful aroma to homemade lemonade.
Try other variations by adding peeled fresh ginger in place of mint, honey in place of sugar,
or strained blueberries in addition to the sliced lemons.

Always start with room temperature lemons. Place each lemon on the counter top
and push down gently as you roll it back and forth. This will help to release the juices
before you slice the lemon.

CHILLED GAZPACHO SOUP

Gazpacho is a terrific cold soup, especially easy to prepare since there is no cooking involved!

2   medium cucumbers, peeled and diced into ½-inch pieces (about 4 cups)
1   large red bell pepper, seeded and diced into ½-inch pieces (about 1 cup)
1   large yellow bell pepper, seeded and diced into ½-inch pieces (about 1 cup)
1   large green bell pepper, seeded and diced into ½-inch pieces (about 1 cup)
1   small red onion, finely diced (about ½ cup)
1   medium jalapeño peppers, seeded and finely diced (about 2 tablespoons)
½   cup chopped fresh cilantro leaves
    Juice of 4 fresh limes (about ½ cup)
1   28-ounce can diced tomatoes
2   medium cloves garlic, minced (about 1 teaspoon)
1   teaspoon granulated sugar
2   tablespoons red wine vinegar

6   slices white bread, crust trimmed and cut into cubes
2   to 6 drops hot pepper sauce (or more)
    Salt and freshly ground pepper

1. Place half of each of the diced cucumbers, peppers onion, and jalapeño pepper into a large bowl.
2. Place the remaining vegetables into a blender (or the bowl of a food processor).
3. Add the cilantro, lime juice, tomatoes, garlic, sugar and vinegar. Pulse to purée.
4. Add the bread and pulse again.
5. Season with hot pepper sauce, salt, and pepper.
6. Pour this mixture into the large bowl containing the diced vegetables. Stir. Cover and chill for at least 2 hours or overnight.

Servings: 6 to 8
Preparation Time: 35 minutes

Gazpacho is a Spanish soup that has as many variations as there are regions in Spain. The commonalities include diced tomatoes, cucumbers, red peppers and bread or croutons to thicken the soup.

Dilled Chicken Salad Sandwiches

Thin slices of red apple add a sweet crunch to this flavorful salad.

2   **6- to 8-ounce skinless boneless chicken breast halves**
    Salt and freshly ground pepper

2   **medium celery ribs, thinly sliced (about 1 cup)**
1   **medium red apple, cored and thinly sliced (about 1 cup)**
¾   **cup mayonnaise**
3   **tablespoons chopped fresh dill**
    Juice of 1 fresh lime (about 2 tablespoon)
    Zest of 1 medium lime (about 2 teaspoons)

12 **slices thin rye bread**
2   **tablespoons mayonnaise**
½   **head iceberg lettuce, shredded (about 4 cups)**
2   **large beefsteak tomatoes, thinly sliced (about 2 cups)**

1. Place the chicken breasts into a saucepan. Cover with water. Season with salt and freshly ground pepper.
2. Simmer over medium heat until the chicken is just cooked through and still very moist, about 15 to 20 minutes. Remove the chicken to a plate and cool.
3. In a large bowl stir together the celery, apple slices, mayonnaise, fresh dill, lime juice and lime zest.
4. Cut the chicken breasts into ½-inch cubes. Stir into the mayonnaise mixture.
5. Season with salt and freshly ground pepper. Chill for at least 30 minutes and up to 4 hours.
6. Lay 6 pieces of bread onto a work surface.
7. Spread each slice with mayonnaise. Top with shredded lettuce, chicken salad, tomato slices, and a second bread slice.
8. Trim the crusts from the sandwiches and cut into triangles.

Serves 6
Preparation Time: 30 minutes

You can poach the chicken the day before and assemble the salad that morning. Keep chilled until you are ready to serve. It should be eaten immediately upon serving.

CURRIED EGG SALAD SANDWICHES

Here is a delightful salad that is full of flavor and makes an excellent sandwich.

12   **hard boiled eggs, peeled, sliced in half**
4   **green onions, thinly sliced (about ¼ cup)**
2   **tablespoons chopped fresh parsley leaves**
½   **cup mayonnaise**
2   **teaspoons curry powder**
      Salt and freshly ground pepper

12   **thin white bread slices**
1   **medium cucumbers, cut into thin diagonal strips (about 2 cups)**

1. Place the eggs, onion, and parsley into the bowl of a food processor. Pulse to chop thoroughly.
2. Add the mayonnaise to the bowl and pulse to combine.
3. Add the curry powder and pulse briefly. Season with salt and freshly ground pepper.
4. Lay 6 pieces of bread onto a work surface.
5. Spread each slice with mayonnaise. Top with 2 thin cucumber slices, egg salad, and a second bread slice.
6. Trim the crusts from the sandwiches and cut into triangles.

Serves 6
Preparation Time: 20 minutes

---

*To cook perfect hard boiled eggs, place fresh eggs into the bottom of a saucepan.
Cover with water. When the water comes to a boil, cover the pan with a lid
and turn off the heat. Set a timer for 12 minutes then remove the eggs into ice water.
The fresher the egg the easier it is to peel.*

TUNA and WHITE BEAN PITAS

Pita bread is the perfect container to catch all of the great goodies in this salad.

1   **6-ounce can solid white tuna packed in oil**
1   **16-ounce can cannellini beans, drained**
1   **tablespoon finely diced red onion**
2   **tablespoons chopped fresh tarragon leaves**
3   **tablespoons chopped fresh parsley leaves**
1   **tablespoon tarragon vinegar**
  Salt and freshly ground pepper
1   **12-ounce jar roasted yellow peppers, sliced into strips**

  Leafy green lettuce
6   **6-inch pita breads, split in the center**

1. Place the tuna (and the oil from the can) and the beans into a bowl.
2. Stir in the onion, tarragon, parsley and vinegar. Season with salt and pepper.
3. Place yellow pepper strips on the bottom half of the pita. Top with lettuce and the tuna bean salad.

Servings: 6
Preparation Time: 15 minutes

Pita is a flat, round shaped bread originating in the Middle East. When the bread bakes, the bread forms a pocket in the center, which is why it is perfect for stuffing. Pita bread is usually made of white or wheat flour and is easily found in your local grocery store.

Raspberry Orange Cupcakes
with Orange Cream Cheese Frosting

These light cupcakes combine the flavors of summer with fresh raspberries and a hint of zesty orange.

2⅓ cups cake flour
2 teaspoons baking powder
½ teaspoon salt
1 pint fresh raspberries (about 2 cups)
1 cup unsalted butter (2 sticks), room temperature
1½ cups granulated sugar
4 large eggs
1 cup milk
2 teaspoons vanilla extract
   Zest of ½ medium orange (about 1 tablespoons)

2 8-ounce packages cream cheese, room temperature
½ cup unsalted butter (1 stick), room temperature
4 cups confectioners' sugar
   Zest of ⅓ medium orange (about 2 teaspoons)
1 tablespoon fresh orange juice

Preheat the oven to 350°.
1. Place paper muffin cups into a muffin tin.
2. Combine cake flour, baking powder and salt in a small bowl. Set aside.
3. Place the raspberries into a bowl. Sprinkle with 1 tablespoon of the flour mixture. Toss and set aside.
4. Use an electric mixer to beat the butter and sugar together until fluffy.
5. Mix in the eggs, one at a time.
6. Mix in the flour and milk in 3 additions alternating ⅓ flour with ⅓ milk until just blended.
7. Stir in the vanilla and orange zest.
8. Use a large wooden spoon to gently stir in the raspberries.
9. Pour the batter into the muffin cups about ¾ full. Bake for 20 to 25 minutes or until a toothpick inserted into the center comes out clean. Cool on a rack.
10. Use an electric mixer to beat together the cream cheese, butter, sugar, orange zest, and orange juice. Chill for 5 to 10 minutes.
11. Spread the tops of the cupcakes with the frosting.

Yield: 18 cupcakes
Preparation Time: 30 minutes plus baking

Obtain the zest of citrus fruit from the colored portion of the outside peel, which contains all of the flavorful oils needed to perk up any dish. A hand held grater will produce minced zest. A handy tool known as a zester will produce fine, thin strips that are terrific for garnishing.

Paella Party Plan

Party Motivation

Grazing. The need to munch and munch on great dishes that hold well on a buffet table. The late arrivals have plenty to keep them interested but the early birds enjoy the entire experience.

Party Menu
Party Sangria
Roasted Eggplant Tapenade
Chicken, Sausage, and Seafood Paella **
Herbed Focaccia Bread with Caramelized Onions and Tomatoes
Simple Rice Pudding with Macerated Strawberries

**** Over-the-Top Suggestion**

There is a ton of seafood in the paella—shrimp, squid, clams and mussels. But, for a real treat include a lobster tail or two.

Party Strategy

Serve everything buffet style allowing guests to nibble on each dish or pile their plates high with all the goodies in the main dish.

The day before: Dice the veggies for the paella. Store separately in airtight containers.

The evening before: Make the pudding and chill.

That morning: Prepare the tapenade and store in an airtight container.

Four hours before: Place focaccia ingredients into bread machine. Macerate berries. Make Sangria. Prepare bread for tapenade.

Two hours before: Bake focaccia bread.

One hour before: Prepare paella.

Shortcuts

There are several terrific pre-made tapenade products on the market. If time is short—or the party grows, purchase additional tapenade for extra appys. Macerating the strawberries lends a wild taste treat to the subtle pudding—but fresh berries work just as well.

Party Backdrop

An antique pine table dressed with a Mexican striped blanket—or an outdoor table on the porch set with citronella candles.

Hot and spicy. A pitcher of Sangria cools the heat of the feisty paella. Hang a piñata and dare your guests to strike.

The Table Setting

Buy or borrow a heavy duty, deep, six-quart skillet with a long handle at one end and an easy grasping handle at the other. This pan will easily hold and serve the paella. Or, if you really want to splurge you can purchase a copper paella pan, hand hammered and lined with tin, a great pan perfect for cooking Spain's national dish on your kitchen stovetop. Serve the Sangria from a crystal clear pitcher so that you can see the fruit in the drink. Break the bread into pieces and offer olive oil and balsamic vinegar for "dip buddies." Place separate dessert dishes next to the pudding so that the guest can enjoy dessert when they are ready.

Party Sangria

Choose a wine that has a fruity base rather than a dry red wine for this drink. The simple syrup and orange juice will add just enough sweetness.

½   **cup simple syrup**
1   **750 ml bottle fruity red wine**
½   **cup orange juice**
½   **cinnamon stick**
1   **tablespoon brandy**
1   **large orange, sliced into thin rounds**
1   **large lime, sliced into thin rounds**
1   **large lemon, sliced into thin rounds**
1   **cup club soda**

1.   Prepare simple syrup by placing 1 cup sugar and 1 cup water in a pan. Bring the mixture to a boil and cook until the sugar dissolves. Remove the simple syrup from the heat and allow to cool.

2.   Place the simple syrup, wine, orange juice and cinnamon stick in a large pitcher.

3.   Stir in the brandy and the fruit.

4.   Cover and chill for at least 2 hours or as much as overnight.

5.   Just before serving, pour in the club soda and stir.

6.   Serve the Sangria in a glass filled with ice.

Serves a crowd
Preparation Time: 10 minutes

ROASTED EGGPLANT TAPENADE

The intensity of the flavors in this dish makes for a stunning appetizer—with promises of great things to come!

1   **medium eggplant, peeled and cut into 1 inch cubes (about 4 cups)**
2   **medium cloves garlic**
1   **tablespoon olive oil**
2   **tablespoons capers, drained**
1   **2-ounce jar Spanish pitted olives (about 20)**
1   **tablespoon chili sauce**
1   **tablespoon balsamic vinegar**
    Juice of 1 lemon (about 2 tablespoons)
2   **tablespoons chopped fresh rosemary**
¼   **cup olive oil**
    Freshly ground pepper

1   **loaf crusty bread**
    Olive oil
    Garlic cloves

Preheat the oven to 400°.

1. Place the eggplant and 2 garlic cloves on a baking sheet. Sprinkle with olive oil. Bake until soft, about 20 to 30 minutes.
2. Place the roasted eggplant, garlic, capers, olives, chili sauce, vinegar, lemon juice, and rosemary in the bowl of a food processor. Pulse.
3. With the blade running slowly pour the olive oil through the food tube until it is incorporated into the eggplant mixture.
4. Season with pepper.
5. Cut the bread into ½-inch slices. Brush one side of the bread with a small amount of olive oil. Grill the bread slices (or toast in a 350 degree oven) until golden. Rub a garlic clove over the grilled side of the bread.

Yield: 2 cups
Preparation Time: 15 minutes plus roasting

True Spanish tapenade is an olive spread that usually integrates the flavors of capers, garlic and anchovies. The word tapenade is taken from the word tapeno meaning capers. In addition to spreading tapenade on bread it is also used as a pizza topping, on focaccia bread and as a dip for veggies. Store extra tapenade in an airtight container in the refrigerator for several days.

Chicken, Sausage, and Seafood Paella

Paella can vary from region to region from cook to cook. This combination of chicken pieces, chorizo sausage and shellfish has something for everyone.

2	**cups bottled clam juice**
1½	**cups chicken stock**
¼	**teaspoon saffron**
½	**cup dry white wine**
4	**4 to 6-ounce chicken thighs**
4	**4 to 6-ounce chicken legs**
	Salt and freshly ground pepper
2	**tablespoons olive oil**
1	**pound sausage links (like Chorizo), sliced into rings**
2	**large yellow onions, diced (about 2 cups)**
4	**medium cloves garlic, minced (about 2 teaspoons)**
1	**large green bell pepper, seeded and diced (about 1 cup)**
2	**teaspoons paprika**
2	**cups Arborio rice**
1	**16-ounce can diced tomatoes**
1	**16-ounce can small peas, drained**
1	**pound large uncooked shrimp, peeled and deveined (about 18)**
1	**pound cleaned squid, cut into ½-inch rings**
1	**dozen clams**
1	**dozen mussels**

1. Warm the clam juice, chicken stock, saffron and white wine in a saucepan over low heat.

2. Heat the olive oil in a large, deep skillet over medium high heat.

3. Season the chicken pieces with salt and pepper. Cook each piece in the hot oil until brown about 5 minutes. Remove the chicken to a platter.

4. Add the sausage pieces to the pan. Cook until the pieces begin to brown about 5 minutes. Remove the sausage to the platter.

5. Add the onions, garlic, green pepper, and paprika to the pan. Cook until the vegetables are soft and begin to brown about 10 minutes.

6. Stir the rice into the vegetables. Cook for 2 minutes.

7. Stir in the diced tomatoes and peas.

8. Add the warm broth mixture and bring to a boil. Cook for 3 minutes.

9. Place the chicken and sausage pieces into the pan. Cover and cook over medium heat for 30 minutes.

10. Add the shrimp, squid, clams, and mussels to the pan. Cook for 15 minutes more or until the chicken is cooked through and the clams and mussels open.

Servings: 6 to 8 very generous portions
Preparation Time: 45 minutes plus cooking

Make this dish in a very large skillet on top of the stove. As an alternate, you can combine all of the cooked ingredients in a baking dish, cover with foil, and bake in the oven at 400°.

Saffron is an expensive and rare spice. Although it is not necessary it does heighten the color and earthiness of the dish. You only need to use just a little bit. It will keep for quite a while on the pantry shelf if stored properly. You can purchase Saffron threads, which are the most desirable or powdered Saffron, which is sometimes ground with other ingredients—but okay in a pinch.

HERBED FOCACCIA BREAD with CARAMELIZED ONIONS and TOMATOES

The bread machine makes this an easy bread to prepare. Feel free to vary the toppings. Sun-dried tomatoes and sliced olives are a great alternative.

¾ **cup water**
¼ **cup dry white wine**
¼ **cup olive oil**
½ **teaspoon salt**
1 **tablespoon sugar**
4 **cups bread flour**
2 **tablespoons chopped fresh rosemary**
2 **tablespoons chopped fresh thyme leaves**
1 **tablespoon chopped fresh oregano leaves**
2 **teaspoons yeast**

¼ **cup olive oil**
2 **tablespoons balsamic vinegar**
½ **pint ripe cherry tomatoes, cut in half (about 1 cup)**
Salt and freshly ground pepper

1 **tablespoon olive oil**
1 **small red onion, thinly sliced (about ½ cup)**
½ **teaspoon sugar**

2 **medium cloves garlic, minced (about 1 teaspoon)**
1 **teaspoons course salt**
2 **tablespoons chopped fresh basil leaves**

1. Place the water, white wine, olive oil, salt, sugar, flour, and fresh herbs into the pan of a bread machine.
2. Pour the yeast into the yeast compartment (or follow the bread machine directions).

3. Complete the process for the dough setting on your bread machine.
4. Combine ¼ cup olive oil and 2 tablespoons balsamic vinegar in a bowl. Place the tomatoes in the bowl. Season with salt and pepper. Cover and refrigerate for 30 minutes.
5. Heat 1 tablespoon olive oil in a skillet over medium high heat.
6. Add onions and cook until golden brown.
7. Add the sugar and cook until syrupy. Remove to a bowl.
8. Remove the dough from the machine and gently roll it (or press it with your fingers) onto a baking sheet that has been lightly sprayed with vegetable oil spray.
9. Cover and let rise for 30 minutes.

Preheat the oven to 375°.
10. Make indentations in the dough with your fingers.
11. Remove the tomatoes from the marinade and spread them over the dough. Place the caramelized onion on top of the dough. Sprinkle with minced garlic and course salt. Drizzle with additional olive oil.
12. Bake for 20 to 30 minutes or until the bread is golden brown.
13. Sprinkle with fresh basil. Serve additional olive oil for dipping.

Servings: 6
Preparation Time: 45 minutes plus dough cycle and baking

This flat bread is traditionally baked in a shallow pan and filled with salad or cheese and served for a light snack. The toppings for this bread act like an open sandwich. Feel free to vary the combinations of flavors to create your own favorite Focaccia.

SIMPLE RICE PUDDING with MACERATED STRAWBERRIES

Just like mother used to make, smooth rice pudding is the perfect dessert for a spicy menu. Confectioners' sugar and fresh berries are the perfect garnish.

4	**cups milk**
2	**cups water**
1	**cup arborio rice**
¾	**cup granulated sugar**
¼	**teaspoon salt**
1	**teaspoon vanilla extract**
½	**teaspoon ground cinnamon**
½	**teaspoon ground nutmeg**
	Confectioners' sugar
	Macerated fresh strawberries (see sidebar)

1. Heat the milk and water in a large pot over medium high heat until it begins to boil.

2. Stir in the rice, sugar, and salt.
3. Reduce the heat to medium low and cook uncovered until the pudding is thick and the rice is tender, about 45 minutes to 1 hour.
4. Stir in the vanilla, cinnamon, and nutmeg.
5. Spoon the pudding into bowls, cool, and garnish with confectioners' sugar and berries.

Serves 6
Preparation Time: 10 minutes plus cooking

This basic recipe has its roots in comfort cooking. Feel free to experiment with flavorings like key lime or lemon or garnish with sautéed apples for an easy update on a traditional favorite.

Macerate berries by soaking them in juice, liquor or sugar to soften the fruit and intensify the flavors. Always us a non-reactive bowl and try not to over do it. Just a little bit of added gusto will do!

Informal Get Togethers

(EASY PARTIES FOR EIGHT OR MORE GUESTS)

Continuous Quesadilla
Gotta Have Pasta Feast
Totally Topped Pizza Party
Backyard Barbecue with all the Fixins'

"Don't forget the music! I am always surprised when someone has gone to an enormous amount of effort to clean and decorate his or her home, stock a bar, cook a splendid meal, and then forgets to set the atmosphere. I love to select music to match the time of year or even the cuisine that I am serving. Favorite examples include the soundtrack from *The Big Easy* when I am serving Creole food or golden oldies for a backyard barbecue.

Katherine Hutt
Nautilus Communications
Vienna, Virginia

Continuous Quesadilla Party Plan

Party Motivation

The gang is coming back to town for an impromptu reunion and they expect to gather at your place. You want a menu that is fun, has something for everyone, is relaxed and allows your pals to chip in.

Party Menu

Frozen Strawberry Cocktails
Yellow Rice and Black Bean Salad in Individual Radicchio Cups
Flank Steak, Black Bean, and Toasted Corn Quesadilla **
Oven Roasted Zucchini, Tomato, and White Cheddar Quesadilla
Butternut Squash Quesadilla
Lime Grilled Chicken Breast, Asparagus, and Brie Cheese Quesadilla
Not Your Mama's Guacamole
Super Fresh Salsa
Creme de Menthe Swirl Cheesecake

**** Over-the-Top Suggestion**

Take this party outside and grill a bunch of quesadilla at once. Combine ingredients and create triple-decker masterpieces with input from your pals.

Party Strategy

Make the dessert and the salad days in advance. Prepare all of the quesadilla ingredients before the party begins so that all that remains is the assembly.

Two days in advance: Bake the cheesecake and refrigerate.

One day in advance: Prepare rice and bean salad. Create radicchio cups. Grill flank steak and refrigerate. Grill chicken breasts and refrigerate. Prepare salsa and refrigerate.

Four hours before: Roast zucchini and tomatoes, grate cheese. Roast butternut squash and make filling. Roast asparagus.

Two hours before: Prepare guacamole. Prepare black bean filling.

One hour before: Set out all of the ingredients. Stuff salad bowls. Prepare ingredients for strawberry cocktails.

Shortcuts

There are way more quesadilla ideas here than you will need for a party of 8. Choose 2 or 3, plenty for a crowd.

Party Backdrop

Transform your kitchen (or backyard grill) into a hustling diner. Place several skillets on the stove. With pals gathered—shouting requests, create individual quesadilla. Toss one onto a platter. Have your helpers, cut into quarters, garnish with herbs and sour cream and dollop with salsa and guacamole. Everyone digs in as more and more quesadilla appear. It's continuous food and oh so good!

The Table Setting

Rustic, earthenware platters are terrific for serving the quesadilla. If budget permits, choose one or two that have red clay bottoms and ceramic tops. Enameled platters are colorful often depicting roosters or wine and cheese scenes. Ovenproof is the best. Serve the salsa and guacamole from clay bowls or pitchers. The salad is beautifully presented in individual radicchio bowls. Place them onto a large oval platter. A pitcher of frozen strawberry cocktails and a scattering of martini glasses are placed on a separate table. The centerpiece, a Crème de Menthe Swirl Cheesecake on a whimsical cake stand, adds to the gaiety of the day.

Frozen Strawberry Cocktails

This is a fun, refreshing drink that is a breeze to make. Make as many as your blender will allow and be prepared to make more as your guests drain their glasses! The drink becomes more or less sweet as you increase or decrease the amount of simple syrup. You choose.

8   ounces vodka
1   pint strawberries (reserve 8 for garnish)
1   cup simple syrup
    Juice of 1 lime (about 2 tablespoons)
    Ice

1. Pour half of the vodka into a blender.
2. Remove the stems from the strawberries that are not reserved. Add half of them to the blender.

3. Pour ½ cup simple syrup into the blender.
4. Add 1 tablespoon of lime juice.
5. Fill the blender to the top with ice.
6. Pulse until blended.
7. Pour the mixture into 4 martini glasses. Garnish with the reserved strawberries.
8. Repeat for a second batch of cocktails.

Servings: 8
Preparation Time: 10 minutes

Prepare simple syrup by placing equal parts of sugar and water in a pan. Bring the mixture to a boil and cook just until the sugar dissolves. Remove the simple syrup from the heat and allow to cool.

Yellow Rice and Black Bean Salad in Individual Radicchio Cups

This simple salad comes together in minutes and the presentation is so inviting.

4   cups cooked yellow rice
1   16-ounce can black beans, drained
1   large avocado, diced (about 1 cup)
4   plum tomatoes, seeded and diced (about 1 cup)
4   green onions, thinly sliced (about ¼ cup)
¼   cup chopped fresh parsley leaves
1   teaspoon ground cumin
2   tablespoons balsamic vinegar
1   7-ounce jar sun-dried tomatoes in oil
    Salt and freshly ground pepper

4   small heads Radicchio lettuce

1. Place the rice in a large bowl.

2. Add the black beans and toss.
3. Add the avocado, plum tomatoes, green onion, parsley, cumin, and vinegar.
4. Measure 2 tablespoons of the oil from the sun-dried tomatoes and add this to the salad. Discard the remaining oil.
5. Chop the sun-dried tomatoes into small pieces and add to the salad. Toss well.
6. Season with salt and pepper.
7. Cut each head of radicchio in half. Remove enough of the center leaves to form a bowl. Serve the salad in the radicchio bowls.

Servings: 8
Preparation Time: 20 minutes

Feel free to alter the presentation of this dish. If radicchio is unavailable, serve the salad in iceberg lettuce bowls or hollowed out bell peppers—also a good choice for this fun and festive dish.

Flank Steak, Toasted Corn, and Black Bean Quesadilla

Make these quesadilla one at a time and share the wedges while another batch cooks on the grill.

1   8- to 12-ounce flank steak
    Salt and freshly ground pepper
1   tablespoon olive oil
2   medium jalapeño peppers, seeded and
    diced (about 4 tablespoons)
1   16-ounce can corn, drained
    Salt and freshly ground pepper

1   tablespoon olive oil
¼   small red onion, diced (about 2 table-
    spoons)
2   medium cloves garlic, minced (about 1
    teaspoon)
1   large green bell pepper, seeded and
    diced (about 1 cup)
1   16-ounce can black beans, drained
1   tablespoon tomato paste
1   teaspoon ground cumin

8   10-inch flour tortillas
1½ cups grated sharp Cheddar cheese
1½ cups grated Monterey Jack cheese

1. Season the flank steak with salt and pepper. Grill over medium high heat to medium rare. Allow to rest for several minutes. Cut against the grain into thin strips.
2. Heat 1 tablespoon olive oil in a skillet over medium high heat.
3. Add the jalapeño peppers and cook for 2 minutes.
4. Add the corn and cook for 2 minutes. Season with salt and pepper. Remove to a dish and set aside.
5. Heat 1 tablespoon olive oil in the same skillet over medium high heat.
6. Add the onions, garlic, and bell pepper and cook for 2 minutes.
7. Add the black beans and cook for 2 minutes.
8. Stir in the tomato paste and cumin. Season with salt and pepper. Remove from the heat
9. Lay one tortilla into a skillet that has been sprayed with vegetable oil spray over medium high heat.
10. Top with ¼ of the cheese, ¼ of the bean mixture, ¼ of the corn mixture, and ¼ of the slices of flank steak. Place a second tortilla on top and push down slightly.
11. Cook until beginning to brown on the bottom, about 2 minutes. Use a large spatula and your fingertips to carefully flip the quesadilla. Cook until the cheese begins to melt, about 2 more minutes.
12. Repeat with the remaining ingredients.

Servings: 8
Preparation Time: 40 minutes

An alternate cooking method is to grill the quesadilla, which also allows you to make several at a time. Place 1 tortilla onto a grill over medium high heat. Top with cheese and flank steak. Add another tortilla. Top with bean and corn mixtures. Add an extra sprinkling of cheese. Top with a third tortilla. Use 2 spatulas to flip the triple-decker tortilla when the cheese is melted. Add more cheese as needed to keep the other ingredients in place!

Jalapeño peppers add a great heat to a Mexican inspired dish like quesadilla. When handled properly, jalapeño is easy to work with. Cut the stem from the pepper. Split the pepper in half. Use the tip of a spoon to remove the seeds and veins from the pepper. Dice the pepper into small pieces. Make sure to wash your hands or use rubber gloves when handling the seeds.

Oven-Roasted Zucchini, Tomato, and White Cheddar Quesadilla

Grated white Cheddar cheese adds a diverse taste to fresh, roasted veggies.

3 **medium zucchini, sliced into rounds (about 3 cups)**
8 **to 10 plum tomatoes, sliced into rounds (about 3 cups)**
2 **tablespoons olive oil**
4 **medium cloves garlic, minced (about 2 teaspoons)**
1 **tablespoon chopped fresh oregano leaves**
   Salt and freshly ground pepper

8 **10-inch flour tortillas**
12 **ounces white Cheddar cheese, grated**

Preheat the oven to 375°.

1. Place the zucchini and tomato slices into a baking dish. Drizzle with olive oil. Sprinkle with garlic and oregano. Season with salt and pepper. Roast for 10 to 15 minutes.

2. Lay one tortilla on a griddle or into a skillet that has been sprayed with vegetable oil spray on medium high heat.
3. Top with ¼ of the cheese and ¼ of the roasted vegetables. Place a second tortilla on top and push down slightly.
4. Cook until beginning to brown on the bottom, about 2 minutes. Carefully flip the quesadilla with a spatula. Cook until the cheese begins to melt, about 2 more minutes.
5. Repeat with the remaining ingredients.

Servings: 8
Preparation Time: 30 minutes

Feel free to experiment with your favorite roasted veggies for this simple dish. A favorite addition is roasted garlic and roasted yellow pepper strips.

BUTTERNUT SQUASH QUESADILLA

The slightly sweet taste of the cook squash is enhanced with the spice of red pepper flakes and then tempered by mellow cheese. This dish has something for everyone!

2	**medium butternut squash, peeled and diced into 1 inch squares (about 4 cups)**
1	**medium white onion, diced (about ⅔ cup)**
8	**medium cloves garlic, peeled**
1	**tablespoon olive oil**
1	**teaspoon dried red pepper flakes**
4	**10-inch flour tortillas**
1	**12-ounce jar roasted yellow peppers, drained and cut into strips**
12	**ounces goat cheese, crumbled**

Preheat the oven to 375°.

1. Place the squash cubes, diced onion, and garlic cloves in a baking pan. Toss with olive oil and season with red pepper flakes. Bake for 30 to 40 minutes or until the squash is soft.
2. Transfer the vegetables to a food processor. Pulse until smooth.
3. Lay one tortilla on a griddle or into a skillet that has been sprayed with vegetable oil spray on medium high heat.
4. Top with ¼ of the squash mixture, ¼ of the yellow pepper strips, and ¼ of the cheese. Place a second tortilla on top and push down slightly.
5. Cook until beginning to brown on the bottom, about 2 minutes. Carefully flip the quesadilla with a spatula. Cook until the cheese begins to melt, about 2 more minutes.
6. Repeat with the remaining ingredients.

Servings: 8
Preparation Time: 50 minutes

Butternut squash is a member of the marrow family. It is shaped like a long, large pear. The skin of the squash is smooth and buttery yellow in color. The flesh of the squash is bright orange. Have some patience when peeling and dicing, as it is quite dense!

Lime-Grilled Chicken Breast, Asparagus, and Brie Cheese Quesadilla

Roasted asparagus and marinated chicken slices give a fresh update to traditional Quesadilla ingredients.

2 6 to 8-ounce skinless, boneless chicken breast halves
Salt and freshly ground pepper
Juice of 2 limes (about ¼ cup)

12 to 16 medium asparagus spears, tough stems removed
1 tablespoon olive oil

8 10-inch flour tortillas
12 ounces Brie cheese, thinly sliced

Preheat the oven to 375°.

1. Season the chicken breasts with salt and pepper. Marinate in lime juice for 30 minutes or up to several hours, covered and chilled in the refrigerator.
2. Grill over medium high heat. Allow to rest for several minutes. Slice into thin strips.
3. Place the asparagus spears on a rack onto a baking sheet. Drizzle with olive oil and season with salt and pepper. Roast for 10 to 15 minutes.
4. Lay one tortilla on a griddle or into a skillet that has been sprayed with vegetable oil spray on medium high heat.
5. Top with ¼ of the cheese, ¼ of the chicken strips, and ¼ of the roasted asparagus spears. Place a second tortilla on top and push down slightly.
6. Cook until beginning to brown on the bottom, about 2 minutes. Carefully flip the quesadilla with a spatula. Cook until the cheese begins to melt, about 2 more minutes.
7. Repeat with the remaining ingredients.

Servings: 8
Preparation Time: 30 minutes

Asparagus is most often thought of as a harbinger to springtime. Truthfully, great asparagus is available all year round. Asparagus can be pencil thin or almost an inch thick. Choose a thicker spear when roasting. Thin asparagus are easily blanched or steamed for a crispy deep green result.

NOT YOUR MAMA'S GUACAMOLE

Straying just a touch from the traditional dish, this guacamole has substance and a distinctive flavor.

2	**large ripe avocados, diced (about 2 cups)**
	Juice of 1 lime (about 2 tablespoons)
1	**cup cottage cheese**
2	**plum tomatoes, seeded and diced (about ½ cup)**
1	**small jalapeño pepper, seeded and diced (about 1 tablespoons)**
4	**green onions, thinly sliced (about ¼ cup)**
2	**medium cloves garlic, minced (about 1 teaspoon)**
2	**to 6 drops hot pepper sauce**
1	**teaspoon chili powder**
1	**tablespoon chopped fresh cilantro leaves**
	Salt and freshly ground pepper

1. Place the avocado in a bowl and mash with a fork. Sprinkle with lime juice.
2. Stir in the cottage cheese until just combined.
3. Add the tomatoes, pepper, onions, garlic, and as much hot pepper sauce as you like. Stir to combine.
4. Stir in the chili powder and fresh cilantro.
5. Season with salt and pepper.
6. Chill for at least 30 minutes or overnight.

Yield: 2 cups
Preparation Time: 20 minutes

Traditional Mexican guacamole consists of mashed avocado, finely diced onion, lime or lemon juice and fresh cilantro. The addition of cottage cheese changes the consistency slightly and the chili powder gives this dip a feisty flavor. Make sure that you chose a very ripe avocado for this dish, one that yields to the pressure of your fingers. Do not choose an avocado that feels mushy—that's too ripe! Keep unripe avocados in a cool, dark place for two to three days to ripen. To make sure that the avocado does not turn brown while refrigerating, place the pit into the guacamole. Remove before serving.

Super Fresh Salsa

Preparing fresh salsa is as easy as dicing and tossing. The results are so very yummy and only get better the next day.

6   to 8 plum tomatoes, seeded and diced (about 2 cups)
2   medium jalapeño peppers, seeded and diced (about 4 tablespoons)
2   medium cloves garlic, minced (about 1 teaspoon)
1   bunch (6 to 8) green onions, chopped (about 1 cup)
2   tablespoons chopped fresh basil
2   tablespoons chopped fresh cilantro
    Juice of 2 limes (about ¼ cup)
1   tablespoon balsamic vinegar
1   tablespoon olive oil
    Salt and freshly ground pepper

1. Place the tomatoes, jalapeño, garlic, green onion, basil, and cilantro into the bowl of a food processor.
2. Pour in the lime juice, balsamic vinegar, and olive oil. Pulse briefly. The salsa should be chunky.
3. Season with salt and pepper.
4. Cover and refrigerate for at least 30 minutes or for several hours.
5. Drain the salsa in a colander before serving.

Yield: 2 cups
Preparation Time: 10 minutes

Salsa is a spicy sauce that can be prepared fresh or cooked. Salsa most often includes tomatoes, peppers onions and garlic. Terrific additions include mango, avocado, bell pepper, diced olives, and green chilies.

CRÈME de MENTHE SWIRL CHEESECAKE

Serve this cool cake after a spicy meal to please your guests and "leave 'em laughing!"

1	**9-ounce package chocolate wafer cookies, crushed (about 2 cups)**
3	**tablespoons unsalted butter, melted**
4	**8-ounce packages cream cheese, room temperature**
1	**cup granulated sugar**
4	**large eggs**
2	**cups sour cream**
2	**teaspoons vanilla extract**
½	**cup green Crème de Menthe**
1	**cup whipping cream**
½	**cup confectioners' sugar**
	Chocolate mint sandwich candies

Preheat the oven to 350°.

1. Place the cookies in the bowl of a food processor. Pulse to form crumbs.
2. Add the melted butter through the feed tube.
3. Press the mixture in the bottom and 1-inch up the sides of a 10-inch springform pan.
4. Bake the crust for 8 minutes.
5. Use an electric mixer to combine the cream cheese and the sugar until fluffy.
6. Add the eggs one at a time.
7. Stir in the sour cream and vanilla.
8. Pour half of the batter into the chocolate crust.
9. Stir the Crème de Menthe into the remaining batter.
10. Place the batter flavored with Crème de Menthe by tablespoons onto the plain batter. Use the tip of a sharp knife to swirl the two together.
11. Bake in the center of the oven for 50 to 60 minutes or until the center is just set.
12. Remove the cheesecake from the oven. Cool for 5 minutes. Run a sharp knife around the sides of the cheesecake. Cool completely. Cover and refrigerate overnight.
13. Beat the whipping cream and sugar until soft peaks form.
14. Use a vegetable peeler to shave the candies into soft curls.
15. Remove the cheesecake from the sides of the pan. Spread the cake with whipped cream and sprinkle the candy curls on top.

Servings: 8 to 10
Preparation Time: 30 minutes plus baking

Cheesecakes all have one thing in common—a rich wonderful base that blends well with all types of great garnishes like berries, coconut, chocolate curls, kiwi and mango. You can also add many variations to the cheese base like candy or cookie pieces, chocolate, or cinnamon flavorings, and other liqueurs like Amaretto or Cointreau. The crumbly crust is easily made from ginger snaps, vanilla wafers, or chocolate sandwich cookies. Feel free to experiment with your favorite ingredients to create a special cheesecake.

As an alternate baking method guaranteed to produce a perfectly baked cheesecake try this method. Preheat the oven to 500°. Place the cheesecake on the center rack and bake for 15 minutes. Reduce the heat and bake for 1 hour or until the center is set. Turn the oven off. Allow the cheesecake to remain in the oven for 1 hour longer. Cover and refrigerate overnight.

Gotta Have Pasta Feast Party Plan

Party Motivation

You absolutely cannot decide which of your favorite Italian dishes will satisfy your pasta craving. So, you prepare them all and invite good friends to share in the fun. The recipes are designed for four—but when sharing more than one—there will be plenty of pasta for everyone.

Party Menu

Frozen Tangerine Margaritas
Romaine Salad with Crumbled Gorgonzola Cheese
Penne with Marinated Tomatoes and Herbed Ricotta Cheese
Three Cheese Fettuccine with Toasted Pine Nuts **
Farfalle with Grilled Chicken, Wilted Spinach, and Sun-Dried Tomatoes
Rosemary Olive Quick Bread
Honey Cheese Pie with Sweetened Berries

** Over-the-Top Suggestion

Pasta with cream sauce is an Italian menu standard. But, what happens if you add not one, not two, but three amazing cheeses to the cream? The result is a dish so very rich that you'll only need a spoonful per person to satisfy the longing.

Party Strategy

Prepare the sauces for the pastas in advance. Use a pasta pan with built-in colander to place dried pasta into the boiling water. After the pasta is cooked, remove, but retain the boiling water. Transfer the cooked pasta to the prepared sauce. Place another dried pasta into the colander and into the boiling water, thus saving reheating time.

Two days ahead: Prepare dessert. Cover and refrigerate.

The evening before: Prepare ingredients for salad. Grill chicken breasts. Bake bread.

The morning of: Prepare the buffet table.

Two hours before: Prepare fettuccine sauce. Toast pine nuts. Squeeze juice for Margaritas. Whisk salad dressing. Marinate tomatoes for penne.

Thirty minutes before: Prepare boiling water for pasta. Gently warm fettuccine sauce and sliced chicken.

Shortcuts

For a less ambitious party approach, choose one pasta and double the recipe to serve 8 people. Or, eliminate the home-baked bread and purchase fresh rolls.

Party Backdrop

Serve each pasta from its own large bowl. Prepare one at a time and bring to the dining table. Offer salad to munch on between pasta number 1 and 2. Offer Rosemary bread between pasta number 2 and 3. Guests are relaxed and confident that the good, great food will keep coming from your kitchen.

The Table Setting

Chill 9-inch, glass plates for the salad. Use the same size plates or shallow bowls for each pasta course. Matching pasta and serving bowls are the perfect idea for this party. Borrow a set or two from your pals so that cleaning in between pasta courses is not necessary. Replenish cocktails from an over-sized margarita pitcher and garnish margarita glasses with tangerine pinwheels.

FROZEN TANGERINE MARGARITAS

This refreshing drink begins a terrific party with a bang. If tangerines are hard to find, feel free to substitute with orange juice.

4 cups tangerine juice
8 ounces tequila
4 ounces Cointreau
Juice of 3 limes (about 6 tablespoons)
Margarita salt
Lime pinwheels

1. Place half of the tangerine juice, tequila, Cointreau, and lime juice in a large blender.
2. Fill the blender to the top with ice.
3. Pulse until the mixture is well blended.
4. Pour into Margarita glasses that have been dipped in Margarita salt. Garnish with lime pinwheels.
5. Repeat with remaining ingredients for a second batch of cocktails.

Servings: 8
Preparation Time: 15 minutes

ROMAINE SALAD with CRUMBLED GORGONZOLA CHEESE

Chill the lettuce and the serving dish to ensure a crisp, tart salad that is refreshing and inspiring.

2 medium heads romaine lettuce, washed, dried and torn into 1-inch pieces, about 6 cups

Juice of 2 lemons (about ¼ cup)
1 tablespoon sherry vinegar
1 large shallot, minced (about 1 tablespoon)
1 teaspoon Dijon mustard
2 tablespoons chopped fresh dill
½ cup olive oil
Salt and freshly ground pepper
1 cup crumbled Gorgonzola cheese

1. Toss the romaine leaves into a salad bowl.
2. In a small bowl whisk together the lemon juice, vinegar, shallot, mustard, and dill until combined.
3. Whisk in the olive oil.
4. Season with salt and pepper.
5. Drizzle the dressing over the lettuce. Toss.
6. Add the cheese and toss again.

Servings: 8
Preparation Time: 10 minutes

Gorgonzola cheese is a semisoft cow's milk cheese with a distinctive flavor and creamy texture. It is a bit subtler than most blue-veined cheeses.

PENNE with MARINATED TOMATOES and HERBED RICOTTA CHEESE

This pasta is simple, delicious and a great quick and easy midweek supper. Combine all of the ingredients in a pasta bowl and watch as the hot penne melts the cheese and warms the tomatoes.

½ cup olive oil
¼ cup balsamic vinegar
½ teaspoon red pepper flakes
4 medium cloves garlic, finely sliced (about 2 teaspoons)
1 pint ripe cherry tomatoes, cut in half (about 2 cups)
  Salt and freshly ground pepper
8 ounces ricotta cheese (about 2 cups)
2 tablespoons chopped fresh oregano leaves
1 pound penne, cooked al dente

1. In a medium bowl whish together the olive oil, vinegar, and red pepper flakes.
2. Stir in the garlic and tomatoes. Season with salt and pepper. Marinate for at least 15 minutes at room temperature.
3. Stir the oregano into the ricotta cheese.
4. Place the tomatoes and cheese in a pasta bowl. Add the warm pasta and stir until the cheese just begins to melt.

Serves 4
Preparation Time: 10 minutes

Great cooks argue the proper way to prepare dried pasta. My rule is to generously salt the water for pasta but to refrain for adding oil. You can adjust the seasoning in the sauce to reflect the scant amount of salt absorbed by the pasta. Conversely your sauce will have difficulty clinging to pasta that has been introduced to oil while cooking.

THREE CHEESE FETTUCCINE with TOASTED PINE NUTS

The wonderful flavors of three cheeses are melted into rich, heavy cream and tossed with warm pasta.

2	cups heavy cream
4	ounces Gorgonzola cheese, crumbled (about ½ cup)
8	ounces Fontina cheese, cut into pieces
8	ounces whole ricotta cheese (about 2 cups)
	Salt and freshly ground pepper
½	teaspoon ground nutmeg
1	pound fettuccine pasta, cooked al dente
4	ounces pine nuts, toasted (about ½ cup)
2	tablespoons chopped fresh Italian parsley leaves

1. In a saucepan over medium high heat bring the cream to a slow boil.

2. Stir in the Gorgonzola cheese. Stir until smooth.
3. Stir in the Fontina and ricotta cheese. Stir until smooth.
4. Season with salt, pepper, and nutmeg.
5. Pour half of the sauce over the cooked pasta. Let sit for a few minutes. Pour the remaining sauce over the pasta.
6. Toss with toasted pine nuts and sprinkle with fresh parsley.

Serves 4
Preparation Time: 20 minutes

There are countless ways to lighten the calorie count of this dish. Start by substituting milk for cream and skim Ricotta for whole.

Toasting pine nuts bring out their buttery quality. Spread the nuts on a baking sheet. Bake at 350°. for just a few minutes. The nuts are toasted when they are golden not dark brown.

Farfalle with Grilled Chicken, Wilted Spinach, and Sun-Dried Tomatoes

This easy-to-make pasta comes together quickly and is an invitation for ingredient substitution. Use whatever you have on hand. After all, it is your party!

4   **6 to 8-ounce skinless boneless chicken breast halves**
1   **teaspoon dried oregano**
    Salt and fresh ground pepper
½   **cup chicken stock**
    Juice of 3 lemons (about ½ cup)
1   **7-ounce jar sun-dried tomatoes in oil, julienned**
½   **cup olive oil**
6   **ounces fresh spinach leaves, torn (about 2 cups)**
8   **ounces fresh mozzarella, cubed**
1   **pound farfalle, cooked al dente**
    Parmigiano Reggiano cheese, shaved

1. Cook the chicken breast in a grill pan over medium high heat. Season with dried oregano, salt, and freshly ground pepper. Remove from the heat and allow to sit for 5 minutes. Slice the chicken breast into diagonal strips. Set aside.
2. Pour the chicken stock, lemon juice, and sun-dried tomatoes with the oil from the jar into a large bowl. Stir.
3. Whisk in the olive oil.
4. Place the spinach leaves and mozzarella into the bowl.
5. Add the warm pasta. Toss.
6. Lay the sliced chicken pieces on top of the pasta. Garnish with curls of shaved cheese.

Serves 4
Preparation Time: 10 minutes

Parmigiano Reggiano is a distinctive, salty, Parmesan cheese that adds a wonderful flavor to pasta. Feel free to substitute with other varieties of Parmesan or Romano cheese.

For a wetter sauce, take a tip from the Italian kitchen and add a ladle full of pasta water to the dish. Toss well.

ROSEMARY OLIVE QUICK BREAD

The cake-like nature of this savory bread makes it a perfect addition to a party table.

2½ cups all-purpose flour
¾ cup granulated sugar
2 teaspoons baking powder
2 teaspoons dried rosemary
Zest of 1 medium lemon (about 1 tablespoons)
2 large eggs
¾ cup white wine
½ cup olive oil
½ cup sliced green olives

Preheat the oven to 350°.

1. Place the flour, sugar, baking powder, rosemary, and lemon zest in a bowl. Set aside.
2. In a mixing bowl, stir together the eggs, wine, and olive oil.
3. Add the flour mixture and stir well.
4. Stir in the olives.
5. Pour the batter into a loaf pan that has been sprayed with vegetable oil spray.
6. Bake for 50 to 60 minutes or until a toothpick inserted into the center of the loaf comes out clean.

Servings: 8
Preparation Time: 10 minutes plus baking

Olives were first cultivated in the Mediterranean thousands of years ago.
Olives are the fruit of a very old tree and must be cured before they are palatable. The color of the olive depends on its age. Green olives are picked the earliest, while black olives have been left on the tree to ripen fully. You can chose from all varieties of olives for this recipe.
My favorites are the easy to find pitted Spanish olives.

Honey Cheese Pie with Sweetened Berries

This delicious dessert is a cross between a cheesecake and a custard tart.

¼ **cup butter (½ stick)**
2 **tablespoons honey**
40 **vanilla wafer cookies**
¾ **cup whole almonds**
¾ **cup whole walnuts**

2 **8-ounce packages cream cheese, room temperature**
1 **15-ounce container ricotta cheese**
½ **cup granulated sugar**
½ **cup honey**
4 **large eggs**
2 **teaspoons vanilla extract**
1 **teaspoon lemon extract**
Zest of 1 medium lemon (about 1 tablespoon)

1 **pound fresh berries (about 3 cups)**
⅓ **cup honey**

Preheat the oven to 350°.
1. Prepare a 10-inch spring-form pan by wrapping it along the bottom and up the sides with plastic wrap and then aluminum foil.
2. In a saucepan over medium high heat bring the butter and 2 tablespoons of honey to a boil. Remove from the heat.
3. Place the cookies and nuts in the bowl of a food processor. Pulse to form crumbs.
4. Add the honey mixture to the crumb mixture.
5. Spread this mixture on the bottom and up the sides of the pan.
6. Bake for 10 minutes.
7. Use an electric mixer to combine the cream cheese, ricotta cheese, sugar, and honey until fluffy.
8. Add the eggs one at a time.
9. Stir in the vanilla, lemon extract, and lemon zest.
10. Pour this mixture into the crust.
11. Place the spring-form pan into a larger baking dish and fill half way up the sides with hot water. Bake pie 60 to 70 minutes or until the center is puffed and moves only slightly when shaken. Carefully remove the pan from the water bath. Cool completely. Cover and refrigerate overnight.
12. Place the berries and the honey in a bowl. Toss, cover and chill for at least 30 minutes.
13. Top each serving with a spoon full of berries.

Servings: 8
Preparation Time: 30 minutes plus baking

Baking in a water bath provides a moist even-tempered environment for delicate desserts like cheesecakes, custards and puddings. The water insulates the food from the direct heat of the oven. Make sure that you start with a least warm—if not boiling water for the most even cooking. Pour the water only half way up the sides of the pan. You may need to check the water level after a while to make sure that you compensate for evaporation.

Totally Topped Pizza Party Plan

Party Motivation

You just returned from a weekend in Lugano, Switzerland where your host taught you to create home-baked pizza from the wood burning stove in the center of his home and now you are just dying to show your friends your newly learned skill. Or, you are tired of over-priced, luke-warm, pizzas delivered in cardboard boxes and have a burning need to twirl dough. Whatever the reason, this is a great way to party with good pals.

Party Menu

Chianti Cooler
Tri-Colored Tomato Salad with Zesty Olive Dressing
Roasted Tomato and Portobello Mushroom Pizza
Four Cheese Pizza
Pizza with Roasted Peppers and Ricotta Cheese **
Great Big Ginger Cookies

** Over-the-Top Suggestion

Everyone can bake pizzas with slices of pepper and onions, but roast the peppers first and the satiny taste adds a depth of flavor that just twangs your taste buds.

Party Strategy

Prepare a few pizzas in advance and bake several at a time using a double oven or a single oven with several racks. Have extra pizza dough and toppings for those creative pals that want to build their own.

The day before: Bake ginger cookies. Prepare pizza dough. Roast tomatoes and peppers.
Two hours before: Assemble salad. Roll out pizza dough.
One hour before: Heat the oven and begin to build pizzas.

Shortcuts

Frozen pizza dough is an acceptable substitute. If tri- colored tomatoes are unavailable use the reddest, most ripe tomato in the market.

Party Backdrop

A counter in the kitchen is the perfect place to begin this fun party. Allow guests to mingle over Chianti coolers while they create their own individual pizza.

The Table Setting

Use a pizza stone in the oven to guarantee great results. Serve pizzas from a cornmeal-dusted paddle and slide onto a serving platter. Use a pizza cutter to cut the pies into wedges. Serve slices on buffet plates that will also hold slices from the tomato salad. Serve ginger cookies from a wicker basket.

CHIANTI COOLER

Offer your guests a cocktail that uses Chianti as a base and freshens up with a splash of soda and a hint of citrus.

1   **750-mililitre bottle Chianti**
1   **1-liter bottle club soda**
     Orange peel cut into curls

1. Pour Chianti into 8 tall glasses filled with ice half way to the top.
2. Pour in a splash of club soda.
3. Garnish with an orange curl.

TRI-COLORED TOMATO SALAD with ZESTY OLIVE DRESSING

This pretty salad is easy to assemble. Olive paste is available in a tube and adds an intense flavor to the dressing. Start with a touch and feel free to add as much as you like. A wonderful variation is to substitute with anchovy or tomato paste.

4   **cups fresh salad greens**
3   **medium red tomatoes, cut into wedges (about 2 cups)**
3   **medium yellow tomatoes, cut into wedges (about 2 cups)**
3   **medium green tomatoes, cut into wedges (about 2 cups)**
1   **bunch (6 to 8) green onions, chopped (about 1 cup)**
1   **tablespoon fresh tarragon leaves**
     Zest of 1 medium lemon (about 1 tablespoons)
2   **medium cloves garlic**

¼   **cup balsamic vinegar**
     Juice of 1 lemon (about 2 tablespoons)
1   **tablespoon anchovy paste**
1   **teaspoon Worcestershire sauce**
½   **cup olive oil**

1. Place the salad greens on a large platter.
2. Arrange the tomato wedges on top of the greens.
3. Place the green onions, tarragon leaves, lemon zest, and garlic in the bowl of a (mini) food processor. Pulse to mince.
4. Sprinkle the onion mixture on top of the tomatoes.
5. Whisk together the balsamic vinegar, lemon juice, anchovy paste, and Worcestershire sauce in a small bowl.
6. Slowly whisk in the olive oil.
7. Drizzle the dressing on top of the tomatoes and onto the greens.

Servings: 8
Preparation Time: 15 minutes

Green tomatoes are a specific type of tomato like beefsteak or cherry. However, green tomatoes are also often marketed as an unripe red tomato. For this recipe choose the ripest tomatoes possible. Although mixing the three colors is eye appealing, a great tasting tomato is most important in this dish!

Roasted Tomato and Portobello Mushroom Pizza

Prepare the roasted tomatoes in the morning and slow cook all day long. The rest of the pizza comes together in minutes.

1	**10-ounce prepared pizza dough (or see sidebar)**
½	**pound portobello mushrooms, cut into strips (about 1½ cups)**
	Salt and freshly ground pepper
1	**tablespoon olive oil**
¼	**cup sour cream**
	Roasted Tomato slices (see below)
3	**ounces Gorgonzola cheese, crumbled (about ½ cup)**
½	**teaspoon dried oregano**
	Oil for drizzling

4	**medium tomatoes, cut into ½-inch slices**
1	**medium clove garlic, minced (about ½ teaspoon)**
1	**teaspoon dried cilantro**
1	**tablespoon olive oil**

Preheat the oven to 500°.:
1. Roll out the pizza dough to a large circle.
2. Place the dough onto a pizza paddle (or baking sheet) that has been dusted with cornmeal.
3. Season the mushrooms with salt and pepper.
4. Heat the olive oil over medium high heat. Cook the mushrooms until just beginning to turn brown. Drain on paper towels.

5. Spread the sour cream onto the dough.
6. Place the cooked mushroom strips over the sour cream.
7. Top with roasted tomato slices.
8. Sprinkle with Gorgonzola cheese.
9. Season with dried oregano, salt, and freshly ground pepper. Drizzle olive oil over top.
10. Bake for 12 to 15 minutes until the cheese bubbles.

Yield: 8 slices
Preparation Time: 15 minutes plus baking and roasting tomatoes

FOR ROASTED TOMATOES:
Preheat the oven to 250°.
1. Place the tomatoes on a baking sheet.
2. Place a small amount of minced garlic on each tomato.
3. Sprinkle the dried cilantro over each.
4. Season with salt and freshly ground pepper.
5. Drizzle olive oil over the tomatoes.
6. Bake the tomatoes on low heat for several hours depending on available time. Cook the tomatoes for as much as 6 hours at 250°. or as little as 2 hours at 300°.

Making your own pizza dough is as easy as 1-2-3.
1.) Combine 1 teaspoon sugar and 1 package yeast (about 2¼ teaspoons) with 1 cup warm water. Place 2½ to 3 cups flour and 1 teaspoon salt in the bowl of a food processor. Pulse to combine. With machine running add 1 tablespoon olive oil and the yeast mixture through the feed tube. Process for 1 to 2 minutes or until a ball forms and the dough becomes smooth. You may need to add more or less flour.
2.) Turn out the dough to a floured surface and knead for at least 10 minutes adding more flour if the dough is too sticky.

3.) Spray a large bowl with vegetable oil spray. Place the dough in the bowl, turning to cover with the oil. Cover with plastic wrap and allow the dough to rise for about 1 hour or until almost doubled in size. Punch the dough down and let rest for 5 minutes more. Divide the dough in half and roll each half into a ½-inch thick circle.

FOUR CHEESE PIZZA

Four different cheeses combine to make this yummy pizza. Start with the ones listed in the recipe. Then, feel free to choose your own.

1   10-ounce prepared pizza dough
1   medium white onion, sliced into rings (about ⅔ cup)
1   tablespoon olive oil
1   clove garlic, minced (about ½ teaspoon)
1   cup sliced fresh mozzarella
½   cup ricotta cheese
½   cup grated Parmesan cheese
2   tablespoons grated Asiago cheese
1   teaspoon dried oregano
      Salt and freshly ground pepper
1   tablespoon truffle oil
1   tablespoon chopped fresh parsley leaves

Preheat the oven to 500°.
1. Roll out the pizza dough to a large circle.
2. Place the dough onto a pizza paddle (or baking sheet) that has been dusted with cornmeal.
3. Heat a skillet over medium high heat. Add 1 tablespoon olive oil. When the oil is hot, add the onion and cook until well browned but not burned. Add the garlic and cook for 2 minutes more.
4. Place the mozzarella cheese on the pizza dough.
5. Place the onion mixture on top of the cheese.
6. Top with the ricotta cheese.
7. Sprinkle with Parmesan and Aseago cheeses.
8. Season with dried oregano, salt, and freshly ground pepper.
9. Bake for 12 to 15 minutes until the cheese bubbles.
10. Drizzle the pizza with truffle oil and fresh chopped parsley.

Yield: 8 slices
Preparation Time: 15 minutes plus baking

A pizza stone is a terrific gadget to use when baking pizza. Heat the stone in the oven on the center rack. Assemble the pizza onto a paddle that has been sprinkled with cornstarch. When you are ready to bake, slide the pizza onto the heated stone. Make sure to also use the paddle to remove the pizza from the oven.

Fresh mozzarella is great in this recipe. It is available rolled into balls and surrounded by a small amount of whey.

Pizza with Roasted Peppers and Ricotta Cheese

Prepare the roasted peppers in the morning and slow cook all day long. The rest of the pizza comes together in minutes.

1   **10-ounce prepared pizza dough**
½   **cup ricotta cheese**
1   **large green bell pepper, roasted, charred skin removed, seeded**
1   **large red bell pepper, roasted, charred skin removed, seeded**
1   **large yellow bell pepper, roasted, charred skin removed, seeded**
1   **2-ounce tin anchovy fillets**
½   **cup grated Parmesan cheese**
½   **teaspoon dried basil**
2   **tablespoons olive oil**
    Salt and freshly ground pepper

Preheat the oven to 500°.
1. Roll out the pizza dough to a large circle.
2. Place the dough onto a pizza paddle (or baking sheet) that has been dusted with cornmeal.
3. Spread the ricotta cheese onto the pizza dough.
4. Slice the peppers into thin strips and place on top of the ricotta cheese.
5. Top with anchovy fillets.
6. Sprinkle with Parmesan cheese, dried basil, olive oil, salt, and freshly ground pepper.
7. Bake for 12 to 15 minutes until the cheese bubbles.

Yield: 8 slices
Preparation Time: 15 minutes plus baking and roasting peppers

---

To roast a pepper place it on a broiler pan at on the top rack in a preheated 500° oven. Turn the pepper one quarter turn as the skin blackens. (When you are roasting a large quantity of peppers use an outside barbecue grill.) Char the skin of the pepper until it is black. Place the pepper in a large brown bag to steam for at least 10 minutes. Remove the pepper from the bag. Peel away the black skin and remove the inside seeds.

GREAT BIG GINGER COOKIES

These were a favorite cookie in my grandmother's kitchen. She prepared enough dough to fill a deep ceramic crock and baked sheets and sheets at a time. For those of us that helped, she would replace the raisins with a sliver of almonds or a wedge of chocolate!

2½ cups all-purpose flour
2 teaspoons ground ginger
1 teaspoon baking soda
¾ teaspoon ground cinnamon
½ teaspoon ground cloves
½ teaspoon salt
¾ cup margarine (1½ sticks), room temperature
1 cup granulated sugar
1 large egg
¼ cup molasses

¼ cup granulated sugar
1 cup raisins

Preheat the oven to 350°.
1. Combine the flour, ginger, baking soda, cinnamon, cloves, and salt in a medium bowl.
2. With an electric mixer beat the margarine and 1 cup of sugar in a large bowl until fluffy.
3. Add the egg and stir.
4. Add the molasses and stir.
5. Add the flour mixture in 3 additions.
6. Use a tablespoon to portion out the dough. Roll into 2-inch balls.
7. Roll the balls in granulated sugar.
8. Place onto a cookie sheet lined with a Silpat liner.
9. Bake for 10 to 12 minutes or until the cookies are puffed and the edges beginn to turn light brown.
10. Place the cookie sheet on a cooling rack. Place 1 to 2 raisins in the center of each cookie.
11. Cool the cookies on the baking sheet for several minutes. Transfer to a rack to cool completely.

Yield: 2 dozen cookies
Preparation Time: 20 minutes plus baking

These cookies are even better the next day, as they get softer and softer.
Store in an airtight container and they will keep well in the refrigerator.

Backyard Barbeque with all the Fixins' Party Plan

Party Motivation

A three-day weekend, an afternoon before the big game, Sunday supper with family—all are great leisurely occasions that deserve good friends getting together with great good food.

Party Menu

Bourbon Minted Tea
Butterflied Chicken on the Grill **
Spicy Baked Bean Casserole
Potato Salad with Sour Cream and Garbanzo Beans
Crisp Coleslaw with Mustard Dressing
Deep Dish Apple Pie

**** Over-the-Top Suggestion**

Use red bricks or a large stone to weight the chicken on the grill while you are cooking. It makes for a few raised eyebrows, but the result is an evenly cooked bird.

Party Strategy

While the chicken rests before carving, bring the other dishes to the table. Pass the platters and bowls family style.

The day before: Prepare the salads and the bean casserole for baking (without the topping).
The morning of: Bake the apple pie. Marinate the chickens.
Two hours before: Set the table. Bake the beans.
One hour before: Make tea for Minted Tea. Start up the grill.

Shortcuts

Although the pie dough is as easy as can be, frozen dough is an acceptable substitute. Chicken pieces work just as well in the grilled chicken recipe.

Party Backdrop

An outdoor picnic is the perfect setting. Place the table under shade trees or an umbrella canopy. Pots of flowering plants make a perfect centerpiece. A brightly-colored tablecloth or festive placemats are a welcome addition to the table.

The Table Setting

Prepare salads in large pottery bowls. Serve with oversized spoons. Cook baked beans in a deep casserole dish or Dutch oven. Covered, the dish will stay warm for a long time. A deep pie dish holds the yummy desert and cools on a counter as the gang gathers outside.

Bourbon Minted Tea

Here is a refreshing twist on a traditional Southern favorite.

Juice of 4 lemons (about ½ cup)
1½ cups simple syrup
12 ounces bourbon
5 cups prepared iced tea
Fresh mint sprigs for garnish

1. Place lemon juice, simple syrup, bourbon, and iced tea into a large pitcher. Stir.
2. Pour into 8 large glasses that have been filled with ice.
3. Garnish with mint sprigs.

For the iced tea portion of this drink you can make your own or purchase your favorite already prepared iced tea drink. If your pitcher is not large enough to hold all of the ingredients—feel free to make the drink in 2 batches.

Butterflied Chicken on the Grill

This is a great outdoor dish. The chickens cook on the grill while your guests enjoy cocktails.

1 cup olive oil
Juice of 4 limes (about ½ cup)
8 medium cloves garlic, sliced (about 4 teaspoons)
1 cup fresh mint leaves
4 2½-pound chickens, butterflied
Salt and freshly ground pepper

1. Mix together the olive oil, lime juice, garlic and mint leaves in a shallow baking dish.
2. Place the chicken in the marinade turning to coat both sides. Marinate for at least 2 hours or overnight.
3. Remove the chicken from the marinade. Season with salt and pepper.
4. Place the chicken, skin side down on a grill over medium heat. Grill for 4 to 5 minutes to seal in the juices.
5. Turn the chicken over. Cook for 15 to 20 minutes or until the juices run clear when you pierce the chicken with a fork in the thigh area.
6. Let the chickens rest before carving into leg, thigh, and breast portions.

Servings: 8
Preparation Time: 10 minutes plus marinating and grilling

Butterfly the chickens by splitting the backbone with a sharp knife. Flatten the chicken pressing down firmly with your hands. (Watch out for sharp bones!) Marinate overnight with the breast side facing down in the pan. For an over-the-top presentation, you can place clean bricks on top of the chicken to weight it down while grilling. Make sure the bricks are as clean as possible. If this is hard to do—add a piece of aluminum foil between the chicken and the bricks!

SPICY BAKED BEAN CASSEROLE

Take those everyday beans over-the-top with the addition of some spicy ingredients and a cheesy topping.

1	**28-ounce can kidney beans, drained**
1	**16-ounce can pinto beans, drained**
1	**16-ounce can black beans, drained**
1	**small red onion, diced (about ½ cup)**
2	**medium jalapeño peppers, seeded and diced (about 4 tablespoons)**
2	**medium cloves garlic, minced (about 1 teaspoon)**
¼	**cup Worcestershire sauce**
⅓	**cup packed brown sugar**
¼	**cup yellow mustard**
¼	**cup ketchup**
1	**teaspoon to 1 tablespoon hot pepper sauce**
	Salt and freshly ground pepper
½	**pound bacon, diced**
30	**saltine crackers**
6	**ounces white Cheddar cheese, grated**

Preheat the oven to 350°.

1. Place the canned beans, onion, pepper, and garlic into a large baking dish or Dutch oven.
2. Add Worcestershire sauce, brown sugar, mustard and ketchup. Stir to combine.
3. Stir in as much hot pepper sauce as you like and season with salt and pepper.
4. Bake uncovered for 45 minutes.
5. Cook the bacon in a skillet over medium high heat. Drain on paper towels.
6. Place the saltine crackers into the bowl of a food processor. Pulse to form fine crumbs.
7. Remove the casserole from the oven. Stir.
8. Sprinkle the top with cooked bacon, cracker crumbs, and grated cheese.
9. Place the casserole back into the oven and bake uncovered for 10 to 15 minutes or until the topping browns and the casserole bubbles.

Servings: 8 to 12
Preparation Time: 30 minutes plus baking

This recipe serves a crowd. For smaller parties, prepare as directed but divide into 2 baking dishes. Freeze one until next week's party!

POTATO SALAD with SOUR CREAM and GARBANZO BEANS

Here is an interesting twist on run-of-the-mill potato salad. Letting the potatoes soak in the vinaigrette adds a concentration of flavor. The crisp veggies and firm beans add just the right amount of pizzazz.

3	pounds small creamer potatoes cut into ½–inch pieces
2	tablespoons red wine vinegar
1	medium clove garlic, minced (about ½ teaspoon)
½	teaspoon dry mustard
½	teaspoon chili powder
¼	cup olive oil
1	16-ounce can garbanzo beans, drained
1	bunch (6 to 8) green onions, chopped (about 1 cup)
2	medium celery ribs, thinly sliced (about 1 cup)
1	large red bell pepper, seeded and diced (about 1 cup)
1	large green bell pepper, seeded and diced (about 1 cup)

½	cup sour cream
2	tablespoons chopped fresh parsley leaves
	Salt and freshly ground pepper

1. Boil the potato pieces until tender, about 10 minutes.
2. In a small bowl whisk together the vinegar, garlic, mustard, and chili powder until combined.
3. Slowly whisk in the olive oil.
4. Drain the potatoes. Place in a large bowl.
5. Add the vinegar mixture to the potatoes and let sit for 10 minutes.
6. Add the beans, onions, celery, and peppers to the potatoes. Toss.
7. Stir in the sour cream and parsley.
8. Season with salt and pepper.
9. Chill for at least 30 minutes or overnight.

Servings: 8 to 10
Preparation Time: 30 minutes

Garbanzo beans are also known as chickpeas. They have a rich, nutty taste and are often used to add depth to salads. You will also find them in Mediterranean cooking, as they are the main ingredient in hummus.

CRISP COLESLAW with MUSTARD DRESSING

Every great Southern cook has her own version of this traditional dish—often served over pulled pork sandwiches and always seen on the barbeque buffet table. This rendition adds an ample amount of mustard to the mayonnaise-based sauce. Feel free to add as much or as little as you like to create your own tradition.

1	**small head green cabbage, shredded (about 4 cups)**
½	**small head red cabbage, shredded (about 2 cups)**
1	**medium white onion, shredded (about ⅔ cup)**
2	**large carrots, shredded (about 1 cup)**
2	**medium celery ribs, shredded (about 1 cup)**
	Stems of 1 medium bunch broccoli, shredded (about ½ cup)
½	**cup prepared yellow mustard**
½	**cup apple cider vinegar**
½	**cup sour cream**
¼	**cup ketchup**
¼	**cup mayonnaise**

2	**tablespoons granulated sugar**
2	**tablespoons snipped fresh garlic chives**
½	**teaspoon red pepper flakes**
	Salt

1. Toss the cabbage, onion, shredded carrots, celery, and broccoli stems into a large bowl.
2. Mix together the vinegar, sour cream, mustard, ketchup, mayonnaise, sugar, chives, and red pepper flakes in a small bowl until combined.
3. Pour the mustard mixture into the vegetables. Toss. Season with salt. Cover and refrigerate for at least 1 hour or overnight.

Servings: 8
Preparation Time: 30 minutes

Coleslaw is a salad made of shredded vegetables, most often cabbage, onion and sometimes peppers and carrots. Pre packaged shredded vegetables make this salad a no-brainer. Feel free to choose from the wide selection offered in the produce market. The dressing is easily spiced up or down with the addition of cayenne pepper, or upping the amount of sugar.

Deep Dish Apple Pie

The sweet pastry for this dish is easy to work with and makes baking pies an every week treasure.

3½	**cups all-purpose flour**
½	**cup granulated sugar**
¼	**teaspoon salt**
1	**cup (2 sticks) butter, chilled, cut into small pieces**
1	**large egg**
2	**to 4 teaspoons ice water**
1	**5-pound bag Granny Smith apples**
1	**tablespoon all-purpose flour**
⅓	**cup granulated sugar**
1	**teaspoon cinnamon**

Preheat the oven to 400°.

1. Place the flour, sugar, and salt in a food processor.
2. Add the butter and pulse until course crumbs form.
3. Separate the egg. Add the yolk to the flour mixture. Reserve the egg white.
4. Add the chilled water 1 tablespoon at a time through the feed tube until the dough begins to clump together.
5. Remove the dough and divide into halves. Form each half into a disk, wrap in plastic, and refrigerate.
6. Peel and thinly slice the apples.
7. Sprinkle the apple slices with 1 tablespoon flour, ⅓ cup sugar, and cinnamon. Toss.
8. Roll out one disk of pastry into a round about ⅛ inch thick. Place in a pie pan.
9. Mound the pastry with sliced apples.
10. Roll the second pastry disk into a round. Cover the apples, form a decorative crust, and slit the top crust so that the steam will escape.
11. Brush the top of the pie with the egg white mixed with 1 tablespoon water. Sprinkle with extra sugar. Bake for 50 to 60 minutes or until the crust is golden brown.

Serves 8
Preparation Time: 30 minutes plus baking

For a foolproof way to handle your favorite pastry crust, place two sheets of plastic on your work surface with the long edges overlapping slightly. Place the pastry disk in the middle of the overlapping edge. Cover the top of the pastry disk with two more sheets of plastic. Roll out the dough to desired thickness. To transfer the dough to a pie dish, fold it in half (with the plastic still in place. Transfer to the dish and remove one of the bottom sheets of plastic. Fold the dough into the dish. Now, fold the pastry in half again and remove the second bottom sheet. The bottom of the pastry will now be in the dish without plastic. Remove the top plastic sheets and gently push the dough in place. See how easy? And we didn't even need flour!

Bashes that Are Best with a Bunch

(BUFFET PARTIES FOR EIGHT OR MORE)

It's Tapas Time

Milk Shake and Cookie Bar

Game's On Party

Almost a Pig Roast

"I have been planning parties for almost ten years and have worked on large events for Fortune 500 companies including Disney and Coca Cola in Japan. The tip that I can offer to every host and hostess is that when planning a buffet menu, remember to make the food easy to eat. Try not to serve anything with a stick, bone, or shell that will need to be discarded after it has been eaten. Guests can find it difficult to manage a beverage and a canape while standing. When you add the element of something that needs to be discarded, people begin looking for creative places to discard things. If you do choose to serve slightly more complicated hors d'oeuvres, you might want to check your plants after the party!"

Darren Roberts
Owner of CarryOn Communications
Los Angeles, California
www.CarryOnpr.com

It's Tapas Time Party Plan

Party Motivation

It's your turn to host the annual company cocktail party and you feel like breaking with tradition. Just say "NO" to mini quiches and stuffed mushroom caps. Instead it's time to partee like a toreador.

Party Menu

Individual Tequila Martinis
Warm Olives with Fennel and Orange
Quick Crab and Goat Cheese Empanadas
A Trio of Tapenades
Tuna and Caper-Stuffed Hard Boiled Eggs with Almond Garnish
Roasted Peppers, Roasted Garlic and Grilled Endive with Blue Cheese
Sautéed Chicken Wings in Garlicky Broth
Garlic Shrimp with Lime **
Cinnamon Vanilla Flan with Toasted Coconut

** Over-the-Top Suggestion

Serve the garlicky shrimp from individual shells that have been warmed under a broiler for 2 minutes. Wow!

Party Strategy

Style this party in the tradition of the many Tapas Bars that dot the landscape of Spain. Inside, numerous earthenware crocks hold bite-size tastes of delicious treats, which are eaten between sips of dry sherry. We will diversify a bit to include Martinis as the cocktail of choice.

Two days before: Make sure that you have plenty of serving pieces and all of the ingredients that you will need.

One day before: Prepare flan and chill. Prepare empanadas through step 8 so that they are ready to bake. Make the tapenades, cover and chill. Prepare crostini for the tapenades and the roasted vegetable dish. Prepare the tuna-egg dish. Roast the peppers and garlic. Clean shrimp.

The morning of: Chop all remaining vegetables and herbs. Prepare and sauté chicken wings. Assemble ingredients for the accompanying broth.

Two hours before: Prepare olive dish and keep warm. Bake empanadas and keep warm. Display tapenades and bring to room temperature. Roast garlic and grill endive to assemble vegetable platter. Prepare the garlic broth for the wings. Complete dish and keep warm.

One hour before: Complete shrimp dish. Remove eggs and flan from the refrigerator.

Shortcuts

Purchase puff pastry dough or pie dough in place of making the dough for empanadas if wonton wrappers are not authentic enough for your taste. Choose only those tapas treats that you have time to make—it is not necessary to make them all. Increase the amount of the recipes that you do make to be sure you have plenty of food on hand. Purchase roasted peppers in a jar if you do not have time to roast and peel your own. Purchase peeled and deveined shrimp for a little bit more money—but a definite time saver.

Party Backdrop

For this cocktail party set a table in the center of the party space—your living room, great room or outdoor patio. Alternatively, cluster several tables in the center of the space. Dress the serving table(s) in brightly-colored fabric. Place cabaret tables and chairs around the perimeter of the area. Set the bar at the furthest space from the entrance to make sure that your guests circulate around the room. Music from a Spanish acoustical guitar is a perfect mood setter.

The Table Setting

Sticking to tradition, use as many earthenware casserole dishes as you can. Serve the garlicky chicken wings, lime shrimp and roasted pepper dish from casseroles. A small covered crock will hold the olives and keep them warm at the same time. The empanadas sit pretty in a straw basket, as do the hard-boiled eggs. Bring the dessert out at the end of the evening and serve with cups of dark, rich coffee.

INDIVIDUAL TEQUILA MARTINIS

Shaken—not stirred is the secret to this great martini!

2   ounces tequila
½   teaspoon Triple Sec
4   to 6 ice cubes
Twist of lime peel

1. Combine the tequila and Triple Sec in a cocktail shaker.
2. Add the ice cubes. Place the top onto the shaker and shake vigorously.
3. Rub the lime peel around a chilled martini glass.
4. Strain the liquid into the glass.
5. Garnish with a fresh twist of lime.

Servings: 1
Preparation Time: 5 minutes

The sophisticated martini imbiber knows the formula for the perfect martini—James Bond's famous splash of vodka, poured over two cubes of ice, then shaken (never stirred) with a twist of lemon. But if you and your pals are the kind of friends that long to wear loud floral shirts— untucked, this martini is the one for you!

WARM OLIVES with FENNEL and ORANGE

The selection of olives that you can use in this dish is endless. Feel free to experiment with Kalamata, Niçoise, and Spanish varieties.

2   cups assorted olives
2   tablespoons olive oil
1   tablespoon fresh cilantro leaves
1   medium clove garlic, minced (about ½ teaspoon)
1   fennel bulb, cut into ¼-inch thin strips (about 2 cups)
     Zest of ½ medium orange (about 1 tablespoon)
1   tablespoon white wine vinegar

1. Place the olives in a colander and rinse to remove excess salt.
2. Place the rinsed olives in a saucepan over medium heat.
3. Add olive oil, cilantro, garlic, sliced fennel, and orange zest.
4. Cook for 5 minutes or until the olives are warmed through.
5. Remove from heat and stir in the white wine vinegar.
6. Place the olives in a bowl. Spoon some of the cooking liquid over top and add a few of the fennel strips for garnish. Serve warm.

Serves 8
Preparation Time: 15 minutes

Fennel is a fun veggie to include in your recipes. Cut the bottom stem and top leaves from the bulb to expose the compacted white part. Break apart the layers and wash thoroughly. Slice the bulb into thin strips and proceed with the recipe.

QUICK CRAB and GOAT CHEESE EMPANADAS

Empanadas can be large pies designed to serve an entire family or petite, bite size pastries perfect for a tapas party. This recipe uses a quick substitution trick that yields light, crisp treats.

1   tablespoon olive oil
1   large yellow onion, diced (about 1 cup)
4   medium cloves garlic, minced (about 2 teaspoons)
½   medium jalapeño peppers, seeded and diced (about 1 tablespoons)
1   pound lump crabmeat
8   ounces goat cheese, room temperature
2   tablespoons chopped fresh thyme leaves
2   tablespoons chopped fresh cilantro leaves
    Salt and freshly ground pepper

36 won ton wrappers
1   tablespoon cornstarch mixed with 2 to 3 tablespoons cold water

Preheat the oven to 400°.
1. Heat the olive oil in a skillet over medium high heat.
2. Cook the onion, garlic, and jalapeño pepper until soft, about 5 minutes. Remove from the heat and cool to room temperature.

3. In a mixing bowl combine the crabmeat, goat cheese, and herbs.
4. Stir in the onion mixture.
5. Place 1 tablespoon crab mixture into the center of 1 wonton wrapper.
6. Brush the edges of the wrapper with the cornstarch mixture.
7. Bring 1 corner of the wrapper to the opposite side to form a triangle. Seal the edges by pressing down with the tines of a fork.
8. Place the empanada on a wire rack. Repeat with the remaining wrappers and crab mixture.
9. Lightly brush a baking sheet with olive oil. Place the empanadas on the sheet. Brush the tops of the empanadas with olive oil. Bake for 5 to 8 minutes. Turn each empanada over and cook for 3 minutes more or until they are golden brown.

Yield: 18 empanadas
Preparation Time: 45 minutes

Traditional empanadas include various fillings like beef, pork and potato, but are most often made from pastry dough. Wonton wrappers are a fun, less work intensive choice. Make sure that you keep the wonton wrappers covered with a damp towel to keep them from drying out.

If you prefer the more traditional approach, prepare the dough by combining 2 cups all-purpose flour, 1 teaspoon salt, ½ cup butter (cut into small pieces)and 2 to 4 tablespoons cold water. Place the flour, salt and butter in the bowl of a food processor. Pulse to form medium size crumbs. Add just enough cold water to form the dough. Form into a disk, wrap with plastic wrap and chill for 30 minutes. Roll out the dough to ¼-inch thickness. Cut 3-inch circles from the dough. Place the filling in the center of the circle and continue with the recipe.

These empanadas need to be baked at 325° for about 10 to 15 minutes.

A Trio of Tapenades

Choose one or all of these tangy tapenades to perk up your Tapas buffet table.

WHITE BEAN TAPENADE
1   16-ounce can white beans, drained
¼   cup chopped fresh parsley
½   medium celery ribs, finely diced (about 2 tablespoons)
½   medium carrots, finely diced (about 2 tablespoons)
1   teaspoon Dijon mustard
1   tablespoon olive oil
    Salt and freshly ground pepper

TUNA AND ROSEMARY TAPENADE
1   6-ounce can solid white tuna
12 green olives (about ½ cup)
2   tablespoons chopped fresh rosemary
    Juice of 1 lemon (about 2 tablespoons)
2   tablespoons olive oil

OLIVE AND ANCHOVY TAPENADE
1   16-ounce jar Kalamata olives, pitted and drained
2   medium cloves garlic
4   to 5 anchovy fillets
1½ tablespoon capers
2   tablespoons chopped fresh thyme leaves
    Juice of 1 lemon (about 2 tablespoons)
½   cup olive oil

WHITE BEAN TAPENADE
1. Mash all but 2 tablespoons of white beans and place into a bowl.
2. Place the parsley, celery, and carrots in the bowl of a food processor. Pulse to finely chop. Add this mixture to the mashed beans.
3. Sir in the mustard, 2 tablespoons of unmashed beans, and olive oil. Season with salt and pepper.

TUNA AND ROSEMARY TAPENADE
4. Drain the tuna.
5. Place the green olives, rosemary, and lemon juice in the bowl of a food processor. Pulse to combine.
6. Add the tuna and pulse just to combine. Add just enough olive oil to produce a silky sheen.
7. Season with pepper.

OLIVE AND ANCHOVY TAPENADE
8. Place the olives, garlic, anchovies, capers, thyme leaves, and lemon juice in the bowl of a food processor. Pulse to combine.
9. With the blade running, pour the olive oil through the feed tube until smooth and creamy. Season with pepper.

Yield: 1 to 2 cups
Preparation Time: 10 minutes each

The perfect accompaniment to the spunky flavors of tapenade is crostini, thin slices of bread baked until just golden. Slice 1 loaf of French bread into ¼-inch rounds. Brush one side of the bread slices with olive oil that has been infused with ½ teaspoon garlic powder. Bake for 10 to 15 minutes at 350°.

TUNA and CAPER-STUFFED HARD BOILED EGGS with ALMOND GARNISH

This is a great up-scaling of traditional deviled eggs. Feel free to substitute with other ingredients like anchovies and olives to create a unique appetizer.

8   large eggs, hard boiled and peeled
1   6-ounce can solid white tuna packed in water, drained
1   tablespoon capers
2   tablespoons mayonnaise
Salt and freshly ground pepper

2   tablespoons sliced almonds, toasted
1   tablespoon chopped fresh parsley leaves

1. Cut the eggs in half. Remove the yolks and place them into a bowl.

2. Add the drained tuna, capers and mayonnaise to the bowl. Mash well to combine.
3. Season with salt and pepper.
4. Fill each egg half with the tuna mixture.
5. Toast the almonds in a toaster oven at 350°. until just beginning to brown. Cool.
6. Place the almonds and the parsley in the bowl of a (mini) food processor. Pulse to chop well.
7. Sprinkle the almond mixture over the eggs.

Yield: 16 eggs
Preparation Time: 20 minutes

To boil eggs that peel easily, purchase the freshest egg you can find.
Place the eggs in a pan and cover with water. Cover and place the pan over medium high heat.
Bring to a boil and cook for 10 minutes. Remove the pan from the heat.
Drain and immediately immerse the eggs into ice water.

ROASTED PEPPERS, ROASTED GARLIC, and GRILLED ENDIVE with BLUE CHEESE

Simple vegetables take the spotlight when they are perfectly prepared and beautifully presented.

2	**large red bell peppers**
2	**large yellow peppers**
4	**heads garlic**
2	**tablespoons olive oil**
1	**teaspoon dried oregano leaves**
	Salt and freshly ground pepper
4	**heads endive**
2	**tablespoons olive oil**
4	**ounces blue cheese, crumbled**

ROAST PEPPERS

Preheat the oven to broil

1. Place the peppers on a broiler pan at the top of the oven.
2. Turn the peppers until all of the skin is blackened.
3. Place the peppers in a brown bag and steam for 20 minutes.
4. Remove the black skin and seeds from the peppers and cut into strips.

ROASTED GARLIC

Preheat the oven to 350°.

5. Slice the tops from the heads of garlic and place on a sheet of aluminum foil. Drizzle with olive oil, sprinkle with dried oregano, and season with salt and pepper.
6. Wrap the ends of the foil around the garlic and bake for 30 to 40 minutes at 350°. The garlic cloves will turn golden and begin to pop from the bulb.

GRILLED ENDIVE

7. Cut each endive into quarters. Drizzle generously with olive oil and season with salt and pepper.
8. Place into a hot grill pan over medium high heat and cook, turning once until brown on the edges and soft about 6 to 8 minutes.
9. Place the peppers, whole heads of roasted garlic and grilled endive on a platter.
10. Sprinkle with crumbled blue cheese, drizzle with additional olive oil, and sprinkle with freshly grated pepper.

Servings: 8
Preparation Time: 30 minutes

Feel free to alter this simple starter with your favorite fresh veggies. Roast eggplant and tomatoes or grill artichokes and zucchini!

Sautéed Chicken Wings in Garlicky Broth

Serve these wings from a bowl so that they are swimming in the fragrant sauce. Serve slices of crusty bread as "dip buddies."

1	to 2 pounds chicken wings, cut into 2 pieces, tips discarded (24 pieces)
½	cup all-purpose flour
1	tablespoon paprika
1	teaspoon cumin
	Salt and freshly ground pepper
¼	to ½ cup olive oil
2	leeks, white part only, sliced into thin rings
8	to 10 cloves garlic, thinly sliced
	Juice of 2 lemons (about ¼ cup)
⅓	cup dry sherry
2	tablespoons chopped fresh oregano leaves
2	cups chicken broth
1	bay leaf
¼	teaspoon crushed saffron threads
¼	teaspoon dried red pepper flakes

1. Rinse and thoroughly dry wings.
2. Combine flour, paprika, cumin, salt and pepper in a zip lock bag. Place the wings, 6 at a time, into the bag and shake to coat.
3. Heat ¼ cup olive oil in a skillet over medium high heat. Cook the wings in batches, turning once, until golden and crisp, about 4 minutes per side. Remove the wings to a platter. Continue until all of the wings are cooked. You may need to add additional oil to the pan.
4. Add the leeks to the pan and cook until just beginning to brown, about 5 minutes.
5. Add the garlic to the pan. Cook for 2 minutes.
6. Add the lemon juice and sherry to the pan. Cook until reduced, about 3 to 5 minutes.
7. Add the chicken broth to the pan.
8. Add the bay leaf, saffron, and red pepper flakes to the sauce. Season with salt and pepper.
9. Add the chicken pieces back to the pan. Cover and reduce the heat. Simmer for 15 minutes. Discard the bay leaf.

Yield: 24 wing pieces
Preparation Time: 30 minutes

Prepare the wings by slicing them into 3 pieces, cut at the joint. Discard the tip. Rinse well and make sure the chicken is very dry before sautéing. Remember not to overcrowd the pan to maintain the temperature of the oil thus insuring a crisp result.

GARLIC SHRIMP with LIME

A take-off on the butter rich recipe for Shrimp Scampi, this dish is sure to please shrimp lovers.

2 **tablespoons olive oil**
   Juice of 2 fresh limes (about ¼ cup)
2 **tablespoons Worcestershire sauce**
4 **medium cloves garlic, minced (about 2 teaspoons)**
2 **teaspoons granulated sugar**
   Zest of 1 medium lime (about 2 teaspoons)
¼ **teaspoon cayenne pepper**
1½ **pounds large uncooked shrimp, peeled and deveined (about 24)**
2 **tablespoons chopped fresh mint leaves**
   Salt and freshly ground pepper

1. Heat the olive oil in a skillet over medium high heat.
2. Add the lime juice, Worcestershire sauce, garlic, sugar, lime zest, and cayenne pepper.
3. Add the shrimp and cook until they turn pink and opaque, about 4 to 5 minutes.
4. Stir in the mint leaves and season with salt and freshly ground pepper.

Serves 4
Preparation Time: 15 minutes

To shell a shrimp begin by gently pulling off the legs on the underside of the curve near the top of the shrimp. Pull the shell towards the tail. You may either remove the tail or let it stay on the shrimp. I prefer "tails-on" for this dish. Devein the shrimp by using a very sharp knife to cut an incision on the center of the top side of the shrimp. Gently lift up the black vein and pull it out using your finger tips.

Cinnamon Vanilla Flan with Toasted Coconut

Make this dessert the day before and unmold onto an earthenware platter for an utterly Spanish experience.

2 cups granulated sugar
¼ cup water

3 cups milk
1 cinnamon stick
⅓ cup granulated sugar
4 large eggs
2 large egg yolks
2 teaspoons vanilla extract

1 cup sweetened, shredded coconut, lightly toasted

Preheat the oven to 350°.

1. Place the sugar and water in a saucepan over medium high heat. Swirl the pot as the sugar begins to melt to prevent burning. Remove the pot from the heat when the sugar has turned caramel colored.
2. Pour the caramel into bottom of a shallow oval baking dish.
3. Place the milk, cinnamon stick, and ⅓ cup sugar in a saucepan over medium high heat. Bring to a boil, stirring constantly. Remove from the heat.

4. Whisk the eggs and egg yolks in a large bowl. Stir in the vanilla.
5. Slowly pour the warm milk mixture into the eggs, whisking constantly.
6. Strain the custard through a colander into the baking dish.
7. Wrap the dish in aluminum foil (to prevent water from getting into the custard). Place it into a roasting pan that is larger than the baking dish. Pour warm water halfway up the top of the baking dish.
8. Bake for 40 to 50 minutes or until the center is just set. Remove the baking dish from the water bath. Remove the foil.
9. Cover with plastic wrap and chill overnight.
10. Toast coconut on a baking sheet at 350° for several minutes until the flakes just begin to brown.
11. Unmold the flan by placing the baking dish into very hot water. Place a platter on top of the dish. Turn the dish with the platter over and let the caramel dribble down the sides of the custard. Drizzle with toasted coconut.

Servings: 8
Preparation Time: 30 minutes plus baking and refrigeration

Caramelizing sugar develops a more complex and appetizing flavor, which is a natural accompaniment to rich custard. Officially sugar is caramelized when it reaches a temperature between 320 and 350° on a candy thermometer. Use this check if you are concerned about burning!

Milkshake and Cookie Bar Party Plan

Party Motivation

A blast from the past concept—milk and cookies before bedtime—is just the right reason to throw a midnight dessert buffet party. Good friends gathering after a performance at the local theatre, a gallery opening, an evening ball game or a long week at work fill tummies with sweet plums. Offer bedtime story conversation and "tuck-in" hugs as the party dwindles down.

Party Menu

Thick and Creamy Milkshakes
Lemony Squares
Chocolate Toffee Bars
Our Favorite Peanut Butter Squares
Chocolate Chip Oatmeal Bars with Plum Filling
Chocolate Lovers Turtle Brownies

** Over-the-Top Suggestion

Add an ice cream sundae bar by placing scoops of flavored ice cream into a large bowl. Keep cold in the freezer until ready to serve. Surround the bowl with all the ice cream toppings that you can think of like marshmallows, coconut, chocolate shavings, M&Ms, chopped toffee, caramel sauce, strawberry sauce, warm chocolate sauce and anything else that you can imagine.

Party Strategy

Everything is done in advance for this party and can sit on the table until you come home from the early portion of the evening.

One to 2 days before: Make the cookie bars, cover and store.

The afternoon before: Cut the bars into squares and place on platters. Cover with plastic wrap.

Shortcuts

Make 1 batch of bars a day and freeze. This way you can start days—if not weeks in advance of your party.

Party Backdrop

Pull the chairs away from the dining room table. Overlap colorful placemats in the center. Place platters, baskets, and bowls full of bars onto the placemats. Stack small dessert or appetizer dishes all around. Serve milkshakes from a blender in the kitchen—and keep them coming.

The Table Setting

Vary the height of the platters to create interest on the table. Serve lemony bars on a pedestal cake plate, chocolate toffee bars on a platter tipped on one end by resting on a small bowl. Place peanut butter squares in a basket on top of an inverted basket. Decorate the platters by laying a layer of chocolate bits on the bottom of a shallow pasta bowl and nesting chocolate chip oatmeal bars on top of the bits. Likewise, a layer of coconut flakes serves as an excellent "nest" for chocolate lovers turtle brownies. The idea is to serve bit-size bars in interesting presentations using food as both a decoration and a garnish.

THICK and CREAMY MILKSHAKES

This is a really basic recipe for rich, thick, moustache-leaving milk shakes. Create your own favorites by adding your favorite flavorings and best quality ice creams.

1   quart best quality vanilla ice cream
1   teaspoon vanilla extract
1   cup milk
1   cup half and half

1. Place all of the ingredients in a blender and pulse to combine.

2. Serve with whipped cream, chopped nuts and top with a cherry.

Servings: 4
Preparation Time: 10 minutes

Try these variations on this basic theme:

1. Substitute with chocolate ice cream and ¼ cup chocolate syrup.

2. Add ¼ cup brewed coffee and substitute half of the vanilla ice cream with chocolate for a mocha flavor.

3. Substitute with strawberry ice cream and add ½ cup sliced strawberries.

4. Substitute half of the ice cream with praline-flavored ice cream and add 2 tablespoons of maple syrup.

LEMONY SQUARES

This delicate bar can hold it's own on a dessert buffet table. The contrast between sweet and tart is so refreshing!

2 **cups all-purpose flour**
½ **cup confectioners' sugar**
¾ **cup butter (1½ sticks), chilled, cut into pieces**

6 **large eggs**
2 **cups granulated sugar**
1 **teaspoon baking powder**
   Zest of 2 medium lemons (about 2 table-spoons)
   Juice of 4 lemons (about ¾ cups)

Preheat the oven to 325°.
1. Place the flour, confectioners' sugar, and butter in the bowl of a food processor.
2. Pulse until the mixture resembles course crumbs.
3. Press the crumb mixture into the bottom of an 11 x 9 x 2-inch baking pan.
4. Bake for 20 minutes or until the crust begins to turn golden brown on the edges.
5. Whisk the eggs and the sugar together in a bowl until fluffy.
6. Whisk in the baking powder, lemon zest, and juice.
7. Pour the filling over the crust.
8. Bake for 30 to 40 minutes or until the center is just set.
9. Cool the bars, dust with additional confectioners' sugar and cut into 1½-inch squares.

Yield: 24 bars
Preparation Time: 30 minutes plus baking

This traditional bar can be personalized with your favorite flavorings. For lime or orange bars substitute with either lime or orange juice or zest.

CHOCOLATE TOFFEE BARS

These buttery bars are sure to be a crowd pleaser.

2 cups packed brown sugar
1 cup butter (2 sticks), room temperature
1 cup margarine (2 sticks), room temperature
2 large egg yolks
2 teaspoons vanilla extract
4 cups all-purpose flour
½ teaspoon salt

12 ounces milk chocolate
½ cup chopped pecans
½ cup chopped walnuts

Preheat the oven to 350°.

1. Use an electric mixer to beat together the brown sugar, butter, and margarine until fluffy.
2. Mix in the egg yolks and vanilla extract.
3. Combine the flour and salt. Stir in the flour in 3 additions.
4. Spread the dough into a 11 x 9 x 2-inch baking dish that has been sprayed with vegetable oil spray.
5. Bake for 25 to 30 minutes or until golden brown.
6. Melt the chocolate in a double boiler over simmering water.
7. Spread the warm chocolate over the toffee base.
8. Sprinkle with chopped nuts. Allow the mixture to cool. Cut into 2-inch squares.

Yield: 12 bars
Preparation Time: 20 minutes plus baking

A large pan will yield a thinner bar and as you might expect, a smaller, square pan will yield a thick cookie bar. The choice is yours. Alter the cookie time in connection with the size of your pan.

OUR FAVORITE PEANUT BUTTER SQUARES

Here is a very easy recipe that is guaranteed to please young and old alike—one that you can whip up in minutes for the answer to the drop-in guest question.

½   **cup creamy peanut butter**
½   **cup margarine (1 stick)**
1½ **cups granulated sugar**
2   **large eggs**
1½ **teaspoon baking powder**
½   **teaspoon salt**
1   **teaspoon vanilla extract**
1   **cup all-purpose flour**

Preheat the oven to 350°.

1. Melt the peanut butter and margarine in a saucepan over medium high heat until smooth and shiny.

2. Remove the saucepan from the heat.
3. Stir in the sugar, eggs, baking powder, salt, vanilla, and flour.
4. Pour this mixture into an 11 x 9 x 2-inch pan than has been sprayed with vegetable oil spray and dusted with flour.
5. Bake for 25 to 30 minutes or until the top begins to turn golden brown.
6. Cool and cut into 1½-inch squares.

Yield: 24 bars
Preparation Time: 15 minutes plus baking

Top these bars with a layer of melted chocolate and you have a double whammy of a treat.

Chocolate Chip Oatmeal Bars with Plum Filling

The variations on this simple recipe are endless—which is why these bars cookies are so really, really good!

2   cups all purpose flour
2   cups old-fashioned rolled oats
1   teaspoon baking soda
½   teaspoon salt
1   cup brown sugar
1   cup butter (2 sticks), room temperature
12   ounces semi-sweet chocolate chips
1   cup red plum jam

Preheat the oven to 375°.

1. Place the flour, oats, baking soda, and salt in a bowl and set aside.
2. Use an electric mixer to combine the brown sugar and butter until fluffy.
3. Add the flour/oat mixture and stir. The dough will be very crumbly.

4. Place 2 cups of the dough mixture into a bowl.
5. Add the chocolate chips to the bowl and stir.
6. Press the remaining dough into the bottom of an 11 x 9 x 2-inch baking dish.
7. Spread the dough with the jam.
8. Sprinkle the flour/chocolate chip mixture over the top.
9. Bake for 30 minutes or until the top begins to look golden brown.
10. Cool completely on a wire rack. Cut into 1 ½-inch squares.

Yield: 2 dozen bars
Preparation Time: 20 minutes plus baking

Jam is different from jelly in that jelly is made from fruit juice and strained to remove all other pieces of fruit. Jam is prepared by cooking whole fruit or fruit pieces in sugar and water until the mixture sets. While red plum jam provides the perfect flavoring for this terrific dessert, feel free to substitute with strawberry, raspberry or even blueberry jams.

Chocolate Lovers Turtle Brownies

A rich, fudgy caramely bar, this recipe is perfect for the final period of the game. Everyone wins with this great dessert.

1	**14-ounce bag caramels**
⅓	**cup evaporated milk**
2	**sticks unsalted butter**
16	**ounces semisweet chocolate**
6	**ounces unsweetened chocolate**
6	**eggs**
2	**tablespoons vanilla extract**
1	**cup packed dark brown sugar**
⅔	**cup granulated sugar**
1	**cup all-purpose flour**
1	**tablespoon baking powder**
1	**teaspoon salt**
4	**ounces pecan halves (1 cup), chopped**
1	**6-ounce package semi-sweet chocolate chips**

Preheat the oven to 350°.

1. In a double boiler over medium heat stir together the caramels and evaporated milk until smooth, about 20 minutes. Remove from heat. Set aside.

2. In a double boiler over simmering water melt the butter, semisweet chocolate, and unsweetened chocolate. Stir until smooth and shiny. Cool to room temperature.
3. Whisk together the eggs, vanilla, brownsugar, and granulated sugar in a large bowl.
4. Add the chocolate mixture and stir well.
5. Stir in the flour, baking powder, and salt.
6. Stir in the chopped pecans until just mixed.
7. Spray a 13 x 9 x 2-inch baking dish with vegetable oil spray. Press half of the batter mixture into the bottom of the baking dish.
8. Sprinkle the chocolate chips over the batter.
9. Spread the melted caramel mixture on top of the chips.
10. Sprinkle the remaining batter on top of the caramel.
11. Bake for 25 to 30 minutes or until the center is set. Cool and cut into 2-inch squares.

Yield: approximately 18 bars
Preparation Time: 30 minutes plus baking.

A double boiler is used when melting chocolate, and in this case, caramels, to prevent burning. Place an inch or more of water into the bottom of the pan. Place a bowl or smaller pan over the water. You do not want the water to be in contact with the pan holding the caramels. Bring the water to a simmer—not a rapid boil. Stir constantly to guarantee the result.

Game's On Party Plan

Party Motivation

Are you ready for some FOOTBALL? Or maybe it's "Take me out to the ball game" season. Whatever the sport—what ever the time of year, sports watching means feeding the watchers. That means brining pals together and serving plenty of great food, while not missing one single play.

Party Menu

"The Wannstedt Crush"
Game Day Crab Dip
Warm Sausage Dip Served in a Bread Bowl
Soft Shell Crab Po Boys with Roasted Red Pepper Aioli **
Fiery Beef and Black Bean Chili
Grilled Harvest Best Veggies
Grandma's Blackberry Cake with Caramel Frosting

** Over-the-Top Suggestion

There is plenty of great food to choose from in this menu, but if you love soft shell crabs, score this dish to put your party way, way over the top.

Party Strategy

Make as much of the menu as you can in advance so that you can enjoy the game and cheer on your team. Allow for arranging and warming during commercial interruptions.

Two days before: Make the chili. Seal tightly and refrigerate.

One day before: Bake the cake and frost. Prepare aioli, crab dip and sausage dip. Assemble or slice dippers.

The morning before: Arrange buffet tables and tableware.

Two hours before: Grill veggies and keep warm.

One hour before: Fry soft shell crabs and keep warm. Warm dips.

Shortcuts

Use caramel frosting and fresh fruit over prepared pound cake if you don't have time to bake.

Party Backdrop

If you want to feed your game-watching crowd, there is no better way than to offer the meal buffet-style. A buffet table permits the guests to serve themselves from lots of platters of easy-to-eat, deliciously-prepared food. Don't feel that you are limited to using your dining room table for your buffet. You can create an interesting presentation for your sports party anywhere that you please. How about using the island in your kitchen or the counter top next to the stove? A dining room sideboard or a family room bar makes an excellent buffet area. In warm weather an outside barbecue grill area and teacart provides just enough space. If the weather is inclement, set low tables in front of your big screen T.V. All of these ideas work equally well when you envision your buffet. There are two tips that make any section of your home a great place to set a buffet. First, make the buffet accessible so that your guests aren't stumbling over each other. Secondly, begin at the beginning. Build the meal with each dish and be mindful of time outs and penalties when planning to serve. You certainly don't want to be forced into an overtime situation when you are in the lead.

The Table Setting

Pre-game offers refreshing beverages. Serve warm crab dip in an oven proof crock. Place the crock on a tray. Fill pilsner glasses with all of the dippers and set those around the crock. First period ends and out comes a new tray hosting the bread bowl filled with warm sausage dip and all the trimmings. Half time invites guests to serve themselves from a tureen filled with fiery chili. Accompanying bowls of condiments are set nearby. Buffet plates hold both the bowl of chili and the grilled veggies.

Spectacular soft shell po boys are assembled—complete with aioli—and heaped into a large basket. Dessert outshines the final score of the game as Grandmas' cake tops a beautiful pedestal plate. Regardless of the game score—we get "W" in the party column. Everybody's a winner.

"THE WANNSTEDT CRUSH"

What's more perfect than a fun cocktail supplied by a winning coach? Well, perhaps a victory for the home team!

8 **ounces spiced rum**
8 **ounces lite rum**
4 **ounces coconut milk**
4 **ounces orange juice**
4 **ounces pineapple juice**
1 **teaspoon grenadine**
Orange pinwheels

1. Pour all of the ingredients into a large pitcher and stir to combine.
2. Pour into 8 tall glasses filled with ice cubes.
3. Garnish the glasses with orange pinwheels

Servings: 8
Preparation Time: 10 minutes

Coach Dave Wannstedt and wife Jan generously published their favorite cocktail at a
fund raiser for the Museum of Discovery and Science in Fort Lauderdale.
Suffice it to say—the fans went wild!

GAME DAY CRAB DIP

An easy-to-make dip, this one can be assembled ahead and served warm as the referee tosses the coin.

2	**tablespoons olive oil**
1	**medium white onion, finely diced (about ⅔ cup)**
1	**medium jalapeño peppers, seeded and finely diced (about 2 tablespoons)**
4	**medium cloves garlic, minced (about 2 teaspoons)**
1	**pound lump crabmeat**
1	**6-ounce jar roasted yellow peppers, drained and diced**
1	**bunch (6 to 8) green onions, chopped (about 1 cup)**
8	**ounces white Cheddar cheese, grated**
1	**cup sour cream**
1	**cup mayonnaise**
1	**tablespoon tomato paste**
¼	**teaspoon dry mustard**
2	**to 4 drops hot sauce**
	Salt and freshly ground pepper

Preheat the oven to 350°.

1. Heat the olive oil in a skillet over medium high heat.
2. Cook the white onion, jalapeño pepper, and garlic until soft about 5 minutes.
3. Place the onion mixture into a deep baking dish.
4. Add the crabmeat, yellow pepper, green onion, cheese, sour cream, and mayonnaise to the dish. Stir to combine.
5. Add the tomato paste and dry mustard. Stir. Season with hot sauce, salt and pepper.
6. Bake for 20 minutes or until the mixture is bubbling and beginning to brown on the top.
7. Serve with your favorite dippers like chips, bread sticks, celery, carrot sticks, and endive leaves.

Yield: 3 cups
Preparation Time: 15 minutes plus baking

When purchasing fresh cooked crabmeat from the market, the most desirable is "lump" crabmeat that can also be known as jumbo. These are the best pieces of the crab taken from the center part of the body. The result are large, white pieces of tender crab.

You can purchase less expensive flaked crabmeat, which is darker, smaller, and taken from the center and legs of the crab. Drain the crabmeat of excess moisture before you incorporate it into the dish. Imitation crabmeat is a product made from fish pieces other than crab and is a good substitute for guests with shellfish allergies.

WARM SAUSAGE DIP SERVED in a BREAD BOWL

This is a super dish because you can make it in advance and serve it as the game begins.

16 ounces mild Italian sausage
16 ounces hot sausage
2   cups sour cream
1   cup mayonnaise
½   cup Parmesan cheese
1   6-ounce jar chopped pimento, drained
1   bunch (6 to 8) green onions, chopped
    (about 1 cup)

1   large round bread loaf
    Crackers
    Bread sticks
    Carrot slices

Preheat the oven to 350°.
1. Crumble the sausage. Cook over medium high heat until browned. Drain and set aside.

2. In a bowl mix together the sour cream, mayonnaise, and Parmesan cheese.
3. Stir in the pimento and sliced green onion.
4. Add the sausage and stir to combine.
5. Pour the mixture into a baking dish.
6. Cook for 20 to 25 minutes until it is warmed through.
7. Slice the top from the bread loaf. Use your hands to remove the inside of the loaf tearing the bread into bite size pieces.
8. Pour the warm mixture into the bread bowl. Serve with bread pieces, extra bread sticks, crackers and carrot slices.

Yield: approximately 6 cups
Preparation Time: 15 minutes plus baking

This recipe makes plenty of warm dip for a crowd. Pour in enough to fill the bread bowl and keep the remaining mixture warm. Refill the "bowl" as needed. You may want to buy an additional loaf to make extra bread pieces for dipping.

SOFT SHELL CRAB PO BOYS
with ROASTED RED PEPPER AIOLI

Here is a takeoff on the tradition foot-long hoagie that one might consider to be the usual sports buffet mainstay. This sub is sure to attract fans!

1 **cup all-purpose flour**
1 **teaspoon seafood seasoning such as Old Bay**
   Salt and freshly ground pepper
   Canola oil for frying
8 **soft-shell crabs, cleaned**

8 **hoagie rolls or split-top rolls**
4 **tablespoons butter, melted**
½ **teaspoon garlic powder**

2 **large red bell peppers, charred, steamed, seeded, and peeled**
2 **cups mayonnaise**
3 **tablespoons capers, drained**
3 **tablespoons chopped fresh cilantro leaves**
   Juice of ½ lemon (about 1 tablespoon)

   Shredded iceberg lettuce
   Beefsteak tomato slices

1. Place the flour, seafood seasoning, salt, and pepper into a plastic bag.
2. Pour canola oil ⅓ to ½ way up the sides of a deep pot. Heat over medium high heat until just beginning to smoke (about 350°).

3. Place 1 crab into the plastic bag, seal and shake to coat. Dust off excess flour and slowly place into the hot oil. Fry until golden, 2 to 4 minutes. Remove from the oil and drain on paper towels. Repeat with the remaining crabs.
4. Slice the hoagie rolls halfway through. Mix together the melted butter and garlic powder. Brush the insides of the roll with melted butter mixture and lay onto a hot grill pan. Grill for 2 minutes.
5. Place the roasted peppers, mayonnaise, capers, cilantro, and lemon juice in the bowl of a food processor. Pulse to combine. Season with salt and pepper.
6. Assemble the sandwiches by spreading a generous amount of aioli on both sides of the grilled hoagie bun. Layer with lettuce and tomato slices. Place a fried soft shell crab on top.

Servings: 8
Preparation Time: 30 minutes

Soft shell crabs are available frozen from a reputable fish monger all year long.
Fresh crabs are found in the waters near Baltimore from late spring to early fall.
Soft shell crabs are blue crabs that shed their hard shells and then grow new ones.
They are meant to be eaten soft shell and all and are worth the time it may take you to find
them. If soft shells are impossible to find, substitute fried shrimp or oysters for this recipe!

FIERY BEEF and BLACK BEAN CHILI

What's more perfect than a big bowl of spicy chili while watching your favorite game? Only a victory at the end! Calm down the heat by serving the chili around a mound of brown rice.

2	to 4 tablespoon olive oil
3	pounds boneless beef chuck roast, cut into ½-inch cubes
	Salt and freshly ground pepper
1	medium red onion, chopped into ¼-inch pieces (about 1 cup)
1	red bell pepper, chopped into ½-inch pieces (about 1 cup)
2	garlic cloves, minced (about 1 tablespoon)
1	to 2 chipotle peppers in adobo sauce, minced
1	16-ounce can sweet corn, drained
2	28 ounce cans chopped tomatoes
2	tablespoons tomato paste
1	16-ounce can black beans
2	tablespoons chili powder, more or less
½	teaspoon cumin
1	cup sour cream
1	tablespoon chopped fresh cilantro
	Salt and freshly ground pepper
4	cups cooked brown rice
	Sliced green onions
	Grated Monterey Jack cheese

1. Heat 1 tablespoon olive oil in a large pot over medium high heat.
2. Season the beef cubes with salt and pepper. Brown the beef in batches. Remove to a platter. Use additional oil if needed.
3. Add the red onion, red pepper, and garlic to the pot. Cook until soft, about 5 minutes.
4. Add the chipotle peppers, corn, canned tomatoes, and tomato paste. Simmer for 5 minutes.
5. Add the black beans and the beef cubes to the sauce.
6. Stir in chili powder and cumin.
7. Cover and simmer over medium heat for 20 to 30 minutes.
8. Place the sour cream into a small bowl. Spoon a ladle full of hot sauce from the pot into the sour cream. Stir this mixture back into the chili.
9. Stir in the cilantro and adjust seasonings.
10. Place a mound of rice in the center of a shallow bowl. Ladle the chili around the rice. Top with sliced green onions and shredded cheese.

Servings: 8
Preparation Time: 60 minutes

The spice in this dish comes from chipotle pepper, which is a dried and smoked jalapeño pepper that is very, very hot. They can be purchased dry or in a jar or can packed in a tomato mixture called adobo sauce. You can add or detract from the heat of this dish by adjusting how many peppers you add to the sauce.

GRILLED HARVEST BEST VEGGIES

Feel free to use the freshest, best looking vegetables in the market for this impressive dish. You will be surprised how the grilling sweetens the veggies and bolsters their natural flavor.

2	**small eggplants, cut in half from stem to bottom**
2	**large red onions, cut in half from stem to bottom**
2	**large red bell peppers, cut in half from stem to bottom**
2	**large yellow bell peppers, cut in half from stem to bottom**
2	**large beefsteak tomatoes, cut in half from stem to bottom**
8	**large asparagus spears**
	Olive oil
	Salt and freshly ground pepper

1. Brush both sides of the vegetables with olive oil.
2. Season with salt and freshly ground pepper.
3. Grill over hot coals (or in a grill pan over medium high heat) until the vegetables are soft and begin to char about 15 to 20 minutes.
4. Arrange the veggies on a large platter and drizzle with additional olive oil.

Servings: 8
Preparation Time: 30 minutes

Arrange the vegetables onto a simple platter for the perfect presentation of this easy-to-make side dish.

GRANDMA'S BLACKBERRY CAKE with CARAMEL FROSTING

This cake is reminiscent of one that has roots in the foothills of West Virginia. It's everything you could want for a celebration dessert.

2 cups granulated sugar
1 cup butter (2 sticks), room temperature
1 cup buttermilk
3 large eggs
3¼ cups all-purpose flour
2 teaspoons baking powder
1 teaspoon baking soda
2 teaspoons ground cinnamon
1 teaspoon ground allspice
1 teaspoon grated nutmeg
1 cup fresh blackberries tossed with 1 tablespoon all-purpose flour

¼ cup butter (½ stick)
½ cup packed brown sugar
¼ teaspoon salt
1 teaspoon vanilla extract
¼ cup milk
2 cups confectioners' sugar
1 cup fresh blackberries

Preheat the oven to 350°.
1. Use an electric mixer to combine the sugar and butter until fluffy.
2. Add the eggs, one at a time. Mix until smooth.
3. Combine the flour, baking powder, baking soda, cinnamon, allspice, and nutmeg.
4. Stir in the flour mixture and buttermilk in 3 additions, alternating ⅓ of the flour and ⅓ of the buttermilk until just blended.
5. Gently fold in the berries.
6. Pour the batter into 2 8-inch round cake pans that have been sprayed with vegetable oil spray.
7. Bake in the center of the oven for 30 to 35 minutes or until a toothpick inserted into the center comes out clean. Cool on wire racks.
8. For frosting, cook ½ stick butter, ½ cup brown sugar, salt, and 1 teaspoon vanilla in a saucepan over medium high heat for 3 to 5 minutes until the mixture is brown and bubbling and the sugar is dissolved. Remove from the heat.
9. Gradually stir in the milk and sugar. Stir until thickened.
10. Remove the cakes from the pans and cool completely.
11. Place one cake onto a cake plate.
12. Spread the frosting on top of the cake. Top with blackberries and then the second cake.
13. Spread the frosting on the top of the second cake and allow to drizzle down the sides.

Servings: 8 or more
Preparation Time: 30 minutes plus baking

Mixing fresh fruit with a little flour is a good way to prevent the fruit from bleeding into the batter. Make sure that the fruit is as dry as possible and that you do not pour excess juices into the batter. Use a wooden spoon or large spatula to fold in the berries in a upward motion from the center of the bowl, turning the bowl one time around.

Almost a Pig Roast Party Plan

Party Motivation

Tropical breezes beckon you and your pals to shed business attire, pull up a lounge chair and graze on great food while sipping a week-ending concoction.

Party Menu

Hurricane Brew
Chili Cheese Dip
Raspberry and Goat Cheese Salad
Slow-Roasted Pulled Pork with Southern-Style Barbecue Sauce
Two Potato Gratin
Cheese-Stuffed Party Bread
Tropical Trifle **

** Over-the-Top Suggestion

An authentic trifle is built in a glass trifle pedestal dish with layers of fresh fruit, rich pudding and dense cake. This one rivals the original and adds just enough of a tropical twist to render oohs and ahs from all of your guests.

If time permits, whip up a batch of Crisp Coleslaw with Mustard Dressing (page 151) to top pork sandwiches.

Party Strategy

Pull out your loudest shirt and crank up Jimmy Buffet while preparing the majority of this menu way in advance of the weekend.

Two days before: Prepare all of the ingredients for the trifle.

One day before: Prepare dip, cover and refrigerate. Assemble trifle, cover and refrigerate.

The evening before: Prepare pork for overnight roasting method.

The morning of: Arrange buffet and tableware.

One hour before: Prepare and bake cheese bread, keep warm. Assemble and bake gratin, keep warm. Warm dip.

Immediately before serving: Assemble salad

Shortcuts

Substitute with prepared pound cake and packaged pudding mix for trifle. Substitute with readily available strawberries and Brie cheese in the salad. Purchase terrific barbeque sauce to serve with the pork.

Party Backdrop

A great buffet line flows well. I bet you have been at parties where the table is set with duplicate food dishes on each side of a long table. A guest grabs a plate at one end of the table then works his way down either side. You know what happens. Some guest will stroll around the entire table so as not to miss a dish. Others collide at the opposite end and have to turn around—plates in hand—to avoid running into each other. Avoid guest-to-guest contact by arranging your buffet table in an area with ample space. You may have to push the table against the wall to create up-front space thereby directing your guests to help themselves

The Table Setting

Serve fun iced beverages while offering chips with the tangy dipping sauce.

Ease your guests into the meal by setting a simple buffet. Direct them to the proper starting location by placing all of the utensils, dishes, and napkins at the beginning of the buffet. For trouble-free handling, you may consider wrapping utensils in napkins so they are easily held. Place the wrapped utensils in a large basket at the front of the buffet for easy identification.

Serve the colorful salad from a wooden bowl at the beginning of the buffet. Guests can fill salad bowls and set them at their place. Room temperature pulled pork is the star of the meal and is mounded onto a platter. Over-sized buns and a pitcher of warm sauce sit alongside. The warm gratin comes straight from the oven to the table. Guests can tug at slices of cheesy bread served from a shallow bowl to catch all of the butter sauce.

Hurricane Brew

Where are those paper umbrellas when you need them? This cocktail will have your looking all over for them!

8	ounces light rum
8	ounces dark rum
½	cup grenadine
½	cup fresh orange juice
½	cup fresh lime juice
1	tablespoon granulated sugar
	Lime wedges for garnish

1. Place all of the ingredients except the lime wedges in a large pitcher.
2. Stir well to dissolve sugar
3. Pour the mixture into 8 tall glasses that have been filled with ice.
4. Garnish each glass with a lime wedge to rub around the rim.

Chili Cheese Dip

Make this dip in moments and keep warm until your guests arrive. Then watch as everyone dips in.

2	tablespoons olive oil
1	small red onion, finely diced (about ½ cup)
2	medium cloves garlic, minced (about 1 teaspoon)
2	medium jalapeño peppers, seeded and diced (about 4 tablespoons)
1	8-ounce package cream cheese, room temperature
8	ounces Cheddar cheese, shredded
6	to 8 plum tomatoes, seeded and diced (about 2 cups)
1	teaspoon chili powder
	Salt and freshly ground pepper
1	tablespoon chopped fresh cilantro leaves

Tortilla chips

1. Heat the olive oil in a skillet over medium heat.
2. Add the onion, garlic and jalapeño to the pan and cook until the vegetables are soft, about 5 minutes.
3. Add the cream cheese to the pan. Stir constantly until the cheese melts.
4. Add the Cheddar cheese to the pan. Stir constantly until the cheese melts.
5. Add the tomatoes to the cheese mixture. Stir.
6. Season with chili powder, salt, and freshly ground pepper.
7. Reduce the heat to medium low and simmer for 5 minutes.
8. Garnish with fresh cilantro.

Servings: 8
Preparation Time: 20 minutes

This simple-to-make dip is terrific for drive by drop-in guests. It comes together quickly, stays well and makes enough to hold off the hungry while you regroup in the kitchen!

RASPBERRY and GOAT CHEESE SALAD

The sweet flavor of the fruit and the crunch of the walnuts add an interesting twang to a simple toss salad.

8   **cups fresh salad greens**
1   **cup fresh raspberries**
1   **cup chopped walnuts**
1   **small red onion, thinly sliced (about ½ cup)**

⅓   **cup raspberry vinegar**
1   **teaspoon Dijon mustard**
2   **tablespoons chopped fresh mint leaves**
⅔   **cup olive oil**
     Salt and freshly ground pepper
4   **ounces goat cheese, crumbled**

1. Combine the greens, raspberries, walnuts, and red onion in a large salad bowl. Toss
2. Whisk together the raspberry vinegar, mustard, and fresh mint leaves.
3. Slowly whisk in the olive oil. Season with salt.
4. Pour enough of the dressing into the salad to lightly coat the leaves. Season with pepper.
5. Add the goat cheese and toss.

Servings: 8
Preparation Time: 15 minutes

Classic vinaigrettes require three fourths part oil to one-fourth part vinegar, but you need not be limited by that ratio. If you prefer your dressings on the tangy side, add more vinegar or a touch of citrus juice. Vary the dressing by substituting with different vinegars like balsamic, tarragon, champagne or a combination of vinegar and citrus juices (lemon, orange and lime). Season the vinaigrette with fresh herbs, condiments and vegetables to create your own fabulous salad dressing. Whisk the vinegar, herbs and condiments in a bowl. Continue whisking while you slowly pour the oil into the mixture. You may use a food processor to accomplish this task. The oil will be emulsified into the vinegar forming a richly flavored vinaigrette.

Slow-Roasted Pulled Pork with Southern-Style Barbecue Sauce

Slow cooking insures that the meat is "fall-off-the-bone" tender and full of flavor.

½   **cup balsamic vinegar**
¼   **cup minced shallots**
¼   **cup finely chopped sage leaves**
2   **tablespoons Dijon mustard**
2   **tablespoons cayenne pepper**
2   **tablespoons minced garlic**
1   **7- to 8-pound bone-in pork shoulder**
     Salt and freshly ground pepper

3   **cups apple cider vinegar**
1   **cup ketchup**
¾   **cup packed brown sugar**
1   **6-ounce can tomato paste**
2   **tablespoons yellow mustard**
1   **tablespoon Worcestershire sauce**
1   **teaspoon garlic powder**
1   **teaspoon dried red pepper flakes**
⅛   **teaspoon ground cloves**

Preheat the oven to 300°.

1. Mix together the balsamic vinegar, shallots, chopped sage, mustard, cayenne pepper, and garlic in a bowl.
2. Rub this mixture all over the pork shoulder.
3. Season generously with salt and pepper.
4. Wrap the shoulder in aluminum foil. Place on a rack in a large roasting pan.
5. Cook until the meat is very tender, about 1 hour per pound. Let the roast stand for at least 30 minutes before pulling. Remove excess fat and bones.
6. Prepare the sauce by combining the remaining ingredients in a deep saucepan. Bring to a boil and simmer for 15 minutes. Turn off the heat and let the sauce stand to absorb all of the flavors.
7. Season with salt and pepper.

Servings: 8 or more
Preparation Time: 30 minutes plus roasting

"Pulled pork" is the term used when describing shredding the cooked meat and discarding fat and bones. As an alternate cooking method you can place the roast in an oven set on low (250°.) before you go to bed. The meat will be ready sometime the next afternoon! Serve the shredded pork with barbecue sauce on the side and plenty of large rolls for sandwiches.

TWO POTATO GRATIN

Way better than au gratin potatoes, this combination of sweet and white tomatoes blend together when baked with a creamy sauce.

12 ounces bacon, diced
1   large yellow onion, diced (about 1 cup)
6   medium cloves garlic, minced (about 1 tablespoon)
3   cups heavy cream
2   tablespoons chopped fresh rosemary
2   tablespoons chopped fresh thyme leaves
Salt and freshly ground pepper
3   medium sweet potatoes
4   medium Idaho potatoes
¼   cup grated Parmesan cheese

Preheat the oven to 350°.

1. Cook the bacon in a skillet over medium high heat until brown and crisp. Remove the pieces to a paper towel and drain.
2. Cook the onions and garlic in 1 tablespoon bacon drippings over medium heat until just soft. Do not brown the onions and garlic.
3. Add the cream to the pan. Bring to a boil. Reduce the heat and simmer for 5 minutes.
4. Stir the bacon into the cream.
5. Sir in the herbs and season with salt and pepper. Set aside.

6. Peel the potatoes and cut into very thin slices.
7. Spray a baking dish with vegetable oil spray.
8. Place an overlapping layer of white potatoes on the bottom of the dish. Season with salt and pepper.
9. Drizzle some of the cream mixture on top of the potatoes.
10. Cover with an overlapping layer of sweet potatoes. Season with salt and pepper and drizzle with the cream mixture.
11. Continue until all of the potato slices have been used. Press down on the top layer of the gratin. Pour the remaining cream over top.
12. Sprinkle with Parmesan cheese.
13. Bake for 50 to 60 minutes or until the gratin is bubbly and the top is golden brown. Let rest for 20 minutes before cutting into squares.

Servings: 8
Preparation Time: 30 minutes plus baking

What is the difference between sweet potatoes and yam? Well, there is a difference,
but the truth is that most of the product that you see in the market is really sweet potato even
though it may be labeled a yam. A sweet potato has pointed ends and an orange flesh.
A yam has a dark brown, bark-like skin with a white, dry flesh.
Yams are starchier than sweet potatoes and don't taste sweet at all.
They are found mostly in the tropics and are not widely available in the United States.

Cheese-Stuffed Party Bread

You can make a meal out of this yummy bread with the simple addition of prepared deli meat like sliced roasted turkey, baked ham or corned beef.

1	**1-pound round loaf crusty bread**
10	**ounces Swiss cheese, grated**
1	**cup butter (2 sticks)**
2	**tablespoons sesame seeds**
1	**large shallot, minced (about 1 tablespoon)**
	Juice of ½ lemon (about 1 tablespoon)
½	**teaspoon dry mustard**

Preheat the oven to 350°.

1. Cut the bread into ½-inch slices, cutting ¾ of the way down the loaf. Cut the loaf down the middle so that each slice is cut in half. (Keep the slices attached at the bottom of the bread.)
2. Place the sliced bread onto aluminum foil.
3. Stuff the bread slices with the grated cheese.
4. Melt the butter in a saucepan over medium high heat.
5. Stir in the sesame seeds, shallot, lemon juice and dry mustard.
6. Pour the butter mixture between the bread slices and over top of the loaf.
7. Wrap the bread completely with aluminum foil. Place onto a baking sheet.
8. Bake for 20 to 30 minutes or until the cheese is melted and the top of the bread is golden brown.

Servings: 8
Preparation Time: 20 minutes plus baking

If a large round loaf of bread is unavailable, you can substitute with a loaf of French or Italian bread. It will taste just as great!

TROPICAL TRIFLE

There are a lot of steps to making this dessert but the visual presentation alone is worth the preparation. Check out the party plan for shortcuts and remember that you can make this dish a day before the party.

CAKE
3   **cups cake flour**
1   **tablespoon baking powder**
½   **teaspoon salt**
1   **cup butter (2 sticks), room temperature**
1½   **cups granulated sugar**
4   **large eggs**
1   **cup milk**
       Juice of 1 medium lime (about 2 tablespoons)
       Zest of 1 medium lime (about 2 teaspoons)

CUSTARD
4   **egg yolks**
¼   **cup granulated sugar**
¼   **cup Cointreau (plus extra for brushing on cake)**
½   **cup orange juice**
½   **cup heavy cream**

1   **pint strawberries, sliced (about 2 cups)**
1   **mango, peeled, pitted, cut into ½-inch cubes (about 2 cups)**
1   **papaya, peeled, seeded, cut into ½-inch pieces (about 3 cups)**
1   **medium pineapple, peeled, cored, cut into ½-inch pieces (about 3 cups)**

FOR CAKE
Preheat the oven to 325°.
1. Combine the cake flour, baking powder and salt in a small bowl and set aside.
2. Use an electric mixer to beat the butter until fluffy.
3. Add the sugar and mix on medium speed, scraping down the sides of the bowl, for several minutes.
4. Add the eggs, one at a time, stirring well after each addition.
5. Stir in the flour mixture and milk in 3 additions, alternating ⅓ of the flour with ⅓ of the milk until just blended.
6. Stir in the lime juice and zest.
7. Pour the batter into 2 8-inch cake pans that have been sprayed with vegetable oil spray and dusted with flour. Bake for 20 to 25 minutes or until the tops begin to turn golden on the edges and a toothpick inserted into the center comes out clean.
8. Cool the cakes on metal racks for 10 minutes. Invert the cakes onto the racks and cool completely. Use a serrated knife to trim the cakes to fit into a 7-inch trifle bowl.

FOR CUSTARD
1. Whisk the egg yolks and sugar together in the top part of a double boiler over simmering water.
2. Whisk in the Cointreau and orange juice.
3. Continue whisking until the sauce has doubled in volume. It will thicken, become fluffy and turn pale yellow, about 5 to 8 minutes.
4. Remove the top of the double boiler to a large bowl filled with ice. Continue whisking the custard until it cools.
5. Use an electric mixer to beat the cream until soft peaks form.
6. Fold the whipped cream into the custard mixture. Chill until ready to serve.

TO ASSEMBLE
1. Spoon ⅓ of the custard into the bottom of a trifle dish.
2. Use a pastry brush to lightly coat the cakes with Cointreau. Fit one cake layer on top of the custard. Feel free to cut the cake into pieces.

3. Arrange half of the fruit on top of the cake.
4. Repeat with ⅓ more custard, the remaining cake pieces and a layer of fruit.
5. Top with the remaining custard.

Servings: 8 or more
Preparation Time: 90 minutes

This recipe is an invitation to be creative. Use any fruit that is readily available. Likewise you can vary the liqueur or eliminate it and substitute with a sugar glaze. Shortcuts include buying store-bought cake or whipping us a batch of instant pudding. Be as inventive as you can—and create your own favorite trifle.

Family Parties

(PARTIES FOR EIGHT OR MORE)

Sunday Supper
Indoor/Outdoor Family Feast
Birthday Bashes for Kids and Big Kids
Sparkling Spa Teen Sleepover

"The first impression is always important in life. This definitely applies to party invitations. The best ones are unique and fun. The invitation should draw the attention of the invitee as soon as it is opened. The party theme is evident so guests are immediately aware of the mood. Recently, for a one-year-old birthay party we dressed the baby only in a diaper. With a white backdrop we gave her a birthday cake and took pictures as she explored every sugary morsel. We chose the best shot of her laughing and painted in cake for the front of the invitation. The party was a huge success and everyone that received an invitation came."

Andrea Mildrad
Owner of Little BIG Man
Coral Springs, Florida
www.LittleBigMan.org

Sunday Supper Party Plan

Party Motivation

That one special day a week when families come together to celebrate each other deserves a wonderful meal. Traditions are created, recipes are passed on to the next generation and bonds are formed.

Party Menu

Warm Mushroom Salad with Maple Lime Dressing
Herb-Roasted Leg of Lamb with Browned Vegetables
Sautéed Green Beans with Blood Orange Ginger Sauce **
Maple-Glazed Butter Cake

**** Over-the-Top Suggestion**

Blood oranges add a sweet twist to a Sunday supper staple. Picture Grandma meeting Emeril. Bam!

Party Strategy

Platters and bowls are passed from hand to hand. Bring everything to the table and linger over a super supper.

The morning of: Bake the simple cake and glaze with frosting.

Two hours before: Prepare and roast the lamb and vegetables.

Thirty minutes before: Prepare green beans and keep warm.

Immediately before serving: Sauté the mushrooms and assemble salad.

Shortcuts

If portobello mushrooms are hard to find, substitute with sliced button mushrooms in the salad. Scored veggies will quickly brown and crisp, however it is not necessary in preparation for roasting.

Party Backdrop

Sunday supper is set on the dining room kitchen table. If there are more people than chairs, set another table nearby. Turn off the television and listen to the chatter as platters are passed and seconds are requested.

The Table Setting

Lay out a tablecloth the night before to eliminate wrinkles. Set each place, starting at the left with a salad fork, dinner fork, dinner plate, steak knife and spoon. Place dessert forks at the top of the plate. Place salad bowls to the left of the plate above the forks. Iced tea and or water glasses sit on the right of the plate at the top of the knife.

Serve the salad from a chilled bowl. Slice the roast in the kitchen. Place lamb and roasted vegetables on a platter. Garnish with rosemary sprigs. Place a small bowl of mint jelly on the table for those that love this traditional accompaniment. Green beans are served from a shallow bowl with the sauce drizzled on top. After the table is cleared, bring the buttery cake to the table and slice.

WARM MUSHROOM SALAD with MAPLE LIME DRESSING

A nice break from the simple tossed salad, the warm mushrooms and maple vinaigrette twist offer a great first course.

	Juice of 2 limes (about ¼ cup)
3	**tablespoon maple syrup**
1	**teaspoon soy sauce**
1	**teaspoon sesame oil**
	Freshly ground pepper
1	**tablespoon olive oil**
1	**8-ounce package baby portobello mushrooms, sliced (about 2 cups)**
1	**8-ounce package shiitake mushrooms, sliced (about 3 cups)**
2	**tablespoons chopped fresh rosemary**
8	**cups fresh salad greens**
1	**bunch (6 to 8) green onions, chopped (about 1 cup)**
	Toasted pecans
	Gorgonzola cheese

1. Whisk together the lime juice, maple syrup, soy sauce, sesame oil, and pepper in a small bowl.
2. Heat 1 tablespoon olive oil in a skillet over medium high heat.
3. Add the mushrooms to the pan and cook for 5 minutes.
4. Add the rosemary to the pan. Toss.
5. Remove the mushrooms from the heat.
6. Pour the maple lime dressing over the mushrooms. Toss.
7. Place the salad greens and green onion in a large bowl.
8. Add the warm mushrooms to the salad greens and toss.
9. Pass bowls of toasted pecans and gorgonzola cheese to garnish.

Servings: 8
Preparation Time: 20 minutes

In days past, mushrooms grew wild in the forest and were foraged by farmers for use in traditional dishes. Today's farmers cultivate most of the new and interesting varieties of mushrooms that are readily available for our kitchen. "Baby bello" mushrooms are one example of this trend. Similar in shape and coloring to the larger portobello mushroom, a "baby bello" is closer in size to a button mushroom and is easily interchanged with this very common ingredient. Shiitake mushrooms were wildly popular in Japan and are now found on the grocery shelf in American markets. The stems are sometimes tough and are most easily removed before incorporating the shiitake into a recipe.

Herb-Roasted Leg of Lamb with Browned Vegetables

Called to the table for Sunday supper by the aroma of a savory roast, let's see how many family members are seated before the oven door is opened.

1 **4 ¼-pound boneless leg of lamb**
4 **medium cloves garlic, thinly sliced**
1 **tablespoon olive oil**
1 **tablespoon chopped fresh thyme leaves**
1 **tablespoon chopped fresh rosemary leaves**
1 **tablespoon chopped fresh sage leaves**
1 **tablespoon chopped fresh mint leaves**
1 **teaspoon course salt**
1 **teaspoon course pepper**

1 **pound carrots, peeled and cut into 2-inch pieces (about 5 to 6 medium)**
6 **medium potatoes, peeled and sliced into 2-inch wedges**
2 **medium white onions, cut into 2-inch wedges**

Preheat the oven to 375°.

1. Use a sharp knife to make small slits, about 1-inch deep, in the lamb. Insert the garlic pieces into the slits.
2. Brush the lamb with olive oil.
3. Place the herbs, salt and pepper into the bowl of a mini food processor. Pulse to finely chop.
4. Rub the herb mixture all over the lamb.
5. Place the lamb onto a rack into a large roasting pan.
6. Use the tines of a fork to score the carrots, potatoes and onion on all sides.
7. Place the vegetables in the roasting pan around the lamb.
8. Roast for 1 hour and 15 minutes or until a thermometer inserted in the thickest part of the meat reaches a temperature of 135°. for medium rare. Remove lamb to a cutting board and let stand at least 15 minutes before carving.
9. Turn the vegetables in the roasting pan and return to the oven until crisp and golden brown.

Servings: 8
Preparation Time: 30 minutes plus roasting

Lamb has a very distinctive taste that is wonderfully enhanced by fresh garlic and herbs.
Choose a roast with firm flesh that is finely grained and reddish pink.
Leg of lamb is purchased with the bone in, or by asking the butcher to remove the bone,
it can be rolled and tied. If you purchase a roast with the bone-in, the cooking time will increase.
A most common accompaniment to lamb is mint jelly—a favorite of my namesake grandfather.

Sautéed Green Beans
with Blood Orange Ginger Sauce

The addition of citrus juice and a hint of ginger make this sauce a must for a Sunday supper veggie.

2 pounds green beans (about 6 cups)
2 tablespoons olive oil
**2 medium cloves garlic, minced (about 1
    teaspoon)**
**1 ½-inch piece ginger, grated (about 1
    tablespoon)**
**Juice of 2 large blood oranges (about ⅓
    cup)**
1 tablespoon soy sauce
1 tablespoon sesame seeds
Salt and freshly ground pepper

1. Place the green beans in casserole dish. Pour in 1-inch water. Cover.
2. Steam the beans in a microwave on high for 4 minutes. Beans will be crisp tender.
3. Heat the olive oil in a skillet over medium high heat.
4. Add the garlic and ginger and cook for 1 minute.
5. Drain the beans in a colander.
6. Add the beans to the skillet. Toss.
7. Add the blood orange juice and soy sauce to the skillet.
8. Simmer and toss for 3 minutes.
9. Add the sesame seeds to the beans. Season with salt and pepper.

Servings: 8
Preparation Time: 20 minutes

Blood oranges are sweet oranges originally from Sicily and easily identified by their distinctive red flesh and juice. Use them as you would a navel, Valencia, or other variety of sweet orange.

Maple-Glazed Butter Cake

A decorative cake pan adds an original presentation to this buttery cake. But, it is so good—any pan will do.

3   **cups cake flour**
3   **teaspoons baking powder**
¼   **teaspoon salt**
1   **cup butter (2 sticks), room temperature**
1½   **cups granulated sugar**
4   **large eggs, beaten**
1   **cup milk**
2   **tablespoons maple syrup**

2½   **cups confectioners' sugar**
1   **teaspoon vanilla extract**
¼   **cup maple syrup**
½   **cup corn syrup**
½   **cup milk**

Preheat the oven to 325°.

1. Prepare a Bundt cake pan by spraying with vegetable oil spray and dusting with flour.
2. Combine the flour, baking powder, and salt in a bowl and set aside.
3. Use an electric mixer to beat the butter and sugar until light and fluffy.
4. Mix in the eggs. Stir until fluffy.
5. Add the flour and milk in 3 additions, alternating ⅓ flour mixture and ⅓ milk until just blended.
6. Stir in the maple syrup.
7. Pour the batter into the prepared pan.
8. Bake for 45 to 55 minutes or until a toothpick inserted into the center comes out clean.
9. Remove the cake to a rack. Run a knife around the edge of the pan. Cool for 5 minutes. Invert the cake onto the rack.
10. Whisk together the confectioners' sugar, vanilla, maple syrup, corn syrup, and milk in a bowl.
11. Place waxed paper under the rack holding the cake.
12. Use a skewer to poke holes into the cake.
13. Pour the maple glaze over the cake allowing it to soak into the holes.
14. Recover the excess glaze from the waxed paper and again pour the glaze over the cake.
15. Allow to stand for at least 1 hour. Dust with additional confectioner's sugar to serve.

Servings: 8
Preparation Time: 30 minutes plus baking

This cake easily turns into the citrus cake of your choice by substituting citrus juice like lemon, lime or orange in place of maple syrup. A touch of citrus zest takes the taste over-the-top! Experiment with the basic butter cake and come up with your own special combination of flavors.

Indoor/Outdoor Family Feast Party Plan

Party Motivation

Invite the aunts, uncles, cousins and their aunts, uncles and cousins to a family party that is easy to prepare and a blast to serve. Young and old come together with sleeves rolled to elbows and fingers dripping with butter. What could be better?

Party Menu

Jalapeño-Spiked Artichoke Dip
Romaine and Red Leaf Salad with Yellow Tomato Vinaigrette
Low Country Kitchen Clambake **
Baked Lima Beans with Bacon and Caramelized Onion
Down Home Peach Shortcake with Cinnamon Biscuits

** Over-the-Top Suggestion

The idea of an indoor clam bake is a simple twist on the outdoor version. But why choose? Prepare low country clambake on the stove and cook the real thing on the outdoor grill at the same time. More to choose from—just as easy to prepare.

Party Strategy

Serve an easy dip while the clambake boils on top of the stove. Toss everything into a large bowl and let the group choose their favorite pieces.

The day before: Prepare the dip, cover and refrigerate. Prepare vinaigrette for salad. Prepare peaches.

The morning of: Prepare lima bean casserole. Bake biscuits.

Two hours before: Husk corn, prepare sausage and shrimp.

One hour before: Prepare oven top clambake. Bake beans and keep warm. Warm dip.

Immediately before serving: Assemble and toss salad.

Shortcuts

Use canned beans in the lima bean casserole. Purchase fresh biscuits or prepared scones for the shortcake.

Party Backdrop

This party is definitely best served on the kitchen table—or if the weather permits, an outdoor picnic table. The most important aspect is that everyone can gather at the table at the same time.

The Table Setting

Greet guests with hugs and offer a nibble. Place a crock full of warm dip onto a tray. Surround the crock with your favorite dippers such as carrots, celery, endive, breadsticks or crackers.
Serve the salad from a wooden bowl. Place a cruet full of vinaigrette nearby. Drain the clambake ingredients. Use a slotted spoon to move everything into a large shallow bowl or platter with rim. Sprinkle with fresh chopped herbs and set out bowls of melted butter. Place the warm bean casserole from the oven onto the table. Pass around oversized plates and invite everyone to dig in. Place empty bowls on the table for empty shells and corncobs. Cleanup is a breeze if you line the table with newspapers!

Pass individual bowls of peach shortcake that are overflowing with whipped cream.

Jalapeño-Spiked Artichoke Dip

There are many variations on this easy dish—and no wonder—it's soooo good no matter how you bake it!

2	**8-ounce packages cream cheese, room temperature**
½	**cup sour cream**
¼	**cup mayonnaise**
	Juice of 1 lemon (about 2 tablespoons)
1	**tablespoon Dijon mustard**
1	**medium clove garlic, minced (about ½ teaspoon)**
1	**teaspoon Worcestershire sauce**
2	**to 6 drops hot pepper sauce**
1	**16-ounce can artichoke hearts, drained**
1	**cup grated Parmesan cheese**
4	**green onions, thinly sliced (about ¼ cup)**
1	**medium jalapeño peppers, seeded and diced (about 2 tablespoons)**

Preheat the oven to 400°.

1. Place the cream cheese, sour cream, mayonnaise, lemon juice, mustard, garlic, Worcestershire, and hot pepper sauce in the bowl of a food processor. Pulse to combine.
2. Add the artichoke hearts, Parmesan cheese, green onions, and jalapeño pepper. Pulse.
3. Pour the artichoke mixture into a shallow baking dish.
4. Bake uncovered for 20 to 30 minutes or until the dip is hot and bubbling.
5. Serve with vegetable crudités and breadsticks.

Servings: 8
Preparation Time: 20 minutes plus baking

The baking time will vary based on the size of the dish that you choose. A shallow dish will bake in less time than a deeper dish. Choose one that goes with the party theme and adjust accordingly.

ROMAINE and RED LEAF SALAD with YELLOW TOMATO VINAIGRETTE

This easy salad comes together in minutes and cries out for substituting with the freshest tomatoes that you can find.

2   medium heads romaine lettuce, washed, dried, and torn into 1-inch pieces (about 6 cups)
1   medium head red leaf lettuce, washed, dried, and torn into 1-inch pieces (about 3 cups)
1   cup grated Swiss cheese
1   cup croutons

4   medium yellow tomatoes, seeded and quartered
¼   small red onion, chopped (about 2 table-spoons)
2   cloves garlic
¼   cup rice wine vinegar
4   tablespoons fresh basil leaves
½   cup olive oil
     Salt and freshly ground pepper

1. Place the lettuce, Swiss cheese, and croutons in a large salad bowl.
2. Place the yellow tomatoes, red onion, garlic, rice wine vinegar, and basil leaves into a blender. Pulse to emulsify.
3. Slowly add the olive oil with the machine running. Season with salt and pepper.
4. Pour just enough vinaigrette over the salad to lightly moisten the leaves. Toss.

Servings: 8
Preparation Time: 10 minutes

Today's tomatoes are grown in many varieties. In your local market you will easily find white tomatoes, purple black to reddish black tomatoes and even zebra striped green tomatoes. Experiment with the many different types of tomatoes to see which ones are your crowd's pleasers.

LOW COUNTRY KITCHEN CLAMBAKE

A take off on the famous New England clambakes, this meal comes together on top of your kitchen stove—and no one has to dig the pit! The substitution of shrimp for whole lobsters makes this an affordable family party dish.

1	medium celery rib
1	medium carrot
4	fresh parsley sprigs
4	fresh thyme sprigs
2	bay leafs

10	to 12 small red potatoes
8	ears of fresh corn, husked, cut into 3-inch pieces
2	pounds cooked andouille sausage, cut into 3-inch pieces
1½	pounds large uncooked shrimp, peeled and deveined (about 24)
4	dozen clams, scrubbed

Salt and freshly ground pepper
Melted herbed butter
Chopped parsley
Lemon wedges
Garlic bread (see sidebar, below)

1. Place the celery, carrot, parsley, thyme, and bay leaves on a piece of cheesecloth. Roll up and tie with a string.

2. Place the potatoes in the bottom of a very large pan pan. Place the corn on top of the potatoes. Cover the vegetables with water (filling the pot about halfway full). Place the herb bundle in the water. Cook over medium high heat for 10 minutes.

3. Place the sausage on top of the vegetables. Cook for 10 minutes or until the potatoes are tender.

4. Place the shrimp and the clams on top of the sausage. Cover the pot with a lid (or piece of aluminum foil). Steam until the clams open and the shrimp is cooked, about 10 to 12 minutes.

5. Remove the cooked seafood, sausage, corn and potatoes to a large bowl. Sprinkle the vegetables with salt, pepper and parsley.

6. Serve with individual bowls of melted herbed butter and garnish with lemon wedges.

Servings: 8
Preparation Time: 40 minutes

There are many varieties of clams will work well in this dish such as littleneck, cherrystone or the soft-shell steamers. Choose the freshest clams that you can find. Scrub them under cold water. Discard any clams that do not open after cooking.

Prepare herb butter by melting 1 stick butter with 2 garlic minced cloves 1 teaspoon of dried oregano and 1 teaspoon of dried basil in a saucepan over medium heat. Remove from heat, cover and let the flavors combine. Warm the butter just before serving.

Make terrific garlic bread by making ½-inch diagonal slices in an Italian or French loaf of bread. Cut down ¾ of the way leaving the loaf in tact. Combine 1 stick softened butter with 2 to 3 cloves very finely minced garlic. Add 1 tablespoon very finely chopped parsley. Spread this mixture between each slice. Wrap the bread in aluminum foil and bake for 10 to 15 minutes.

BAKED LIMA BEANS with BACON and CARAMELIZED ONION

This terrific side dish takes those unloved beans to new heights. Give them a try and see if your guests won't come back for more.

1	**pound fresh lima beans (about 3 cups)**
½	**pound bacon, diced**
1	**medium red onion, diced (about 1 cup)**
2	**tablespoons balsamic vinegar**
2	**tablespoons brown sugar**
2	**tablespoons Dijon mustard**
1	**cup chicken broth**
	Salt and freshly ground pepper

Preheat the oven to 350°.

1. Place the lima beans into salted boiling water and cook for 10 minutes.
2. Cook the bacon in a skillet on medium high heat until crisp. Remove and drain on a paper towel.
3. Remove all but 1 tablespoon of the bacon drippings.
4. Cook the onion in the skillet until soft.
5. Add the balsamic vinegar and continue cooking until the onions are brown and syrupy.
6. Drain the beans and place in a bowl.
7. Stir in the brown sugar and mustard.
8. Stir in the bacon and onions.
9. Place the beans into a baking dish that has been sprayed with vegetable oil spray.
10. Pour in 1 cup chicken broth. Season with salt and pepper. Cover with aluminum foil.
11. Bake for 30 minutes or until the beans are very tender.

Servings: 8
Preparation Time: 30 minutes plus baking

Fresh lima beans are available in the produce section of the market. Dried lima beans are easily substituted. Soak the beans overnight or cook the beans in boiling water for 30 minutes until tender. Continue with the recipe using 3 cups of cooked beans. You may also substitute with canned beans by reducing the cooking time. Substitute with 2 16-ounce cans, drained.

Down Home Peach Shortcake with Cinnamon Biscuits

Nothing tops off a terrific meal better than this Southern favorite. A hint of cinnamon updates the traditional biscuit, but the secret is in handling the dough.

8   **medium peaches, peeled and sliced (about 8 cups)**
     Juice of 1 medium orange (about ⅓ cup)
     Zest of 1 medium orange (about 2 tablespoons)
¼   **cup granulated sugar**
½   **cup water**

1   **cup granulated sugar**
2   **cups all-purpose flour**
2   **cups cake flour**
4   **teaspoons baking powder**
½   **teaspoon salt**
1   **teaspoon ground cinnamon**
¼   **teaspoon baking soda**
¾   **cup butter (1½ sticks), chilled, cut into pieces**
2   **large eggs, beaten**
1   **cup sour cream**

2   **tablespoons granulated sugar**
1   **teaspoon cinnamon**

     Vanilla ice cream
     Whipped cream

1. Place the peach slices, orange juice, orange zest, ¼ cup sugar, and water in a bowl. Toss. Cover and chill for at least 1 hour or overnight.
Preheat the oven to 400°.
2. Combine 1 cup of sugar, flour, cake flour, baking powder, salt, cinnamon, and baking soda in the bowl of a food processor.

3. Add the butter pieces and pulse until the mixture resembles coarse crumbs.
4. Reserve 1 tablespoon of the beaten egg in a small bowl.
5. Add the remaining eggs and the sour cream to the bowl. Pulse until the mixture comes together to form a dough.
6. Pour the dough onto a lightly floured surface. Gently knead the dough until it just holds together. Do not overwork the dough or the biscuits will be tough.
7. Roll out the dough to 1-inch thickness. Cut out 3-inch rounds with a biscuit cutter dipped in flour.
8. Place the biscuits on a Silpat-lined baking sheet. Brush the tops of the biscuits with reserved beaten egg.
9. Combine 2 tablespoons of sugar with 1 teaspoon of cinnamon. Sprinkle the tops of the biscuits with this mixture.
10. Bake for 10 to 15 minutes or until the tops are golden.
11. Slice each warm biscuit in half horizontally. Place the bottom half in a fruit bowl. Top with a scoop of ice cream. Top the ice cream with peaches and a drizzle of the juices. Add the biscuit top. Add another layer of peaches and juice. Top with a generous dollop of whipped cream.

Yield: about 12 biscuits
Preparation Time: 20 minutes

Take a simple recipe for shortcake and add your own special touches to create your favorite dessert. Try lemon and poppy seed biscuits with blueberries, or chocolate biscuits with strawberries and chocolate fudge syrup.

Birthday Bash for Kids and Big Kids Party Plan

Party Motivation

A milestone birthday for your little one is the perfect occasion to gather family to celebrate with balloons, party hats, noisemakers and plenty of festive food.

Party Menu

Shirley Temple Martoonies
Fish and Chips with Roasted Tomato Ketchup **
Individual Salmon Pot Pies
Grilled Veggie and Fruit Kabobs
Chocolate Mocha Sheet Cake with Peanut Butter Frosting

**** Over-the-Top Suggestion**

In addition to roasted pepper ketchup add another sauce for the yummy fish fingers. Peppery Tartar Sauce is just the sauce for dipping battered fish as it has a nice hint of heat that works well with milder varieties of fish. Combine 2 cups mayonnaise, 1 tablespoon drained capers, 1 tablespoon fresh garlic chives, 1 tablespoon fresh tarragon, 1 chipotle pepper in adobo sauce, the juice of 1 lemon (about 2 tablespoons) and 2 teaspoons Dijon mustard in the bowl of a food processor. Pulse to combine.

Party Strategy

Keep little ones out of the kitchen as you prepare fun fried fingers. Allow others to organize games and activities while you prepare the family feast.

Two days before: Prepare roasted tomato ketchup and peppery tartar sauce.

One day before: Prepare cake and frosting. Prepare fruit and veggie skewers. Prepare the salmon filling and potatoes for the pot pies.

The morning of: Assemble the pot pies. Cover and refrigerate.

Two hours ahead: Grill veggies and fruit and keep warm. Prepare batter for fish. Cut fish into strips.

One hour before: Bake pot pies. Heat oil. Precook fries.

Immediately before: Deep fry fish and chips.

Shortcuts

Prepare the salmon pot pie in a casserole dish and allow guests to serve themselves.

Party Backdrop

An outdoor patio and backyard is just enough space to allow little ones to run around. Birthday party essentials include tons of balloons, at least one piñata, game stations, art stations, and at least a smidge of play dough. High chairs keep babies contained. Manning each adult with a disposable camera is guaranteed to keep smiles smiling.

The Table Setting

Use paper cups to serve the fish and chips. Choose a festive design. Place an unfolded napkin into the cup. Fill with 2 to 3 fish pieces and 4 to 5 fries. Serve the ketchup on the side and a dollop of Peppery Tartar Sauce. Don't forget a squeeze bottle of prepared ketchup for those that smother everything in the children's condiment of choice. A platter hold skewers of grilled fruit and veggies. For parties with lots of little ones, remove both the fruit and vegetables from the skewers in advance of serving. Place individual pot pies on a tray and serve the grown ups at their own special table. Decorate the chocolaty cake with "Happy Birthday" written with prepared tubes of frosting.

Shirley Temple Martoonies

Perfect for the really underage guests at your child's party, serve these fun drinks with a flare.

1   liter lemon-lime soft drink, chilled
**   Grenadine**
1   12-ounce bottle red cherries

1. Pour chilled soda into plastic martini glasses.
2. Add a drop or two of grenadine.
3. Garnish with a toothpick holding 1 to 2 cherries.

Fish and Chips with Roasted Tomato Ketchup

Little hands love "hands-on" food and this fun dish fits the bill for your little one's next big bash.

6	**medium red tomatoes cut into wedges (about 2 cups)**
3	**tablespoons olive oil**
	Salt and freshly ground pepper
2	**large shallots, minced (about 2 tablespoons)**
4	**medium cloves garlic, minced (about 2 teaspoons)**
½	**cup sherry vinegar**
¼	**cup granulated sugar**
½	**teaspoon ground cinnamon**
½	**teaspoon ground allspice**
1½	**cups all-purpose flour plus extra for dredging**
1	**tablespoon olive oil**
2	**egg yolks, beaten**
2	**tablespoons chopped fresh dill**
1	**tablespoon soy sauce**
1	**cup beer**
1½	**pounds firm-fleshed fish fillets such as dolphin, grouper, flounder, or salmon, cut into 1-inch strips**
6	**large potatoes, peeled and sliced into ¼-inch strips**
	Canola oil for frying
	Paprika

FOR ROASTED TOMATO KETCHUP
Preheat the oven to 350°.

1. Place the tomatoes onto a baking sheet. Sprinkle with 1 tablespoon olive oil and season with salt and pepper. Roast for 10 to 15 minutes or until the tomatoes are soft.
2. Transfer the tomatoes to the bowl of a food processor. Pulse to emulsify. Use a food mill to remove seeds and excess pulp (alternatively strain the tomatoes through a sieve).
3. Heat 2 tablespoons olive oil in a saucepan over medium high heat.
4. Add the shallots and cook until soft, about 2 to 4 minutes.

5. Add the minced garlic and cook for 2 minutes more.
6. Add the tomato purée, sherry vinegar, sugar, cinnamon, and allspice. Reduce heat to medium. Simmer for 20 to 30 minutes, stirring occasionally until thickened. Cool, cover and refrigerate.

FOR FISH AND CHIPS:

1. In a medium bowl stir together the flour, olive oil, egg yolks, dill, and soy sauce.
2. Slowly whisk in the beer. Cover and refrigerate for at least 2 hours.
3. Place the potato strips into a bowl filled with cold water.
4. Pour oil into a deep pot ⅓ full. Heat the oil over medium high heat until it reaches about 300°.
5. Remove several fries from the bowl. Use paper toweling to pat dry. Fry the potatoes in the oil for 2 minutes.
6. Use a slotted spoon to remove the fries to paper toweling to drain. The potatoes will remain white. Repeat until all of the potato strips have been cooked. Set aside.
7. Heat the oil to 350°.
8. Dredge each fish piece in extra flour. Shake off excess. Remove the batter from the refrigerator. Dip each fish piece into the batter. Immediately place into the hot oil in batches. Cook for 2 to 4 minutes or until just golden brown. Transfer to paper toweling to drain. Continue until all of the fish has been fried.
9. Reheat the oil to 350°. Place the pre-cooked potato strips into the hot oil. Cook 2 to 4 minutes until golden brown. Transfer to paper toweling. Generously sprinkle with salt, pepper, and paprika.

Servings: 8
Preparation Time: 2 hours

INDIVIDUAL SALMON POT PIES

For the big kids, here is a dish that is sure to please—a grown up version of the fish and chips theme.

2   **pounds fresh salmon, skin removed**
        Salt and freshly ground pepper

¼   **cup butter (½ stick)**
¼   **cup all-purpose flour**
2   **8-ounce bottles clam juice**
2   **cups heavy cream**

½   **pound bacon, diced**
1   **large yellow onion, diced (about 1 cup)**
1   **large red bell pepper, diced (about 1 cup)**
1   **16-ounce can peas, drained**
1   **teaspoon Dijon mustard**
⅓   **cup chopped fresh dill**
2   **tablespoons chopped fresh parsley**
        Juice of 1 lemon (about 2 tablespoons)
        Zest of 1 medium lemon (about 1 tablespoons)

4   **to 5 large russet potatoes, peeled and cut into pieces (about 4 pounds)**
¼   **cup butter (½ stick)**
½   **cup sour cream**
3   **large egg yolks**

Preheat the oven to 350°.

1. Season the salmon with salt and pepper. Place on a baking sheet. Bake for 15 to 20 minutes. The salmon should be cooked through but still rare, pink, and moist in the center. Flake the salmon into bit size pieces.
2. Melt ¼ cup butter in a large pot over medium heat.
3. Whisk in the flour. Cook until bubbly and golden.
4. Whisk in the clam juice and cream. Cook, stirring until thick, about 8 to 10 minutes. Remove from the heat.
5. Cook the bacon in a skillet over medium high heat. Remove to a paper towel to drain. Pour off all but 1 tablespoon of the drippings.
6. Cook the onion and pepper in the drippings until soft, about 5 minutes.
7. Stir the cooked bacon and vegetables into the sauce.
8. Stir in the peas, mustard, dill, parsley, lemon juice, and lemon zest.
9. Fold in the salmon. Season with salt and pepper.
10. Cook the potatoes in salted, boiling water until tender, about 20 minutes.
11. Drain the potatoes in a colander and allow to cool to remove excess moisture.
12. Pass the potatoes through a vegetable mill or ricer and place into a bowl.
13. Melt ¼ cup butter in a small saucepan over medium high heat. Stir in the sour cream. Add this to the potatoes. Stir in the egg yolks.

Preheat the oven to 375°.

14. Pour the salmon mixture into 8 1½- to 2-cup ovenproof crocks. Spread each crock with the potato mixture.
15. Place the crocks onto 2 baking sheets. Place each sheet into the oven. Bake for 20 to 30 minutes or until the tops are golden and crusty and the salmon is warmed. Rotate the pans in the oven for even browning.

Servings: 8
Preparation Time: 1 hour

You can easily make these pot pies in advance and refrigerate, covered overnight. You may also prepare the dish by placing the salmon filling into a large casserole. Cover the entire casserole with the potato mixture and bake for 35 to 45 minutes. Allow your guests to serve themselves.

GRILLED VEGGIE and FRUIT KABOBS

Such a simple treat, skewers of grilled veggies and grilled fruit are a scrumptious way to include these important food groups into any great party.

Vegetable oil
1   medium pineapple, peeled, cored, and cut into 1-inch pieces
1   pint strawberries
4   large pears, peeled and cut into 1-inch pieces
4   large Granny Smith apples, peeled and cut into 1-inch pieces

8   ears fresh corn, cut into 2-inch rounds
1   medium eggplant, peeled and cut into 1-inch cubes
4   medium zucchini, sliced into 1-inch rounds
6   to 8 plum tomatoes, halved
1   cup prepared sweet and sour sauce

Preheat the grill to medium high heat. Brush the grill with vegetable oil.

1. Alternate fruit pieces on metal skewers. Brush with sweet and sour sauce.
2. Grill for 2 minutes on each side, or until beginning to char.
3. Alternate vegetable pieces on metal skewers. Brush with sweet and sour sauce.
4. Grill for 2 to 4 minutes on each side, or until beginning to soften and turn golden.

Servings: 8
Preparation Time: 30 minutes

A grill pan will accommodate grilled veggies and fruit for inside parties. Use bamboo skewers that have been soaked in water for several hours. Lightly brush the fruit and veggie pieces with a small amount of olive oil. Grill over medium high heat as specified in the recipes.

Serve the skewers with your preferred dipping sauce. For fruit skewers, a mixture of vanilla yogurt, honey, and raspberries makes a super accompaniment. Your favorite bottled salad dressings work well as veggie dips, as will soy sauce.

CHOCOLATE MOCHA SHEET CAKE with PEANUT BUTTER FROSTING

Mocha flavor is achieved by adding brewed coffee to the chocolate batter. Peanut butter frosting adds a lip-smacking topping—sort of like that candy bar, but even yummier.

2	**cups all-purpose flour**
2	**cups granulated sugar**
½	**teaspoon salt**
1	**cup butter (2 sticks), room temperature**
1	**cup brewed coffee**
¼	**cup cocoa powder**
1	**teaspoon baking soda**
2	**large eggs, beaten**
1	**teaspoon imitation black walnut flavoring**
½	**cup sour cream**

1	**16-ounce package semisweet chocolate chips**
½	**cup butter (1 stick), cut into pieces**
¾	**cup peanut butter**
2	**tablespoons heavy cream**

Preheat the oven to 350°.

1. Spray a 15 x 10-inch jelly roll pan with vegetable oil spray and dust with flour. (Alternatively use a 17 x 12 x 1-inch half sheet pan.)
2. Combine the flour, sugar, and salt in a small bowl. Set aside.
3. Melt the butter in a saucepan over medium heat.
4. Stir in the coffee and cocoa. Bring to a boil.
5. Add the flour mixture and stir. Remove from the heat.
6. Stir in the baking soda, eggs, black walnut flavoring and sour cream.
7. Pour the batter into the prepared pan.
8. Bake for 15 to 20 minutes or until a toothpick inserted into the center comes out clean. Cool completely.
9. Melt the chocolate chips in the top of a double boiler over simmering water, stirring until smooth.
10. Remove the pan from the heat.
11. Whisk in the butter, peanut butter, and cream. Stir until smooth.
12. Place the pan into a large bowl filled with ice. Stir until the frosting becomes thick and spreadable.
13. Frost the cake.

Servings: 8 or more
Preparation Time: 30 minutes

This cake is a take-off on the very popular "Texas Sheet Cake," a favorite among young and old alike. The more traditional frosting is chocolate and is poured onto the cake and allowed to set up. Feel free to give this one a try in lieu of peanut butter frosting.

Melt ½ cup of butter (1 stick) in a saucepan over medium heat. Stir in ⅓ cup of cocoa powder and ⅓ cup of milk. Bring to a boil. Stir in 2 cups of confectioners' sugar, 1 teaspoon of vanilla extract, and 1 cup of chopped walnuts or pecans.

Sparkling Spa Teen Sleepover Party Plan

Party Motivation

You're looking for a way to spend a little "bonding time" with your teen. What better approach than to plan a party together? This one combines the traditions of a "sleep-over" with the indulgences of a "spa day." There are lots of fun activities that mom and daughter can do to get everything ready for the girls. The party plan can be adapted for every age from preteens to those more sophisticated and "spa wise." As a matter of fact—this party could be a fun activity for teen girls to throw for tired out moms! The connection is in the preplanning—the fun is in the pampering.

Party Menu

Cucumber, Tomato, and Olive Bruschetta
Yogurt Dip with Toasted Pitas
Curried Shrimp served with White Rice
Strawberry, Peach, and Banana Smoothie **
Power Waffles with Brown Sugar Syrup, Bananas, and Almonds

**** Over-the-Top Suggestion**

Set up a smoothie bar complete with fresh fruits, juices, and chilled glasses for an ongoing great refresher.

Party Strategy

All of these activities create a healthy appetite. The order of the day—Splendid Spa Food. The secret is to make light fare that is irresistible because the flavor is punched up to match the event. Start with a bruschetta buffet. These build-your-own treats are great appetizers and will stay fresh while hair and nails dry. Another fun appetizer is one that combines chopped spinach and yogurt.

Shrimp Curry is a most Splendid Spa Supper. Make individual rice bowls by packing cooked white rice into small ramekins or bowls. Invert the ramekin onto the dinner plate and serve the shrimp curry over top. Garnish with lemon zest and a sprinkle of red pepper flakes. Late night snacks are a breeze if they include fresh fruit smoothies. Rest assured that there will be some sleepy girls. When morning comes, they may need a boost. Power waffles made with a batter of buckwheat flour, rolled oats, a touch of cinnamon and beaten egg whites are the perfect choice, especially when served with warm maple syrup, sliced bananas and sugared sliced almonds.

Three weeks before: Send out invitations and arrange for spa helpers.

Two days before: Set up smoothie bar.

One day before: Prepare veggies for bruschetta and yogurt dip.

Two hours before: Prepare ingredients and accompaniments for shrimp curry. Prepare syrup for power waffles, cover and refrigerate.

Immediately before serving: Prepare shrimp curry.

The morning of: Make batter for power waffles. Heat syrup.

Shortcuts

A Sparkling Spa Party sounds ambitious—and it may be. But, it is a doable party that need not be intimidating. If your teen wants to run the gamut and offer tons of activities, you might consider splitting the party with her best friend and her mother to help in the preparations. You might also consider a trip to a local day spa that you take over for a couple of hours the evening of the party and head everyone back home for videos and a touch of spa popcorn. Maybe your spa party turns out to be you and your baby and her best buddy in the backyard hot tub. You braid their hair, do their nails, and offer foot rubs while eating pizza (with veggies of course). However you fashion your most special spa party—I guarantee you that it will turn out to be splendid fun.

Party Backdrop

Set the mood with an enticing invitation that is sure to set the entertaining tone for the party. In place of a perky printed note why not send a long handled wooden scrub brush—you know the kind used to get to those hard to reach places when you are taking a shower. Use a permanent marker to write the solicitation on the back paddle: "You are invited to Jenny's Splendid Spa Sleepover." Attach a card that includes all of the details—time, date, address and r.s.v.p. Punch a hole in the card. Tie a brightly colored ribbon through the hole to attach the card to the brush. If you are mailing the invitations, use a tube mailer and make sure to check for extra postage requirements. Just think of the faces on the gal pals when they open up that tube!

The Table Setting

Set the bruschetta on a tray and invite the girls to serve themselves. The same is true for the yogurt dip. Serve shrimp curry during a spa activity "time out." Shallow bowls easily house inverted rice and shrimp. Serve accompaniments in bowls on the side. Invite sleepy girls to the breakfast table with eye-opening poser waffles served on buffet plates with individual pitchers of warm syrup at each place.

CUCUMBER, TOMATO, and OLIVE BRUSCHETTA

A terrific munchie, bruschetta is easily adapted to any COOL party.

1	loaf French or Italian bread
1	tablespoon olive oil
1	medium clove garlic, peeled
1	medium cucumber, peeled, seeded, and diced
6	to 8 plum tomatoes, seeded and diced (about 2 cups)
½	cup chopped pitted black olives
2	tablespoons chopped fresh cilantro leaves
1	tablespoon tarragon vinegar
2	tablespoons olive oil

1. Cut the bread into ½-inch diagonal slices.
2. Brush one side of the bread with olive oil.
3. Grill the bread, brushed side down, over medium high heat until just toasted. (Alternatively, grill the bread in a grill pan on top of the stove.)
4. Rub the garlic over the grilled bread.
5. Combine the cucumber, tomatoes, olives, cilantro, vinegar, and oil in a small bowl. Toss well.
6. Mound the cucumber mixture onto the bruschetta.

Servings: 8
Preparation Time: 30 minutes

Experiment with all types of toppings for this easy dish. Be sure to use the freshest herbs and ripest veggies that are at the height of their flavor season. Here are some suggestions:

Diced yellow pepper, red onion and fresh tarragon.

Sliced avocado, sliced green onion and roasted red peppers with basil.

White bean, diced carrot, minced garlic, and chopped chives.

YOGURT DIP with TOASTED PITAS

Here is an easy-to-prepare veggie dip that is short on fat and tall in taste!

2	medium cloves garlic
4	green onions, sliced
1	medium carrot, cut into pieces
1	8-ounce can water chestnuts, drained
1	medium bunch broccoli florets (about 2 cups)
1	cup plain low fat yogurt
1	cup low fat sour cream
2	to 4 drops hot pepper sauce
	Salt and freshly ground pepper
4	4-inch pita rounds
1	tablespoon olive oil
2	tablespoons grated Parmesan cheese

1. Place the garlic, onions, carrot, water chestnuts, and broccoli into the bowl of a food processor. Pulse until the vegetables are very finely diced.

2. Add the yogurt and sour cream. Pulse to combine.
3. Season with hot pepper sauce, salt, and pepper.
4. Chill for 1 hour or overnight.

Preheat the oven to 400°.

5. Brush each pita round with olive oil. Sprinkle with Parmesan cheese. Cut into triangles.
6. Place the triangles onto a baking sheet.
7. Bake for 10 minutes, or until just beginning to turn golden.

Yield: 2 cups dip
Preparation Time: 30 minutes

Alter the veggies in this yummy dip to create a family favorite.

CURRIED SHRIMP served with WHITE RICE

Spectacular spa food takes only moments to make and depends on an attractive presentation—like the one found here.

2	**tablespoons olive oil**
1	**large yellow onion, diced (about 1 cup)**
1	**2-inch piece ginger, grated (about 2 tablespoons)**
4	**medium cloves garlic, minced (about 2 teaspoons)**
1	**tablespoon curry powder**
½	**teaspoon turmeric**
1	**14-ounce can unsweetened coconut milk**
2	**cups chicken broth**
3	**pounds large uncooked shrimp, peeled and deveined (about 48)**
	Salt and freshly ground pepper
¼	**cup chopped fresh parsley leaves**
	Zest of 1 medium lime (about 2 teaspoons)
4	**cups cooked white rice**
4	**green onions, thinly sliced on the diagonal**

1. Heat the olive oil in a skillet over medium high heat.
2. Cook the onion in the oil until soft, about 5 minutes.
3. Add the ginger and garlic and cook for 2 minutes more.
4. Stir in the curry powder and turmeric.
5. Pour in the coconut milk and chicken broth. Bring to a boil.
6. Simmer until the sauce reduces slightly and begins to thicken, about 10 minutes.
7. Add the shrimp. Cook until opaque, about 5 minutes.
8. Season with salt, pepper, parsley, and lime zest.
9. Place ½ cup rice into an 8-ounce ramekin or small bowl. Press to mold.
10. Invert the rice in a larger, shallow bowl.
11. Ladle the shrimp around the rice.
12. Garnish with thin pieces of green onion.

Servings: 8
Preparation Time: 30 minutes

Most of the shrimp in the market place has been previously frozen and then thawed for display. Many chefs recommend buying shrimp frozen and thawing only as many as you need for the dish. It is not advisable to freeze the shrimp after they have been thawed.

Curry is traditionally served with accompaniments. Select from any of the following: chopped green onion, chopped hard boiled eggs, chutney, shredded coconut, peanuts, diced cooked bacon, and raisins.

STRAWBERRY, PEACH, and BANANA SMOOTHIE

What a yummy, refreshing, fruit laden drink. Try one for a pick-me-up between workouts.

1   **cup white grape juice**
1   **cup low fat vanilla yogurt**
2   **peaches, sliced (about 2 cups)**
1   **pint strawberries, sliced (about 2 cups)**
1   **large banana, sliced (about 1 cup)**

Additional fruit for garnish

1. Chill the fruit in the freezer for 5 minutes.

2. Place half of each ingredient in a large blender.
3. Fill the blender with ice cubes. Pulse on high until the ingredients are emulsified.
4. Pour into 4 glasses. Garnish with peach and strawberry slices.
5. Repeat with remaining ingredients.

Servings: 8
Preparation Time: 15 minutes

Chilling the fruit before puréeing adds a terrific texture to the smoothie and guarantees a smoothie mustache on all the faces.

Power Waffles with Brown Sugar Syrup, Bananas, and Almonds

Holding the waffles in a warm oven directly on the rack maintains their crispness. Warm sugar syrup adds a real depth of flavor.

1½	cups all-purpose flour
½	cup old-fashioned oats
1	teaspoon ground cinnamon
1	teaspoon ground ginger
½	teaspoon salt
1	tablespoon sugar
2	teaspoons baking powder
3	egg yolks, beaten
¼	cup canola oil
1½	cups milk
1	teaspoon vanilla extract
3	egg whites

1	cup packed dark brown sugar
1	cup granulated sugar
¼	cup corn syrup
2	cups water
3	tablespoons butter
	Zest of ½ medium orange (about 1 tablespoons)

¼	cups sliced almonds
2	large bananas, sliced

Preheat a waffle iron.
Preheat the oven to 200°.

1. Whisk together in a large bowl the flour, oats, cinnamon, ginger, salt, sugar, and baking powder.
2. Whisk in the egg yolks, oil and milk.
3. Stir in the vanilla.
4. Use an electric mixer to beat the eggs until stiff peaks form.
5. Fold the egg whites into the batter.
6. Pour the batter onto the waffle iron and cook according to the manufacturers directions.
7. Place cooked waffles directly onto the rack in the warm oven. Continue until all of the batter has been used.
8. Cook the brown sugar, granulated sugar, corn syrup, and water in a saucepan over medium heat until it begins to boil.
9. Reduce the heat and simmer until the mixture begins to thicken, about 15 to 20 minutes.
10. Stir in the butter and orange zest. Let the syrup cool slightly to thicken.
11. Serve warm waffles with warm syrup and garnish with sliced almonds and bananas.

Servings: 8
Preparation Time: 40 minutes

For terrific waffles remember these tips:

Brush even non-stick waffle iron surfaces with a small amount of oil or a spray of vegetable oil spray to prevent sticking.

Use a rubber spatula to remove the waffle from the iron in place of a metal fork to maintain the surface of the iron.

Try not to over-pour the batter onto the iron. Start with half as much as you need and add more only after the batter has expanded to fill the surface.

Do not peek at the waffles while they are cooking. Instead depend on the timer or watch for the steam to reduce to almost nothing.

Experiment with savory waffles by omitting the sugar from the batter and adding fresh herbs, diced ham or bacon, and a sprinkling of grated cheese. Serve with sautéed chicken livers or mushrooms for a terrific first course.

Guilt-Free Parties

(LOW CALORIE PARTIES FOR EIGHT OR MORE)

Rustic Supper Party
Kitchen Soup Party
Very Veggie Celebration
Seaside Soiree

"As a professional party planner, I have five basic, yet not to be overlooked, key elements to a successful party. First, make sure you have great tasting food—and plenty of it. Presentation is important, but wonderful flavor is essential. Second, make sure that you have fun beverages that break the ice and put your guests at ease. Third, make sure you are playing continuous, appropriate, mood music. Fourth, make sure that your guest list is made up of a wide range of personalites. Hosts tend to believe that by bringing together similar groups of people that the collection will naturally be cohesive. Actually, the reverse is true. Our most successful parties are those where the mix includes everyone from the handyman to the CEO of one of Fortune's top 500 companies. The final, yet vital element to a successful party is to distinguish your event from all others—the element of surprise. This is crucial. A special theme for a unique occasion guarantees that your event will not blend into the woodwork."

Marley Majcher
The Party Goddess! Inc.
Pasadena, California
www.ThePartyGoddess.com

Rustic Supper Party Plan

Party Motivation

The girls getting together to celebrate a special occasion, a couple's block party, good pals reuniting for the evening. All are great reasons to celebrate in relaxed style.

Party Menu

Tomato, Onion, and Cucumber Salad with Black Bean Vinaigrette
Hearty Fisherman's Stew **
Multigrain Molasses Bread
Rustic Peach and Blueberry Tarts

** Over-the-Top Suggestion

This rustic stew is jam-packed, full of great tasting shellfish and chunks of diced fish. You need only use what you are comfortable with and feel free to substitute with your choice of the freshest fish you can find.

Party Strategy

Everything is prepared in advance for this party plan so that you can enjoy your guests and your supper.

One day ahead: Prepare the stew broth, cover and refrigerate.

The evening before: Prepare vegetables for salad. Make vinaigrette.

Four hours before: Bake bread in bread machine.

Two hours before: Prepare rustic tarts.

One hour before: Warm broth for stew.

Immediately before: Place fish in broth and simmer until cooked. Toss salad. Bake tarts.

Shortcuts

Make the tarts the day before and reheat just before serving.

Party Backdrop

Set the mood as a last glimpse of summer in Maine, on a wooden porch overlooking the ocean. An outdoor table works well. Indoors, a kitchen table is perfect. Use casual placemats and plenty of cloth napkins. This is a really hands-on menu, so roll up your sleeves and invite the group to dig in.

The Table Setting

Arrange the salad on a large platter or stacked into a shallow bowl. Serve vinaigrette from a ceramic pitcher. Pour the stew into a large bowl—or better yet, serve it from a huge soup pot. Provide a slotted spoon to scoop out fish and a ladle for the yummy broth. Set each place with bread plates, salad plates, a shallow bowl for the stew and an empty bowl for the shells. Fish forks and shell crackers are the perfect utensils for the meal. Serve the dessert warm on confectioner's sugar dusted plates with a scoop of ice cream and a sprig of mint.

TOMATO, ONION, and CUCUMBER SALAD with BLACK BEAN VINAIGRETTE

Sweet red and yellow peppers combine with spicy jalapeño to flavor fiber filled beans in this simple—yet tasty dressing. Choose a sweet Vidalia onion or one similar in taste for just the right balance of flavors in the salad.

4   **large beefsteak tomatoes, thinly sliced (about 4 cups)**
1   **large yellow onion, diced (about 1 cup)**
2   **medium cucumbers, thinly sliced (about 4 cups)**
1   **tablespoon chopped fresh cilantro leaves**

1   **large red bell pepper, seeded and cut into fourths**
1   **large yellow bell pepper, seeded and cut into fourths**
2   **medium jalapeño peppers, seeded and cut in half**
2   **medium cloves garlic, minced (about 1 teaspoon)**
3   **tablespoons sherry vinegar**
2   **tablespoons honey**

1   **tablespoon Dijon mustard**
¼   **cup olive oil**
1   **cup canned black beans**
    Salt and freshly ground pepper

1. Arrange slices of tomato, onion, and cucumber on a platter.
2. Sprinkle with chopped cilantro.
3. Use a blender or food processor to combine the peppers, garlic, vinegar, honey, mustard, oil, and black beans. Pulse to combine.
4. Season with salt and pepper.
5. Drizzle the dressing over the salad. Place additional dressing in a gravy boat alongside the platter.

Servings: 8
Preparation Time: 20 minutes

A mandoline is the perfect tool to use when cutting vegetables into very thin slices. It is a rectangular device that usually comes with an assortment of blades that are perfect for cutting into julienne, waffle cut or any desired thickness of slices. When choosing a mandoline, the most important component is the hand guard used to hold the vegetable while slicing.

Hearty Fisherman's Stew

The rich flavor of the stew broth seasons the seafood as it cooks. The dish works well for a party menu, because you can prepare the broth the day before and reheat it to simmer the seafood as guests arrive. Feel free to use the freshest seafood available and to substitute with lobster or clams.

3   tablespoons olive oil
1   large yellow onion, diced (about 1 cup)
2   large red bell peppers, diced (about 2 cups)
2   medium celery ribs, thinly sliced (about 1 cup)
6   medium cloves garlic, minced (about 2 teaspoons)
2   28-ounce cans diced tomatoes
1   6-ounce can tomato paste
6   8-ounce bottles clam juice
1½ cups white wine
2   tablespoons chopped fresh rosemary
2   tablespoons chopped fresh thyme leaves
1   tablespoon chopped fresh oregano leaves
2   tablespoons chopped fresh basil leaves
2   bay leaves
    Salt and freshly ground pepper

1   medium head escarole lettuce, washed, dried and torn into 1-inch pieces (about 4 cups)
1½ pounds salmon fillet, skinned, cut into 2-inch pieces
1½ pound grouper fillet, skinned, cut into 2-inch pieces
16 large sea scallops
1½ pounds large uncooked shrimp, peeled and deveined (about 24)
1½ pounds small mussels

2   tablespoons chopped fresh parsley leaves
    Garlic croutons

1. Heat the olive oil in a large Dutch oven over medium high heat.
2. Add onion, peppers, celery, and garlic and cook until soft, about 5 minutes.
3. Add the canned tomatoes. Stir in the tomato paste.
4. Stir in the clam juice, white wine, fresh herbs and bay leaves. Reduce the heat, simmer uncovered for 5 minutes. Season with salt and pepper. Remove the bay leaves.
5. Use an immersion blender to purée the stew base. (Alternatively, you may purée the stew base in a food processor or a blender.)
6. If the sauce is too thin, thicken it by adding a mixture of cornstarch and cold water. Thin a thick sauce by adding more clam juice or chicken stock.
7. Add the escarole and cook for 5 minutes.
8. Nestle the salmon, grouper, and sea scallops into the stew. Cook for 5 minutes.
9. Add the shrimp and mussels to the stew. Cook for 5 minutes or until the mussels have opened, the shrimp is opaque and the fish is cooked through.
10. Ladle the stew into shallow bowls. Garnish with chopped parsley and garlic croutons.

Servings: 8
Preparation Time: 1 hour

Prepare garlic croutons by slicing a loaf of French or Italian bread into 1 inch pieces. Place the cubed bread into a bowl. Sprinkle with garlic powder, dried oregano or basil, and a small amount of olive oil. Toss to coat the cubes. Place the bread on a baking sheet. Sprinkle with grated Parmesan Cheese. Bake at 350° for 5 to 10 minutes or until the croutons are golden brown.

MULTIGRAIN MOLASSES BREAD

Make this bread so that it is just done baking as your guests arrive. The aroma of fresh baked bread sets the tone for a warm and toasty party.

3½	**cups bread flour**
1	**cup water**
½	**cup milk**
¼	**cup yellow cornmeal**
¼	**cup old-fashioned rolled oats**
¼	**cup wheat flour**
¼	**cup molasses**
2	**tablespoons butter, cut into pieces**
1	**teaspoons salt**
2½	**teaspoons yeast**

1. Place the bread flour, water, milk, cornmeal, oats, wheat flour, molasses, butter, and salt into the bucket of a bread machine.
2. Pour the yeast in the yeast compartment (or follow the specific directions for your bread machine).
3. Select the bake cycle and start the bread machine.

Yield: 1 loaf
Preparation Time: 15 minutes plus bake cycle.

Molasses is syrup used to sweeten baked goods and sometimes as a topping on pancakes or ice cream. It is prepared by repeatedly boiling cane sugar. The darker the molasses, the more distinctive and bitter the taste. Molasses is easily stored in a jar with an air-tight lid in your pantry. A fairly good substitute for molasses is honey.

RUSTIC PEACH and BLUEBERRY TARTS

This rustic dessert is as fancy or as every day as you choose to present it. Garnish with a scoop of cinnamon vanilla ice cream, fresh mint leaves, and a sprinkle of confectioners' sugar to take it over-the-top.

1 17-ounce frozen package puff pastry

6 peaches, peeled and sliced (about 6 cups)
8 ounces fresh blueberries (about 1½ cups)
¼ cup granulated sugar
4 tablespoons apricot preserves
Candied Orange Peel (see sidebar)

Preheat the oven to 425
1. Thaw 2 sheets of puff pastry according to the package directions.
2. Roll out each pastry to ¼-inch thickness.
3. Place each pastry on a baking sheet lined with a Silpat liner (or with parchment paper).
4. Warm the apricot preserves in a small pan over low heat until just melted.
5. Brush each pastry sheet with 2 tablespoons melted preserves.
6. Combine the peaches and blueberries in a bowl with the sugar.
7. Place half of the peach mixture in the center of a pastry rectangle leaving a 3-inch border.
8. Fold the pastry toward the center of the peach mixture, pressing gently to seal. (The dough will only partially cover the fruit.) Repeat with remaining peaches and pastry.
9. Bake for 10 minutes. Reduce the heat to 350°. Bake for 20 minutes more or until the pastry crust is puffed and golden.
10. Serve warm or at room temperature. Cut each tart into 4 pieces. Garnish with candied orange zest.

Servings: 8 to 12
Preparation Time: 45 minutes

To prepare candied orange peel, simmer long, thin strips of peel in equal parts of water, sugar, and grenadine syrup for 10 to 15 minutes. Place in a bowl, cover, and refrigerate until needed.

Kitchen Soup and Salad Party Plan

Party Motivation

The soup and salad bar's calling your name. A great way to choose veggie-filled meals—why not share the plan with your pals!

Party Menu

Beet, Apple, and Goat Cheese Salad with Orange-Shallot Vinaigrette
Harvest Vegetable Soup with Corn Dumplings **
Down Home on the Ranch Salad
Southwestern-Style Chicken Soup
Cocoa Angel Food Cake with Raspberry Sauce

**** Over-the-Top Suggestion**

Fresh corn and sliced okra takes Harvest Soup way, way over the top!

Party Strategy

Make the soups in advance. Cover and refrigerate in their pots. Reheat as guests begin to arrive. Prepare all of the ingredients and dressings for the salad and toss at the last moment.

Two days in advance: Prepare chicken soup, cover and refrigerate.

One day in advance: Prepare vegetable soup, cover and refrigerate. Prepare dumplings, cover and refrigerate.

The morning of: Prepare salad dressings. Chop veggies for salads.

One hour before: Warm soups on stovetop.

Immediately before: Toss salads. Add dumplings.

Shortcuts

Feel free to substitute frozen spinach in Harvest Vegetable soup to save time.

Party Backdrop

This really is a kitchen party. Bubbling hot soups stay hot on the stove top while chilled salads sit on the counter. Place the airy cake onto a pedestal cake plate in the center of the table to make sure everyone saves room for dessert.

The Table Setting

Stack bowls and soup spoons near the pots of soup with ladles nearby. Serve the salads from wooden or ceramic salad bowls with extra dressing nearby. Use a fork-tined cake slicer or two forks to gently pull slices from the angel food cake. Drizzle raspberry sauce from a pitcher directly onto the dessert place. Dust with a shaker filled with confectioner's sugar.

Beet, Apple and Goat Cheese Salad
with Orange-Shallot Dressing

Beets are a popular addition to salads because they are packed full of healthy stuff. Beware of handling, lest your fingers are dyed red for days to come.

2   pounds medium red beets
     Salt and freshly ground pepper
     Olive oil for drizzling
1   pound Granny Smith apples
6   medium heads Boston lettuce, washed, dried and torn into 1-inch pieces, about 12 cups

4   large shallots, minced (about ¼ cup)
     Juice of 1 medium orange (about ⅓ cup)
2   tablespoons red wine vinegar
1   teaspoon granulated sugar
⅓   cup olive oil
     Salt and freshly ground pepper
6   ounces goat cheese, crumbled

Preheat the oven to 400°.

1. Roast the beats by placing them on a sheet of aluminum foil. Season with salt and pepper and a drizzle of olive oil. Wrap the foil around the beets. Place the aluminum foil onto a baking sheet. Bake for 60 minutes or until the beets are tender. Cool.
2. Peel the beets and slice into thin strips.
3. Cut the apples into thin slices.
4. Place the lettuce into a large salad bowl.
5. Toss in the beets and apples.
6. Whisk together the shallots, orange juice, red wine vinegar, and sugar in a small bowl.
7. Slowly whisk in the olive oil. Season with salt and pepper.
8. Drizzle the salad dressing over the salad and toss until the leaves are just moistened.
9. Top with crumbled goat cheese.

Servings: 8
Preparation Time: 30 minutes plus roasting

There are many varieties of beets available in the market place from pink, white, golden, and even striped. The most popular are the deep red beets that are most often the size of a medium lemon. Choose beets that have the greens and about 2 inches of root attached. They should be firm and smooth with no signs of bruising. Because of their dark color, you may want to use plastic gloves when handling and work on parchment paper rather than your best wood cutting board.

Harvest Vegetable Soup with Corn Dumplings

Use the freshest vegetables that you can find for ingredients in this simple soup. The corn dumplings add a nice surprise.

2	**tablespoons olive oil**
2	**large yellow onions, diced (about 2 cups)**
4	**medium cloves garlic, minced (about 2 teaspoons)**
1	**large red bell pepper, cut into ½-inch dice (about 1 cup)**
4	**quarts chicken broth**
1	**28-ounce can diced tomatoes**
3	**medium sweet potatoes, cut into ½-inch dice (about 2 cups)**
8	**ounces green beans, cut into 1-inch pieces (about 1 cup)**
2	**large carrots, diced (about ½ cup)**
2	**medium zucchini, cut into ½-inch dice (about 2 cups)**
1	**pound spinach leaves, chopped (about 5 cups)**
1	**15-ounce can navy beans, drained**
¼	**cup chopped fresh parsley leaves**
1	**teaspoon dried red pepper flakes**
	Salt and freshly ground pepper
1	**cup all-purpose flour**
1	**tablespoon cornmeal**
1½	**teaspoons baking powder**
1	**teaspoon sugar**
½	**teaspoon salt**
1	**tablespoon butter, cut into pieces**
2	**tablespoons chopped fresh basil leaves**
⅓	**cup milk**
½	**cup canned corn, drained**

1. Heat the olive oil in a large pot over medium high heat.
2. Add the onions, garlic, and red pepper to the pan. Cook until the vegetables are soft, about 5 minutes.
3. Pour the chicken broth into the pan. Stir in the diced tomatoes.
4. Add the sweet potatoes, green beans, carrots, and zucchini. Reduce heat and simmer for 20 minutes or until the vegetables are soft.
5. Stir in the spinach, navy beans, and parsley. Season with red pepper flakes, salt, and pepper. Simmer for 5 minutes more.
6. Place the flour, cornmeal, baking powder, sugar and salt into the bowl of a food processor.
7. Place the butter pieces into the bowl and pulse until the mixture resembles course crumbs.
8. Place this mixture into a bowl. Stir in the basil, milk, and corn. Stir until just moist.
9. Bring the soup to a boil.
10. Form 8 dumplings by rounded tablespoon. Drop each one into the soup.
11. Cover the soup pot. Reduce the heat to medium low and simmer for 10 minutes or until the dumplings are cooked through.

Servings: 8
Preparation Time: 1 hour

Dumplings are small balls of dough that can be either savory or sweet. The dough is then poached in flavorful liquid and the dumpling is served as an accompaniment to the main dish.

Down Home on the Ranch Salad

A terrific salad that you can make in minutes—is just as good for you as it is great-tasting.

1 cup buttermilk
½ cup prepared salsa
¼ cup mayonnaise
2 tablespoons chopped fresh cilantro leaves
Juice of ½ lime (about 1 tablespoon)
1 tablespoon mustard
1 teaspoon granulated sugar
Salt and freshly ground pepper

12 cups fresh salad greens
1 pint ripe grape tomatoes (about 2 cups)
12 whole radishes, sliced (about 1 cup)
4 green onions, thinly sliced (about ¼ cup)
1 cup canned red beans, drained

1 cup tortilla chips, broken into pieces
1 cup grated extra sharp Cheddar cheese

1. Mix together in a small bowl the buttermilk, salsa, mayonnaise, cilantro, lime juice, mustard, and sugar. Season with salt and pepper.
2. Place the salad greens in a large bowl.
3. Toss in the tomatoes, radishes, onions, red beans, and tortilla pieces.
4. Sprinkle with grated Cheddar cheese.
5. Serve the salad chilled with the dressing on the side.

Servings: 8
Preparation Time: 30 minutes

This salad begs for ingredient substitutions with anything that you keep on hand in your pantry and fridge. Try black beans in place of red, Monterey Jack cheese in place of Cheddar, garlic croutons in place of crumbled tortilla chips, or chili sauce in place of salsa.

SOUTHWESTERN-STYLE CHICKEN SOUP

A fun twist on traditional chicken soup, this one is guaranteed to diminish sniffles while increasing smiles!

2	**6- to 8-ounce chicken breast halves with rib**
4	**4- to 6-ounce chicken thighs**
4	**quarts chicken broth**
2	**medium celery ribs, cut into thin slices (about 1 cup)**
2	**large carrots, cut into thin slices (about ½ cup)**
2	**medium white onion, diced (about 1⅓ cup)**
4	**medium cloves garlic, minced (about 2 teaspoons)**
2	**medium jalapeño peppers, seeded and diced (about 4 tablespoons)**
4	**ears fresh corn, corn sliced from cob (about 2 cups)**
1	**16-ounce can black beans, drained**
1	**16-ounce can diced tomatoes**
1	**teaspoon ground cumin**
1	**teaspoon chili power**
1	**tablespoon chopped fresh parsley leaves**
	Salt and freshly ground pepper

Guacamole
Yogurt
Baked tortilla strips

1. Place the chicken pieces in the bottom of a large pot.
2. Pour the chicken stock into the pan and bring to a boil over medium high heat.
3. Add the celery, carrots, onion, garlic, and jalapeño pepper to the pot. Reduce heat to medium and simmer for 20 to 30 minutes or until the chicken is cooked through.
4. Remove the chicken to a platter.
5. Add the corn, black beans, and tomatoes to the pot.
6. Stir in the cumin, chili powder, and parsley. Season with salt and pepper. Simmer for 10 minutes.
7. Remove the skin from the chicken pieces. Remove the meat from the bone and shred or cut into small pieces.
8. Place the meat back into the pot. Adjust seasonings.
9. Ladle the soup into bowls. Garnish with guacamole, yogurt, and baked tortilla strips.

Servings: 8
Preparation Time: 40 minutes

Prepare baked tortilla strips for garnish by cutting 4 (6-inch) corn tortillas into ¼-inch strips. Place the strips onto a baking sheet that has been lightly coated with vegetable oil spray. Sprinkle with garlic powder. Bake for 5 minutes, turning once so the strips are just golden brown.

Cocoa Angel Food Cake with Raspberry Sauce

This airy cake takes a little time, but is well worth the effort. Sifting is an important part of maintaining the lightness of the batter. Try not to skip this step.

1   cup cake flour
½   cup confectioners' sugar
½   teaspoon salt
1   cup granulated sugar
¼   cup cocoa powder
10   egg whites
1   teaspoon cream of tartar
½   teaspoon salt
1   teaspoon vanilla extract

1   pint fresh raspberries (about 1½ cups)
⅓   cup raspberry preserves
⅓   cup water
½   cup granulated sugar

Preheat the oven to 350°.

1. Sift the cake flour with ½ cup confectioner's sugar and the salt. Set aside.
2. Sift the granulated sugar with the cocoa powder. Set aside.
3. Use an electric mixer to whip the egg whites until foamy.
4. Add the cream of tartar. Continue beating until the egg whites form stiff peaks.
5. Fold in the vanilla.
6. Fold in ¼ of the flour/confectioners' sugar mixture.

7. Fold in ¼ of the sugar/cocoa mixture.
8. Continue until all of the flour and sugar mixtures have been incorporated into the batter.
9. Pour the batter into an ungreased 10 x 3-inch tube pan. Bake in the lower third of the oven for 45 minutes.
10. Remove the cake from the oven. Invert the pan onto a funnel or bottle. Let cool completely. Loosen the cake from the sides of the pan with a knife. Turn out the cake onto a platter.
11. Place the raspberries, raspberry preserves, water, and granulated sugar into a pan. Bring to a boil over medium high heat. Cook for 1 minute. Use the back of a wooden spoon to mash the fruit. (Alternatively, you may purée the sauce with an immersion blender or a food mill.) The sauce will be thick and syrupy. Cook for 1 minute. Cool.
12. Place a swirl of raspberry sauce on a plate. Slide a slice of cake on top. Garnish with a shake of confectioners' sugar and fresh mint sprigs.

Servings: 8 to 12
Preparation Time: 25 minutes plus baking

If your electric mixer comes with a copper bowl, now is the time to use it.
The combination of a copper bowl and a bit of cream of tartar stabilizes the egg whites and makes for a very light cake. Do not slice the cake with a knife, it will smoosh like a sponge.
Instead use two forks to flake the cake slices. Or use a cake divider, which is a comb-like serving utensil that has a set of long tines held together by a strong handle.

Very Veggie Celebration Party Plan

Party Motivation
Card night and you are in charge of the food. The emphasis is on the game, so you want everything ready when the group gets hungry.

Party Menu

Jicama Slaw with Sesame Dressing
Veggie Burgers with Spicy Cranberry Mayonnaise
Roasted Root Vegetables with Balsamic Glaze
Lemon Pound Cake with Blueberry Sauce **

** Over-the-Top Suggestion
Add strawberries and raspberries to blueberries for a super berry sauce that is great on lemon cake and everything else that you can think of!

Party Strategy
Indoor grilling is the key to this fun menu. The salad and cake are prepared a day in advance and the veggies roast while the burgers cook.
One day ahead: Bake cake and prepare berry sauce. Slice veggies for slaw. Prepare dressing.
The evening before: assemble salad, cover and refrigerate.
The morning of: Prepare veggies for roasting.
Two hours before: Make veggie patties and refrigerate. Prepare cranberry sauce.
One hour before: Roast veggies and prepare glaze.

Shortcuts
If fresh jicama is unavailable, try your supermarket freezer. If not, fennel is a good substitute. Dice casserole veggies into small, similar size pieces for a shorter roasting time.

Party Backdrop
Set up a game table in the middle of the family room. Set s small table with beverages, ice and glasses. Throw a tablecloth or light blanket over the kitchen counter. Set platters and baskets on top.

The Table Setting

A buffet plate is the only dish required for the meal. Serve the salad from a large bowl. Pile assembled veggie burgers into a large basket lined with colorful napkins. Serve cranberry mayonnaise from a bowl on the side. Roasted veggies come to the counter in the baking pan that they have roasted in. When the game ends, serve the lemony cake. The looser gets the first slice!

JICAMA SLAW with SESAME DRESSING

This crisp salad is easily made in advance and then tossed at the last second for a refreshing side dish that is meant to be an evolution of traditional coleslaw.

¼ cup honey
   Juice of 1 medium orange (about ⅓ cup)
2 tablespoons sesame oil
1 tablespoon soy sauce
1 ½-inch piece ginger, peeled and minced (about 1 teaspoon)
½ cup olive oil
   Salt and freshly ground pepper

1 large jicama, peeled and cut into matchstick-size pieces (about 2 cups)
2 large cucumbers, peeled, seeded and cut into matchstick-size pieces
1 large red bell pepper, seeded and cut into matchstick-size pieces (about 1 cup)
1 large yellow bell pepper, seeded and cut into matchstick-size pieces (about 1 cup)

1 large carrot, peeled and cut into matchstick size pieces (about ¼ cup)
1 tablespoon sesame seeds
¼ cup fresh parsley leaves

1. Whisk together the honey, orange juice, sesame oil, soy sauce, and minced ginger in a small bowl.
2. Slowly whisk in the olive oil. Season with salt and pepper.
3. Combine the vegetables in a large bowl. Sprinkle with sesame seeds and parsley and toss. Drizzle with enough dressing to just coat the vegetables.
4. Serve chilled.

Servings: 8
Preparation Time: 30 minutes

To peel jicama, cut the vegetable in half horizontally. Cut off the root and stem ends. Use a paring knife to cut the peel from the horizontal cut down to the root. Turn and repeat on all sides. The peel is way too thick to use a vegetable peeler. But, if you are tenacious, you can try to peel it off in strips with your fingers.

Veggie Burgers with Spicy Cranberry Mayonnaise

Perfect for an outdoor grill or just as easily baked or sautéed, these burgers are an easy treat and designed to be made in advance of your guest's arrival.

2	cups dry lentils
4	cups water
1	tablespoon olive oil
2	8-ounce packages portobello mushrooms, chopped into ¼-inch dice (about 3 cups)
1	16-ounce can red kidney beans, drained and mashed
1	cup whole wheat bread crumbs
½	medium white onion, finely diced (about ⅓ cup)
4	medium cloves garlic, roasted and mashed
1	tablespoon Worcestershire sauce
2	tablespoons chopped fresh thyme leaves
1	large egg
	Salt and freshly ground pepper
1	cup mayonnaise
½	cup canned whole berry cranberry sauce
½	medium jalapeño pepper, seeded and finely diced (about 1 tablespoon)
1	teaspoon cumin
8	whole wheat buns, toasted
	Beefsteak tomatoes
	Red onion

1. Place the lentils in a pot over medium heat. Cover with 4 cups of water. Simmer until the lentils are soft, about 30 minutes. Remove 1 cup of the cooked lentils to a large bowl. Mash the remaining lentils.

2. Heat the olive oil in a skillet over medium high heat. Cook the diced mushrooms until softened, about 5 minutes.

3. Place the mashed lentils and mushrooms into a large bowl.

4. Add the kidney beans, bread crumbs, onion, roasted garlic, and Worcestershire to the bowl. Mix well.

5. Add the thyme, reserved whole lentils, and egg. Season with salt and pepper.

6. Use your hands to form the mixture into 8 large patties. Place each patty on a baking sheet and refrigerate for 2 hours.

7. Mix together the mayonnaise, cranberry sauce, jalapeño, and cumin in a small bowl.

8. Cook the patties over a hot grill or in a grill pan for 5 minutes per side or until golden brown.

9. Serve on toasted whole wheat buns with slices of ripe beefsteak tomatoes, red onion, and a dollop of the mayonnaise.

Servings: 8
Preparation Time: 45 minutes plus refrigeration

Roast whole heads of garlic for use in every day recipes. Cut the top from the bulb. Place onto a sheet of aluminum foil. Sprinkle with olive oil, dried oregano, salt and pepper. Loosely wrap the garlic in the foil. Bake for 30 to 45 minutes at 350°., or until the cloves are golden and beginning to burst from the garlic. Cool and refrigerate extras in an airtight container, or remove the cloves and place the roasted garlic into a small container.

ROASTED ROOT VEGETABLES with BALSAMIC GLAZE

The simple glaze adds a little oomph to the garden fresh veggies in this dish.

1	medium rutabaga, cut into 1-inch pieces (about 3 cups)
6	to 8 small red potatoes, cut into wedges (about 2 cups)
2	medium parsnips, peeled and cut into 1-inch pieces (about ½ pound)
3	medium turnips, peeled and cut into 1-inch pieces (about 1 pound)
6	medium carrots, peeled and cut into 1-inch pieces (about 1 pound)
1	fennel bulb, cut into 1-inch pieces (about 2 cups)
½	cup sesame oil
1	teaspoon dried oregano
¼	cup fresh thyme leaves
	Salt and freshly ground pepper
½	cup balsamic vinegar
2	tablespoons mustard
1	teaspoon dried oregano

Preheat the oven to 375°.

1. Place all of the vegetables into a large baking dish.
2. Toss with sesame oil, 1 teaspoon of dried oregano, and thyme sprigs. Season with salt and pepper.
3. Roast for 1 hour or until the vegetables are golden brown and tender.
4. Place the vinegar in a small saucepan over medium high heat. Stir in mustard and 1 teaspoon dried oregano. Simmer for 2 minutes or until reduced slightly.
5. Pour the vinegar sauce over the roasted veggies. Roast for 5 minutes more.

Servings: 8
Preparation Time: 30 minutes plus roasting

Roasted root vegetables are an elegant yet simple enhancement to any party menu. Although most are available year round, feel free to use only your favorites or those that are abundantly in season for this recipe.

LEMON POUND CAKE with BLUEBERRY SAUCE

This tangy cake is the perfect ending to a veggie laden meal. Enjoy the syrupy sauce over every delicate slice.

2 **cups cake flour**
1 **teaspoon baking powder**
½ **teaspoon salt**
1 **cup granulated sugar**
½ **cup butter, room temperature (1 stick)**
1 **large egg**
½ **cup milk**
  Zest of 1 medium lemon (about 1 tablespoon)
½ **teaspoon lemon extract**
2 **large egg whites**

  Juice of 3 lemons (about ½ cup)
⅓ **cup granulated sugar**
1 **teaspoon ground ginger**
½ **teaspoon ground cinnamon**
8 **ounces fresh blueberries (about 1½ cups)**

  Confectioners' sugar

Preheat the oven to 350°.
1. Combine the cake flour, baking powder, and salt in a bowl. Set aside.
2. Use an electric mixer to beat 1 cup of sugar and the butter together until light and fluffy.
3. Mix in the egg.
4. Add the flour mixture and milk in 3 additions alternating ⅓ flour mixture with ⅓ milk until all of the milk and flour are incorporated into the batter.
5. Stir in the lemon zest and extract.
6. Use an electric mixer to beat the egg whites until stiff peaks form.
7. Fold the egg whites into the batter.
8. Pour the batter into an 8 x 4-inch loaf pan that has been sprayed with vegetable oil spray.
9. Bake for 45 to 50 minutes or until a toothpick inserted into the center of the cake comes out clean.
10. Pour the lemon juice into a saucepan over medium high heat.
11. Stir in the sugar, ginger and cinnamon. Bring to a boil.
12. Gently stir in the blueberries. Cook for 1 minute. Cool.
13. Serve each slice of cake with a drizzle of blueberry sauce and a splash of confectioners' sugar.

Servings: 8
Preparation Time: 45 minutes plus baking

To insure even baking, place the cake in the middle of a preheated oven. Once it is in—do not open the door because the heat escapes every time that you do. Cakes bake best when the heat is even. Check the cake with 10 minutes left in the baking time. You will be able to tell if the cake is done by gently pushing your finger into the top. When the cake springs back check to see if it is finished.

Seaside Soirée Party Plan

Party Motivation

You and the gang are getting together for an informal supper at the beach. Everyone brings a dish and you coordinate the menu. Upscale take-out is definitely in order. Include foods that are delicious served at room temperature and keep those that are served cool on ice.

Party Menu

Seviche in a Martini Glass
Sweet and Sour Pearl Onions
Roasted Butternut Squash and Toasted Corn Ratatouille with Paprika Oil
Wild Rice and Veggie Pilaf
Banana Bread Cookies **

** Over-the-Top Suggestion

Dip cooled cookies into warm chocolate for a dessert that is totally yummy.

Party Strategy

Prepare foods that are easy to pack, transport and present. Non fussy but great-tasting dishes are a must.

One day before: Prepare ratatouille. Cover and refrigerate. Bake cookies, store in an airtight container. Prepare onions, cover and refrigerate.

The morning of: Prepare rice pilaf, cover and refrigerate.

Four hours in advance: Prepare seviche, cover and refrigerate.

One hour before: Pack up party and go to the beach.

Shortcuts

Use frozen pearl onions to eliminate boiling and peeling. Use quick cooking rice in place of the slower cooking wild rice.

Party Backdrop

Throw a beach blanket onto a picnic table or onto the sand. Make sure that there are plenty of lounge chairs, plastic cups for beverages, plastic utensils and plates for easy clean up and some vintage Beach Boy albums playing on the boom box.

The Table Setting

Pack a large picnic basket with tablecloths, plates, utensils and cups. Plastic martini glasses are perfect for the seviche. Set the container holding the seviche in a cooler on ice. The flavors are best when served at room temperature—not too chilled and definitely not warm. Spoon seviche into the glasses and toast each pal.

Serve the ratatouille, wild rice and sweet and sour onions from individual Chinese take-out containers packed in advance. These are available at restaurant supply stores and make for great picnic presentation. A large Chinese take-out container holds the yummy cookies and passes from one friend to another. Fortune telling anyone?

SEVICHE in a MARTINI GLASS

Here is a light first course that is presented whimsically signally the start of a fun meal.

2   pounds fresh snapper fillet, skin
    removed, cut into ½-inch cubes
1   medium white onion, diced (about ⅔
    cup)
3   cups lime juice

6   to 8 plum tomatoes, seeded and diced
    (about 2 cups)
2   medium jalapeño pepper, seeded and
    diced (about 4 tablespoons
2   large oranges, peeled, sectioned, and
    roughly chopped (about 1 cup)
1   4¼-ounce can, green olives, chopped
    (about ⅔ cup)
2   tablespoons chopped fresh cilantro
    leaves
2   large avocados, diced (about 2 cups)
    Salt and freshly ground pepper

1. Place the snapper and diced onion in a large
   bowl.
2. Cover the snapper mixture with lime juice.
   The fish should be completely covered with
   liquid.
3. Cover the bowl and refrigerate for 3 to 4
   hours until the fish is "cooked through" and
   opaque in color.
4. Gently drain the mixture through a colander.
5. Add the chopped tomatoes, peppers, orange
   sections, olives, cilantro, and avocado to the
   fish. Stir gently.
6. Season with salt and freshly ground pepper.
7. Place a spoonful of the seviche into a martini
   glass. Garnish with a sprig of fresh cilantro
   and a green olive on a toothpick.

Serves 8
Preparation Time: 20 minutes plus "cooking"

Lime juice acts as the cooking agent for the snapper in this dish. The acidity of the citrus changes the elements of the fish to produce the desired result. Feel free to substitute with other types of fish or shellfish. Try fresh grouper or scallops for an equally yummy result.

SWEET and SOUR PEARL ONIONS

This dish takes the place of chutney or savory marmalade.

1½ **pounds pearl onions, peeled**
½ **cup white wine vinegar**
3 **tablespoons olive oil**
3 **tablespoons honey**
3 **tablespoons tomato paste**
1 **bay leaf**
½ **cup fresh mint sprigs**
½ **cup golden raisins**
 Salt and freshly ground pepper

1. Place the onions, vinegar, olive oil, honey, tomato paste, bay leaf, mint sprigs,k and raisins in a saucepan over medium heat with 2 cups water. Simmer uncovered for 30 to 45 minutes or until the onions are soft and the liquid is syrupy.
2. Season with salt and pepper.
3. Remove bay leaf and mint sprigs.
4. Serve warm.

Servings: 8
Preparation Time: 20 minutes plus cooking.

Peeling pearl onions is easy if you blanche them first. Use a pairing knife to place two crossed slits in the root end of each onion. Bring a saucepan half full with water to a boil over medium high heat. Place the onions in the boiling water. When the water returns to a boil, cook the onions for 1 minute. Place the onions in ice water to stop the cooking process. Pinch the onions to remove the skin.

ROASTED BUTTERNUT SQUASH and TOASTED CORN RATATOUILLE with PAPRIKA OIL

Ratatouille is a vegetable stew originating in the Provence region of France and traditionally consists of eggplant, zucchini, onion, and yellow squash. I've taken some gigantic liberties here to offer a hearty vegetable stew with a hint of the conventional dish.

2	medium butternut squash, peeled and diced into 1-inch squares (about 4 cups)
¼	cup olive oil
4	ears fresh corn, corn sliced from cob (about 2 cups)
2	large green bell peppers, chopped into 1 inch pieces (about 2 cups)
1	medium red onion, diced (about 1 cup)
2	large zucchini, sliced into rounds (about 4 cups)
	Salt and freshly ground pepper
1	28-ounce can tomatoes, crushed
1	16-ounce can cannellini beans
2	tablespoons chopped fresh basil
2	tablespoons chopped fresh parsley
	Salt and freshly ground pepper
3	ounces Gorgonzola cheese, crumbled (about ½ cup)
½	cup olive oil
4	medium cloves garlic
1	tablespoon Hungarian paprika (or any hot paprika)

Preheat the oven to 350°.

1. Place the squash cubes in a baking pan. Toss with 1 tablespoon olive oil. Bake for 30 to 40 minutes or until the squash is soft.

2. Heat 1 tablespoon olive oil in a skillet over medium high heat. Toast the corn kernels until just beginning to brown, about 5 minutes. Remove from the pan.

3. In the same skillet heat the remaining 2 tablespoons olive oil over medium high heat.

4. Add the bell pepper, onion, and zucchini to the pan and cook until just soft, about 10 minutes.

5. Add the roasted squash and toasted corn to the pan. Season with salt and pepper.

6. Stir in the tomatoes and beans.

7. Stir in the herbs and adjust seasonings.

8. Pour the mixture into a large baking dish. Sprinkle with Gorgonzola cheese. Bake for 20 to 30 minutes or until the cheese is melted and the casserole is bubbling.

9. Heat ½ cup of olive oil over medium heat. Add the garlic and cook until golden, about 4 minutes. Stir in the paprika. Remove from the heat. Remove the garlic and reserve for another use. Pour the oil into a squeeze bottle.

10. Season the hot ratatouille with paprika flavored oil.

Servings: 8
Preparation Time: 1 hour plus baking

Paprika is made from ground red peppers. Depending on the peppers used, paprika can be found sweet, half-sweet or hot. Hungary and Spain are the biggest suppliers of paprika. This spice works well as a flavoring in savory dishes, as a coloring in soups or stews, and as a garnish when dusted onto a serving plate.

WILD RICE and VEGGIE PILAF

This simple side dish is easily prepared and cooks while you assemble the rest of the meal. Feel free to substitute with any veggie that you have on hand to create your own favorite rice dish.

1	**tablespoon olive oil**
1	**bunch (6 to 8) green onions, chopped (about 1 cup)**
1	**large red bell pepper, seeded and diced (about 1 cup)**
½	**pound shiitake mushrooms, diced (about 1½ cups)**
1	**cup frozen corn**
1	**cup wild rice**
1	**teaspoon ground coriander**
	Salt and freshly ground pepper
2½	**cups water**

1. Heat the olive oil in a saucepan over medium high heat.

2. Add the onions and pepper and cook until soft.
3. Add the mushroom and corn and cook for 2 minutes.
4. Add the rice and stir.
5. Season with coriander, salt, and freshly ground pepper.
6. Cover the rice with water and bring to a boil. Reduce the heat to a simmer, cover, and cook until all of the water is absorbed and the rice is tender and fluffy, about 45 minutes for wild rice.

Serves 4
Preparation Time: 15 minutes plus cooking

Different varieties of rice require different amounts of water and cooking time. For best results follow the directions on the package. When using true wild rice first rinse the rice under cold water. Add enough water to cover the amount of rice that you are using by 3 inches. Pour in the rice and cook for 30 to 45 minutes.

Banana Bread Cookies

Good friend Gail contributes this recipe. She says that these cookies are not fancy. In fact, they are the ones that you whip up in the morning for impromptu guests or neighborhood bake sales. Perfect for parties!

2   **cups all-purpose flour**
¼   **teaspoon salt**
1   **teaspoon baking soda**

¾   **cup margarine (1½ sticks), room temperature**
¾   **cup granulated sugar**
1   **large egg**
½   **teaspoon vanilla extract**
2   **ripe bananas, mashed**

Preheat the oven to 350°.

1. Combine the flour, salt, and baking soda in a small bowl.
2. Use an electric mixer to beat the shortening and sugar until light and fluffy.
3. Stir in the egg, vanilla, and mashed bananas.
4. Stir in the flour in 3 additions.
5. Place the cookies by rounded teaspoons onto a baking sheet that is lined with a Silpat liner, parchment paper, or coated with vegetable oil spray.
6. Bake for 8 minutes or until the cookies just begin to brown on the edges.
7. Remove the cookies to a rack to cool.

Yield: 2 dozen cookies
Preparation Time: 15 minutes

This simple cookie lends itself to all types of additions. Gail suggests adding nuts, raisins or chocolate chips to the batter. My favorite is to dip one half of the cookie into melted chocolate and allow to set up on a rack.

Sparkling Sit Down Affairs

(SIT-DOWN PARTIES FOR EIGHT OR MORE)

Guess Who's Coming to Dinner
Monthly Supper Club
Saturday Night's Special
Dazzling New Year's Eve

"Planning and preparation are the keys to participation. A hostess should be helpful to her guests, educating them on dress and other party details so that there are no surprises. The more information given, the more comfortable the guests will be. Courtesy suggests that hosts and hostesses appear relaxed, yet be absolutely attentive to the needs of each of their guests."

Dana May Casperson
Author of *Power Etiquette: What You Don't Know Can Kill The Deal*
Power Etiquette Group
Santa Rosa, California
www.PowerEtiquette.com

Guess Who's Coming To Dinner Party Plan

Party Motivation

You are entertaining your spouse's big client, or perhaps meeting future in-laws. The perfect party solution is a sit-down affair meant to impress your guests and let them know that the time and effort you have put forward is designed to welcome them by offering an evening to remember.

Party Menu

Chilled Three Green Soup with Crab Relish
Arugula, Tomato, and Blue Cheese Salad with Dill Vinaigrette
Sautéed Snapper with Orange Butter Sauce
Rosemary Zucchini Cakes
Coconut Crème Brulée **

** Over-the-Top Suggestion

Bring the individual desserts to the table on a tray. Sprinkle each with granulated sugar. Use a kitchen torch to brown the sugar topping in front of your guests. (Practice first—just to be sure you know how to operate the torch without burning the top of the Brule— or your guests!) Top with a sprinkle of toasted coconut.

Party Strategy

Place both the chilled soup and the fresh salad on the table before you invite your guests to be seated. The zucchini cakes and the fish can be mostly prepared and then held in the oven while your guests enjoy their first (and second) course.

The day before: Prepare desserts, cover and chill.

The evening before: Prepare soup, cover and chill. Prepare ingredients for salad and dressing.

The morning of: Prepare ingredients for zucchini cakes. Set the table. Arrange centerpieces.

Two hours before: Prepare crab relish. Assemble zucchini cakes.

Thirty minutes before: Cook zucchini cakes. Finish baking as your guests come to the table.

Immediately before the guests arrive: Prepare fish by slightly undercooking each fillet. Remove the fish to a platter and keep warm in a warming drawer or in an oven on the lowest setting. Prepare the sauce through step 8. Remove from heat. Just before serving, reheat the sauce, stir in the chilled butter and pour over the fish.

Shortcuts

If time is short, a dollop of sour cream and fresh dill sprigs will suffice as a garnish for the chilled soup.

Party Backdrop

The dining room is the place for this party, unless you set a formal table outside on a patio. Lay a crisp cloth with matching (or complimenting) napkins. Small bowls of roses set down the center of the table makes for a wonderful centerpiece as well as a gorgeous favor for your guests to take home after the meal. Make sure the flowers are low enough so that when seated each guest can see over the arrangement easily. Votive candles add just the right amount of atmosphere.

The Table Setting

Set your best table—with your best china. Feel free to mix and match. Use over-sized white buffet plates as chargers and blue flowered dinner plates for the main course. Use huge rose colored coffee cups for the cold soup and the matching saucer for bread plates. Choose whatever combination you want as long as all of the components compliment each other without clashing.

Place cold soup directly onto a charger plate—or on top of a dinner plate. When your guests have eaten, remove both plates and the utensils. Beginning at the left of the place setting set a salad fork for the salad and a dinner fork for the main course. To the right of the plate set a knife, spoon and soup spoon. Place a dessert fork or extra spoon at the top of the plate. Place butter knives onto the butter plate.

After you (and hopefully a helper) have removed the salad and soup from the table, arrange the main course plate in the kitchen. Remember you are the host/hostess. Your guests will not begin savoring your wonderful meal until you sit down and invite them to begin.

CHILLED THREE GREEN SOUP with CRAB RELISH

The color of this soup matches the brilliance of the flavors.

1	quart chicken stock
2	medium cloves garlic, minced (about 1 teaspoon)
¼	teaspoon red pepper flakes
½	medium head escarole lettuce, washed, dried and torn into 1-inch pieces (about 2 cups)
1	bunch (6 to 8) green onions, chopped (about ½ cup)
½	medium heads romaine lettuce, washed, dried and torn into 1-inch pieces (about 2 cups)
6	ounces fresh spinach leaves, torn (about 2 cups)
1	cup whipping cream
	Juice of 1 lemon (about 2 tablespoons)
	Salt and freshly ground pepper

1	pound fresh crabmeat, chopped
1	large red bell pepper, seeded and diced (about 1 cup)
1	large yellow bell pepper, seeded and diced (about 1 cup)
1	medium cucumbers, peeled, seeded and diced (about 1 cup)

2 tablespoons chopped fresh cilantro leaves

Juice of 1 lime (about 2 tablespoons)

1. Heat the chicken stock, garlic, and red pepper flakes in a large soup pot over medium high heat until it begins to boil.
2. Reduce the heat to medium. Stir in the escarole and green onions. Simmer for 5 minutes.
3. Add the romaine lettuce. Cover the pot and cook for 10 minutes.
4. Add the spinach. Cook for 2 minutes.
5. Use an immersion blender to purée the soup. (Alternatively, you may purée the soup in batches in the bowl of a food processor.)
6. Season with salt and pepper. Chill for at least 2 hours.
7. Combine the crabmeat, peppers, cucumber, cilantro, and lime juice in a bowl. Chill the relish for at least 30 minutes.
8. Add the whipping cream and lemon juice to the chilled soup. Adjust the seasonings.
9. Divide the crab relish into 8 serving bowls. Ladle the soup around the relish.

Servings: 8
Preparation Time: 45 minutes plus refrigeration.

There are so many varieties of lettuce in the market place, that by substituting you could reinvent this soup every week for a year! Feel free to experiment with any combination of green leaf, red leaf, butter, bib, oakleaf, frisee or watercress greens.

ARUGULA, TOMATO, and BLUE CHEESE SALAD with DILL VINAIGRETTE

The mustardy taste of arugula leaves adds a great flavor to a simple tossed salad.

¼ cup sherry vinegar
1 large shallot, minced (about 1 tablespoon)
2 tablespoons chopped fresh dill
½ cup olive oil
Salt and freshly ground pepper

8 cups fresh salad greens
2 cups fresh arugula leaves
1 pint ripe cherry tomatoes, cut in half
(about 2 cups)
4 ounces blue cheese, crumbled
Freshly ground pepper

1. In a small bowl whisk together the vinegar, shallot and dill. Slowly whisk in the olive oil. Season with salt and pepper.
2. Place the salad greens and arugula leaves in a salad bowl.
3. Add the cherry tomatoes. Sprinkle with blue cheese.
4. Drizzle with enough dressing to just moisten the leaves. Toss.
5. Serve with fresh pepper.

Servings: 8
Preparation Time: 10 minutes

This simple salad becomes a household staple with the addition of your favorite flavored vinegar and the market's freshest herbs.

SAUTÉED SNAPPER with ORANGE BUTTER SAUCE

Use the freshest fish to insure the best results in this dish. If snapper is not available you may substitute with any white fish fillet.

2   tablespoon olive oil
2   to 6 tablespoons butter
8   6- to 8-ounce snapper fillets
     Salt and freshly ground pepper
½   cup white wine
     Juice of 4 medium oranges (about 1½ cups)
¼   cup chutney

1. Heat 1 tablespoon of olive oil and 2 tablespoons of butter in a skillet over medium high heat.
2. Score the snapper and season with salt and freshly ground pepper.
3. Cook the fish in batches by placing 2 to 3 fillets skin side up into the skillet. Cook until just brown, 2 to 3 minutes.
4. Use a fish spatula to turn each fillet. Cook for 2 to 3 minutes more. Remove the fillets to a warm platter. The fish will continue to cook.
5. Continue with the remaining fillets, adding more olive oil and butter to the skillet as needed.
6. Deglaze the skillet with white wine, stirring the brown bits from the bottom. Cook for 4 minutes.
7. Add orange juice to the pan and cook for 2 minutes more.
8. Add the chutney to the pan and stir.
9. Reduce the heat and stir in 2 more tablespoons of chilled butter until just melted.
10. Pour the sauce over the fish. Garnish with orange sections and mint leaves.

Serves 4
Preparation Time: 15 minutes

Score the skin of a fish fillet to prevent it from curling up in the hot skillet. Use a sharp knife to cut diagonal slits in the skin but not through to the flesh of the fillet.

ROSEMARY ZUCCHINI CAKES

A great way to incorporate veggies and potatoes into one dish, these cakes are easily made in advance and baked at the last moment.

2   **medium russet potatoes, peeled (about 1 pound)**
2   **medium zucchini, grated (about 2 cups)**
4   **medium cloves garlic, minced (about 2 teaspoons)**
2   **tablespoons chopped fresh rosemary**
1   **tablespoon chopped fresh oregano leaves**
1   **cup fresh breadcrumbs**
½   **cup grated Parmesan cheese**
¼   **teaspoon ground nutmeg**
     Salt and freshly ground pepper
2   **to 4 tablespoons canola oil**

1. Cook the potatoes in boiling water until just tender, about 10 minutes. Drain and cool. Grate the potatoes and place into a bowl.
2. Place the grated zucchini in a colander. Use a paper towel to press out as much moisture as possible. Add the zucchini to the potatoes.

3. Add the garlic, rosemary, oregano, breadcrumbs, cheese, nutmeg, salt, and pepper to the mixture. Use you hands to combine the ingredients. Form the mixture into 8 3-inch cakes. Refrigerate for at least 1 hour.

Preheat the oven to 375°.

4. Heat 2 tablespoons canola oil in a skillet over medium high heat.
5. Cook the cakes in batches until just brown on each side, about 2 minutes per side. You may need to add additional oil to the pan.
6. Place the cakes on a baking sheet and bake for 10 minutes.

Servings: 8
Preparation Time: 30 minutes plus refrigeration

Fresh breadcrumbs are prepared by placing bread into the bowl of a food processor. Pulse to form crumbs. Fresh breadcrumbs produce a lighter cake. Feel free to use more or less than a recipe calls for. You want only to incorporate enough to just hold the cake together.

COCONUT CRÈME BRULÉE

This basic recipe is easy to master and even easier to modify for your next upscale dinner party.

3 cups heavy cream
½ cup coconut milk
1 1-inch piece vanilla bean
2 eggs
4 egg yolks
6 tablespoons sugar, plus more for crust
6 ounces toasted coconut

Preheat the oven to 325°.

1. Heat the cream, coconut milk, and vanilla bean in the top of a double boiler over simmering water.
2. Whisk the eggs, egg yolks, and sugar in a bowl until light and fluffy.
3. Remove the vanilla bean from the cream. Pour a small amount of the warm cream into the eggs. Whisk. Pour the egg mixture back into the cream.
4. Stir the custard in the double boiler until it thickens enough to coat the back of a spoon.
5. Pour the custard into 8 4-ounce brulée molds.

6. Place the molds into 2 baking dishes. Place enough water in the baking dishes to come half way up the sides of the molds.
7. Bake until the custard is set around the edges (about 30 to 40 minutes). The internal temperature of the custard will reach 170° to 175°. You may loosely cover the pans with aluminum foil to prevent browning. Transfer the molds to a rack to cool and then to the refrigerator. Chill for at least 2 hours or overnight.
8. Sprinkle 1 tablespoon granulated sugar evenly over the top of each brulée. Use a kitchen torch 2 inches above the surface to brown the sugar to form a crust. (Or, place the brulée under the broiler element of your oven.)
9. Top each brulée with toasted coconut.

Servings: 8
Preparation Time: 40 minutes plus baking and refrigeration.

Create your own favorite crème brulée by adding interesting flavors to the custard. Stir in shaved chocolate, lemon juice, amaretto, or crystallized ginger. Flavored sugars will also add a distinctive taste. Try maple sugar or a mixture of brown sugar and cinnamon.

Monthly Supper Club Party Plan

Party Motivation

Good friends getting together once a month to share great food and stunning conversation. It is your turn and you want to do something special for the gang.

Party Menu

Salmon "Tartar" in New Potato Jackets
Fresh Green Salad with Sliced Apples and Ginger Lime Vinaigrette
Paprika-Spiced Cornish Game Hen with Lemon Tarragon Sauce
Tuscan-Style Lentils
Southern-Style Warm Berry Cobbler **

** Over-the-Top Suggestion

Take Southern-charmed cobbler over the top by adding a scoop of homemade ice cream and a drizzle of warm fudge sauce.

Party Strategy

Pass the elegant appetizers on a silver platter. Pre-set the salads on chargers at the place settings before you invite your guests to the table. Serve the hens and lentils from the kitchen. Relax over warm cobbler in the living room.

The evening before: Prepare potatoes for appetizer. Prepare salad dressing, cover and chill.

The morning of: Set the table.

Two hours before: Prepare hens for roasting. Prepare salad ingredients. Prepare salmon tartar, cover and chill.

One hour before: Roast hens. Prepare and bake cobbler, keep warm.

Thirty minutes before: Prepare lentils. Cover and keep warm.

Immediately before: Prepare sauce for hens. Toss salad.

Shortcuts

Substitute with smoked salmon if sushi-grade salmon is not available.

Party Backdrop

Cocktails in the living room, dinner at the dining table and desserts and coffee in the den. This party moves from room to room at the easy direction of you—the relaxed host/hostess. Coordinate centerpieces in all of the rooms. Add candles lit just as your guests enter.

The Table Setting

A silver tray holds liquors and mixers. A silver ice bucket holds opened wine. Glasses, cocktail napkins and ice tongs are placed nearby so that each guest can serve himself or herself. Pass the bite size appetizers from your best tray lined with a crisp paper doily. If the potatoes are small enough, only a napkin is needed, although an appetizer-sized plate is fine.

Chill glass salad plates in the freezer. Place the tossed salad on the plates and place these on a charger set at each place. Remove the salad plate and the charger when guests are finished with this course.

Place one half of a game hen on a dinner plate. Place a tablespoon of lentils alongside. Drizzle the hen with the lemon sauce. Feel free to place a gravy boat of extra sauce on the table. Dessert is served from the kitchen. Place a scoop of cobbler in a shallow bowl. Place this bowl onto a dessert plate with a dessert spoon. Garnish with ice cream, mint leaves and chocolate fudge sauce. Use a tray to present the individual desserts to each guest with a clean napkin for dribbles.

SALMON "TARTAR" in NEW POTATO JACKETS

This fussy looking starter is easy to assemble and a delight to serve.

16 small new potatoes

1 pound fresh salmon fillet, all skin and bones removed
1 large shallot, minced (about 1 table-spoon)
2 tablespoons chopped fresh chives
Juice of 1 lemon (about 2 tablespoons)
2 tablespoons olive oil
Salt and freshly ground pepper

1 small cucumber, peeled, seeded and finely diced (about 1 cup)
1 tablespoons sesame oil

Preheat the oven to 350°.

1. Roast the new potatoes in a baking dish until soft, about 20 minutes. Cool.
2. Remove the top of the potatoes. Scoop out the inside leaving about ½-inch potato shell.
3. Use a very sharp knife to cut the salmon into ¼-inch dice.
4. Mix together the salmon, shallot, chives, lemon juice, and olive oil in a bowl. Season with salt and pepper. Chill.
5. Place the cucumber and sesame oil in a bowl. Toss and chill.
6. Place a spoonful of the salmon tartar into the potato jacket. Top with diced cucumber.

Yield: 16 hors d'oeuvres
Preparation Time: 30 minutes

Use the freshest salmon for this dish, purchased from a reputable fishmonger. Make sure that the tartar remains chilled until you are ready to serve the dish. If this is not doable, feel free to substitute with smoked salmon.

Fresh Green Salad with Sliced Apples and Ginger Lime Vinaigrette

The spicy dressing for this salad comes together quickly and offers a tangy dinner starter. Serve fresh pear slices or mandarin orange sections in place of apples for a fun salad treat.

8   cups fresh salad greens
2   medium apples, sliced into thin wedges
    (about 2 cups)

¼   cup rice wine vinegar
    Juice of 1 fresh lime (about 2 table-
    spoons)
1   medium clove garlic
1   1-inch piece ginger, peeled and cut into
    pieces
2   green onions, thinly sliced (about 2
    tablespoons)
1   tablespoon honey
½   cup peanut oil
    Salt and freshly ground pepper

1. Place the fresh greens and apple slices into a serving bowl. Chill.
2. Place the rice wine vinegar, lime juice, garlic, ginger, onion, and honey into the bowl of a food processor. Pulse to combine.
3. With the blade running, slowly pour in all of the peanut oil until the dressing is emulsified.
4. Season with salt and freshly ground pepper.
5. Toss the salad with a drizzle of the ginger dressing. Use additional dressing to garnish the plate.

Serves 8
Preparation Time: 15 minutes

If you are preparing the salad ahead of time, sprinkle the apple slices with lime or lemon juice to prevent browning.

Paprika-Spiced Cornish Game Hen with Lemon Tarragon Sauce

A dry spice rub flavors the hens and begins the simple sauce reduction.

4	**Cornish game hens**
2	**tablespoons brown sugar**
2	**teaspoons paprika**
1	**teaspoon chili powder**
1	**teaspoon cumin**
½	**teaspoon turmeric**
2	**tablespoons olive oil**
	Juice of 2 lemons (about ¼ cup)
	Fresh tarragon leaves
	Salt and freshly ground pepper

½	**small red onion, diced (about ¼ cup)**
1	**tablespoon olive oil**
½	**cup white wine**
	Juice of 3 lemons (about ½ cup)
2	**tablespoons chopped fresh tarragon**

Preheat the oven to 425°.

1. Cut the hens into halves. Place the 8 halves into a large baking dish.
2. Mix together the brown sugar, paprika, chili powder, cumin, and turmeric. Rub the skin side of the hens with this mixture.
3. Drizzle the hens with 2 tablespoons of olive oil and the lemon juice, and dot with fresh tarragon leaves. Season with salt and pepper.
4. Place the baking pan in the oven and immediately reduce the heat to 350°. Cook until the juices from the hen run clear, about 30 to 40 minutes. Remove the hens to a platter and keep warm.
5. Heat 1 tablespoon olive oil in a skillet over medium high heat.
6. Add the diced onion to the pan and cook until soft.
7. Add wine and lemon juice to the pan and cook for 1 minute.
8. Add the juices from the baking pan to the skillet. Cook until the sauce reduces to about ½ cup.
9. Toss in fresh chopped tarragon. Stir. Drizzle the sauce over the hens. Garnish with thin lemon slices.

Serves 8
Preparation Time: 15 minutes plus roasting

Feel free to experiment using this recipe as a guideline. You can substitute the ground spices that you have on hand and the fresh herbs that are available in your garden!

TUSCAN-STYLE LENTILS

The mild flavor of lentils goes nicely with the "heat" of the game hens. Pump up the flavor by substituting with a flavored olive oil like truffle or walnut oil.

2	quarts chicken stock
1	pound dried lentils
2	large carrots, diced (about ½ cup)
3	tablespoons olive oil
4	medium cloves garlic, minced (about 2 teaspoons)
¼	cup chopped fresh parsley
2	tablespoons chopped fresh rosemary
1	tablespoon Dijon mustard
	Salt and freshly ground pepper

1. Bring the chicken stock to a boil over medium high heat in a large pot.
2. Reduce the heat to medium. Cook the lentils and the carrots in the simmering stock until soft, about 30 minutes.
3. Drain the lentil mixture through a colander. Transfer to a bowl.
4. Toss the lentils with the olive oil, garlic, parsley, rosemary, and mustard.
5. Season with salt and pepper.

Servings: 8
Preparation Time: 45 minutes

Lentils are a member of the dried bean family. Small and flat they are found either green, brown, yellow or red. Lentils cook much more quickly than other types of dried beans and are thus very useful for quick cook recipes.

SOUTHERN-STYLE WARM BERRY COBBLER

This easy cobbler can be baked with any fruit that you prefer and served warm or at room temperature.

1	**pint raspberries (about 2 cups)**
1	**pint blueberries (about 2 cups)**
2	**tablespoons granulated sugar**
½	**cup butter, melted (1 stick)**
1	**cup all-purpose flour**
1	**cup granulated sugar**
1	**cup packed brown sugar**
3	**teaspoons baking powder**
¼	**teaspoon salt**
1	**cup milk**
½	**teaspoon ground nutmeg**
	Confectioners' sugar

Preheat the oven to 375°.

1. Mix the berries together with the sugar in a small bowl.
2. Pour the melted butter into a 13 x 9 x 2-inch baking dish.
3. Mix together the flour, sugars, baking powder, salt, and milk in a medium bowl.
4. Pout the batter into the baking dish. Do not stir into the melted butter.
5. Sprinkle the berries over the batter. Do not stir them into the batter.
6. Sprinkle with nutmeg.
7. Bake for 40 to 45 minutes or until the top begins to brown.
8. Dust with confectioners' sugar.

Servings: 8
Preparation Time: 15 minutes plus baking

Serve a spoonful of cobbler with a scoop of vanilla ice cream for a traditional Southern dessert. You can also garnish with a swirl of raspberry sauce and a dollop of whipped cream.

Saturday Night's Special Party Plan

Party Motivation

Getting the gang together for a night of great fun. You fuss on the food, but your friends arrive relaxed and informal. A blend of casually fussy entertaining is terrific way to host a party.

Party Menu

Brandy-Sautéed Scallops with Broccoli Purée **
Fig and Goat Cheese-Stuffed Chicken Breasts with Madeira Wine Sauce
Baked Potatoes with Mushrooms and Fontina Cheese
Mocha Fudge Cake with Caramel Pecan Center

**** Over-the-Top Suggestion**

This elegant first course is enhanced by a garnish of thinly sliced, fried leeks. Wash and dry a large leek. Cut into very thin strips. Heat olive oil in a pot to 350°. Place the leek strips into the hot oil and cook for 1 to 2 minutes. Drain on paper toweling.

Party Strategy

Serve each course from the kitchen. Allow guests to savor each bite and luxuriate over the blend of flavors in this menu.

The evening before: Prepare the cake. Prepare stuffing for potatoes and bake. Assemble the potatoes, cover and refrigerate.

The morning of: Set the table. Prepare the stuffing for the chicken. Stuff, cover and refrigerate.

Four hours before: Prepare the broccoli purée, cover and refrigerate. Prepare the fried leeks.

One hour before: Bake chicken and potatoes.

Immediately before serving: Sauté scallops, warm purée. Make sauce for chicken.

Shortcuts

The cake filling and frosting is a huge flavor binge. If time is really short, substitute with a boxed chocolate cake mix.

Party Backdrop

Set the kitchen table with great placemats and a combination of china. Miniature pots of fresh herbs by each place setting are perfect name card holders as well as party favors for each guest. A large basket filled with various fresh herbs makes for a casual, yet aromatic centerpiece. Alternate sizes of pillar candles around the table.

The Table Setting

Mix and match china is the key here. Your best thrift shop find is blended with your Grandma's patterned china. Coordinate a salad plate to sit on a larger supper plate for the appetizer. Serve with a salad fork and fish knife. Remove both plates when your guests have finished the first course. Serve the chicken and potato on a coordinating dinner plate. Individual salt cellars by each plate are a fun way to introduce a little seasoning. After the main course is removed, bring out the show-stopping cake on a pedestal cake stand. Slice the cake at the table and invite guests to pass plates to each other until everyone has been served.

BRANDY-SAUTÉED SCALLOPS with BROCCOLI PURÉE

Prepare the purée and sauté the scallops in advance. As your guests arrive, assemble this stunning first course.

2	**medium bunch broccoli florets (about 4 cups)**
4	**medium cloves garlic, minced (about 2 teaspoons)**
½	**teaspoon turmeric**
½	**teaspoon cumin**
2	**tablespoons sour cream**
	Salt and freshly ground pepper
16	**medium sea scallops**
2	**tablespoons butter**
2	**tablespoons brandy**
	Sour cream
	Chopped fresh chives

1. Steam the broccoli until just tender, about 8 minutes.

2. Place the broccoli into the bowl of a food processor. Pulse to emulsify.

3. Add the garlic, turmeric, cumin, and sour cream. Pulse to purée until smooth. Season with salt and pepper.

4. Melt 2 tablespoons butter in a skillet over medium high heat. Add the brandy.

5. Place the scallops into the skillet. (You may do this in batches if your scallops are too large for your pan.)

6. Cook for 2 to 4 minutes or until golden. Turn, cook for 2 to 4 minutes more. Remove the scallops to a warm plate.

7. Place a spoonful of the broccoli purée onto a small plate. Top with 2 scallops. Garnish with additional sour cream and chopped chives.

Servings: 8
Preparation Time: 30 minutes

To take this elegant first course over-the-top, add a garnish of fried leeks. Cut the white part of a cleaned leek into very thin match-stick size strips. Heat a small amount of olive oil in a skillet over medium high heat. Cook the leeks in the hot oil until golden. Remove with a slotted spoon and drain on paper toweling. Place a clump of fried leeks on top of the scallops.

Fig and Goat Cheese-Stuffed Chicken Breasts with Madeira Wine Sauce

The combination of sweet figs and tart wine sauce are an impressive match in this yummy dish.

8   6 to 8-ounce chicken breast halves with rib
    Salt and freshly ground pepper

1   **tablespoon olive oil**
½   **large yellow onion, diced (about ½ cup)**
2   **medium cloves garlic, minced (about 1 teaspoon)**
1   **tablespoon chopped fresh basil leaves**
4   **ounces dried figs, plumped in hot water, drained and chopped**
8   **ounces goat cheese**

1   **tablespoon olive oil**
4   **large shallots, minced (about ¼ cup)**
1   **cup Madeira wine**
2   **cups beef broth**
2   **tablespoons tomato paste**
1   **tablespoon fresh basil, rolled and cut into julienne strips**

Preheat the oven to 375°.

1. Season the chicken breasts with salt and pepper and place skin side up in a baking dish.
2. Heat 1 tablespoon of olive oil in a skillet over medium high heat.
3. Add the onion and cook until soft, about 5 minutes.
4. Add the garlic and cook until soft, about 2 minutes.
5. Add the basil leaves and figs. Stir. Remove from heat.
6. Add the goat cheese to the mixture. Cool.
7. Gently lift the skin from the flesh of a chicken breast, leaving a portion attached. Place ⅛ of the filling under the skin and pat to evenly distribute. Repeat with the remaining chicken breasts and filling.
8. Place the baking pan in the oven and roast for 30 to 40 minutes.
9. Heat 1 tablespoon olive oil in a skillet over medium high heat. Cook the shallots in the oil until soft.
10. Pour the wine into the skillet. Simmer until reduced by half, about 10 minutes.
11. Pour the beef stock into the skillet. Simmer until reduced to 2 cups, about 10 minutes.
12. Stir in the tomato paste, basil, and season with salt and pepper.
13. Serve the chicken breast on a puddle of sauce.

Servings: 8
Preparation Time: 40 minutes

Dried figs are sweeter and chewier than their fresh counterparts. Choose dried figs that are not packaged too tightly and remain somewhat soft. Packaged in an airtight containers, dried figs will last up to 2 months when stored in a cool, dry place.

BAKED POTATOES with MUSHROOMS and FONTINA CHEESE

These potatoes can be prepared the day before a party and then quickly heated just before serving.

4	**large baking potatoes**
½	**cup butter (1 stick)**
2	**pounds button mushrooms, sliced (about 4 cups)**
4	**green onions, thinly sliced (about ¼ cup)**
½	**8-ounce package cream cheese**
½	**cup sour cream**
1½	**cups shredded Fontina cheese**
2	**tablespoons chopped fresh garlic chives**
	Salt and freshly ground pepper

Preheat the oven to 375°.

1. Scrub the potatoes and pierce each one with the tines of a fork. Place on the rack in the oven and cook until soft, about 45 minutes.
2. Heat 2 tablespoons butter in a skillet over medium high heat.
3. Add the mushrooms. Cook until soft, about 8 minutes.
4. Add the green onion. Cook until soft, about 2 minutes. Season with salt and pepper. Remove from the heat.
5. Remove the cooked potatoes from the oven. Cut the hot potatoes in half. Scoop out the potato leaving a ½-inch shell.
6. Place the potato in the bowl of an electric mixer.
7. Mix in the cream cheese, sour cream and the remaining 6 tablespoons butter. Season with salt and pepper.
8. Mix in the mushrooms and ¾ cup cheese.
9. Fill the potato jackets with the potato and mushroom mixture and place onto a baking sheet.
10. Sprinkle with the remaining cheese and fresh garlic chives.
11. Bake until the cheese melts about 30 minutes.

Servings: 8
Preparation Time: 30 minutes plus roasting and baking

There are many types of potatoes and all of them will work well in this recipe. But the overall favorite potato for baking is the Russet because it is starchy and will have less moisture when cooked than other varieties. Store potatoes in a cool dry area for up to 2 weeks. Do not place them in the refrigerator.

Mocha Fudge Cake with Caramel Pecan Center

Mocha flavored frosting and a nutty caramel center makes this cake a candy bar treat.

2	cups cake flour
2	teaspoons baking soda
¼	teaspoon ground nutmeg
½	teaspoon salt
2	cups packed brown sugar
½	cup shortening, room temperature
3	large eggs
4	ounces unsweetened baking chocolate, melted
½	cup buttermilk
1	cup brewed coffee
1	teaspoon vanilla extract
½	cup prepared caramel sauce
4	tablespoons chopped toasted pecans
6	cups confectioners' sugar
¾	cup cocoa powder
6	tablespoons butter, melted
½	teaspoon salt
½	cup hot brewed coffee
⅓	to ½ cup milk

Preheat the oven to 350°.

1. Combine the flour, baking soda, nutmeg and salt in a bowl. Set aside.
2. Use an electric mixer to combine the brown sugar and shortening until fluffy.
3. Add the eggs one at a time.
4. Stir in the melted chocolate.
5. Add the flour and buttermilk in 3 additions, alternating ⅓ flour mixture with ⅓ milk until just blended.
6. Stir in the coffee and vanilla.
7. Pour the batter into 2 9-inch round cake pans that have been sprayed with vegetable oil spray and dusted with flour.
8. Bake in the center of the oven for 30 to 35 minutes or until a toothpick inserted in the center comes out clean.
9. Remove the cake pans to a rack and cool. Invert the cakes onto the racks to cool completely.
10. Stir the caramel sauce and toasted pecans together.
11. Use an electric mixer to combine the confectioners' sugar, cocoa, melted butter, salt, and ½ cup of coffee. Add enough milk to produce a frosting consistency.
12. Place one cake on a cake platter. Spread the caramel sauce onto the cake. Cover with the second cake.
13. Spread the frosting on the sides and top of the cake. Garnish with additional pecans.

Servings: 8 to 10
Preparation Time: 30 minutes plus baking

Over mixing cake batter will produce air holes and make the cakes rise unevenly. Under mixing will produce a dense, grainy cake. The secret is to combine the sugar and butter very well, and then mix only just enough to incorporate the rest of the ingredients. Refrigerate extra frosting in an air-tight container for later "cookie-dipping."

Dazzling New Year's Eve Party Plan

Party Motivation

It's New Year's Eve! Time to get dressed up, sip champagne and wear funny hats. What better way to ring in the New Year than to invite great pals to a really fussy supper?

Party Menu

Caviar with Accompaniments
Lobster Bisque **
Roasted Salmon with Peppercorn Sauce
Spinach Dumplings with Sage Cream Sauce
Strawberry Cheesecake with Chocolate Cookie Crust

** Over-the-Top Suggestion

Lobster Bisque is over-the-top by itself. Prepared with freshly caught lobster and garnished with fresh lobster meat—this stunning starter is quite impressive.

Party Strategy

The lobster stock takes some time—so begin days in advance. Shop for great party favors and decorations. Order the freshest caviar you can find and have it delivered no more that 3 days before the event. The sumptuously rich dessert is designed to be prepared the day before—which leaves plenty of time for you to open the champagne! Serve the meal late in the evening, so that the last bite of cheesecake is eaten at midnight

At least two weeks in advance: Order caviar.

At least 2 days in advance: Prepare lobster stock, cover and refrigerate.

One day in advance: Prepare cheesecake.

The morning of: Set the table. Finish bisque, cover and refrigerate. Prepare accompaniments for caviar.

Two hours before: Prepare dumplings for boiling. Prepare sauce, cover.

One hour before: Prepare salmon and keep warm. Prepare sauce through step 9.

Immediately before serving: Boil dumplings. Complete sauce for salmon.

Shortcuts

Substitute with spinach tortellini in place of spinach dumplings if time grows short, but don't forget the sage cream sauce.

Purchase stock for bisque in place of making your own.

Party Backdrop

Your dining room is perfect—but if you are partying in a tropical climate, pitch a gauze tent, lit with hundreds of twinkle lights, next to your crystal clear pool. (One can dream...)

In a den, dining room or living room, serve the caviar on a silver tray that holds all of the accompaniments. Toast with chilled champagne or frozen vodka.

The Table Setting

Place a flat mirror onto the center of the table. Fill and surround the table with all sizes and heights of white candles. Fill small bowls with blooming white roses. A white tablecloth is set with coal black chargers. Coordinate with crisp napkins tied with a piece of glittering lace.

Serve lobster bisque from a cream soup bowl (a bowl with handles on two sides). In many cases the cream soup bowl comes with a matching saucer and/or cover to keep the soup warm.

Serve the salmon and the spinach dumplings on a dinner plate. Garnish the rim of the plate with multi-colored, freshly ground pepper.

Draw a swirl of warm chocolate on each of the desert plates and lay a slice of cheesecake on top.

Don't forget coffee for the late night ride home.

CAVIAR with ACCOMPANIMENTS

Nothing says New Years better than the rich, salty taste of delectable and delicate caviar. Choose the best that you can afford and savor every bite.

1	**ounce Beluga, Osetra, or Sevruga caviar**
2	**large eggs, hardboiled, whites and yolks separated, finely chopped**
4	**large shallots, finely chopped (about ¼ cup)**
2	**tablespoons capers, drained**
	Sour cream
	Chopped fresh chives
	Toast

1. Serve the caviar in a bowl that sits in a larger bowl of crushed ice. Open the caviar immediately before you present it. Use a non-metallic utensil to serve each guest.
2. Traditional accents to caviar are chopped egg, diced shallot or red onion, capers, sour cream, and chopped fresh chives.
3. Melba toast, crackers, or triangles of brown bread are common accompaniments.

Servings: 8
Preparation Time: 20 minutes

Caviar is the roe or eggs of the sturgeon fish. It ranges in color from black to gray and in size from a small pinhead to pearl size. Red caviar is the roe of salmon or lumpfish and not "true" caviar. Keep caviar chilled at all times. If unopened, store in the refrigerator for up to two weeks. If opened, caviar should be eaten within 24 hours.

LOBSTER BISQUE

Nothing defines an elegant dinner party like a velvety, rich bisque soup as a first course. This recipe is worth all of the steps involved. You can prepare the stock days in advance of the party. Finish the soup just as your guests arrive—the aroma is so inviting.

2	**pounds lobster shells**	2	**cups dry white wine**
½	**cup butter (1 stick)**	1	**cup Madeira wine**
2	**tablespoons olive oil**	6	**cups chicken stock**
2	**medium white onions, unpeeled and cut into pieces (about 1⅓ cups)**	4	**cups tomato juice**
2	**large carrots, cut in pieces (about ½ cup)**	8	**garlic cloves, unpeeled**
2	**medium celery ribs, cut into pieces (about 1 cup)**	2	**bay leaves**
	Salt and freshly ground pepper	½	**cup fresh parsley**
		2	**tablespoons fresh thyme**

2 tablespoons butter
4 large shallots, minced (about ¼ cup)
½ pound shiitake mushrooms, finely diced (about 1½ cups)
1 cup brandy
1 cup Madeira wine
6 cups lobster stock (above)
2 tablespoons butter, room temperature
2 tablespoons flour
2 cups heavy cream
  Juice of 1 lemon (about 2 tablespoons)
2 to 4 drops hot pepper sauce

FOR LOBSTER STOCK

1. Remove the meat from the lobster and reserve for another use. Use a hammer to pound the shells into small pieces
2. In a large pot over medium high heat melt together the butter and olive oil.
3. Add the onions, carrots, and celery. Cook until just beginning to brown, about 10 minutes. Season with salt and pepper.
4. Add the lobster shells. Cook for 5 minutes.
5. Add the white wine and 1 cup of Madeira.
6. Add the chicken stock followed by the tomato juice. Bring to a boil and stir.
7. Add the garlic, bay leaves, parsley, and thyme to the pot.
8. Reduce the heat and allow the stock to simmer, uncovered for at least 2 hours or until the liquid is reduced by half.
9. Strain the stock through a colander. Cover and refrigerate.

FOR BISQUE

1. Heat 2 tablespoons of butter over medium high heat in a large pot.
2. Add the shallots and mushrooms to the butter. Cook for 5 minutes.
3. Remove the pot from the stovetop. Stir in the brandy. Return the pot to the stove. Bring the soup to a boil over medium high heat and cook until the liquid is reduced by half, about 5 minutes.
4. Add 1 cup of Madeira wine to the pot and cook until reduced by half.
5. Add the lobster stock to the pot and bring to a boil. Cook for 5 minutes.
6. Strain the soup through a colander using the back of a spoon to separate all of the solids from the liquid.
7. Return the soup to the pot and bring to a boil.
8. Use a whisk to combine the softened butter and flour in a small bowl. Whisk this mixture into the soup and cook for 5 minutes. The soup will thicken slightly.
9. Reduce the heat to medium and stir in the cream.
10. Season with lemon juice, salt, and fresh pepper.

Serves 8
Preparation Time: 30 minutes plus cooking for stock
30 minutes for bisque

This recipe was developed using Florida lobster. Florida lobsters do not have claws like Maine lobster. I harvested the thick antennae appendages and the side legs for shells. You can easily substitute with shrimp or crawfish in lieu of lobster shells. Use cooked lobster meat as an imipressive garnish for this soup.

Roasted Salmon with Peppercorn Sauce

The peppercorns pack a wallop of a flavor boost to subtle salmon in this easy-to-serve dish.

2   **teaspoon white peppercorns**
2   **teaspoon black peppercorns**
2   **teaspoons pink peppercorns**
1   **teaspoon salt**
8   **6-ounce salmon fillets**
2   **to 4 tablespoons olive oil**

1   **7-ounce jar sun-dried tomatoes in oil, sliced lengthwise into strips**
1   **bunch (6 to 8) green onions, chopped (about ½ cup)**
1   **cup white wine**
1   **tablespoon chopped fresh parsley leaves**
2   **tablespoons butter, chilled**

Preheat the oven to 350°.

1. Use a mortar and pestle to grind the peppercorns together with the salt. (Alternatively you can crush the peppercorns with a rolling pin or meat mallet.)
2. Press the peppercorn mixture onto one side of the salmon fillets.
3. Heat 2 tablespoons olive oil in a skillet over medium high heat.
4. Place several of the salmon fillets peppercorn side down in the hot oil. Cook for 2 to 3 minutes or until golden. Use a fish spatula to turn the fillets and cook for 2 to 3 minutes more. Place the fillets into a baking dish. Repeat until all of the fillets have been sautéed. You may need to add more oil to the pan.
5. Roast the salmon for 8 to 10 minutes depending on the thickness of the fillets. The salmon should be medium rare in the center.
6. Add the sun-dried tomatoes and oil to the skillet.
7. Add the onion and cook for 2 minutes.
8. Pour in the white wine and cook until reduced by half, about 5 minutes.
9. Stir in the parsley. Remove the pan from the heat.
10. Stir in the butter until just melted.
11. Pour the sauce over the fillets.

Servings: 8
Preparation Time: 30 minutes

White and black peppercorns are really the same pungent spice picked at varying times of ripeness. Pink peppercorns are not really peppercorns at all, but instead they are small berries that come from a type of rose plant. Grinding the peppercorns release the aroma and piquancy of the spice.

Spinach Dumplings with Sage Cream Sauce

These dense dumplings takes the place of potatoes or rice while sprucing up a dinner plate.

1 10-ounce package frozen chopped spinach, cooked

1 tablespoon butter
1 tablespoon flour
1 cup milk
½ teaspoon nutmeg
½ teaspoons cayenne pepper
Salt and freshly ground pepper

2 large eggs
2 tablespoons grated Swiss cheese
½ cup all-purpose flour

1 cup heavy cream
1 large shallot, minced (about 1 tablespoon)
6 to 8 large sage leaves, rolled and cut into julienne

1. Drain the spinach in a colander using paper toweling to remove as much moisture as possible.
2. Heat the butter in a pan over medium heat. Whisk in the flour until golden and bubbling.
3. Whisk the milk into the flour mixture. Cook until the sauce is thick, about 10 minutes.
4. Season with nutmeg, cayenne, salt, and pepper. Cool.
5. Place the eggs and cheese into a large bowl.
6. Stir in the spinach until smooth.
7. Stir in the sauce. Add enough flour to bind the mixture. The dumplings will just hold their shape when formed.
8. Use two tablespoons to form the dumplings into egg-like shapes. Make 16 or more dumplings.
9. Bring a ¾ full saucepan of water to boil. Add salt to the water.
10. Place several dumplings into the boiling water. When they float to the top, cook for 3 minutes more. Remove with a slotted spoon and keep warm while you cook the remaining dumplings.
11. Heat the cream, shallot, and sage in a saucepan over medium high heat until reduced by ⅓ and slightly thickened. Season with salt and pepper. Serve the sauce over the dumplings.

Servings: 8
Preparation Time: 40 minutes

Form the dumplings into oval-shaped quenelles by moving the dumpling dough back and forth with 2 teaspoons. The end result is a smooth, egg-like form that looks as fantastic as it tastes.

STRAWBERRY CHEESECAKE with CHOCOLATE COOKIE CRUST

An extra drizzle of warm fudge sauce is the perfect accompaniment to this delicious dessert.

1   **9-ounce package chocolate wafer cookies (about 40 cookies)**
5   **tablespoons butter, melted**

3   **8-ounce packages cream cheese, room temperature**
1   **cup granulated sugar**
2   **tablespoons all-purpose flour**
3   **large eggs**
    Zest of 1 medium lemon (about 1 tablespoon)
    Juice of ½ lemon (about 1 tablespoon)
1   **teaspoon vanilla extract**
1   **pint strawberries, hulled and chopped (about 2 cups)**

1½ **cups sour cream**
¼   **cup strawberry jam**
1   **teaspoon vanilla extract**
1   **pint strawberries, hulled and sliced**

Preheat the oven to 325°.

1. Place the cookies in the bowl of a food processor. Pulse to form into crumbs. Add the melted butter and pulse again.
2. Press the cookie curst into the bottom and up the sides of a 9-inch springform pan that has been sprayed with vegetable oil spray. Bake for 8 minutes.
3. Use an electric mixer to combine the cream cheese and sugar until fluffy.
4. Stir in the flour.
5. Add the eggs one at a time, mixing after each addition.
6. Stir in the lemon zest, lemon juice, and vanilla.
7. Gently fold in the strawberries. Pour the batter into the prepared crust.
8. Bake until the edges begin to turn golden and the center is just set, about 1 hour and 15 minutes.
9. Combine the sour cream, jam, and vanilla in a small bowl.
10. Spread this mixture on top of the warm cheesecake.
11. Place the cake back into the oven and bake for 5 more minutes.
12. Remove the cake to a rack and cool thoroughly. Loosen the sides of the cake from the pan with a sharp knife. Refrigerate at least 4 hours or overnight.
13. Remove the outer ring of the pan. Garnish by placing sliced strawberries on top of the cheesecake.

Servings: 8 to 10
Preparation Time: 30 minutes plus baking and refrigeration

A common lament among bakers is why does my cheesecake crack? There are two answers to the question—over baking and over mixing. Remove a cheesecake from the oven when the center is still quivering. The cheesecake will continue to bake as it cools. Beat room temperature cream cheese until it is smooth before adding other ingredients. Then stir in the ingredients until just incorporated.

Holidays at Home

(HOLIDAY THEMED PARTIES FOR TEN TO TWELVE)

Easter Basket Picnic Lunch
Labor Day "Cook-In"
Haunted Halloween Open House
Tree Trimming Supper

"A simple and elegant centerpiece that works for every holiday occasion is a silver Revere bowl overflowing with beatiful fragrant flowers in an array of color. This works well in a traditional setting with cabaret lamps that feature white pleated shades or in a contemporary setting with soft votive tea candles that surround the flowers.

The secret to the most successful party is in the detail. A well-schooled host or hostess makes a statement of style. You do this by coordinating each and every detail from the invitation to the fold of the napkin."

Sylvie Lawless
Party Planning Specialist
Lauderdale Flower Shop
Fort Lauderdale, Florida

Easter Basket Picnic Lunch Party Plan

Party Motivation

A gorgeous spring morning with flowers in bloom and everyone dressed in bonnets and ties begs for an outdoor occasion. A perfect picnic is in order with individual baskets for each guest. When emptied, the same baskets work wonderfully for an egg hunt!

Party Menu

Crispy Fried Chicken Fingers
Herb and Sour Cream Muffins with Diced Tomato
Chilled Macaroni Salad
Six-Veggie Slaw with Tarragon
Individual Lemon Tarts **

** Over-the-Top Suggestion

Take the suggestion on page 284 and add a peak of meringue to each lemon tart.

Party Strategy

Gather fun disposable containers to hold each dish. Create baskets filled with containers and utensils.

Two days before (or more): Gather containers and baskets.

One day before: Prepare the lemon tarts, cover and refrigerate. Prepare the veggies for the slaw.

The evening before: Marinate chicken fingers. Prepare macaroni salad, cover and refrigerate.

The morning of: Bake muffins. Assemble slaw. Prepare macaroni salad.

Two hours before: Place salads in individual containers. Refrigerate.

One hour before: Cook chicken fingers.

Immediately before: Arrange containers in picnic baskets.

Shortcuts

Purchase prepared lemon curd and pre-made tarts to expedite dessert.

Party Backdrop

A well manicured backyard, a favorite park, grandma's garden all are perfect backgrounds for a picnic lunch. Make sure there is plenty of room for little ones to run around collecting colored eggs—and just enough seating for everyone to enjoy their "packed lunch."

The Table Setting

A cloth-lined table holds all of the baskets. A simple centerpiece of long gladiolas in a tall vase signals the simplicity of the afternoon. Each basket is lined with colorful linen napkins to act as both the placemat and the serviette. Two containers, such as Chinese food take-out cartons or the simpler, reusable plastic tubs hold the salads. Wrap the muffin in a nest of aluminum foil. Stand the chicken fingers in a tall paper cup. Add plastic utensils, miniature salt and pepper shakers, and a colored hard-boiled egg stenciled with the guest's name. The after-egg-hunt perfect refresher is a tray full of lemon tarts next two a pitcher of iced-tea and a second pitcher of lemonade.

CRISPY FRIED CHICKEN FINGERS

Oversized "fingers" marinated in buttermilk and dipped in light breadcrumbs are a cool picnic treat—perfect for all ages.

12 6 to 8-ounce skinless boneless chicken breast halves
1 cup buttermilk
½ cup olive oil
1 bunch (6 to 8) green onions, chopped (about ½ cup)
2 tablespoon Dijon mustard
1 teaspoon dried red pepper flakes
Salt and freshly ground pepper

2 cups Japanese-style (panko) breadcrumbs
1 cup cornmeal
2 teaspoons finely chopped fresh thyme
2 teaspoons finely chopped fresh rosemary
1 teaspoon paprika

Canola oil

1. Cut each chicken breast in half vertically creating 2 long fingers.
2. Place the buttermilk, olive oil, green onions, mustard and red pepper flakes into a blender or food processor. Pulse to combine.
3. Place the chicken strips into a large baking dish. Pour in the marinade. Cover and chill for at least 2 hours or overnight.

Preheat the oven to 350°.
4. Combine the breadcrumbs, cornmeal, thyme, rosemary, and paprika in a large bowl.
5. Heat canola oil in a deep skillet over medium high heat.
6. Remove one chicken finger from the marinade. Shake off excess.
7. Place the chicken into the breadcrumb mixture coating both sides. Shake off excess.
8. Place the chicken into the hot oil. Cook until golden brown, about 3 to 5 minutes. Turn and cook until the other side is golden brown.
9. Remove the chicken to a cooking rack placed onto a baking sheet.
10. Continue with the remaining chicken. Season with salt and pepper.
11. Bake the chicken fingers for 20 minutes or until cooked through but not dry.

Servings: 12
Preparation Time: 45 minutes plus baking.

Japanese style breadcrumbs also called panko are sold in Asian markets and are finding their way into your local grocery store. They are a very light, snow-flake size crumb that produce a very crisp and airy texture to fried food.

HERB and SOUR CREAM MUFFINS with DICED TOMATO

Serve these savory muffins at room temperature or warm from the oven. Split in half and slather with sweet butter or jam.

2½	**cups all-purpose flour**
2	**teaspoons baking powder**
1	**teaspoon salt**
½	**teaspoon baking soda**
1	**cup buttermilk**
2	**large eggs**
⅓	**cup sour cream**
4	**tablespoons butter, melted**
1	**tablespoon chopped fresh chives**
1	**tablespoon chopped fresh basil**
1	**tablespoon chopped fresh dill**
1	**tablespoon chopped fresh rosemary**
2	**plum tomatoes, seeded and diced (about ½ cup)**

Preheat the oven to 350°.

1. Combine the flour, baking powder, salt, and baking soda in a small bowl.
2. Stir together the buttermilk, eggs, sour cream, and 2 tablespoons melted butter in a large bowl.
3. Stir in the fresh herbs.
4. Stir the flour mixture into the buttermilk mixture until just combined.
5. Fold in the diced tomatoes.
6. Place the batter into a 12-cup muffin tin that has been sprayed with vegetable oil spray.
7. Brush the tops of the muffins with the remaining melted butter.
8. Bake for 30 minutes or until the tops are golden and a toothpick inserted into the center comes out clean.

Yield: 12 muffins
Preparation Time: 20 minutes plus baking

The best muffins are made with the least effort. Stir until the ingredients just come together. Ignore lumps. The batter should be clumpy—not smooth. Over-mixing will produce a dry muffin. Make your own favorite muffins by using the freshest herbs available. Substitute with grated cheese, sun-dried tomatoes or chopped olives for a special twist.

CHILLED MACARONI SALAD

Sweet peas and tangy Dijon flavor this classic pasta salad. The crunchy veggies make all of the chopping well worth the effort.

1½ pounds elbow macaroni
2   large green bell peppers, seeded and diced (about 2 cups)
4   medium celery ribs, thinly sliced (about 2 cups)
1   bunch (6 to 8) green onions, chopped (about ½ cup)
1   10-ounce package frozen peas, cooked
1   6-ounce jar chopped pimento, drained
⅓   cup chopped fresh parsley

    Juice of 2 lemons (about ¼ cup)
¼   cup white wine vinegar
2   tablespoons Dijon mustard
1   teaspoon granulated sugar
½   cup sour cream
½   cup mayonnaise
    Salt and freshly ground pepper

1. Cook the macaroni according to package directions. Drain and rinse with cold water to stop the cooking process.
2. Place the macaroni into a large bowl.
3. Add the pepper, celery, onions, peas, pimento, and parsley. Toss.
4. Whisk together the lemon juice, vinegar, mustard, sugar, sour cream, and mayonnaise in a small bowl.
5. Pour the dressing over the pasta. Toss. Season with salt and pepper. Chill before serving.

Servings: 10 to 12
Preparation Time: 30 minutes

Cook the pasta al dente, which means that the macaroni is still chewy, but is cooked through. Chill for at least an hour so that the pasta will absorb the flavor and aroma of its salad-mates. Mushy pasta will not hold up as well in this dish.

Six-Veggie Slaw with Tarragon

The thinner the veggies, the better the slaw. Use a mandoline or the julienne disk of a food processor to help you achieve the desired results.

½   **small head Savoy cabbage, shredded (about 2 cups)**
6   **large carrots cut into matchstick size julienne strips (about 2 cups)**
1   **fennel bulb, cut into matchstick size julienne strips (about 2 cups)**
2   **large yellow bell peppers, seeded and cut into matchstick size julienne (about 2 cups)**
12   **whole radishes, sliced into thin strips (about 1 cup)**
2   **medium zucchini, sliced into matchstick size julienne strips (about 2 cups)**

   Juice of 6 to 8 limes (about 1 cup)
2   **tablespoons honey**
1   **1-inch piece ginger, grated (about 1 tablespoon)**
2   **medium cloves garlic (about 1 teaspoon)**

2   **tablespoons chopped fresh tarragon leaves**
1   **cup olive oil**
   Salt and freshly ground pepper

1. Cut the vegetables into similar size very thin strips.
2. Place all of the vegetables into a bowl.
3. Use a blender or food processor to combine the lime juice, honey, ginger, garlic, and tarragon. Pulse to emulsify.
4. With the machine running, slowly add the oil. Season with salt and pepper.
5. Pour the dressing into the bowl and toss with the vegetables. Chill the slaw before serving.

Servings: 10 to 12
Preparation Time: 30 minutes

Vary the veggies with your favorite and those that are readily available. The secret is in the slicing for this dish. Feel free to substitute with yellow squash, cucumber, green or red pepper or even a touch of jalapeño.

Individual Lemon Tarts

A huge tray of individual tarts is a must on a spring buffet table. If time is limited, bake two larger tarts, cut into wedges and serve on individual dessert plates.

3   **cups all-purpose flour**
⅓   **cup confectioners' sugar**
½   **teaspoon salt**
1   **cup butter (2 sticks), chilled and cut into pieces**
1   **large egg yolk**
6   **tablespoons ice water**

4   **large eggs**
2½   **cups granulated sugar**
     Zest of 1 medium lemon (about 1 tablespoon)
     Juice of 3 lemons (about ½ cup)
2   **cups heavy cream**

     Whipped cream
     Strawberries

Preheat the oven to 375°.
1. Place the flour, sugar, and salt into the bowl of a food processor. Pulse to blend.
2. Place the butter into the bowl. Pulse until course crumbs form.
3. Whisk the egg yolk with the ice water.
4. Add enough of the egg yolk/water mixture to bring the crumbs together into dough.

5. Turnr the dough out onto a floured surface. Use your hands to form 2 flat disks. Wrap the disks in plastic and refrigerate for 30 minutes.
6. Roll out one disk onto a lightly floured surface. Cut out 6 rounds. Place each round into an individual tart pan. Trim excess. Line the shell with foil. Place pie weights on top of the foil. Bake for 10 to 15 minutes or until just lightly golden. Remove from the oven. Repeat with the second disk.

Preheat the oven to 325°.
7. Whisk together the eggs, sugar, lemon zest, lemon juice, and cream together in a bowl.
8. Pour the filling into the tart shells. Bake for 30 minutes or until the filling is just set and the tops are golden. Transfer to a rack to cool.
9. Garnish each tart with whipped cream and a fanned strawberry.

Servings: 12
Preparation Time: 1 hour plus baking

To take this dish over-the-top add a meringue topping to the tarts just before baking. Use an electric mixer to whip 4 egg whites until frothy. Add ½ teaspoon cream of tartar. Beat this mixture until the egg whites are stiff, but not dry. Beat in 8 tablespoons of confectioners' sugar one tablespoon at a time. Beat in 1 teaspoon of vanilla extract. Place a generous amount of meringue on each tart and bake as directed above.

Labor Day "Cook In" Party Plan

Party Motivation

Labor Day signals the end of summer and the beginning of the fall season. But, the heat of the dog days of summer has really intensified and rather than a day long cook out at the beach—perhaps a little air-conditioning is just what is needed. Move the party indoors by eliminating the grill but not sacrificing one morsels of cook-out flavor!

Party Menu

Margaritas for a Crowd **
Cucumber, Tomato, and Bread Salad with French Dressing and Roquefort Cheese
Jalapeño-Spiced Barbecue Beef Stew *
Toasted Corn Pudding
Cheesy Potato Casserole
Pumpkin Swirl Cheesecake

** Over-the-Top Suggestion

A pitcher of Margaritas is a perfect outdoor drink. Indoors, you can easily make frozen margaritas by pouring margarita mix into a blender. Add tequila, Triple sec and ice. Pulse until slushy. Pour into margarita glasses and let the fun begin.

Serve the shredded beef stew on oversized buns and top with Jicama Slaw with Sesame Dressing (page 237).

Party Strategy

Prepare all of the casserole dishes the day before and reheat just as the party begins to warm up.

One day before: Bake cheesecake, cover and chill.

The evening before: Prepare corn pudding through step 9, cover and chill. Prepare potato casserole through step 4, cover and refrigerate. Prepare barbecue beef, cool, cover and refrigerate.

The morning of: Prepare ingredients for salad. Arrange buffet table.

One hour before: Bake potato casserole, keep warm. Bake corn pudding, keep warm.

Thirty minutes before: Reheat barbecue beef. Assemble and toss salad.

Shortcuts

To save a bit of work, purchase canned jalapeño peppers in place of roasting your own.

Party Backdrop

Guests are ready for a cook-out and you changed the plan but not the mood. Serve the meal buffet-style from a kitchen table or counter. Guests can take their plates to any chair in the room, as all of the food is lap-friendly.

The Table Setting

Checkered tablecloths, disposable china and candles in lanterns are all the props you need. You can keep the bug spray in the cupboard!

Serve the salad from a clear trifle bowl or pedestal salad bowl. Baking dishes hold all of the casseroles right from the oven. Serve wedges of cheesecake on simple dessert plates.

Margaritas for a Crowd

The citrus mix for these Margaritas can be made up to 3 days ahead, covered, and refrigerated until party time.

4 cups Simple Syrup (see step 1, below)
6 cups freshly squeezed lemon juice
3 cups freshly squeezed orange juice
3 cups freshly squeezed lime juice
Lime wedges
Lime pinwheels
Tequila
Triple Sec

1. Prepare Simple Syrup by adding 4 cups granulated sugar to 4 cups water in a saucepan over medium high heat. Stir until the sugar is dissolved. Cool.

2. Combine the lemon juice, syrup, orange and lime juices in a large pitcher. Chill.

3. Prepare individual margaritas by placing 1 part tequila and 3 parts margarita mix in a shaker. Add ice and a splash of Triple Sec. Shake well.

4. Prepare margarita glasses by running a lime wedge around the rim. Dip the glass into a dish filled with salt.

5. Pour the chilled margarita into the glass and garnish with a lime wedge.

Yield: 1 gallon mix
Preparation Time: 15 minutes

For a large crowd you can easily pre-mix the margaritas by adding the liquor directly into the mix. Pour over ice cubes.

CUCUMBER, TOMATO, and BREAD SALAD
with FRENCH DRESSING and ROQUEFORT CHEESE

Diced bacon and hard-boiled egg make this tempting salad a meal by itself.

4	large cucumbers, peeled, seeded and cut into ½-inch dice (about 6 cups)
12	plum tomatoes, seeded and diced (about 4 cups)
1	1–pound round loaf crusty bread, cut into 1-inch dice, toasted
8	hard-boiled eggs, peeled, sliced in half
1	pound bacon, cooked and diced
4	medium cloves garlic, minced (about 2 teaspoons)
¼	cup chopped fresh basil leaves
1	cup ketchup
½	cup cider vinegar
6	tablespoons granulated sugar
	Juice of 2 lemons (about ¼ cup)
1	bunch (6 to 8) green onions, chopped (about ½ cup)
1	teaspoon paprika

⅔ cup olive oil
Salt and freshly ground pepper
1 cup crumbled Roquefort cheese

1. Place the cucumbers, plum tomatoes, bread cubes, egg, and bacon in a large salad bowl.
2. Add the minced garlic and basil to the bowl.
3. In a separate bowl whisk together the ketchup, vinegar, sugar, and lemon juice.
4. Stir in the onion and paprika.
5. Slowly whisk in the olive oil. Season with salt and pepper.
6. Pour in enough dressing to moisten the salad. Toss and let stand 10 minutes before serving.
7. Top with crumbled cheese and fresh pepper.

Servings: 10
Preparation Time: 20 minutes

Panzanella is a simple bread salad that combines chunks of stale bread, fresh tomatoes and a bit of garlic and fresh herbs. This recipe starts with panzanella basics and adds a few dicey ingredients. The gutsy French dressing brings everything together with a flare and just a hint of the traditional Italian favorite.

JALAPEÑO-SPICED BARBECUE BEEF STEW

Make this terrifically spiced shredded beef dish the day before and slow cook your way to an easy entrée.

Olive oil
5   pounds boneless beef chuck roast, cut into 1-inch cubes
    Salt and freshly ground pepper
2   large red onions, diced (about 2 cups)
2   12-ounce cans beer
2   cups cider vinegar
1   cup ketchup
⅓   cup packed dark brown sugar
⅓   cup Worcestershire sauce
2   tablespoons Dijon mustard
1   tablespoon ground cumin
4   medium jalapeño peppers, roasted, charred skin removed, seeded and diced (about ½ cup)

Preheat the oven to 325°.
1. Heat the olive oil in a large skillet over medium high heat.
2. Brown the beef in the hot oil in batches. Do not crowd the pan. Remove the meat to a bowl and continue until all of the cubes have been browned.

3. Add the onions and sauté until just beginning to brown.
4. Place the meat and onions into a large roasting pan.
5. Stir in the beer, cider vinegar, ketchup, brown sugar, Worcestershire, mustard, cumin, and roasted jalapeño.
6. Cover the pan and roast for 2 to 2½ hours or until the meat is easily shredded with a fork.
7. Uncover the casserole and place it on the top of the stove. Bring the meat mixture to a boil over medium high heat. Cook until the liquid is reduced to about half and thickened slightly.
8. Serve the spicy beef on over-sized buns and top with a tangy vegetable slaw.

Serves 10 to 12
Preparation Time: 30 minutes plus cooking

To roast jalapeño peppers place them on a baking sheet on the top rack of the oven.
Char the skin of the peppers turning until the peppers are blackened on all sides.
Place the peppers in a bowl and cover with foil for 10 to 15 minutes.
Peel off the black skin and discard. Remove the stem and seeds, and dice.

TOASTED CORN PUDDING

You can make this easy recipe in advance and freeze it. Just remember to defrost in time for the party!

¼ **cup bread crumbs**
½ **pound bacon, diced**
2 **large yellow onions, diced (about 2 cups)**
1 **large red bell pepper, diced (about 1 cup)**
1 **large green bell pepper, diced (about 1 cup)**
8 **ears fresh corn sliced from cob (about 4 cups)**
4 **medium cloves garlic, minced (about 2 teaspoons)**
   Salt
½ **teaspoon cayenne pepper**
4 **cups heavy cream**
2 **cups milk**
6 **large eggs**
1 **teaspoon ground nutmeg**
1 **cup Parmesan cheese**
1 **cup white cornmeal**

Preheat the oven to 350°.

1. Prepare a 13 x 9 x 2-inch baking pan by spraying it with vegetable oil spray and sprinkling with bread crumbs.
2. Cook the diced bacon in a large skillet over medium high heat until just beginning to crisp.
3. Add the onions and peppers and cook until soft.
4. Add the corn and cook until just beginning to brown.
5. Add the garlic and cook for 2 minutes more. Season with salt and cayenne pepper.
6. In a large mixing bowl whisk together the heavy cream, milk, and eggs.
7. Stir in the nutmeg and cheese.
8. Stir in the toasted corn mixture.
9. Stir in the cornmeal.
10. Pour the mixture into the prepared pan and bake for about 1 hour or until the center is set.

Serves 10 to 12
Preparation Time: 30 minutes plus baking

Fresh corn begins to lose moisture as soon as the husk is removed. For best results store fresh corn in the husk in a cool dry place in your kitchen.

CHEESY POTATO CASSEROLE

This dish is best served right out of the oven, but holds well on a buffet table.

1   **32-ounce bag frozen hash brown pota-toes, thawed**
2   **cups sour cream**
2   **10¾-ounce cans cream of mushroom soup**
2   **cups grated extra sharp Cheddar cheese**
1   **bunch (6 to 8) green onions, chopped (about 1 cup)**
½   **cup grated Parmesan cheese**
    Salt and freshly ground pepper
½   **cup cornflake crumbs**

Preheat the oven to 350°.

1. Mix all of the ingredients except the cornflake crumbs together in a large bowl.
2. Prepare a 13 x 9 x 2-inch baking pan by spraying it with vegetable oil spray.
3. Spread the mixture into the pan.
4. Sprinkle the cornflake crumbs over top.
5. Cover the casserole with aluminum foil. Bake for 30 minutes.
6. Uncover the pan and cook for an additional 30 minutes or until the top begins to brown and the casserole bubbles.

Serves 10 to 12
Preparation Time: 15 minutes

This simple casserole is perfect for your buffet table. Feel free to add your own special touches. Substitute with various cheese, add your favorite vegetable, or try tater tots in place of hash browns. It all works!

PUMPKIN SWIRL CHEESECAKE

The best thing about this yummy dessert is that you can prepare it a day or two in advance of a party and it is at it's best on the day that you serve it.

18 to 20 gingersnap cookies
7 ounces hazelnuts, toasted (about 1½ cups)
¼ cup packed light brown sugar
½ cup butter (1 stick)

4 8-ounce packages cream cheese, room temperature
1⅔ cups granulated sugar
¼ cup heavy cream
4 eggs
1 15-ounce can pumpkin
1 teaspoon ground cinnamon
1 teaspoon allspice

Preheat the oven to 350°.

1. Place the gingersnap cookies, hazelnuts, and sugar in a food processor. Pulse until combined. Add the melted butter and pulse briefly.
2. Press the crumb mixture into the bottom and up the sides about ½ inch in a 10-inch diameter springform pan using the back of a fork
3. With an electric mixer beat the cream cheese and sugar.
4. Mix in the whipping cream. Stir in the eggs one at a time.
5. Pour half of the filling into a small bowl.
6. Add the pumpkin and spices to the remaining filling and mix well.
7. Place the filling into the pan by alternating between plain and pumpkin batter. With a knife gently swirl together.
8. Bake for 60 to 75 minutes. The cheesecake will puff and may crack on the sides. The center does not have to be set. Cool the cake on a rack. Run a sharp knife around the side of the pan. Cover with plastic wrap and refrigerate overnight.

Serves 10 to 12
Preparation Time: 20 minutes plus baking and refrigeration

Hazelnuts are grape-sized nuts whose shells are tough to crack. For that reason, they are usually sold shelled with a thin skin that is removed by toasting the nut and rubbing with a clean dry towel.

Haunted Halloween Open House Party Plan

Party Motivation

Your house is the oasis in the midst of little trick or treaters and overwrought/undercostumed parents. Greet them all in style by hosting a terrific party that will last long after the kids wear out.

Party Menu

Bibb Lettuce Bowls with Chopped Bacon, Tomatoes, and Blue Cheese
Old-Fashioned Mushroom Soup
Apple Cheddar Muffins
Creamy Tomato Soup
Spicy Cornbread with Sun-Dried Tomato and Jalapeño
Sweet Potato Cake with Orange Glaze

** Over-the-Top Suggestion

If you are expecting tons and tons of tricksters, whip up a batch of paint brush cookies. Use your favorite sugar cookie recipe to cut out Halloween shapes—ghosts, bats, witches and pumpkins. Beat two eggs together with two tablespoons of water. Divide this mixture into several bowls. Use drops of food coloring in each bowl to create "paint." Allow little ones to brush the cookie shapes with paint. Sprinkle with granulated sugar. Bake until golden and serve warm.

Party Strategy

Prepare the soups the day before and reheat as the evening approaches. Bake the muffins and cornbread so that they are warm, tucked into baskets as the first ghost rings the bell.

The day before: Prepare soups, cover and refrigerate.

The evening before: Bake cake, frost, cover and refrigerate.

The morning of: Set the buffet table. Prepare the salad ingredients.

One hour before: Prepare and bake muffins and corn bread.

Thirty minutes before: Assemble salad and dressing.

Immediately before: Place candy in bowl, put on your costume, and answer the door.

Shortcuts

For a larger group, eliminate the lettuce bowls. Instead, tear the leaves and toss with the rest of the salad ingredients.

Party Backdrop

Place the buffet as strategically close to the front door as possible. Guests will be "dropping by" for a taste of muffin or a spoonful of soup. A living room coffee table or an entry sideboard will work well. A kitchen or dining table is perfect if your group plans on lingering awhile.

The Table Setting

Serve warm soups from a tureen or hollowed out pumpkins. Place plenty of mugs and a pile of soup spoons nearby. Cloth lined-baskets hold warm muffins and cornbread, while lettuce bowls sit on a large platter. Pre-slice the cake into easy to grab pieces. Place a tub full of chilled water bottles near the door for those thirsty travelers.

BIBB LETTUCE BOWLS with CHOPPED BACON, TOMATOES, and BLUE CHEESE

This festive salad can be duplicated with any fresh greens. However, the rosette shape of a Bibb lettuce head creates tons of charm on a holiday buffet.

10 **to 12 small heads bibb lettuce**

2 **tablespoons Dijon mustard**
⅓ **cup champagne vinegar**
1 **cup olive oil**
2 **tablespoons chopped fresh chives**
Salt and freshly ground pepper

¼ **pound bacon, diced**
6 **to 8 plum tomatoes, seeded and diced (about 2 cups)**
4 **ounces blue cheese, crumbled**

1. Peel the outer leaves from the lettuce and trim the stem so that the head of lettuce sits on its stem on a platter. Slice off the top fourth of the head. Use your fingers to pull the leaves away from the center creating a "bowl."

2. Whisk together the mustard and champagne vinegar in a bowl.

3. Slowly whisk in the olive oil. Stir in the chives and season with salt and pepper.

4. Cook the bacon in a small skillet over medium high heat. Drain on paper toweling.

5. Assemble the salad by placing the lettuce bowls on a large platter.

6. Sprinkle each lettuce bowl with equal amounts of bacon, chopped tomatoes, and blue cheese.

7. Pour the vinaigrette over the top and into the lettuce bowl.

Servings: 10 to 12
Preparation Time: 20 minutes

For this dish, choose heads of Bibb lettuce that are the size of a man's fist. Larger heads can be divided into two halves. The leaves are pale and tender and the head should be washed well.

Old-Fashioned Mushroom Soup

Just like mama would have made (if she had the time), this soup is easy, yummy, and down-home good!

2	tablespoons olive oil
2	tablespoons butter
2	leeks, white part only, chopped
2	large yellow onions, diced (about 2 cups)
6	medium cloves garlic, minced (about 1 tablespoon)
2	pounds mushrooms such as button, shiitake, portobello, cut into ¼-inch pieces
¼	cup all-purpose flour
2	quarts chicken stock
¼	cup fresh thyme
1	cup heavy cream
	Salt and freshly ground pepper

1. Heat the olive oil and butter in a large soup pan over medium high heat.
2. Cook the leeks, onions, and garlic until soft, about 10 minutes.
3. Add the mushrooms to the pot. Cook until soft, about 5 minutes.
4. Sprinkle the flour over the vegetables and stir. Cook for several minutes.
5. Reduce the heat to medium. Stir in the broth and simmer for 30 minutes.
6. Stir in the thyme and cream. Simmer for 10 minutes more.
7. Season with salt and pepper.

Servings: 10 to 12
Preparation Time: 45 minutes

For a creamier soup feel free to use a food processor or an immersion blender to purée the mushrooms after they are simmered and before the cream is added. Stir the cream into the puréed soup and continue with the recipe.

APPLE CHEDDAR MUFFINS

Just like apple pie with a slice of melted cheese on top, these muffins savor American traditions.

1½ **cups all-purpose flour**
¼ **cup old-fashioned rolled oats**
2 **teaspoons baking powder**
½ **teaspoon baking soda**
2 **tablespoons granulated sugar**
¾ **cup milk**
2 **large eggs**
¼ **cup butter (½ stick), melted**
1 **medium apple, peeled, cored and cut into ⅛ inch dice (about 1 cup)**
¾ **cup finely grated sharp Cheddar cheese**

Preheat the oven to 400°.
1. Combine the flour, oats, baking powder, baking soda, and sugar in a bowl. Set aside.
2. Whisk together the milk and eggs in a large bowl.
3. Stir in the butter.
4. Stir the flour mixture into the milk mixture until just combined.
5. Fold in the diced apples and cheese.
6. Place the batter into a 12-cup muffin tin that has been sprayed with vegetable oil spray.
7. Bake for 30 minutes or until the tops are golden and a toothpick inserted into the center comes out clean.

Yield: 12 muffins
Preparation Time: 20 minutes plus baking

There are an abundant variety of apples to choose from in baking and cooking. Some of the most popular are Granny Smith, a green apple with a sweet and tart taste; Golden Delicious, a milder tasting apple that is often recommended in baking; Red Delicious, which is a popular apple to eat when just harvested; and McIntosh, which is readily available in the fall and has a crispy firmness. Experiment with all the different types and remember to use the freshest apple you can find in all of your cooking.

CREAMY TOMATO SOUP

Curry and paprika spice up this traditional favorite but the creamy texture reminds you of home.

¾	cup butter (1½ sticks)
4	medium celery ribs, thinly sliced (about 1½ cups)
1	large yellow onion, diced (about 1 cup)
2	large carrots, cut into pieces (about ½ cup)
½	cup all-purpose flour
3	28-ounce cans diced tomatoes
1	tablespoon granulated sugar
2	bay leaves
2	quarts chicken stock
1	tablespoon chopped fresh basil
3	cups whipping cream
½	teaspoon paprika
½	teaspoon curry powder
	Salt and freshly ground pepper

1. Melt the butter in a large soup pot over medium high heat.
2. Cook the celery, onion, and carrots in the butter until soft, about 12 minutes.
3. Stir the flour into the vegetables.
4. Stir in the tomatoes, sugar, bay leaves, and chicken stock.
5. Reduce heat and simmer for 30 minutes.
6. Remove the bay leaves from the soup.
7. Use an immersion blender (or food processor) to purée the soup.
8. Stir in the basil, cream, paprika, and curry. Simmer for 10 minutes.
9. Season with salt and pepper.

Servings: 10 to 12
Preparation Time: 60 minutes

Bay leaves are found in the spice section of the grocery store and are the dried leaf of the evergreen bay tree found in the Mediterranean. Bay leaves are most often used to flavor soups and stews as they impart their earthy flavor and aroma when simmered. Bay leaves are tough and should be removed before serving.

SPICY CORN BREAD with SUN-DRIED TOMATO and JALAPEÑO

A bit of chili powder in the batter and chopped veggies add a special zing to this quick bread

¾ **cup all-purpose flour**
2 **teaspoons baking powder**
¼ **teaspoon salt**
1 **teaspoon chili powder**
1½ **cups yellow cornmeal**
6 **tablespoons butter, melted**
¾ **cup milk**
3 **large eggs, beaten**
1 **7-ounce jar sun-dried tomatoes in oil, drained and finely chopped**
2 **medium jalapeño peppers, seeded and diced (about 4 tablespoons)**

Preheat the oven to 350°.

1. Place the flour, baking powder, salt, and chili powder into a large bowl.
2. Whisk in the cornmeal.
3. Whisk in the butter, milk, and eggs until just combined.
4. Fold in the tomatoes and peppers.
5. Place the batter into a loaf pan that has been sprayed with vegetable oil spray.
6. Bake for 45 to 50 minutes or until a toothpick inserted into the center of the loaf comes out clean.

Servings: 10 to 12
Preparation Time: 15 minutes plus baking

Cornmeal is a light flour made from grinding dried corn kernels.
It is most commonly pale yellow in color although white cornmeal is readily available.
Cornmeal is cooked into polenta or baked into muffins or cornbread.
It is also used for coating fried foods like chicken or fish.

Sweet Potato Cake with Orange Glaze

The aroma of this baking cake fills the house with holiday scents matched only by the scrumptious taste.

3	**medium sweet potatoes, peeled and diced (about 2 cups)**
3	**cups all-purpose flour**
1	**teaspoon baking soda**
½	**teaspoon salt**
½	**teaspoon ground ginger**
½	**teaspoon ground nutmeg**
½	**teaspoon ground cinnamon**
½	**cup butter (1 stick), room temperature**
1	**cup granulated sugar**
1	**cup packed brown sugar**
3	**large eggs**
1	**teaspoon vanilla extract**
½	**cup heavy cream**

Zest of 1 medium orange (about 2 tablespoons)

2½	**cups confectioners' sugar**
1	**teaspoon vanilla extract**
	Juice of 3 medium orange (about ¾ cup)

Preheat the oven to 375°.

1. Pace the sweet potatoes in boiling water and cook until soft, about 15 minutes. Drain well and mash.

2. Combine the flour, baking soda, salt, ginger, nutmeg, and cinnamon in a bowl.
3. Use an electric mixer to combine the butter and sugars.
4. Add the eggs one at a time.
5. Stir in the mashed sweet potatoes and vanilla.
6. Add the flour and cream in 3 additions, alternating ⅓ flour mixture with ⅓ cream until just blended.
7. Pour the batter into a Bundt pan that has been sprayed with vegetable oil spray and dusted with flour.
8. Bake for 50 to 60 minutes or until a toothpick inserted into the center of the cake comes out clean. Cool the cake in the pan for 10 minutes. Remove the cake to a rack placed on top of sheets of waxed paper.
9. Whisk together the orange zest and confectioners' sugar.
10. Whisk in the orange juice and vanilla.
11. Use a skewer to poke holes in the cake. Pour the glaze over the cake. Repeating with the glaze that runs off onto the waxed paper.

Servings: 12 to 18
Preparation Time: 45 minutes plus baking.

Glaze will readily be absorbed into a warm cake. Layer several sheets of waxed paper under the cooling rack. As the glaze runs off and onto the top sheet, fold it into a funnel and pour the excess over the cake again. Repeat with remaining waxed paper sheets until all of the glaze is absorbed. Then allow the cake to cool completely.
If glaze is too thick, thin with a few drops of warm water.

Tree Trimming Supper Party Plan

Party Motivation

Invite your best pals for an evening of holiday fun. The requirement is that each one must bring an ornament for your tree. During cocktails the ornaments are attached and the twinkle lights illuminated. Now that your guests have worked up an appetite, it's time to serve a traditional holiday meal.

Party Menu

Stunning Seafood Crepes
Standing Rib Roast with Red Wine Mushroom Gravy
Herbed Parmesan Popovers
Creamed Spinach
Baby Rosemary Baked Potatoes
Warm Ginger Pudding with Butter Rum Sauce

** Over-the-Top Suggestion

Add an eggnog punch by combining chilled prepared eggnog and your best bourbon in a crystal punch bowl. Garnish with grated fresh nutmeg.

Party Strategy

A combination of make ahead and last minute dishes work their way into this doable dinner. Ask a designated helper to assist you when serving the first course.

Two days before: Prepare crepes, stack, cover and refrigerate.

One day before: Set up tree and arrange lights.

The evening before: Prepare ginger pudding and sauce. Cover and refrigerate separately.

The morning before: Prepare seafood filling for crepes. Set table.

Three hours before: Prepare roast, bake as estimated for medium rare.

Two hours before: Prepare batter for popovers. Prepare creamed spinach. Prepare potatoes.

One hour before: Bake spinach and potatoes.

Thirty minutes before: Bake popovers. Warm crepes, seafood, dessert and sauce.

Immediately before: Warm plates for crepes and assemble first course. Carve roast.

Shortcuts
Purchase prepared crepes and warm just before serving.

Party Backdrop
Set a sparkling holiday table and invite your friends to enjoy a special dinner. Small ornaments with each guest's name act as both place card and favor. Mounding pine cones and glass balls into a crystal bowl is an easy centerpiece. Tie napkins with festive ribbon—and don't forget the English poppers.

The Table Setting
Invite your guests to sit at your stunning table. Serve warm seafood crepes on warm plates directly onto chargers set at each place setting. As you enjoy your first course, the herbed popovers bake, the roast potatoes and spinach is kept warm, the roast rests before carving, and the pudding warms in the oven.

You and your designated helper remove first course plates—charger and all and prepare the balance of the meal in the kitchen.

Alternatively, serve the crepes while you and your guests are trimming the tree. When ready, serve the rest of the meal buffet style. Invite guests to fill plates from a sideboard or kitchen island and then sit at the dining table. In this case, serve the roast from a silver platter with a carving well to catch the juices. Serve the potatoes on a platter, opened with a slice of butter and a dollop of sour cream. Creamed spinach is served from a covered vegetable dish, and a silver basket holds nested popovers.

STUNNING SEAFOOD CREPES

This dazzling starter is easily prepared in advance and then assembled just before your guests are seated.

¾ cup all-purpose flour
½ teaspoon salt
1 teaspoon baking powder
2 large eggs, beaten
6 tablespoons butter, melted
1 cup milk

½ pound white sole fillets
½ pound salmon fillets
Juice of 1 lemon (about 2 tablespoons)
Salt and freshly ground pepper
2 tablespoons butter
2 tablespoons all-purpose flour
½ cup clam juice
½ cup white wine
½ cup heavy cream
½ teaspoon ground nutmeg
1 tablespoon chopped fresh dill
¼ cup grated Parmesan cheese

1. Place the flour, salt, and baking powder in a small bowl.
2. Whisk in the beaten eggs.
3. Stir in 1 tablespoon melted butter.
4. Whisk in the milk. Chill the batter for 1 hour.
5. Heat a crepe pan or small skillet over medium heat.
6. Place a small amount of melted butter in the pan.
7. Pour 2 to 3 tablespoons of batter into the pan. Swirl the pan to coat the bottom with the batter. Cook until just golden on the bottom, about 2 minutes. Use a spatula to flip the crepe and cook until golden. Continue with remaining batter, using additional butter as needed.

Place the oven temperature on the broil setting.

8. Place the sole and salmon on a baking sheet that has been sprayed with a vegetable oil spray. Drizzle lemon juice over the fish and season with salt and pepper. Broil until just cooked through, about 5 minutes.
9. Melt 2 tablespoons of butter in a saucepan over medium high heat.
10. Stir in 2 tablespoons flour until golden and bubbling.
11. Add the clam juice, white wine, and cream, stirring until the sauce thickens.
12. Stir in the nutmeg. Remove from heat and stir in the dill. Season with salt and pepper.
13. Flake the fish and place into a bowl. Add half of the sauce to the bowl and toss.
14. Place 2 tablespoons of seafood mixture in the center of a crepe. Fold the crepe in half and then in half again. Place the crepe onto a serving plate and drizzle with additional sauce. Sprinkle with Parmesan cheese and freshly ground pepper.

Yield: 12 to 16 crepes; servings: 12
Preparation Time: 45 minutes

Crepes, with their roots in French cooking are very thin pancakes.
When preparing dessert crepes, add a small amount of sugar to the batter. Crepe batter is best made in advance and allowed to chill for at least an hour or up to 12 hours to allow the flour to absorb all of the liquid. It should be very smooth and can be prepared by hand or by using an electric mixer or blender. Finished crepes can be stacked, wrapped, and stored in the refrigerator, and also keep well when frozen.

STANDING RIB ROAST with RED WINE MUSHROOM GRAVY

There is nothing more traditional than a standing rib roast holiday dinner with all of the trimmings. This roast is so easy to make that you can incorporate it into your meal plan way more often than once a year!

7	**to 8 pound beef rib roast with 4 to 5 ribs, trimmed**
¼	**cup Dijon mustard**
¼	**cup chopped fresh parsley**
2	**tablespoons granulated sugar**
	Salt and freshly ground pepper
2	**pounds button mushrooms, sliced (about 4 cups)**
1	**cup red wine**
3	**cups beef stock**
¼	**cup all-purpose flour, mixed with 1 cup cold water**

Preheat the oven to 475° (the hottest setting).

1. Combine the mustard, parsley, and sugar in a small bowl.
2. Brush the mixture over the entire roast. Season with salt and pepper.
3. Place the roast fat side up on a rack in a roasting pan. Place the roasting pan into the preheated oven. Immediately reduce the heat to 350°. and roast for 18 minutes per pound or until a thermometer inserted into the thickest part of the roast reaches 140° for rare to 170° for well done.
4. Remove the roast from the oven and let stand for 15 minutes before carving.
5. Sauté the mushrooms in the pan drippings, over medium high heat. Remove with a slotted spoon to a bowl.
6. Add the red wine to the pan. Simmer until the liquid is reduced by half, about 5 minutes.
7. Add the beef stock and simmer for 5 minutes more.
8. Add the flour mixture to the pan, a small amount at a time. Cook until the sauce thickens to gravy consistency.
9. Add the mushrooms. Season with salt and pepper.

Servings: 10 to 12 (2 to 3 servings per pound)
Preparation Time: 30 minutes plus roasting

Standing rib roast is the cut of beef where the meat lies between the rib bones. It is the most flavorful, juicy and tender portion and holds a place on the table of special occasions.

HERBED PARMESAN POPOVERS

The perfect accompaniment to traditional standing rib roast is the piping hot, puffed popover some-times referred to as Yorkshire pudding.

4   large eggs
3   cups milk
2   cups all-purpose flour
½ cup finely grated Parmesan cheese
2   tablespoons chopped fresh chives
Salt and freshly ground pepper

¼ cup butter, melted (½ stick)

Heat the oven to 450°.
1. Place a 12-cup muffin tin into the preheated oven. (Or use two 6-cup popover pans.)
2. Place the eggs and milk into a blender. Pulse to combine.
3. Add the flour. Pulse to combine.
4. Add the Parmesan and chives, and season with salt and pepper. The batter should be the consistency of heavy cream.

5. Carefully remove the hot muffin tin from the oven.
6. Pour a small amount of butter into the bottom of each cup. Use a potholder to swirl the pan around to coat.
7. Pour the batter into the pan, filling each cup ¾ full.
8. Place the pan back into the oven. Bake until puffed and golden, about 25 to 30 minutes. Do not open the oven door while the popovers are baking.

Servings: 12
Preparation Time: 20 minutes plus baking

Popovers are best served immediately from the oven. However, you can hold them by piercing the top with a knife to let the steam escape. Place them into a warm (350°) oven and keep warm for up to 15 minutes.

CREAMED SPINACH

Fresh spinach is quickly wilted and then finished in a rich and decadent cream sauce.

2   **tablespoons olive oil**
4   **10-ounce bags fresh spinach**

1   **cup butter (2 sticks)**
1   **cup all-purpose flour**
1   **medium white onion, diced (about ⅔ cup)**
4   **cups milk**
2   **cups heavy cream**
1   **cup Parmesan cheese**
3   **bay leaves**
¼   **teaspoon ground cloves**
   Salt and freshly ground pepper

½   **cup fresh breadcrumbs**

Preheat the oven to 350°.

1. Heat the olive oil in a skillet over medium high heat.
2. Place half of the fresh spinach into the skillet and cook until just beginning to wilt. Remove to a large baking dish. Continue until all of the spinach has been wilted using additional oil as needed.
3. Melt the butter in a large saucepan over medium high heat.
4. Whisk in the flour and cook until golden and bubbling, about 5 minutes.
5. Stir in the onion. Cook for 5 minutes.
6. Whisk in the milk. Reduce the heat to medium.
7. Stir in the Parmesan cheese, bay leaves, and cloves. Continue stirring until the sauce has thickened. Season with salt and pepper.
8. Remove the bay leaves from the sauce. Pour half of the sauce over the spinach. Allow the spinach to wilt in the sauce. Add the remaining spinach and sauce.
9. Sprinkle the breadcrumbs over the casserole.
10. Bake for 20 to 30 minutes or until the casserole is bubbling.

Servings: 12
Preparation Time: 30 minutes plus baking

Fresh spinach is effortless to incorporate into your meal plan because smart farmers have made it easy for us to use. Bags of pre-washed spinach have tough stems and foreign particles removed so that the spinach goes from the bag to your dish without any effort. Fresh is best, however frozen or canned spinach can be substituted in this recipe by eliminating the first step.

BABY ROSEMARY BAKED POTATOES

Course salt rubbed onto the outside of the potatoes makes for a crispy skin while the fragrant herbs flavor the soft flesh.

12 to 18 small red potatoes, about 3-inches in diameter
¼ cup olive oil
2 tablespoons coarse salt
1 bunch fresh rosemary

Butter
Sour cream
Fresh chives

Heat the oven to 375°.

1. Rub each potato with olive oil and sprinkle generously with coarse salt.
2. Place the potatoes into a large, shallow baking dish.
3. Place rosemary sprigs on top and around the potatoes.
4. Roast until just soft, about 30 minutes. Remove rosemary sprigs before serving.

Servings: 12
Preparation Time: 10 minutes plus baking

For this dish choose potatoes that are the same size. Make an "X" in the top of the cooked potatoes. Push the flesh slightly with your fingers. Garnish with butter, a dollop of sour cream, and fresh chopped chives.

Warm Ginger Pudding with Rum Butter Sauce

English pudding steamed for hours and served with brandy hard sauce is the dessert of choice on an English table. This pudding is just as good and is baked in a smidgeon of the time.

2½ **cups flour**
½ **teaspoon baking soda**
2 **teaspoons baking powder**
1 **teaspoon salt**
2 **teaspoons ground ginger**
¼ **cup butter (½ stick)**
2 **large eggs**
1 **cup molasses**
½ **cup finely chopped crystallized ginger**
Zest of ½ medium lemon (about 1 teaspoon)
1 **cup buttermilk**

1½ **cups butter (3 sticks)**
⅔ **cup packed brown sugar**
½ **cup dark rum**
Zest of 1 medium orange (about 2 tablespoons)
½ **cup heavy cream**

Preheat the oven to 325°.

1. Combine the flour, baking soda, baking powder, salt, and ginger in a bowl. Set aside.
2. Use an electric mixer to beat the butter until soft.
3. Add the eggs and molasses and beat until fluffy.
4. Stir in the crystallized ginger and lemon zest.
5. Stir in the buttermilk.
6. Stir in the flour mixture.
7. Pour the batter into a Bundt pan that has been sprayed with vegetable oil spray. Bake for 1 hour.
8. Melt the butter and brown sugar in a saucepan over medium high heat until the sugar is dissolved.
9. Stir in the rum and the orange zest.
10. Stir in the cream.
11. Serve the warm pudding with the warm sauce.

Servings: 10 to 12
Preparation Time: 30 minutes plus baking

Crystallized ginger is ginger that has been candied by cooking in sugar syrup. It is then coated with granulated sugar and is used to add sweetness to desserts. It is found in jars in the spice or baking section of the grocery store.

Really Fussy Festivities

(FUSSY PARTIES FOR A LARGE CROWD—TWENTY OR MORE GUESTS)

Sunset Picnic Supper
They're Getting MARRIED Party
Afternoon Tea Party
Pre-Theatre Coctail Party

"Always create a special cocktail for the event—whether it's a fun summer punch or a classic cocktail with a twist like Mandarin Margaritas. Ultimately you want guests to break out of their shells and loosen up a little. Tempting them to try something new is always a good start and helps to create a fun, festive atmosphere.

For an uncomplicated dessert, leave a splendid impression by overflowing a large urn with every seasonal fruit you can find. Add a wonderful American artisan cheese. To complement this culinary treat pour a sweet liquid confection such as a chilled ice wine, sauterne, or late harvest wine. Another very sexy dessert variation is to bring to the table slightly warmed, spreadable chocolate served with sliced sourdough bread. Finish with an unexpected sparkling red wine.

For larger dinners don't feel obligated to serve a seated meal. These days many hosts and hostesses are skipping the main course and simply serving hors d'oeuvres followed by dessert. Call it "before and after" (the entree, that is)!"

Carl Hedin
Creative Director
Tenation, Potel & Chabot
Catering and Party Planning
New York, New York

Sunset Picnic Supper Party Plan

Party Motivation

A ground breaking celebration, a small seaside wedding, a surprise 50th birthday party. Whatever the occasion, find a gorgeous location, erect a whimsical tent and serve an elegant, family style supper that comes together in days. Upscale picnic fare is the theme for this party— and with a little extra help, you are certain to enjoy every second of the merrymaking.

Party Menu

Authentic Mint Julep
Chilled Avocado Lime Soup with Jalapeño Salsa
Herbed Onion Biscuits
Grilled Baby Artichoke, Shrimp, and Hearts of Palm Salad with Remoulade Dressing
Grilled Flank Steak and Roasted Onion Salad with Poblano Pepper Vinaigrette
Poached Chicken in Rich Tuna Sauce with Capers
Sautéed Fruit and Cheese Platter

** Over-the-Top Suggestion

Set round tables for 6 or 8. Designate one helper per table. Find an experienced helper to head up the food prep area. Each guest receives a picnic basket that includes everything that they will need for their supper. The kitchen helper arranges platters of food, and each table helper delivers the food to the table. Guests pass platters and dig in for second and (perhaps) third helpings. As courses are eaten, table helpers remove dishes and platters, refill glasses and come back with the next course!

Party Strategy

The food for this party is served chilled, or at room temperature to prevent last minute cooking at the party site. Transfer all of the food in large containers, with serving dishes packed separately. Allow plenty of room for a work station to arrange the food on the individual platters.

In advance: Select location, arrange for tent and flooring if necessary. Rent tables and chairs, china, glassware, linens and plants. Plan delivery schedule.

Two days in advance: Prepare soup, cover and refrigerate. Prepare dressing for artichoke salad. Cover and refrigerate. Prepare vinaigrette for flank steak salad. Cover and refrigerate. Prepare tuna dressing for chicken. Cover and refrigerate.

One day in advance: Prepare jalapeños salsa for soup garnish, cover and refrigerate. Prepare ingredients for artichoke salad. Marinate flank steak. Poach chicken, cover and refrigerate whole breasts.

The evening before: Grill flank steak, cover and refrigerate whole steaks. Lay out everything that you will transport to the party site including bar items.

The morning of: Roast onions for flank steak salad. Bake biscuits.

Four hours before: Slice flank steak, cover and refrigerate. Slice chicken breasts, cover and refrigerate. Sauté fruit.

Three hours before: Transport food in coolers with ice to keep chilled. Meet helpers at party site. Direct helpers to set ups tables and prepare bar and food prep areas. Go home, and relax until party time!

Immediately before: Direct helpers to set each place with chilled soup. Place a basket of biscuits on each table. After helpers remove soup course, send out a platter of each salad to each table. Table servers will assist guests in helping themselves to each dish. Set platters on table for extra helpings. After the salads are removed, set platters of sautéed fruit and cheese on each table.

Shortcuts

This party becomes even simpler by serving everything from a buffet table, allowing guests to help themselves.

Party Backdrop

Helpers greet guests with mint juleps as they enter the tent. Pots of plants line the party space, while clusters of potted plants work well as centerpieces. Create cocktail space by arranging the plants to form a corridor directing guests to a bar area. Local musicians play classical music. Round tables are set with coordinating cloths and picnic baskets at each place.

The Table Setting

Each place setting holds a picnic basket. In the basket is a bud vase holding a single flowering stem. Each guests contributes his vase to the table as a centerpiece, and then takes home the vase as his favor. Also inside the basket is a wine glass, water glass, a napkin tied with greenery, a dinner plate, butter plate and dessert plate. Utensils are also tucked into the basket and include a soup spoon, butter knife, steak knife, dinner fork and salad fork. Tuck any special message, photo, place card and memento into the basket for extra special fun.

Authentic Mint Julep

A refreshing cocktail for the perfect sunset supper, the aroma of fresh mint entices every guest.

1 ounce simple syrup
Crushed ice
2 ounces bourbon
1 teaspoon fresh mint leaves, chopped
2 mint sprigs dipped in confectioners' sugar

1. Prepare simple syrup by boiling equal parts of sugar and water until the sugar dissolves.
2. Fill tall (8- to 12-ounce) glasses with crushed ice.
3. Place crushed mint on top of the ice.
4. Pour ½ to 1 ounce simple syrup into the glass.
5. Pour bourbon to the top of the glass.
6. Garnish with mint sprigs that have been dipped into confectioners' sugar and place into the drink.
7. Place a straw into the drink and sip slowly!

CHILLED AVOCADO LIME SOUP with JALAPEÑO SALSA

A refreshing summer soup gains some pizzazz with a hint of spicy heat in the garnish.

6	**tablespoons butter**
2	**medium white onions, cut into pieces (about 1⅓ cups)**
3	**1-inch pieces ginger, grated (about 3 tablespoons)**
3	**quarts chicken stock**
	Juice of 3 limes (about 6 tablespoons)
2	**to 6 drops hot pepper sauce**
6	**large avocados, diced (about 6 cups)**
2	**cups heavy cream**
½	**teaspoon ground cumin**
	Salt and freshly ground pepper
6	**to 8 plum tomatoes, seeded and diced (about 2 cups)**
2	**medium jalapeño peppers, seeded and diced (about 4 tablespoons)**
1	**large red onions, diced (about 1 cup)**
	Juice of 1 lime (about 1 tablespoon)
3	**tablespoons olive oil**
	Fresh garlic chives, snipped
	Sour cream

1. Melt the butter in a large pot over medium high heat.
2. Cook the onion and ginger in the butter until soft, about 5 minutes.
3. Stir in the chicken stock and lime juice. Season with as much hot sauce as you like. Simmer for 5 minutes. Remove from heat.
4. Purée the avocado, cream, and cumin in a food processor or blender.
5. Stir the avocado mixture into the pot. Season with salt and pepper. Chill for at least 2 hours or overnight.

6. Place the tomatoes, jalapeño, red onion, and chives in a bowl.
7. Toss with lime juice and olive oil. Season with salt and pepper. Cover and refrigerate for 1 hour.
8. To serve the soup, ladle the soup into a serving bowl or mug. Drain the salsa and place a spoonful into the center of the bowl. Add a dollop of sour cream and a sprinkling of fresh garlic chives on top.

Servings: 20 or more
Preparation Time: 45 minutes plus chilling

Make this soup for your next "everyday celebration" for 6 to 8 people by decreasing the amount of the ingredients. Save extra salsa to serve with your scrambled eggs in the morning!

2	*tablespoons butter*
1	*medium white onion, cut into pieces (about ⅔ cup)*
1	*1-inch piece ginger, grated (about 1 tablespoons)*
1	*quart chicken stock*
	Juice of 1 lime (about 2 tablespoons)
2	*drops hot pepper sauce*
2	*large avocados, diced (about 6 cups)*
¾	*cup heavy cream*
¼	*teaspoon ground cumin*
	Salt and freshly ground pepper

HERBED ONION BISCUITS

Make these biscuits in advance and serve with slabs of room-temperature butter whipped with a dab of roasted garlic tomatoes. For crowd size entertaining use a heavy duty food processor—or divide the ingredients in half and make the biscuits in batches.

2   **tablespoons butter**
2   **large white onions, chopped (about 2 cups)**
1½ **cups cream**

3   **cups all-purpose flour**
1   **cup whole wheat flour**
4   **teaspoons baking powder**
1   **teaspoon salt**
1   **teaspoon sugar**
1   **teaspoon dried oregano**
1   **teaspoon dried basil**
1   **cup butter, chilled and cut into pieces (2 sticks)**

Preheat the oven to 425°.

1. Heat the butter in a skillet over medium heat.
2. Add the onions and cook until just soft, about 8 minutes.
3. Pour the onions into a blender or food processor. Add cream and pulse until smooth.
4. Place the all-purpose flour, wheat flour, baking powder, salt, sugar, oregano, and basil into the bowl of a food processor.
5. Add the butter and pulse until the mixture resembles course crumbs.
6. Add the onion mixture and pulse until just combined.
7. Turn out the dough onto a floured surface.
8. Knead the dough 6 times. Divide the dough into 2 halves.
9. Roll one half of the dough into 1-inch thickness. Use a 3-inch biscuit cutter to cut out 10 to 12 rounds. Place each round on a Silpat lined baking sheet (or spray a baking sheet with vegetable oil spray).
10. Repeat with the other half of the dough.
11. Bake for 10 to 12 minutes or until the biscuits are golden brown.

Yield: 20 to 24 biscuits
Preparation Time: 30 minutes plus baking

For the lightest, airiest biscuits, handle the dough as little as possible. Turn out the dough to a floured surface and bring together with floured hands. The dough will be sticky. Knead the dough 6 times turning a quarter turn on each fold. Roll out the dough one time (twice if necessary). Do not roll out again and again. This will produce tough biscuits.

GRILLED BABY ARTICHOKE, SHRIMP, and HEARTS OF PALM SALAD with REMOULADE DRESSING

The vibrant colors and fresh flavors of the ingredients in this salad lend themselves to a tempting and indulgent first course.

2   **2-pound bags baby artichokes**
    Lemon slices
¼   **cup olive oil**
4   **to 6 medium cloves garlic, minced**
    (about 3 teaspoons)
10 **cups fresh salad greens**
3   **pounds large shrimp, peeled and**
    deveined (about 48), cooked
2   **14-ounce can hearts of palm, drained,**
    cut into 2-inch diagonal pieces

2   **cups mayonnaise**
2   **tablespoons sweet pickle relish**
2   **tablespoons capers, drained**
1   **tablespoon Dijon mustard**
2   **tablespoons chopped fresh parsley**
2   **tablespoons chopped fresh tarragon**
1   **bunch (6 to 8) green onions, chopped**
    (about ½ cup)
    Salt and freshly ground pepper

1. Prepare the artichokes by removing the dark green outer leaves. The inside leaves will be pale yellow in color. Trim the stem and cut off ¼ of the top of the remaining leaves. Place the trimmed artichokes in a bowl of cold water with a few slices of lemon to prevent them from turning brown until all of the artichokes are trimmed.
2. Cook the artichokes in boiling water until tender, about 8 to 10 minutes. Rinse in cold water to stop the cooking process.
3. Cut each artichoke in half lengthwise. Toss with olive oil and garlic in a bowl.
4. Heat a grill pan over medium high heat. Grill each artichoke, turning once until just beginning to brown.
5. Spread the salad greens on a large platter.

6. Place the grilled baby artichokes on top of the lettuce. Place the cooked shrimp and hearts of palm pieces on the lettuce.
7. Place the mayonnaise, pickle relish, capers, mustard, parsley, and tarragon into a blender or food processor. Pulse to combine.
8. Add the green onion and pulse briefly. Season with salt and pepper.
9. Ladle the dressing around the edges and in the center of the salad.

Servings: 20 or more
Preparation Time: 45 minutes

Make this salad for your next "everyday celebration" for 6 to 8 people by decreasing the amount of the ingredients.

1   ***2-pound bag baby artichokes, outer leaves removed, stems trimmed***
2   ***tablespoons cup olive oil***
2   ***medium cloves garlic, minced (about 1 teaspoon)***
1   ***pound large uncooked shrimp, peeled and deveined (about 20)***
1   ***14-ounce can hearts of palm, drained, cut into 2-inch diagonal pieces***
4   ***cups fresh salad greens***

1   ***cup mayonnaise***
1   ***tablespoon sweet pickle relish***
1   ***tablespoon capers, drained***
2   ***teaspoons Dijon mustard***
1   ***tablespoon chopped fresh parsley***
1   ***tablespoon chopped fresh tarragon leaves***
4   ***green onions, thinly sliced (about ¼ cup)***
    Salt and freshly ground pepper

GRILLED FLANK STEAK and ROASTED ONION SALAD with POBLANO PEPPER VINAIGRETTE

Marinated flank steak, grilled to perfection is enhanced with sweet, roasted onions and spicy vinaigrette in the feisty main course dish.

1	cup olive oil
½	cup balsamic vinegar
¼	cup fresh cilantro leaves
2	tablespoons fresh thyme leaves
4	medium cloves garlic, minced (about 2 teaspoons)
3	12 to 16-ounce flank steaks
18	small white onions, peeled and halved
4	medium poblano peppers, roasted, peeled, and seeded
1	small red onion, chopped (about ½ cup)
	Juice of 3 lemons (about ½ cup)
6	ounces fresh spinach leaves (about 2 cups)
¼	cup chopped fresh cilantro leaves
1	tablespoon honey
2	cups olive oil
	Salt and freshly ground pepper
8	large beefsteak tomatoes, thinly sliced (about 8 cups)
1	pound blue cheese, crumbled

Preheat the oven to 450°.

1. Combine 1 cup olive oil, balsamic vinegar, ¼ cup cilantro, thyme, and garlic into a blender or food processor. Pulse to combine.

2. Place the flank steaks into a shallow baking dish. Pour all but ¼ cup marinade over the steaks. Turn the steaks to coat. Cover and refrigerate for at least 2 hours or overnight.

3. Place the remaining ¼ cup dressing in a bowl. Add the onions. Toss to combine. Place the onions on a baking sheet. Roast until golden brown about 20 minutes.

4. Place the roasted poblano peppers, red onion, lemon juice, spinach leaves, ¼ cup cilantro, and honey into a blender or food processor. Pulse to combine. Add the olive oil and season with salt and pepper.

5. Season the flank steaks with salt and pepper. Grill over medium high heat, turning once about 8 to 10 minutes per side. Allow to rest for 10 minutes. Carve against the grain into thin slices.

6. Place a ring of tomato slices around the edge of a large platter. Sprinkle the cheese over the top of the tomatoes.

7. Pile the flank steak slices inside the ring. Top the steak with roasted onion.

8. Drizzle the platter with the poblano vinaigrette. Serve additional dressing on the side.

Servings: 20 or more
Preparation Time: 1 hour plus marinating

Sunset Picnic Supper

Make this salad for your next "everyday celebra-
tion" for 6 to 8 people by decreasing the amount
of the ingredients.

1   **12 to 16-ounce flank steak**
6   **small white onions, peeled and halved**
½   **cup olive oil**
¼   **cup balsamic vinegar**
2   **tablespoons fresh cilantro leaves**
1   **tablespoon fresh thyme leaves**
2   **medium cloves garlic, minced (about 1**
    teaspoons)
1   **medium poblano pepper, roasted,**
    peeled and seeded

¼   **small red onion, chopped**
    Juice of 1 lemon (about 2 tablespoons)
3   **ounces fresh spinach leaves (about 1**
    cup)
2   **teaspoons chopped fresh cilantro leaves**
1   **teaspoon honey**
¾   **cup olive oil**
    Salt and freshly ground pepper
2   **large beefsteak tomatoes, thinly sliced**
    (about 2 cups)
4   **ounces blue cheese, crumbled**

POACHED CHICKEN in RICH TUNA SAUCE with CAPERS

Based on a traditional Italian meal named Vitello Tonnato, this aromatic dish substitutes poached chicken for the original veal, yet allows for all of the salty flavors to blend into the rich sauce. Designed to be made at least a day ahead in order to soak the essence of the sauce into the chicken, this dish is perfect for a party table.

10	6 to 8-ounce skinless boneless chicken breast halves
1	medium white onion, sliced into rings (about ⅔ cup)
2	large carrots, cut into pieces (about ½ cup)
2	medium celery ribs, cut into pieces (about 1 cup)
2	tablespoons fresh parsley
2	bay leaves
1	tablespoons black peppercorns
1	quart chicken stock
2	cups white wine
2	12-ounce cans solid white tuna packed in oil
2	2-ounce tins anchovy fillets packed in oil
1	3.5-ounce jar capers, drained
1	cup olive oil
	Juice of 6 lemons (about 1 cup)
	Zest of 2 medium lemons (about 2 tablespoons)
3	cups mayonnaise
	Salt and freshly ground pepper
	Lemon slices
¼	cup chopped fresh parsley leaves
2	tablespoons capers

1. Poach the chicken breasts in batches. Place several breasts in a skillet. Add the onion, carrot, celery, parsley, bay leaves, and peppercorns. Pour enough chicken stock and white wine to just cover the breasts. Simmer until just cooked past the pink stage. The breasts should be opaque and very moist. Remove the breasts with a slotted spoon. Cool to room temperature. Repeat until all of the breasts have been poached.
2. Combine the tuna, anchovies, capers, olive oil, lemon juice and zest in a blender or food processor. Pulse to combine.
3. Place the mayonnaise into a mixing bowl.
4. Fold in the tuna mixture. Season with salt and pepper.
5. Cut each chicken breast into ½-inch slices.
6. Place a layer of tuna sauce onto a platter. Place the chicken slices on top. Cover with more sauce. Cover and refrigerate for at least 2 hours or overnight.
7. Bring to room temperature to serve. Garnish with lemon slices, capers, and parsley.

Servings: 20
Preparation Time: 60 minutes plus refrigeration

Make this simple supper for your next "everyday celebration" for 6 to 8 people by decreasing the amount of the ingredients.

4 **6 to 8-ounce skinless boneless chicken breast halves**

½ **medium white onion, sliced into rings (about ⅓ cup)**

1 **large carrot, cut into pieces (about ¼ cup)**

1 **medium celery rib, cut into pieces (about ½ cup)**

1 **tablespoon fresh parsley**

1 **bay leaf**

1 **teaspoon black peppercorns**

2 **cups chicken stock**

1 **cup white wine**

1 **7-ounce can solid white tuna packed in oil**

4 **to 5 anchovy fillets packed in oil**

2 **tablespoons capers, drained**

½ **cup olive oil**

   Juice of 1 lemon (about 2 tablespoons)

   Zest of 1 medium lemons (about 1 tablespoon)

1 **cup mayonnaise**

   Salt and freshly ground pepper

Sautéed Fruit and Cheese Platter

Here is a new twist on the traditional fruit and cheese platter served at the end of a great meal.

½   **cup butter (1 stick)**
2   **cups firmly packed brown sugar**
2   **teaspoons ground cinnamon**
1   **teaspoon ground nutmeg**
2   **medium pineapples, peeled, cored and sliced ¼-inch pieces (about 6 cups)**
6   **medium ripe pears, cored and sliced into ¼-inch wedges (about 6 cups)**
6   **medium apples, cored and sliced into ¼-inch wedges (about 6 cups)**
6   **large bananas, peeled and sliced (about 2 cups)**

Maytag Blue, Stilton, or Roquefort cheese, sliced into wedges

1. Heat 2 tablespoons butter in a skillet over medium heat.

2. Combine the brown sugar, cinnamon, and nutmeg in a bowl.
3. Dip each piece of fruit in the brown sugar mixture.
4. Sauté the fruit in the butter, turning once until just soft and golden. Add more butter to the pan as needed.
5. Transfer the fruit to a baking sheet to hold.
6. Prepare platters by arranging slices of sautéed fruit and cheese wedges on serving dishes.

Servings: 20
Preparation Time: 45 minutes

Make this dessert for your next "everyday celebration" for 6 to 8 people by serving whole pieces of roasted fruit. For example peel, halve and core whole pears and apples. Roll in the brown sugar mixture and roast, cut side down until soft, about 20 minutes at 375°. Team with your favorite cheese or shave pieces of Parmesan or Pecorino Romano on top.

They're Getting MARRIED Party Plan

Party Motivation

After dating—for heaven knows how long—your best friend and her beau decide to take the plunge and you are the one designated to throw THE party. Or, your oldest son comes home with THE girl and announces she is the one and Mom, would ya, could ya, shouldn't ya throw the party to meet the future in-laws? Very special occasions deserve really fussy foods and a party plan that makes all this fussiness doable, so that you too can revel in the milestone celebration!

Party Menu

Creamed Lobster Bruschetta
Chilled Vichyssoise
Cumin-Crusted Sea Bass with Tomato Coulis and Artichoke Salsa
Golden Garlic Mashed Potatoes with Spinach Basil Purée
Warm Carrot Mold with Creamed Peas and Onions
Sesame Seed Dinner Rolls
Red Velvet Cake with Vanilla Frosting **

** Over-the-Top Suggestion

Splurge on individual heart-shaped cake molds and serve one to each guest. Garnish with a dollop of vanilla frosting, a spoon full of champagne macerated berries and a toast to the future bride and groom.

Party Strategy

Helpers are a must as there are plenty of courses and plenty of dishes to be served. Prepare the food at various stages of completion allowing for just a bit of last minute cooking and garnishing.

In advance: Arrange for tables, chairs, china, crystal and linen rental. Find helpers and hire the best jazz guitarist you can find.

Two days in advance: Prepare tomato coulis, cover and refrigerate. Prepare artichoke salsa, cover and refrigerate.

One day in advance: Prepare cake, frost, cover and refrigerate. Prepare potatoes, cover and refrigerate. Prepare spinach purée, cover and refrigerate.

The evening before: Set the table, set up the cocktail area, and chill champagne.

The morning of: Prepare sesame seed rolls. Prepare bread and sauce for bruschetta.

Two hours before: Prepare sea bass through step 4. Cover and refrigerate. Prepare and bake carrot mold. Keep warm.

One hour before: Bring tomato coulis and artichoke salsa to room temperature.

Thirty minutes before: Slowly reheat mashed potatoes and spinach purée. Heat pearl onions and peas in a saucepan over low heat for garnish. Warm the lobster sauce.

To serve: Depending on the size of your bruschetta pass bite size pieces on a tray with extra napkins—or serve larger appetizers on small plates with a fork. While the appetizers are passed, finish the sea bass in the oven. The potatoes with spinach and the carrot mold remain warm.

Shortcuts

In place of passed appetizers, you can prepare the lobster as a first course. See the hint on page 323.

Party Backdrop

A long buffet table with guests on both sides is the perfect setting for this fun party. Or, better yet, make the table into a u-shape with the happy couple in the center. Use white tablecloths and napkins, white taper candles, bowls of white flowers and accent with greenery. Tie napkins with thin green ribbon. White place cards are written in green ink and green chargers are set at each place.

The Table Setting

Pass bite-sized appetizers on a silver tray refilling as more guests arrive. Place toasting glasses at each place setting and encourage guests to audition with great gusto. Baskets of rolls sit on the table. Prepare each dinner plate by swirling tomato coulis onto the dish. Place the sea bass on top. Add a spoonful of salsa on top. Serve the dinner plate to each guest. Divide the potato spinach dish into several bowls. Slice the carrot mold into wedges and place onto several platters. Garnish with warm creamed onions and peas. Alternate a bowl of potatoes with a platter of carrot mold along the length of the table, between several place settings. Guests can pass these treats to each other—the beginning of becoming a united family! Invite the future bride and groom to cut and serve the cake from their position at the head of the table—just for practice!

CREAMED LOBSTER BRUSCHETTA

Slather this terrific sauce on every seafood from scallops to sole fillets for an upscale solution to every-day dining.

2	**tablespoons butter**
1	**tablespoon all-purpose flour**
4	**large shallots, minced (about ½ cup)**
4	**cups heavy whipping cream**
1	**cup grated Swiss cheese**
1	**cup grated Parmesan cheese**
½	**teaspoon ground nutmeg**
	Salt and freshly ground pepper
20	**½-inch slices French bread, toasted**
20	**ounces cooked lobster meat, chopped**
2	**tablespoons chopped fresh parsley**

Preheat the oven to 350°.

1. Melt the butter in a pot over medium high heat.
2. Add the flour and stir until smooth.
3. Add the shallots and cook until soft, about 4 minutes.
4. Add the cream and simmer until reduced to about 3 cups.
5. Stir in the cheeses and nutmeg, and season with salt and pepper. The sauce should be thick.
6. Place toasted bread onto a baking sheet. Place chunks of lobster onto the bread. Spoon the sauce on top of the lobster. Sprinkle with additional Parmesan cheese.
7. Bake for 5 minutes or until just golden. Garnish with fresh chopped parsley.

Servings: 20 appetizers
Preparation Time: 45 minutes

Make this appetizer for your next "everyday cele-bration" for 6 to 8 people by decreasing the amount of the ingredients. For a sit-down starter, serve in individual oven proof dishes. Place the lobster chunks into the dish. Cover with sauce. Sprinkle with cheese and bake until bubbling. Serve with a fork and toast points for dipping.

1	*tablespoon butter*
1	*tablespoon all-purpose flour*
1	*large shallot, minced (about 1 table-spoon)*
2	*cups heavy whipping cream*
½	*cup grated Swiss cheese*
½	*cup grated Parmesan cheese*
¼	*teaspoon ground nutmeg*
	Salt and freshly ground pepper
10	*to 12 ounces cooked lobster meat, chopped*
1	*tablespoon chopped fresh parsley leaves*
	French bread, toasted

Chilled Vichyssoise

This elegant soup has very basic potato roots. The addition of cauliflower adds a yummy dimension. Just for fun you can substitute with carrots, parsnips and seasonings like ginger or cumin.

¾ **cup butter (1½ sticks)**
4 **large leeks, white part only, rinsed and sliced**
1 **large yellow onion, diced (about 1 cup)**
8 **medium celery ribs, thinly sliced (about 4 cups)**
1 **small head cauliflower, cut into flowerets, chopped (about 2½ cups)**
8 **large baking potatoes, peeled and cut into ½-inch dice**
1 **cup all-purpose flour**
4 **quarts chicken stock**
1 **teaspoon ground nutmeg**
   Salt and freshly ground pepper
2 **cups heavy cream**
1 **cup chopped fresh garlic chives**

1. Heat the butter in a large pot over medium high heat.
2. Add the leeks, onion, celery and cauliflower to the pot. Cook until soft, about 15 minutes.
3. Stir in the potatoes. Cook for 5 minutes.
4. Stir in the flour and cook for 2 minutes.
5. Add the chicken broth and nutmeg. Season with salt and pepper.
6. Bring the soup to a boil. Reduce the heat to medium and simmer for 30 minutes or until the potatoes are soft.
7. Use an immersion blender (or a food processor) to purée the soup. Cover and refrigerate for at least 2 hours or overnight.
8. Stir in the heavy cream and garnish with fresh chopped chives.

Servings: 20 or more
Preparation Time: 60 minutes plus refrigeration

Make this soup for your next "everyday celebration" for 6 to 8 people by decreasing the amount of the ingredients.

1 *large leek, white part only, rinsed and sliced*
1 *small yellow onion, diced (about ½ cup)*
2 *medium celery ribs, thinly sliced (about 1 cup)*
¼ *medium head cauliflower, cut into flowerets, chopped (about ¾ cup)*
¼ *cup butter (½ stick)*
2 *large baking potatoes, peeled and cut into ½-inch dice*
¼ *cup all-purpose flour*
1 *quart chicken stock*
¼ *teaspoon ground nutmeg*
   Salt and freshly ground pepper
½ *cup heavy cream*
2 *tablespoons chopped fresh garlic chives*

CUMIN-CRUSTED SEA BASS with TOMATO COULIS and ARTICHOKE SALSA

Sea bass is a very popular fish and an easy one to prepare. It lends itself to an abundant array of flavors as the accompaniments in this dish suggest.

12 plum tomatoes, seeded and diced (about 4 cups)
½ cup olive oil
¼ cup balsamic vinegar
Salt and freshly ground pepper

4 14-ounce cans marinated artichoke hearts, drained and chopped into ½-inch pieces
2 16-ounce jars Kalamata olives, pitted and drained
6 plum tomatoes, seeded and diced (about 2 cups)
1 large red onion, diced (about 1 cup)
½ cup chopped fresh cilantro leaves
½ cup olive oil
¼ cup balsamic vinegar

½ cup chopped fresh cilantro leaves
¼ cup Dijon mustard
¼ cup ground cumin
2 tablespoons paprika
1 tablespoon salt
1 teaspoon pepper
2 to 6 tablespoons olive oil
20 6-ounce sea bass fillets

2 to 4 tablespoons olive oil

1. Place the tomatoes, olive oil, and balsamic vinegar in a blender or food processor. Pulse until smooth. Cover and chill.

2. Place the artichokes, olives, tomatoes, onions, and cilantro in a bowl. Toss with olive oil and vinegar. Season with salt and pepper. Cover and chill.

3. Place the cilantro, mustard, cumin, paprika, salt, and pepper in the bowl of a food processor. Pulse to combine. Brush this mixture onto both sides of the fillets.

4. Warm 2 tablespoons of olive oil in a skillet over medium high heat. Place several fillets into the skillet. Cook until golden, about 2 minutes, turn and cook until golden on the other side, about 2 minutes more. Remove the fillets to a baking dish. Continue until all of the fish has been sautéed adding additional oil as needed.

5. Remove the coulis from the refrigerator and bring to room temperature. Remove the salsa from the refrigerator, drain and bring to room temperature.

Preheat the oven to 375°.

6. Bake the fish for 5 to 10 minutes or until the fish is cooked through, resistant to the touch and flakes easily with a fork.

7. Place a spoonful of coulis onto a dinner plate. Set a fillet on top. Ladle the salsa over top.

Servings: 20
Preparation Time: 1 hour

Make Cumin-Crusted Sea Bass for your next "everyday celebration" for 6 to 8 people by decreasing the amount of the ingredients.

3   to 4 plum tomatoes, seeded and diced (about 1 cup)
2   tablespoons olive oil
1   tablespoon balsamic vinegar
**   Salt and freshly ground pepper**

1   14-ounce can marinated artichoke hearts, drained and chopped into ½-inch pieces
1   cup Kalamata olives, pitted and drained
2   to 3 plum tomatoes, seeded and diced (about ½ cup)

¼   small red onion, diced (about 2 table-spoons)
2   tablespoons chopped fresh cilantro leaves
2   tablespoons cup olive oil
1   tablespoon balsamic vinegar

6   to 8 6-ounce sea bass fillets
2   tablespoons chopped cilantro leaves
2   tablespoons Dijon mustard
1   teaspoon ground cumin
½   teaspoon paprika
½   teaspoon salt
¼   teaspoon pepper
2   tablespoons olive oil

GOLDEN GARLIC MASHED POTATOES
with SPINACH BASIL PURÉE

This super easy dish combines two comfort food favorites. Yukon gold potatoes are buttery and a perfect complement to roasted garlic.

1	**5-pound bag Yukon gold potatoes**
2	**whole heads garlic, roasted and mashed**
1	**cup butter (2 sticks)**
1	**cup milk**
	Salt and freshly ground pepper
2	**to 4 tablespoons olive oil**
2	**large shallots, minced (about 2 tablespoons)**
8	**medium cloves garlic, minced (about ¼ cup)**
4	**10-ounce packages fresh spinach**
2	**cups fresh basil leaves**
2	**cups ricotta cheese**
1	**cup whipping cream**
½	**teaspoon nutmeg**

1. Peel the potatoes and cut into pieces. Place into salted, boiling water and cook until soft, about 15 minutes.
2. Drain the potatoes and place into the bowl of an electric mixer.
3. Add the roasted garlic, butter, and milk. Whip until well combined. Season with salt and pepper. Keep warm.
4. Heat 2 tablespoons olive oil in a skillet over medium high heat. Add the shallots and garlic and cook until soft.
5. Cook the spinach in the pan in batches, until just wilted. Use additional oil as needed.
6. Place the cooked spinach in the bowl of a food processor.
7. Add the basil and ricotta. Pulse to combine.

8. Return the spinach mixture to the skillet. Add the whipping cream and nutmeg. Cook over medium heat until the cream reduces and thickens, about 5 to 10 minutes. Season with salt and pepper.
9. Place the potatoes in a large bowl making a well in the center.
10. Place the spinach mixture into the center of the well.

Servings: 20 or more
Preparation Time: 45 minutes

Make this side dish for your next "everyday celebration" for 6 to 8 people by decreasing the amount of the ingredients.

6	***medium Yukon gold potatoes***
6	***medium cloves garlic, roasted and mashed***
¼	***cup butter (½ stick)***
¼	***cup milk***
	Salt and freshly ground pepper
1	***10-ounce package fresh spinach***
1	***tablespoon olive oil***
1	***large shallot, minced (about 1 tablespoon)***
2	***medium cloves garlic, minced (about 1 teaspoon)***
¾	***cup fresh basil leaves***
¾	***cup ricotta cheese***
½	***cup whipping cream***
¼	***teaspoon nutmeg***

WARM CARROT MOLD with CREAMED PEAS and ONIONS

Growing up, this was my favorite Thanksgiving dinner side dish. Today I serve it for all of my fussy dinner parties. A slice of this mold is like eating dessert with your supper!

2 cups all-purpose flour
1 teaspoon salt
2 teaspoons baking powder
1 teaspoon baking soda
4 large eggs
1½ cups butter (3 sticks), room temperature
1 cup brown sugar
6 medium carrots, peeled and finely grated (about 3 cups)
2 tablespoons cream
Juice of 1 lemon (about 2 tablespoons)

1 10-ounce package frozen pearl onions in cream sauce
1 10-ounce package frozen peas

Preheat the oven to 350°.

1. Blend together the flour, salt, baking powder, and baking soda in a small bowl. Set aside.
2. Separate the eggs. Use an electric mixer to whip the egg whites into soft peaks. Set aside.
3. Use and electric mixer to blend together the butter and brown sugar until light and fluffy.
4. Add the egg yolks one at a time.
5. Stir in the carrots, cream, and lemon juice.
6. Stir in the flour mixture until well combined.
7. Fold in the egg whites.
8. Pour the batter into a Bundt pan that has been sprayed with vegetable oil spray and dusted with flour.
9. Bake in the center of the oven for 1 hour, or until a toothpick inserted into the center come out clean and the cake springs back from the pan. Cool in the pan for 5 minutes. Invert onto a serving platter.
10. Cook the frozen vegetables according to the package directions. Stir together in a bowl.
11. Spoon the vegetables in the center and around the carrot mold. Serve warm.

Servings: 12 to 16
Preparation Time: 30 minutes plus baking

Serve a slice of this rich cake on a dinner plate and top with a spoonful of creamed veggies for the garnish.

Sesame Seed Dinner Rolls

Easily prepared in a bread machine and allowed to rise overnight in the refrigerator, these rolls are a must for your next dinner party.

2   cups milk
3   tablespoons olive oil
3   teaspoons granulated sugar
2   teaspoons salt
4   cups bread flour
2½   teaspoons yeast

1   large egg, beaten with 1 tablespoon water
2   tablespoons sesame seeds

1. Place the milk, olive oil, sugar, salt, and bread flour in the bucket in a bread machine.
2. Pour the yeast in the yeast compartment (or follow the specific directions for your bread machine). Select the dough cycle and start the bread machine.
3. Remove the dough from the machine onto a lightly floured surface.
4. Divide the dough into 24 balls and shape into rolls.
5. Place each roll into a large baking dish.
6. Cover and let rise for 1 hour (or cover and refrigerate overnight).

Preheat the oven to 375°.

7. Brush the tops with beaten egg and sprinkle with sesame seeds.
8. Bake the rolls for 15 to 20 minutes or until golden brown.

Yield: 2 dozen dinner rolls
Preparation Time: 45 minutes plus dough cycle and rising

Experiment with your favorite flavors with these simple rolls. Top with chopped chives, minced shallots, poppy seeds, or Parmesan cheese.

Red Velvet Cake with Vanilla Frosting

Rumor has it that this Southern traditional cake dates back to the Civil War. If that's the truth—then they may have been fighting over the recipe! Well worth every rich bite, food coloring and cocoa powder are the secret ingredients. Take this romantic cake one step further by baking in two heart-shaped pans.

2 **cups all-purpose flour**
2 **tablespoons cocoa powder**
1 **teaspoon salt**
1 **teaspoon baking soda**
1 **teaspoon baking powder**
½ **cup butter (1 stick)**
1½ **cups granulated sugar**
2 **large eggs**
1 **cup buttermilk**
2 **ounces red food coloring (4 tablespoons)**
1 **tablespoon white vinegar**
1 **teaspoon vanilla extract**

1 **cup butter (2 sticks) room temperature**
6 **cups confectioners' sugar**
4 **tablespoons whipping cream**
2 **teaspoons vanilla extract**
½ **teaspoon ground nutmeg**

Preheat the oven to 350°.
1. Combine the flour, cocoa, salt, baking soda, and baking powder in a bowl.
2. Use an electric mixer to combine the butter and sugar until smooth and fluffy.

3. Stir in the eggs one at a time.
4. Stir together the buttermilk, red food coloring, vinegar, and vanilla in a small bowl.
5. Stir in the flour mixture and buttermilk mixture in 3 additions, alternating ⅓ flour mixture with ⅓ buttermilk until just blended.
6. Pour the batter into 2 9-inch round cake pans that have been sprayed with vegetable oil spray and dusted with flour.
7. Bake for 30 to 35 minutes or until a toothpick inserted into the center comes out clean. Cool in pans for 5 minutes. Invert onto a cake rack to cool completely.
8. Use an electric mixer to whip the butter and confectioners' sugar until smooth and fluffy.
9. Mix in the whipping cream, vanilla, and nutmeg. If frosting is too thick, add more cream. If it is too thin, add more sugar.
10. Frost the cake between the layers, on the sides and over the top.

Servings: 10 to 12
Preparation Time: 30 minutes plus baking

For the best technique in mixing cake batter, begin with the shortening (or butter). Beat the butter on low speed until light. Add the sugar and beat on medium speed until well combined. The mixture should resemble whipped cream. Add the eggs one at a time stirring only enough to just combine. Stop the machine after each addition. Use this time to scrape down the sides of the bowl. Use the medium speed to stir in ⅓ of the flour mixture. Stir in ⅓ of the buttermilk. Stop the machine between each addition. Continue until all of the ingredients are combined. The entire process should take only about 2 minutes.

Afternoon Tea Party Plan

Party Motivation

Bridal showers, a baby shower, an afternoon committee meeting, all lend themselves to an upscale afternoon tea party. Take the time to serve the tea with style and set a simple buffet table so that guests feel free to nibble as they sip.

Party Menu

Smoked Salmon and Dill Tea Sandwiches **
Curried Shrimp and Watercress Tea Sandwiches **
Poached Chicken Tea Sandwiches **
Cucumber, Egg, and Arugula Tea Sandwiches **
Layered Fresh Fruit Salad
Lady Marmalade Coconut Layer Cake

** Over-the-Top Suggestion

Make these tea sandwiches the best they can be by preparing your own, rich mayonnaise. Process 1 egg, 1 egg yolk, 2 tablespoons fresh lemon juice and 2 teaspoons Dijon style mustard in the bowl of a food processor. With the blade running, slowly drizzle in ¾ cup olive oil and ½ cup vegetable oil until the mixture is quite thick. Season with a dash of salt.

Party Strategy

Tea sandwiches are easily prepared in advance as long as they are stored correctly. This is a fun party to invite pals to help you prepare. Quite a conversation builds as everyone sits at the table assembling tea sandwiches. Just image the whisperings of the cooks in the castle kitchens of early England.

Two days in advance: Assemble the tea utensils and accessories.

One day in advance: Prepare the cake, cover and refrigerate.

The evening before: Invite pals to prepare tea sandwiches.

The morning of: Prepare fruit salad.

Shortcuts

For a few extra dollars you can purchase fresh fruit for the salad that has been cleaned and sliced. Save some time with this alternative.

Party Backdrop

Afternoon tea was introduced in England by Anna, the seventh Duchess of Bedford in 1840 because she was hungry. It seems that the Duchess had a problem waiting for her household's fashionably late supper served at 8:00 o'clock. She was already craving food by 4:00 o'clock. Her craving for buttered breads and cakes has turned into today's proper afternoon tea fare consisting of dainty tea sandwiches, scones and cream, lemon curd and jams. Aromatic tea is poured from silver pots and into delicate china teacups. The best backdrop for a tea party includes a food laden sideboard, a silver tea service, your best linen napkins, fresh flowers in vases all over the house, soft music and your grandmother's best china.

The Table Setting

Set the sideboard with tiered servers. Vary the heights of each dish. Place an assortment of sandwiches on each serving dish. Serve the fruit salad from a trifle bowl with additional sauce on the side. The cake is a showstopper and deserves a starring role on the buffet table. Use as many tea accessories as you can put your hands on to authenticate the afternoon tea theme. Decorate with a collection of tea pots, placing heirloom pots around the room. Set out tea tongs and sugar ladles, pitchers for cream and milk, bowls for lemon wedges and honey and your best assortment of coordinating cups and saucers—save the mugs for the next coffee clutch.

SMOKED SALMON and DILL TEA SANDWICHES

Choose good quality, flavorful and flaky smoked salmon and garden fresh dill for this elegant sandwich.

½   **cup mayonnaise**
6   **tablespoons butter, room temperature**
1   **large shallot, minced (about 1 table-spoon)**
10 **slices thinly sliced pumpernickel bread**
12 **to 16 ounces smoked salmon, thinly sliced**
½   **cup chopped fresh dill**

1. Place the mayonnaise, butter, and shallot into the bowl of a food processor. Pulse until smooth.
2. Coat one side of each bread slice with the mayonnaise mixture.
3. Place one thin layer of salmon on top of each of 5 bread slices.
4. Sprinkle the chopped dill on top of the salmon.
5. Top with the remaining bread slices.
6. Trim the crusts from the bread and cut each sandwich into 4 triangles.
7. Place each triangle into a plastic container. Cover each layer with a damp paper towel. Seal the container and refrigerate until you are ready to serve. The sandwiches can be made several hours in advance.

Yield: 20 tea sandwiches
Preparation Time: 30 minutes

An interesting twist on the flavors in this sandwich is the substitution of freshly baked and flaked salmon. Bake the salmon with a sprinkle of lemon juice until pink in the center. Allow to cool. Flake the salmon in a bowl. Add a drop or two of olive oil and continue with the recipe. The addition of paper thin slices of very ripe tomato is a further fun extra!

CURRIED SHRIMP and WATERCRESS TEA SANDWICHES

A new twist on the traditional tea sandwich, curried shrimp adds a modern taste treat.

1½   pounds large cooked shrimp, peeled and deveined (about 24)
½   cup mayonnaise
6   tablespoons butter, room temperature
1½   teaspoon curry powder
**   Juice of ½ lemon (about 1 tablespoon)**
10   slices thinly sliced white bread
**   Salt and freshly ground pepper**
¼   cup chopped watercress leaves

1. Place the shrimp in the bowl of a food processor. Pulse until diced. Be careful not to over-process into a paste. Transfer to a bowl.
2. Place the mayonnaise, butter, curry and lemon juice into the bowl of a food processor. Pulse until smooth.
3. Stir the shrimp into the mayonnaise mixture.
4. Spread a layer of the shrimp mixture on top of each of 5 bread slices. Season with salt and pepper.
5. Top the shrimp with a layer of chopped watercress.
6. Top with the remaining bread slices.
7. Trim the crusts from the bread and cut each sandwich into 4 triangles.
8. Place each triangle into a plastic container. Cover each layer with a damp paper towel. Seal the container and refrigerate until you are ready to serve. The sandwiches can be made several hours in advance.

Yield: 20 tea sandwiches
Preparation Time: 30 minutes

Watercress is a peppery flavored green that has its roots in the mustard family.
It is a traditional staple in tea sandwiches. Choose the freshest leaves that you can find.
Rinse and dry well using paper toweling or a salad spinner.

POACHED CHICKEN TEA SANDWICHES

A little touch of nutmeg adds big flavor to moist chicken.

2   **6 to 8-ounce skinless boneless chicken breast halves**
2   **medium celery ribs, cut into pieces**
½   **cup mayonnaise**
6   **tablespoons butter, room temperature**
½   **teaspoon ground nutmeg**
2   **tablespoons chopped fresh thyme leaves**
10 **slices thinly sliced rye bread**
    Salt and freshly ground pepper

1. Poach or bake the chicken until just cooked, yet still moist. Allow to cool and cut into very thin slices.
2. Place the celery in the bowl of a food processor. Pulse until finely diced. Remove to a bowl. Set aside.
3. Place the mayonnaise, butter, nutmeg, and thyme in the bowl of a food processor. Pulse until smooth.
4. Coat one side of each bread slice with the mayonnaise mixture.
5. Place one layer of sliced chicken on top of each of 5 bread slices. Season with salt and pepper.
6. Top the chicken with a layer of diced celery.
7. Top with the remaining bread slices.
8. Trim the crusts from the bread and cut each sandwich into 4 triangles.
9. Place each triangle into a plastic container. Cover each layer with a damp paper towel. Seal the container and refrigerate until you are ready to serve. The sandwiches can be made several hours in advance.

Yield: 20 tea sandwiches
Preparation Time: 30 minutes

Poach the chicken breast for the best results. Place boneless breasts onto a sheet of aluminum foil. Submerge the foil in water, chicken stock, or champagne until just covered. Add celery, onion, and bay leaves to the poaching liquid for flavor. Slowly simmer the breasts until just cooked. The center should be white and opaque but still very moist.
Gently lift out the foil with the breasts from the liquid.

Cucumber, Egg, and Arugula Tea Sandwiches

The peppery flavor of Arugula adds a distinctive taste to this traditional tea sandwich combination.

2   medium cucumbers, peeled and thinly sliced (about 4 cups)
½   cup mayonnaise
6   tablespoons butter, room temperature
10 slices thinly sliced white bread
6   large eggs, hard boiled, thinly sliced
    Salt and freshly ground pepper
2   cups arugula leaves, washed and well dried

1. Place the cucumbers in a colander. Sprinkle with salt and allow to stand for 30 minutes to remove excess moisture.
2. Place the mayonnaise and butter into the bowl of a food processor. Pulse until smooth.
3. Coat one side of each bread slice with the mayonnaise mixture.
4. Place one layer of egg slices on top of each of 5 bread slices. Season with salt and pepper.
5. Top the egg with cucumber.
6. Top the cucumber with Arugula leaves.
7. Top with the remaining bread slices.
8. Trim the crusts from the bread and cut each sandwich into 4 triangles.
9. Place each triangle into a plastic container. Cover each layer with a damp paper towel. Seal the container and refrigerate until you are ready to serve. The sandwiches can be made several hours in advance.

Yield: 20 tea sandwiches
Preparation Time: 30 minutes

Adding salt to the cucumbers will release some of their moisture allowing you to prepare the sandwiches in advance. Just a touch of salt will do the trick. Be careful to not be too generous!

LAYERED FRESH FRUIT SALAD

A tall crystal bowl is a must for a striking presentation of this creative dish.

2   cups plain yogurt
1   teaspoon vanilla extract
¼   cup honey
1   pint fresh raspberries about 2 cups
    Zest of 1 medium lemon (about 1 table-
    spoon)

1   medium pineapple, peeled, cored, cut
    into ½-inch pieces (about 3 cups)
1   medium cantaloupe, cut in 1 inch pieces
    (about 4 cups)
6   medium apples, peeled, cored and sliced
    (about 6 cups) tossed with a few drops
    of fresh lemon juice
4   large bananas, sliced (about 4 cups)
    tossed with a few drops of fresh lemon
    juice
1   pint strawberries, sliced in half about 2
    cups
2   tablespoons fresh mint leaves, chopped

1. Place yogurt, vanilla, honey, raspberries and
    lemon zest in a blender or food processor.
    Pulse until smooth.

2. Place the pineapple chunks in the bottom of
    a large crystal bowl (preferably a trifle bowl).
3. Spoon ¼ of the yogurt sauce over the
    pineapple.
4. Layer the cantaloupe on top of the yogurt.
5. Spoon ¼ of the yogurt sauce over the can-
    taloupe.
6. Layer the apples on top of the yogurt.
    Sprinkle with a few drops of lemon juice.
7. Spoon ¼ of the yogurt sauce on top of the
    apples.
8. Layer banana slices on top of the yogurt.
    Sprinkle with a few drops of lemon juice.
9. Spoon ¼ of the yogurt sauce on top of the
    bananas.
10. Top with strawberries. Garnish with fresh
    mint. Chill for up 2 hours.

Servings: 20 or more
Preparation Time: 30 minutes

Use the freshest fruit that you can find in this dish and feel free to flavor the yogurt sauce with blueberries or cherries in place of raspberries. Let this dish double as dessert with the addition of whipped cream into the yogurt sauce then served over rich pound cake!

LADY MARMALADE COCONUT LAYER CAKE

A soulful dessert perfect for a Duchess, bride-to-be, or chairman of the board, this cake looks elegant on a buffet table.

3	cups cake flour
1	tablespoon baking powder
1	teaspoon salt
1	teaspoons vanilla extract
1	teaspoon coconut extract
1½	cups milk
1	cup butter (2 sticks), room temperature
1	cup granulated sugar
5	large eggs

½	cup milk
2	tablespoons vanilla extract
½	teaspoon coconut extract
	Juice of ½ medium orange (about 2 to 3 tablespoons)
	Zest of 1 medium orange (about 2 tablespoons)
3	cups butter (6 sticks), room temperature
4½	cups confectioners' sugar

1	14-ounce jar orange marmalade
1	7-ounce bag shredded sweetened coconut

Preheat the oven to 350°.

1. Combine the flour, baking powder, and salt in a bowl. Set aside.
2. Add the vanilla and coconut extracts to the milk.
3. With an electric mixer combine 1 cup butter with 1 cup granulated sugar until fluffy.
4. Add the eggs one at a time.
5. Add the flour and milk in 3 additions, alternating ⅓ flour mixture with ⅓ milk until just blended.
6. Pour the batter into 3 8-inch round cake pans that have been sprayed with vegetable oil spray and dusted with flour. Bake for 20 to 25 minutes or until a toothpick inserted into the center comes out clean.
7. Cool the cakes in the pan for 5 minutes. Invert onto a rack and cool completely.
8. Use sewing thread or a serrated knife to cut each cake into 2 pieces.
9. Whisk together ½ cup milk, 2 tablespoons vanilla extract, ½ teaspoon coconut extract, orange juice, and orange zest.
10. With an electric mixer combine 3 cups of butter with the confectioners' sugar until light and fluffy.
11. Stir in the milk in 3 additions on low speed. When incorporated increase the speed to high and beat for 1 minute until fluffy. If frosting it too thick add more milk, if too thin add more sugar.
12. Place one cake half onto a cake plate. Spread with frosting. Sprinkle with coconut.
13. Top with a second cake half. Spread this half with marmalade leaving a 1-inch border around the edge.
14. Repeat with all of the cake halves alternating with layers of frosting and marmalade, finishing with a cake layer.
15. Frost the sides and top of the cake and sprinkle coconut all over.

Servings: 12 to 16
Preparation Time: 1 hour plus baking

This cake is the perfect invitation to experiment with your favorite flavors. Do not hesitate to substitute with your favorite jam like blackberry or plum. You can subtly change the taste of the frosting with the substitution of lime or lemon zest.

Pre-Theatre Cocktail Party Plan

Party Motivation

A dressy occasion before the big affair—pre-theatre, pre-concert, pre-black tie. The guests are dressed to kill and the food must match the occasion. Not a problem—you have plenty of magical yummies to keep the party rocking.

Party Menu

Raspberry Champagne Cocktail **
Bite-Size Salmon Cakes with Yellow Pepper Aioli
Beer Battered Tuna with Wasabi Sauce
Corn Bread Crostini with Sautéed Wild Mushrooms and Blue Cheese
Mini Meatballs in Creamy Gravy
Foie Gras with Port Wine-Glazed Caramelized Onions

** Over-the-Top Suggestion

Offer splendidly pink cocktails from silver trays. Use the best champagne, the freshest raspberries and gorgeous crystal champagne flutes to create one elegant aperitif.

Party Strategy

Designate a helper in the kitchen to complete and present each dish. Another helper can pass trays of hors d'oeuvres while you greet guests.

Two days in advance: Bake corn bread for crostini.

One day in advance: Prepare aioli for salmon cakes, cover, and refrigerate. Prepare wasabi sauce, cover, and refrigerate. Prepare mushrooms for crostini, cover, and refrigerate. Prepare meatballs and gravy, store separately, cover, and refrigerate. Prepare crostini for foie gras.

The morning of: Prepare batter for tuna. Prepare salmon cakes through step 7.

Two hours before: Warm the meatballs and gravy together.

One hour before: Cook the crab cakes, keep warm.

Immediately before: Cook tuna in hot oil. Prepare foie gras.

Shortcuts

Yellow pepper aioli is rich and wonderful. To save some time, prepare mock aioli by blending mayonnaise with roasted peppers, mustard and tarragon vinegar.

Party Backdrop

Guests mingle in the living room as hors d'oeuvres are passed and champagne is offered. Set a bar at the farthest point of the room so that party participants do not gather at the door. Cocktail napkins are a must and an assortment of appetizer plates is desirable.

The Table Setting

Offer raspberry champagne cocktails from a silver tray. Pass salmon cakes on a platter with a bowl of aioli sauce for dipping. Pass chunks of batter cooked tuna on a platter with a bowl of wasabi sauce for dipping. Set down a tray holding a basket of cornbread crostini, a bowl of sautéed mushrooms and a smaller bowl of crumbled blue cheese. Invite guests to build their own crostini. Pour mini meatballs and gravy into a crock pot or chafing dish and keep warm. Offer fish forks or long cocktail toothpicks for easy snatching. Pass the special foie gras appetizer to the guest of honor and watch as everyone else crowds in.

RASPBERRY CHAMPAGNE COCKTAIL

A few drops of raspberry liquor and fresh raspberries make an elegant addition to chilled, crisp champagne.

Fresh raspberries
Framboise liquor
1   bottle chilled champagne

1. Place 1 to 2 fresh raspberries in the bottom of a champagne flute.
2. Add a few drops of Framboise liquor.
3. Pour chilled champagne ¾ full into the flute.

BITE-SIZE SALMON CAKES with YELLOW PEPPER AIOLI

Make this yummy starter in the afternoon and finish cooking just before your guests arrive. Make extras, as they will easily hold in a warm oven for an hour or so.

1½ **pounds salmon fillet**
2 **large eggs, slightly beaten**
1 **bunch (6 to 8) green onions, finely sliced (about 1 cup)**
3 **tablespoons chopped fresh parsley leaves**
3 **tablespoons chopped fresh cilantro leaves**
2 **tablespoons Dijon mustard**
¼ **cup mayonnaise**
3 **cups Japanese breadcrumbs**
Salt and freshly ground pepper
Canola oil for frying

2 **large yellow bell peppers**
2 **tablespoons Dijon mustard**
2 **tablespoons tarragon vinegar**
2 **egg yolks**
3 **medium cloves garlic**
3 **tablespoons chopped fresh cilantro leaves**
1 **cup olive oil**
Salt and freshly ground pepper

1. Place the salmon on baking pan that has been sprayed with vegetable oil spray. Cook until the salmon is opaque and still rare in the center.
2. With a fork flake the salmon in a large bowl.
3. Add the eggs, onion, parsley, and cilantro.
4. Mix in the mustard and mayonnaise.

5. Add enough breadcrumbs to bind the cakes. Reserve extra bread crumbs for later use. Season with salt and freshly ground pepper
6. Form the salmon into 1½-inch balls and flatten into cakes.
7. Dredge each cake through the remaining breadcrumbs. The salmon cakes may be covered with plastic wrap and refrigerated at this point.
8. In a medium skillet heat the oil over medium high heat. Cook the salmon cakes in the oil, turning once until golden brown, about 2 to 3 minutes per side. Drain well.

Preheat the oven to the broil setting.
9. Place the peppers on a baking sheet on the top rack of the oven. Char the skin of the pepper turning until the pepper is blackened. Place the peppers in a bowl and cover with foil for 15 to 20 minutes. Peel off the black skin and discard. Remove the stem and seeds from the peppers.
10. Transfer the roasted peppers and the juices that have collected in the bowl to a blender.
11. Add the mustard, vinegar, egg yolks, garlic, and cilantro. Pulse to emulsify.
12. With the motor running, slowly add the olive oil. Season with salt and pepper.

Yield: about 3 dozen plus 1 cup sauce
Preparation Time: 40 minutes

Salmon is best served with a rare, cool center. However you may cook it to medium and then proceed with the recipe. Don't overcook fish—it continues cooking after it is removed from heat.

Japanese bread crumbs are also known as Panko. They are light in color and have a course texture. Try them as breading for fish, chicken and veggies.

BEER BATTERED TUNA with WASABI SAUCE

The secret to a crispy crust and a rare tuna center is to fry the fish very quickly in hot oil.

2   **cups all-purpose flour**
2   **tablespoons cornstarch**
1   **teaspoon baking powder**
2   **tablespoons chopped fresh dill**
1   **12-ounce can beer**
1   **tablespoon soy sauce**
    Juice of 2 lemons (about ¼ cup)
1   **1-inch piece ginger, grated (about 1 tablespoon)**
    Salt and freshly ground pepper

1½   **pounds fresh tuna, skin removed**

    Canola oil for frying
1   **tablespoon wasabi paste**
⅓   **cup soy sauce**

1. In a medium bowl combine 1½ cups of the flour with the cornstarch and baking powder.

2. In a medium bowl combine the dill, beer, soy sauce, lemon juice, and fresh ginger. Season with salt and pepper.

3. Pour the beer mixture into the flour mixture and stir. The batter should be very wet like pancake batter. Refrigerate the batter for 30 minutes.

4. Heat the canola oil in a deep pot over medium high heat to 360° on a deep fry thermometer.

5. Cut the tuna into 1-inch cubes. Pat the fish dry with paper toweling.

6. Dredge each piece through the remaining flour and then into the chilled batter.

7. Fry the cubes in the hot oil until just lightly brown. Do not crowd the pan. Drain well.

8. Prepare a spicy sauce by mixing wasabi paste into soy sauce to taste.

Yield: about 3 dozen
Preparation Time: 40 minutes

Frying is the process of cooking food in hot oil.
Use these tips to make frying a fool-proof process:

Heat only 2 to 3 inches of oil using a deep pan. As the oil heats, it will bubble up and can spill over. Never leave hot oil unattended.

Do not crowd the pan with too many pieces.

Allow the oil to reheat in between batches.

Use a good quality frying thermometer to help you to maintain the correct temperature.

CORN BREAD CROSTINI with SAUTÉED WILD MUSHROOMS and BLUE CHEESE

This is a simple appetizer that combines the flavors of sweet cornbread with the tang of robust mushrooms and blue cheese.

2   tablespoons vegetable shortening
½   cup granulated sugar
½   cup all-purpose flour
2   cups white cornmeal
¼   teaspoon salt
1   tablespoon baking soda
2   cups buttermilk

2   tablespoons butter
2   pounds assorted mushrooms (shiitake, button, and portobello), chopped
2   tablespoons chopped fresh thyme leaves
        Salt and freshly ground pepper

        Crumbled blue cheese

Preheat the oven to 350°.

1. Divide the shortening into 4 mini-loaf pans. Place the pans in the oven to melt.
2. Sift together the sugar, flour, cornmeal, and salt in a mixing bowl.
3. Stir the baking soda into the buttermilk.
4. Remove the pans from the oven. Pour the batter into the melted shortening in the pans.
5. Bake for 30 to 35 minutes or a toothpick inserted into the center comes out clean. Cool.
6. Melt 2 tablespoons butter in a large pan over medium high heat.
7. Cook the mushrooms in the pan until all of the moisture evaporates. Season with fresh thyme, salt, and pepper. Place the mushrooms into the bowl of a food processor and pulse to chop.
8. Cut the corn bread into ½-inch slices. Brush one side with olive oil. Bake at 350°. until just lightly browned.
9. Place the corn bread crostini on a large platter. Place a spoonful of the mushroom mixture on top of each one. Sprinkle with a touch of crumbled blue cheese.

Yield: about 3 dozen
Preparation Time: 30 minutes plus baking

This cornbread is sweet tasting enough to blend perfectly with the wild mushrooms. Use leftovers for morning breakfast with a slather of fruit jam.

Mini Meatballs in Creamy Gravy

This dish can be made in advance and warmed as your guests arrive. Use a chafing dish or fondue pot set on medium high to keep the meatballs warm.

2   cups fresh breadcrumbs
1   cup milk
1   large shallot, minced (about 1 table-
    spoon)
3   large eggs, beaten
½   teaspoon nutmeg
½   teaspoon allspice
1   pound lean ground beef
1   pound lean ground veal
¾   pound lean ground pork
    Salt and freshly ground pepper
2   to 4 tablespoons butter
¼   to ½ cup all-purpose flour

1   large yellow onion, diced (about 1 cup)
2   tablespoons all-purpose flour
    Salt and freshly ground pepper
2   cups beef stock
1   cup whipping cream
2   tablespoons fresh parsley

1. Soak the breadcrumbs in the milk for 10 minutes in a bowl.
2. Mix in the shallot, eggs, nutmeg, and all-spice.
3. Add all of the meat to the bowl. Use a hand held mixer to combine until fluffy. Season with salt and pepper.
4. Shape into 1-inch meatballs. Place on a baking sheet. Refrigerate for 30 minutes.
5. Heat 2 tablespoons of butter in a skillet over medium high heat.
6. Place ¼ cup of flour in a shallow bowl.
7. Roll each meatball into the flour mixture. Shake off the excess. Cook the meatballs in batches until just cooked through, about 5 minutes.
8. Remove the meatballs with a slotted spoon and drain on paper toweling. Repeat with remaining meat adding additional butter as needed.
9. Remove all but 1 tablespoon of oil from the pan.
10. Cook the onion in the pan until soft, about 3 minutes.
11. Stir the flour into the onion. Cook for 5 minutes. Season with salt and pepper.
12. Stir in the beef broth and cream. Reduce the heat to medium and stir until thickened, about 10 minutes.
13. Place the meatballs in the sauce. Sprinkle with fresh parsley and simmer for 2 to 5 minutes or until cooked through.

Yield: 3 dozen meatballs
Preparation Time: 30 minutes

For an hors d'oeurves party, bite-sized meatballs are a must. However, for everyday celebrations, large meatballs are wonderful especially when served over egg noodles or rice.

FOIE GRAS with PORT WINE-GLAZED CARAMELIZED ONIONS

Wow! This happy hors d'oeuvres will impress even the most worldly guest. Take your time to study the technique as the ingredients are expensive—but worth every rich bite.

2	**14- to 16-ounce goose (or duck) livers**
1	**cup Wonder flour**
	Salt and freshly ground pepper
2	**tablespoons olive oil**
2	**tablespoons butter**
2	**medium white onions, sliced into rings (about 1½ cups)**
2	**tablespoons balsamic vinegar**
1½	**cups port wine**
	Zest of 1 medium orange (about 2 tablespoons)
2	**tablespoons chopped fresh parsley**

Crostini

1. Separate each liver into 2 lobes. Trim the fat and sinew from the liver. Cut into ½-inch thick slices. Dredge each slice in flour. Shake off excess. Season with salt and pepper.
2. Heat a small amount of the olive oil and butter in a skillet over medium high heat. Use only a small amount of hot oil and butter, as the foie gras will yield it's own fat—much like bacon.
3. Quickly brown each slice of liver in the hot butter and oil, cooking only about 1 minute per side. Cook only a few slices at a time. The liver should be brown and crispy. Be very careful not to overcook the liver or it will dissolve to fat.
4. Remove the liver and drain on paper toweling.
5. Add additional oil and butter if needed to get to about 2 tablespoons of fat in the skillet. Place the onions into the hot fat. Cook until golden and soft.
6. Reduce the heat to medium. Add the vinegar and stir.
7. Add the port wine and orange zest.
8. Simmer until the liquid reduces to a thick syrup, about 20 minutes.
9. Serve by placing a spoonful of the syrupy onion mixture onto a crostini. Place a piece of foie gras on top of the onion. Sprinkle with fresh parsley.

Yield: 16 to 24 crostini
Preparation Time: 30 minutes

Foie gras is translated as "fat liver" and is quite essentially that. Purchase good quality goose or duck liver from a gourmet market or specialty store. It is very perishable and should be used within two days of purchase. Choose a liver with no imperfections, one that is large, firm and not spongy. Quickly cook the liver in high heat just until golden on the outside while still pink on the inside. Cook 1 slice to start until you get the feel for the technique.

Wild and Crazy Revelries

(FUN PARTIES FOR TEN TO ONE HUNDRED GUESTS)

Spring Break Partying
New House Warming Party
Candid Camera Party
A Backyard Wedding
Howling at the Moon

"Our company is dedicated to creating unique, personalized experiences with attention to detail and finesse that will make every occasion a memorable expression of the hosts' and hostesses' distinct personalities. One of our most memorable parties was a "Beach-elorette" weeklong event. We rented a beach house on the water. Each bridesmaid entertained with her own distinct style for one day. Depending on the maid's personality we surfed, had a cookout, lazily relaxed, and even had a pirate day. On the last evening we threw a huge party and half our graduating high school class showed up! It was one party that we all will remember for years to come."

Katie Jo Henchir
Co-owner of s i g n a t u r e . s t y l e
Boston, Massachusetts

Spring Break Partying Plan

Party Motivation

The college gang is coming for a visit—you need spicy, filling food that's fun and peppery. Or, perhaps your high school grad has invited the crowd over for a start-of the summer bash. The mood is festive—filled with new doors opening and plenty of new food ideas to get everyone on the right track.

Party Menu

Mojito
Warm Chili Cheese Dip with Diced Tomatoes
Spicy Cuban-Style Skirt Steak with Peppers and Drunken Raisins
Shredded Chicken and Carrot Enchiladas with Roasted Tomato Sauce
Mashed Yuca with Mojo Sauce **
Sautéed Plantains
Pecan Pound Cake with Jamaican Rum Whipped Cream

** Over-the-Top Suggestion

An authentically Cuban dish, mashed yucca is a fun food to incorporate into a wild party. Served warm with a garlicky lime sauce poured over top at the last moment, this dish takes your party menu way, way over the top!

Party Strategy

The recipes in this plan are designed to be multiplied by the number of guests you have invited. Serve all of these dishes warm from the oven right to the buffet table. Each one has enough staying power to make it through a wild and crazy evening.

Two days ahead: Prepare roasted tomato sauce for enchiladas, cover, and refrigerate. Prepare warm chili dip, cover and refrigerate.

The day before: Prepare pound cake, cover, and refrigerate. Marinate flank steak (and raisins). Poach chicken and shred.

The evening before: Peel yuca and place into a pot of cold water, cover, and refrigerate.

The morning of: Set buffet table. Prepare enchiladas through step 13.

Two hours before: Grill flank steak and vegetables. Place into a casserole, keep warm.

One hour before: Warm dip, bake enchiladas, Prepare sauce for yucca. Sauté plantains and remove to a large platter.

Thirty minutes before: Boil and mash yucca, pour sauce over top just before serving. Prepare sauce for plantains, pour sauce over top just before serving.

During the party: Whip cream for pound cake.

Shortcuts

Use left over chicken for the enchiladas—or boil the chicken for easy handling. Substitute a prepared enchilada sauce for the roasted pepper tomato sauce to cut down on prep time.

Party Backdrop

Weather permitting take this one outside! A pool deck is a perfect setting for a summer party. Set up a buffet table and use brightly colored cloths and napkins. Pitchers of sunflowers are all the centerpiece that you need. An aluminum wash tub holds cans of beer and sodas and a special mojito bar offers a glimpse at the spicy mood.

The Table Setting

Serve mojitos from clear, plastic glasses packed with ice. Set bowls of warm cheese dips on several tables. Surround the bowls with baskets of blue corn chips and platters of crudités. Offer skirt steak from a huge earthenware casserole dish. Serve the enchiladas in the same manner. Place the yucca in a shallow bowl and pour the mojo sauce over top. Plantains sit on a platter with a drizzle of sweet sauce over top. As the evening progresses, bring out slices of rich pound cake topped with a dollop of rum flavored whipped cream. Viva de largo la fiesta!

Mojito

A special Cuban tradition, this refreshing drink sets the stage for a fun party.

6   to 8 mint leaves
1   ounce simple syrup
Juice of ½ lime (about 1 tablespoon)
1½ ounces light rum
Club soda
Sugar cane stalks

1. Place fresh mint leaves in the bottom of a tall (high ball) glass.

2. Pour in the simple syrup (equal parts of sugar and water, boiled so that the sugar dissolves).
3. Squeeze in the lime juice.
4. Fill the glass with ice cubes.
5. Pour in the rum.
6. Fill the glass to the top with club soda.
7. Garnish with a stalk or sugar cane or sprigs of fresh mint.

Warm Chili Cheese Dip with Diced Tomatoes

A spicy cheese dip that is great served with chips and equally good on toast with bacon. Yumm …

4   medium poblano peppers, roasted, peeled and seeded
2   tablespoons olive oil
1   large yellow onion, diced (about 1 cup)
2   medium cloves garlic, minced (about 1 teaspoon)
1   pound white Cheddar cheese, shredded
¼   cup sour cream
6   to 8 plum tomatoes, seeded and diced (about 2 cups)

Blue corn chips

1. Roast the poblano peppers under a broiler or over a grill flame until the skin is charred. Place the peppers in a brown bag, seal and steam for 20 minutes. Remove the peppers to a cutting board. Peel off the black skin, cut in half, scrape out the seeds and chop.
2. Heat the olive oil in a skillet over medium high heat.
3. Cook the onion until soft, about 10 minutes.
4. Add the garlic and the roasted peppers. Cook for 10 minutes more.
5. Reduce the heat to medium. Add the cheese and sour cream to the pan. Stir until melted, about 5 minutes.
6. Stir in the tomatoes.
7. Serve warm with blue corn chips.

Yield: about 4 cups
Preparation Time: 20 minutes

Keep this dip warm in a chafing dish or a fondue pot. Add fun dippers like carrot sticks, endive leaves and bread sticks for a break-the-ice starter at your next party.

If poblano peppers are hard to find, substitute with diced, roasted jalapeño or 1 to 2 chipolte peppers in adobo sauce, minced.

Spicy Cuban-Style Skirt Steak with Peppers and Drunken Raisins

Douse the heat of the marinade with a touch of sweet raisins and a hint of rum in this easy-to-make dish.

3	12- to 16-ounce skirt steaks
1	cup fresh grapefruit juice
6	medium cloves garlic, minced (about ¼ cup)
	Juice of 2 fresh limes (about ¼ cup)
1	teaspoon ground coriander
1	teaspoon dried red pepper flakes
1	cup raisins
½	cup light rum
2	to 4 tablespoon olive oil
3	medium white onions, sliced into rings (about 2⅔ cups)
3	large red bell peppers, sliced into strips (about 3 cups)
3	large green bell peppers, sliced into strips (about 3 cups)
4	plum tomatoes, cut in half lengthwise (about 2 cups)
1	teaspoon ground cumin
	Salt and freshly ground pepper

1. Place the skirt steak in a shallow pan.
2. Make a marinade by combining the grapefruit juice, garlic, lime juice, coriander and red pepper flakes in a bowl. Pour the marinade over the steak. Cover and refrigerate for at least 30 minutes and as much as overnight. Turn the meat at least one time.
3. Place the raisins in a small bowl. Pour in the rum. Let stand for 20 to 30 minutes.
4. Heat 2 tablespoons olive oil in a grill pan. Grill the vegetables in batches until just beginning to brown. Do not overcook. (Use additional oil as needed between batches.
5. Stir in the cumin and the raisin mixture. Season with salt and pepper. Remove from heat and keep warm.
6. Season the skirt steak with salt and pepper.
7. Grill over medium high heat turning once about 6 to 8 minutes per side.
8. Cut the skirt steak across the grain into thin slices.
9. Top the steak with the grilled vegetable mixture.

Serves 10 plus
Preparation Time: 45 minutes plus marinating

Skirt steak comes from the "plate" portion of the cow. It is an economical, tender steak and is the cut of choice for fajitas. A traditional Cuban dish named "Vaca Frita" (translating to fried cow) uses flank steak that is boiled, shredded, then fried and served with an array of spicy sauces.

SHREDDED CHICKEN and CARROT ENCHILADAS with ROASTED TOMATO SAUCE

What makes this dish a great party meal is the idea that it can be prepared in advance, and the baked just before placing it onto a buffet table.

4	6 to 8-ounce chicken breast halves with rib
1	teaspoon peppercorns
1	bunch fresh parsley
1	small carrot, cut into pieces
1	celery stalk, cut into pieces
12	plum tomatoes cut in half
2	medium jalapeño peppers, seeded and cut and half
1	medium white onion, cut into quarters
4	medium cloves garlic
2	tablespoons chopped fresh cilantro leaves
2	tablespoons olive oil
2	cups chicken broth
1	tablespoon tomato paste
1	cup heavy cream
	Salt and freshly ground pepper
2	cups shredded Monterey Jack cheese
3	large carrots, shredded (about 1 cup)
	Canola oil
10	6-inch corn tortillas
1	cup shredded fresh mozzarella
1	bunch (6 to 8) green onions, chopped (about ½ cup)

Preheat the oven to 450°.

1. Place the chicken breasts, peppercorns, parsley, carrot, and celery into a large pot. Cover with water. Bring to a boil over medium high heat. Reduce heat and simmer until the chicken is cooked through and beginning to fall off the bone, about 30 to 40 minutes.
2. Place the tomatoes, peppers, onion, and garlic on a baking sheet. Bake until vegetables begin to turn brown, about 10 to 15 minutes.
3. Transfer the vegetables to a blender or food processor. Add the cilantro and pulse until smooth.
4. Heat 2 tablespoons olive oil in a deep skillet over medium high heat.
5. Add the vegetable mixture and cook until the sauce thickens, about 2 minutes.
6. Add the chicken broth and the tomato paste. Simmer for 15 minutes more.
7. Remove from the heat. Stir in the cream. Season with salt and pepper. Set aside.
8. Remove the chicken breasts from the liquid. Cool to room temperature. Use 2 forks to shred the chicken. Place into a bowl.
9. Add the cheese and carrots to the chicken and toss. Season with salt and pepper. Set aside.
10. Heat a small amount of canola oil in a skillet over medium high heat.
11. Place one tortilla into the hot oil. Cook for 30 seconds, turn and cook for 30 seconds more. The tortilla should be soft, pliable and not too crisp.
12. Remove the tortilla to paper toweling to drain.
13. While still warm, fill each tortilla with 2 heaping tablespoons of the chicken/cheese mixture. Roll the tortilla and place it seam side down into baking dish. Repeat until all of the tortillas have been filled.

Preheat the oven to 400°.

14. Cover the enchiladas with the sauce. Cover the sauce with mozzarella cheese and green onions. Bake for 10 to 20 minutes or until the cheese is melted and the casserole is bubbling.

Servings: 10
Preparation Time: 60 minutes plus baking

The name enchilada comes from the word "enchilar" which means to cover or wrap with chili. This traditional Mexican dish is made with corn tortillas that are wrapped around meat, cheese, or vegetables and is often served with rice and beans. Incorporate this easy dish into your week-ly meal plan by using left over beef, roasted chicken or cooked vegetables into an everyday enchilada.

MASHED YUCA with MOJO SAUCE

The Latin version of boiled, buttered potatoes with parsley, this dish is a must for an authentic Cuban party table.

4 to 5 large (8 to 12-inch) yuca

½ cup butter (1 stick)
6 medium cloves garlic, minced (about 1 tablespoons)
Juice of 4 limes (about ½ cup)
Salt and freshly ground pepper
2 tablespoons chopped fresh cilantro leaves

1. Cut the ends from the yuca. Cut each into 3-inch pieces. Trim the outer bark from each piece.

2. Place the yuca into salted, boiling water. Cook until soft, about 10 to 20 minutes depending upon size of pieces.
3. Heat the butter in a pot over medium heat.
4. Add the garlic and cook until translucent and soft, about 2 to 4 minutes.
5. Add the lime juice to the pan. Season with salt pepper.
6. Drain the yuca and place into a serving bowl. Use a potato masher to break up the pieces. Pour the warm mojo sauce over top. Garnish with fresh cilantro.

Servings: 10
Preparation Time: 30 minutes

Yuca is a long tubular root vegetable that is most popular in Latin American cooking but is rap-idly finding its way into your neighborhood grocery store. When cooked it acts much like a pota-to having a buttery taste and a soft texture. Yuca is found in 4 to 12-inch lengths and about 2 to 3-inches in diameter. The bark-like outer skin requires a sharp knife to peel which is best accom-plished by cutting the root into sections, placing each section upright on a cutting board, and slicing down on all sides. You may cut cross-wise slit in both ends of each section to allow the inner fibers to expand while cooking, but this is not necessary. Cooked yucca is served mashed, fried or boiled and is often accompanied by a spicy butter citrus sauce.

SAUTÉED PLANTAINS

Use this sugary side dish as you would a sweet potato. A favorite in Spanish cooking, plantains are readily available in American markets.

5 **to 6 very ripe, black plantains**
Canola oil

4 **tablespoons butter**
4 **green onions, thinly sliced (about ¼ cup)**
1 **tablespoon brown sugar**
½ **teaspoon cinnamon**

1. Peel the plantains by cutting off the ends. Use a sharp knife to cut lengthwise slits in the skin and pry off in sections. Slice lengthwise into ½-inch slices.
2. Place enough canola oil into a skillet to just cover the bottom. Heat the oil over medium heat.
3. Place several plantain slices into the hot oil. Cook until brown and crisp on one side, about 2 minutes. Turn and cook until golden and crisp on the other side, about 2 minutes more.
4. Drain on paper toweling and place onto a rack sitting inside a shallow baking dish. Keep warm. Continue until all of the plantain slices have been cooked using additional oil as needed.
5. Melt the butter in a small pot over medium heat.
6. Stir in the onions, brown sugar, and cinnamon. Cook for 2 minutes.
7. Place the plantains onto a platter. Pour warm sauce over top.

Servings: 10 or more
Preparation Time: 30 minutes

Plantains look like bananas, smell like bananas and are found in the grocery store next to the bananas. However, plantains are a very different food. Green plantains are not ripe and are not sweet. Yellow plantains, looking like a ripe banana are still not sweet enough to use.
Very black plantains that look like the bananas you use to bake in banana bread are the ones you want for this recipe. Although they are incredibly ripe, and very sweet, these plantains are still firm and perfect for frying. They contain a large amount of sugar, so you must watch them when sautéing so that they do not burn.

PECAN POUND CAKE with JAMAICAN RUM WHIPPED CREAM

A very rich, very moist cake is enhanced with silky rum cream. Garnish with tropical fruit and a sprinkle of confectioners' sugar.

1	**tablespoon butter**
1	**tablespoon brown sugar**
1	**cup pecans, coarsely chopped**
3	**cups all-purpose flour**
½	**teaspoon baking soda**
½	**teaspoon salt**
1	**cup butter (2 sticks), room temperature**
3	**cups granulated sugar**
6	**large eggs**
2	**teaspoons rum extract**
1	**cup whipping cream**
2	**cups whipping cream**
6	**tablespoons brown sugar**
3	**tablespoons Jamaican dark rum**

Preheat the oven to 350°.

1. Melt 1 tablespoon butter and 1 tablespoon brown sugar in a skillet over medium heat. Stir in the pecans. Cook for 3 minutes.
2. Place the pecans into a Bundt pan that has been sprayed with vegetable oil spray and dusted with flour.
3. Combine the flour, baking soda, and salt in a bowl. Set aside.
4. Use an electric mixer to combine 1 cup butter and 3 cups granulated sugar until fluffy.
5. Add the eggs one at a time.
6. Stir in the rum extract.
7. Add the flour and 1 cup of whipping cream in 3 additions, alternating ⅓ flour mixture with ⅓ cream until just blended.
8. Pour the batter into the pan.
9. Bake for 1 hour and 20 minutes or until a toothpick inserted into the center of the cake comes out clean.
10. Pour 2 cups of whipping cream in the chilled bowl of an electric mixer. Add the brown sugar and rum. Whip on high speed until soft peaks form.
11. Serve a slice of cake with a generous dollop of rum cream.

Servings: 10 or more
Preparation Time: 30 minutes plus baking

Chill the bowl of an electric mixer as well as the beaters in the freezer for at least 20 minutes before whipping cream. Remember to use cold cream that has been kept in the refrigerator. Using cold utensils and chilled cream will guarantee a rich, yet very light and fluffy whipped cream.

New House Warming Party Plan

Party Motivation

Friends are moving back to town and the gang wants to celebrate their arrival. Or, perhaps dear friends are moving out of town and an impromptu party is just what is needed. Get everyone together and assign each one a dish to bring. Everyone meets at the house at the appointed hour and wham—there is a seriously great party in the making and maybe a little unpacking in the process.

Party Menu

Pesto Torte with Sun-Dried Tomatoes
Bacon, Lettuce, and Tomato Salad
Baked Lemon Chicken
Cauliflower and Potatoes in Ginger Butter Sauce
Macaroni and White Cheddar Cheese Bake **
Asparagus Bread Pudding
Chocolate Spice Cake with Caramel Toffee Frosting

** Over-the-Top Suggestion

Multiply the recipes in this party plan to accomodate your guest list. Turn tummy-cuddling macaroni and cheese into upscale comfort food fare with the addition of sautéed wild mushrooms. Cook the mushrooms in butter, sherry and fresh rosemary until all of the liquid is absorbed. Top the casserole with this mixture and then add the bread crumbs.

Party Strategy

This party comes together easily because everyone chips in to bring a dish. By assigning certain foods, you are guaranteed that there is a terrific balance of dishes that holds at least one favorite per person.

In advance: Assign dishes, pass around recipes, and designate one person to bring disposable china, utensils, glassware, tablecloths, and napkins. Each dish is easily made the day before the party and then baked or reheated just before serving.

Shortcuts

No shortcuts are allowed here. With everyone chipping in there is no need!

Party Backdrop

A way, way casual party, this meal finds it's way to a kitchen counter or on top of a stack of empty boxes. Guests are invited to roll up their sleeves, pitch in and help the new home owners get settled. The reward is great food and a gathering to be remembered.

The Table Setting

Serve the pesto torte on a round platter surround by crackers. Bring the salad in a large bowl and drizzle with dressing just before serving. Transfer baked chicken to a platter. Pour defatted juices into a container, cover and drizzle over the chicken just before serving. Bring the veggies in the skillet they have been cook in. The macaroni and cheese deserves a deep, large baking dish and comes bubbling from the oven. A covered casserole dish works perfectly for the asparagus bread pudding. Use a covered cake plate to transport the dessert.

PESTO TORTE with SUN-DRIED TOMATOES

Make this easy appy ahead of party time and freeze extras for impromptu gatherings.

6   8-ounce packages cream cheese, room temperature
¾   cup butter (3 sticks), room temperature

½   cup fresh basil leaves
½   cup fresh spinach leaves
¼   cup grated Parmesan cheese
¼   cup pine nuts, toasted
2   medium cloves garlic
     Juice of ½ lemon (about 1 tablespoon)
¼   cup olive oil

1   7-ounce jar sun-dried tomatoes in oil, diced

1. Use an electric mixer to combine the cream cheese and butter until light and fluffy. Divide this mixture into 3 bowls.
2. Place ½ cup basil, spinach, cheese, pine nuts, garlic, and lemon juice in a blender or food processor. Pulse to combine. Slowly add the olive oil.
3. Stir the basil mixture into ⅓ of the cream cheese mixture.
4. Stir the sun-dried tomatoes into ⅓ of the cream cheese mixture.
5. Spray a ring mold or deep bowl with vegetable oil spray and line with plastic wrap.
6. Spread the basil layer into the bottom of the mold.
7. Spread ½ of the remaining plain cream cheese mixture on top of the basil layer.
8. Spread the sun-dried tomato layer on top of the cream cheese layer.
9. Top with the remainder of the plain cream cheese layer.
10. Cover the mold with plastic and refrigerate at least 4 hours or overnight. Serve with crackers.

Servings: 10 or more
Preparation Time: 30 minutes

There are countless variations for this simple appetizer. Line basil leaves between the cream cheese layers. You can also layer the mold with plain cream cheese and alternate with a layer of sun-dried tomatoes and pesto. Add toasted pine nuts on the top for a crunchy, nutty garnish.

BACON, LETTUCE, and TOMATO SALAD

Use extra dressing for tomorrow's salad. You want only enough to lightly coat the greens.

10 **to 12 bacon slices, diced**
1 **7-ounce jar sun-dried tomatoes in oil, sliced lengthwise into strips**
8 **cups fresh salad greens**
1 **bunch (6 to 8) green onions, chopped (about ½ cup)**
2 **tablespoons chopped fresh basil leaves**
2 **tablespoons chopped fresh cilantro leaves**
2 **tablespoons chopped fresh tarragon leaves**
¼ **cup red wine vinegar**
2 **tablespoons balsamic vinegar**
½ **cup olive oil**
4 **large hardboiled eggs**
Salt and freshly ground pepper

1. Cook the bacon in a skillet over medium high heat. Remove the pieces with a slotted spoon. Drain on paper toweling.

2. Remove the sun-dried tomatoes from the oil. Reserve the oil for another use.
3. Combine the salad greens and herbs in a large bowl.
4. Whisk together the red wine vinegar and Balsamic vinegar. Slowly whisk in the olive oil.
5. Peel and finely chop the hardboiled eggs.
6. Toss the lettuce with enough dressing to just coat the leaves.
7. Toss with the bacon and sun-dried tomatoes. Garnish with chopped egg.
8. Season with salt and pepper.

Servings: 10
Preparation Time: 20 minutes

The flavor of sun-dried tomatoes adds a real twang to this salad. Roasted tomatoes will work just as well. Cut plum tomatoes in half. Squeeze the pulp and seed from the tomato (reserve this for tomato sauce). Place the tomato halves on a baking sheet. Drizzle with minced garlic or finely chopped shallot. Sprinkle with salt and pepper. Roast the tomatoes in a 300° oven for several hours. Place into an airtight container to use in your best salads, pastas and sauces.

Baked Lemon Chicken

My pal Robin gave me the recipe for this dish—a zillion suppers ago. We love it as much today as we did the first time we prepared it. It's wonderful for an everyday celebration and terrific as a party dish.

1	**cup all-purpose flour**
2	**teaspoons paprika**
	Zest of 1 medium lemon (about 1 table-spoon)
	Salt and freshly ground pepper
4	**tablespoons butter, melted**
4	**6- to 8-ounce chicken breast halves with rib**
6	**4- to 6-ounce chicken thighs**
6	**4- to 6-ounce chicken legs**
½	**cup olive oil**
	Juice of 3 lemons (about ½ cup)
¼	**cup soy sauce**
	Zest of 2 medium lemons (about 2 table-spoon)
1	**bunch (6 to 8) green onions, chopped (about ½ cup)**
	Lemon wheels for garnish
	Chopped fresh parsley for garnish

Preheat the oven to 425°.

1. Place the flour, paprika, 1 tablespoon of lemon zest, salt, and pepper in a plastic bag.
2. Place chicken pieces 2 at a time in the bag and shake to coat.
3. Place the chicken pieces into a baking dish.
4. Drizzle the chicken pieces with melted butter. Bake for 20 minutes.
5. Whisk together the olive oil, lemon juice, soy sauce, remaining lemon zest, and green onions in a bowl.
6. Remove the baking dish with the chicken from the oven. Pour the olive oil mixture over top. Return the pan to the oven. Reduce the temperature to 350°. Bake for 20 minutes more or until the juices of the chicken run clear when pierced with a fork.
7. Place the chicken pieces on a serving platter. Pour the pan juices into a separator cup or measuring cup. After 2 minutes the fat will separate from the juices. Remove the fat and pour the juices over the chicken. Garnish with thinly sliced lemon wheels and fresh chopped parsley.

Servings: 10
Preparation Time: 20 minutes plus baking

Baking chicken can be a bit tricky—especially when the pieces are different sizes. Watch the dish while it is cooking to make sure that you do not overcook small legs and thighs while waiting for the breast to be finished. Simply remove the smaller pieces from the pan to a platter and keep warm until everything else catches up. Ideally for this dish, the breast should be moist and tender (not dry) and the meat of the leg and thigh should be ready to fall away from the bone.

CAULIFLOWER and POTATOES in GINGER BUTTER SAUCE

This flavorful veggie side dish has a hint of Indian spice—a perfect accompaniment for poultry.

2 **to 3 large russet potatoes, peeled and cut into ½-inch pieces (about 2 pounds)**
1 **large head cauliflower, cut into flowerets (about 4 cups)**
½ **cup butter (1 stick)**
2 **1-inch pieces ginger, grated (about 2 tablespoons)**
1 **teaspoon turmeric**
1 **teaspoon chili powder**
½ **teaspoon paprika**
2 **tablespoons soy sauce**
¼ **cup sesame oil**
Salt and freshly ground pepper

1. Cook the potatoes in salted boiling water until soft, about 10 minutes. Drain.
2. Steam the cauliflower in a microwave oven or on the stove top until tender. Drain.
3. Heat the butter in a skillet over medium heat.
4. Add the ginger, turmeric, chili powder, and paprika. Cook for 1 minute.
5. Add the soy sauce and sesame oil.
6. Toss the potatoes and cauliflower in the ginger sauce until coated. Season with salt and pepper.

Servings: 10 or more
Preparation Time: 20 minutes

Develop the intense taste of spice flavors by cooking them when you are creating a sauce. The heat helps the spices merge and add to the pleasure of the dish.

MACARONI and WHITE CHEDDAR CHEESE BAKE

Very rich, very creamy, very yummm, this dish is an easy-to-make addition to your buffet table. Create your favorite by substituting with different cheese, adding diced ham, carrots and peas, or even sautéed wild mushrooms.

2   **pounds elbow macaroni**

1   **cup butter (2 sticks)**
1   **cup all-purpose flour**
2   **medium white onions, finely diced (about 2 cups)**
4   **cups milk**
2   **cups cream**
1   **teaspoon ground nutmeg**
    Salt and freshly ground pepper
2   **pounds white Cheddar cheese, grated**
1   **cup seasoned breadcrumbs**

1. Cook the macaroni in salted boiling water until al dente. Drain in a colander.
2. Melt the butter in a large pot over medium high heat.

3. Stir in the flour until bubbling.
4. Stir in the onions and cook until soft, about 5 minutes.
5. Stir in the milk and cream.
6. Cook until the sauce thickens, about 10 to 15 minutes. Season with nutmeg, salt, and pepper.
7. Place the macaroni in a large baking dish.
8. Toss the cheese into the pasta. Pour the sauce into the pan. Toss to combine.
9. Top with bread crumbs.
10. Bake for 30 minutes or until the top is golden and the casserole is bubbling.

Servings: 10 or more
Preparation Time: 30 minutes plus baking

The secret to terrific baked pasta is to not overcook the pasta in the pot. Al Dente pasta is firm, offering some resistance when pinched. The pasta will continue to cook and absorb the flavor of the sauce when it is baked in the oven. Generously salt the water that the pasta cooks in and add additional spice after you stir in the sauce.

ASPARAGUS BREAD PUDDING

Choose tender, pencil-thin asparagus for this recipe. Savory traces of spicy mustard and fresh basil add all the flavor you will need.

2   pounds small asparagus spears
2   tablespoons olive oil
1   large yellow onion, diced (about 1 cup)
1   1-pound loaf Italian bread, cut into cubes
1   cup grated Swiss cheese
2   cups milk
2   large eggs, beaten
1   bunch (6 to 8) green onions, chopped (about ½ cup)
2   tablespoons Dijon mustard
2   tablespoons chopped fresh basil leaves
2   to 4 drops hot pepper sauce
**   Salt and freshly ground pepper**

Preheat the oven to 375°.

1. Cut each asparagus into 2-inch pieces disregarding the tough stalks.
2. Heat the olive oil over medium high heat. Cook the onion until soft, about 10 minutes.
3. Add the asparagus spears and cook for 2 minutes more.
4. Place the bread cubes into a large baking dish that has been sprayed with vegetable oil spray.
5. Place the asparagus mixture on top of the bread cubes.
6. Sprinkle the cheese on top of the asparagus.
7. Whisk together the milk, eggs, green onion, mustard, and basil in a bowl. Add as much hot sauce as you like. Season with salt and pepper.
8. Pour the milk mixture into the dish. Press down to make sure that the bread absorbs the liquid. Let sit for 20 minutes.
9. Bake for 30 to 40 minutes until the top of the bread pudding is golden.

Servings: 10 or more
Preparation Time: 30 minutes plus baking

Bread puddings are often thought of as the dessert course in flavors like chocolate or pumpkin. However, savory bread puddings are showing up on the menus in upscale restaurants in greater number and unlimited variations. Feel free to create your own personal favorite savory bread pudding by incorporating your best-loved veggie and most favorite spices and herbs.

CHOCOLATE SPICE CAKE with CARAMEL TOFFEE FROSTING

One of my favorite cakes when I was growing up was spice cake with that come hither aroma and mouth licking frosting. This cake has a hint of the traditional but adds a touch of chocolate and a bunch of chopped toffee candy. Ooey gooey!

2	**cups cake flour**
¼	**cup cocoa powder**
1	**teaspoon baking soda**
1	**teaspoons baking powder**
1	**teaspoon cinnamon**
½	**teaspoon ground cloves**
½	**teaspoon salt**
½	**cup butter (1 stick)**
2	**cups packed brown sugar**
½	**cup canola oil**
4	**large eggs**
1	**cup buttermilk**
2	**cups heavy cream, chilled**
¾	**cup prepared caramel topping**
1	**teaspoon vanilla extract**
8	**1.4-ounce bars chocolate-covered English toffee candy, finely chopped (about 2 cups)**

Preheat the oven to 375°.

1. Combine the flour, cocoa, baking soda, baking powder, cinnamon, cloves, and salt in a bowl.
2. Use an electric mixer to combine the butter and brown sugar until light and fluffy.
3. Stir in the eggs one at a time.
4. Add the flour and milk in 3 additions, alternating ⅓ flour mixture with ⅓ milk until just blended.
5. Pour the batter into 2 9-inch cake pans that have been sprayed with vegetable oil spray and dusted with flour.
6. Bake for 20 to 25 minutes or until a toothpick inserted in the center comes out clean. Cool cakes in pans on a rack for 10 minutes. Invert cakes onto a rack and cool completely.
7. Use an electric mixer to beat the cream until it begins to thicken. Add the caramel sauce and vanilla. Continue beating until soft peaks form.
8. Slice the cakes in half using a serrated knife or thread.
9. Place 1 cake layer half on a cake plate. Spread a layer of frosting onto the cake. Sprinkle candy crumbs onto the frosting.
10. Repeat for all layers. Frost the sides and top of the cake. Sprinkle chopped candy pieces on the top and side frosting.

Servings: 10 or more
Preparation Time: 30 minutes plus baking

If the frosting needs to thicken, add a small amount of confectioners' sugar. If it is thicker than you like, add a dab more cream. Let the cake set by refrigerating it for at least one hour.

Candid Camera Party Plan

Party Motivation

Want a great idea for a crazy party? Divide guests into teams. Allow each team to designate a driver. Polaroid cameras are passed out while each team receives a list of places where they must go to have their picture taken. Include wild ideas like sitting in a downtown fountain, a picture with the maître d' at a five-star restaurant, all team members pictured behind the wheel of a taxi cab—you get the idea. Make the challenge as fun—and as rowdy as you like. Set a time limit for everyone to return and send them off with a bang!

Party Menu

Individual Antipasti Packed Coolers **
Classic Meat and Ricotta Lasagna
Lime Chicken with Artichokes and Sun-Dried Tomatoes
Sausage- Stuffed Party Bread
Veggie Filled Bread Torte
Fudgy Chocolate Brownies with Walnut Chunks

** Over-the-Top Suggestion

Talk about drive-through food, these snack filled coolers are the perfect fare for an on-the-run party. Add a chilled beverage and the party gets going.

Party Strategy

Multiply the recipes in this party plan to accomodate your guest list. Have the coolers, cameras and instructions ready in advance of your guest's arrival. After you send them on their way, you have ample time to finish food preparation so that the buffet supper is ready when the photographers return.

In advance of the party: Collect coolers and cameras so that you have as many as you need.

Two days in advance: Prepare lasagna through step 12. Cover and refrigerate.

One day in advance: Bake brownies, cover and refrigerate.

The morning of: Prepare antipasti and pack coolers. Prepare chicken through step 8. Prepare bread dough and stuffing for party bread. Prepare torte through step 9.

After the guests depart: Bake lasagna. Heat chicken dish. Bake party bread. Bake torte.

Shortcuts

Use no-boil noodles for lasagna and frozen bread dough for party bread. Purchase a few of the antipasti ingredients.

Party Backdrop

Set a buffet table with all of the terrific dishes. Assign a helper to collect and evaluate the pictures from each team. After supper, allow guests to vote on the best pictures from each team and supply trophies for the winner. By the way—the winner hosts the same party next year!

The Table Setting

The coolers hold individual containers of bite-sized, easy-to-eat munchies that are eaten on the run. Bubbling hot lasagna is baked in a deep lasagna pan. Serve the lime chicken dish on a large platter or a chafing dish. Cut the bread into slices and serve from a cloth-line basket. Serve the torte on a platter and cut into wedges. Use a cake server to extract each wedge. A platter holds the decadent brownies. A scoop of ice cream guarantees that every guest is a winner.

INDIVIDUAL ANTIPASTI PACKED COOLERS

Here is a fun idea for a moveable feast. The secret is to prepare bite-size antipasti that your guests can pluck from their individual containers.

4   **ounces goat cheese**
8   **ounces Genoa salami, thinly sliced**
1   **tablespoon chopped fresh parsley leaves**

1   **medium head garlic, roasted**
    Crostini
4   **ounces Gorgonzola cheese**

    Roasted red peppers
1   **to 2 heads endive**
    Anchovy fillets
    Freshly ground pepper

1   **pound medium asparagus spears, roasted**
    Marinated assorted olives
    Breadsticks

1. Spread softened goat cheese onto a slice of salami. Sprinkle the cheese with chopped parsley. Roll the salami into a cylinder. Secure with a toothpick if necessary. Place into a disposable plastic container with lid.

2. Spread softened, roast garlic onto a crostini. Sprinkle with Gorgonzola. Place into a disposable plastic container with lid.

3. Place strips of roasted pepper onto half of the endive leaves. Place anchovy fillets into the remaining leaves. Sprinkle with pepper. Place into a disposable plastic container with lid.

4. Place roasted asparagus spears into a disposable plastic container with lid.

5. Place marinated olives into a disposable plastic container with lid.

6. Place breadsticks into a disposable plastic container with lid.

7. Place an ice pack into the bottom of a cooler. Fill the cooler ¾ full with ice. Place each plastic container into the ice.

Servings: 10 or more
Preparation Time: 45 minutes

Antipasti is the Italian term for appetizers, which literally translates to "before the pasta." Traditionally antipasto is created in one of three categories: slices of ham and sausages, cooked veggies, or shellfish. This recipe takes great liberty from the authentic one and allows for a combination of all great tastes. Use this ideas as a guideline. Feel free to intrigue your guests with other tempting morsels. Suggestions include marinated shrimp, grilled calamari, roasted eggplant, cubes of cheese, melon wrapped with Prosciutto, marinated artichoke hearts, and shavings of Parmesan cheese.

Classic Meat and Ricotta Lasagna

Dressed up or down, lasagna is the "basic black dress" of the buffet table. This version has been a hit in our house since I was a little girl. Feel free to add roasted veggies and a layer of thick béchamel for an evening on the town!

2	tablespoons olive oil
1	large yellow onion, diced (about 1 cup)
2	medium cloves garlic, minced (about 1 teaspoon)
1	pound ground Italian sausage
1	pound lean ground sirloin
2	28-ounce cans diced tomatoes
1	6-ounce can tomato paste
1	teaspoon dried basil
1	teaspoon dried oregano
1	teaspoon sugar
	Salt and freshly ground pepper
1	2-pound container ricotta cheese
1	large egg
1	10-ounce package frozen spinach, cooked, excess moisture removed
2	tablespoons chopped fresh basil leaves
½	cup grated Parmesan cheese
1	16-ounce packages lasagna noodles
16	ounces mozzarella cheese, grated
8	ounces Parmesan cheese, grated

Preheat the oven to 375°.

1. Heat the olive oil in a large skillet over medium high heat.
2. Add the onions and cook until soft, about 5 minutes.
3. Add the garlic and cook 2 minutes more.
4. Add the ground sausage and beef. Cook until brown and crumbly.
5. Pour in the tomatoes. Stir in the tomato paste. Season with dried herbs, sugar, salt and pepper. Reduce heat and simmer for 20 minutes.
6. Mix together the ricotta cheese, egg, cooked spinach, basil, and Parmesan cheese in a bowl. Set aside.
7. Cook the lasagna noodles according to the package directions. Drain and rinse under cold water. Lay onto a baking sheet that has been sprayed with vegetable oil spray.
8. In a large lasagna pan place 2 ladles of sauce. Swirl to coat the bottom of the pan.
9. Place a layer of noodles on top of the sauce.
10. Place a layer of sauce on top of the pasta.
11. Place ⅓ of the ricotta cheese mixture on top of the sauce.
12. Sprinkle with ¼ of the mozzarella cheese and ¼ of the Parmesan cheese.
13. Continue layering. End with a layer of noodles, sauce, mozzarella, and Parmesan cheese.
14. Cover the casserole loosely with aluminum foil. Bake for 40 minutes. Remove the foil and bake for 10 minutes more or until the top is golden and the casserole is bubbling. Allow to sit for 15 minutes before serving.

Servings: 10 or more
Preparation Time: 40 minutes plus baking

Lasagna noodles are available dried and in a no-boil category. With no-boil noodles you can skip the tedious step of cooking dried pasta sheets. These accordion shaped dried sheets really do work quite well because they swell to fit the pan while they absorb the flavors of the sauce. Make sure that all of the pasta is covered with sauce. Bare spots will not be tender. Fresh pasta sheets can be made to fit your pan, and if rolled very thin do not require boiling.

LIME CHICKEN with ARTICHOKES and SUN-DRIED TOMATOES

This is a terrific dish that you can make the day in advance for a large crowd, reheat and serve at room temperature. The flavors marry well!

8   6 to 8-ounce skinless boneless chicken breast halves
Juice of 2 limes (about ¼ cup)
2   tablespoons olive oil
Freshly ground pepper

2   14-ounce cans marinated artichoke hearts, quartered
1   7-ounce jar sun-dried tomatoes in oil, sliced lengthwise into strips
1   2-ounce jar Spanish stuffed olives, chopped (about 20)

Preheat the oven to 350°.

1. Season the chicken breasts with salt and pepper. Squeeze fresh lime juice over top and drizzle with 2 tablespoons olive oil. Season with salt and pepper.

2. Place the chicken breasts on a rack in a roasting pan. Bake for 30 to 45 minutes, or until the breasts are just cooked. (In this dish, undercooked is okay.)

3. Cool the breasts slightly. Cut into thin, diagonally slices. Place all of the sliced chicken and the juices into a large roasting pan.

4. Add the artichokes and their marinade to the pan.

5. Add the sun-dried tomatoes and their marinade to the pan.

6. Drain the olives and add to the pan.

7. Season with freshly ground pepper and another drizzle of lime juice. Toss.

8. Cover and refrigerate until 1 hour before serving.

9. Warm the dish in a 350° oven for 45 minutes. Transfer to a chafing dish to serve.

Serves: 10
Preparation Time: 30 minutes plus baking

The marinade from the artichokes and sun-dried tomatoes blend to form the sauce for this dish. Feel free to add white wine, chicken stock or cream to intensify the flavors and create a richer dish.

Sausage-Stuffed Party Bread

Stuff this bread with your favorite filling and take notes. It will disappear before you have time to make it again!

3   tablespoons water
1½ cups sour cream
½   teaspoon salt
½   teaspoon baking soda
1   tablespoon sugar
3½ cups bread flour
2½ teaspoons yeast

1   tablespoon olive oil
1   medium white onion, diced (about ⅔ cup)
2   medium cloves garlic, minced (about 1 teaspoon)
1   pound mild Italian sausage
2   large eggs
2   tablespoons chopped fresh parsley leaves
½   teaspoon dried oregano
¼   cup grated Parmesan cheese
1   cup shredded Cheddar cheese

1. Place the water, sour cream, salt, baking soda, sugar, and bread flour into the bucket in a bread machine.
2. Pour the yeast in the yeast compartment (or follow the specific directions for your bread machine).
3. Select the dough cycle and start the bread machine.
4. Heat the olive oil in a skillet over medium high heat.
5. Cook the onion until soft, about 4 minutes.
6. Add the garlic and cook for 2 minutes more.
7. Add the sausage and cook until browned and crumbly. Remove this mixture to a bowl and cool to room temperature.
8. Combine the sausage, eggs, parsley, oregano, and Parmesan cheese.

Preheat the oven to 350°.

9. Turn out the dough on a lightly floured surface. Roll out to a 12 x 9-onch rectangle.
10. Place the sausage mixture down the long end of the dough rectangle. Sprinkle the Cheddar cheese over top. Roll up jelly-roll style.
11. Place the bread roll seam side down onto a baking sheet that has been sprayed with vegetable oil spray or lined with a Silpat liner. Bake for 40 to 45 minutes or until golden and crisp on the outside. Cool for 10 minutes before serving.

Servings: 10 or more
Preparation Time: 40 minutes plus baking

Party breads were all the rage in the fifties. The bread machine has cut the work load in half. You can also substitute with frozen and thawed bread dough found in the freezer section of the market.

Veggie-Filled Bread Torte

A terrific buffet dish, this torte doubles as a theatrical luncheon meal. Utilize your favorite veggies as long as you choose the best that the market has to offer.

2	tablespoons olive oil
4	large shallots, minced (about ½ cup)
4	leeks, white part only, sliced (about 2 cups)
2	large carrots, diced (about ½ cup)
1	large green bell pepper, seeded and diced (about 1 cup)
1	large red bell pepper, seeded and diced (about 1 cup)
4	medium yellow squash, cut into ½-inch cubes (about 3 cups)
2	medium cloves garlic, minced (about 1 teaspoon)
1	bunch Swiss chard, stems removed (about 4 cups)
1	tablespoon chopped fresh oregano leaves
2	tablespoons chopped fresh basil leaves
	Salt and freshly ground pepper
1	cup heavy cream
½	cup sesame seeds
12	thick slices white bread, crusts removed
8	ounces mozzarella cheese, grated

Preheat the oven to 450°.

1. Heat the olive oil in a large skillet over medium high heat.
2. Add the shallots and leeks. Cook until soft, about 5 minutes.
3. Add the carrots and peppers. Cook until soft, about 10 minutes more.
4. Add the squash and garlic and cook for 5 minutes more.
5. Stir in the Swiss chard and herbs. Cook until wilted, about 2 minutes. Season the vegetables with salt and pepper.
6. Pour the cream into the pan. Reduce heat and simmer until the cream begins to thicken, about 4 minutes. Remove from the heat and cool to room temperature.
7. Spray a 9-inch springform pan with vegetable oil cooking spray. Sprinkle the sides and bottom with sesame seeds.
8. Press the bread slices into the bottom and up the sides of the pan. Cut the bread to so that it fits snugly in the pan.
9. Sprinkle half of the cheese onto the bread. Pour in the vegetable mixture. Top with remaining cheese.
10. Place the torte on a baking sheet. Bake for 25 to 30 minutes or until the top is golden and the torte is set in the center. Cool for 5 minutes. Release the sides of the pan and gently place the torte onto a serving platter.

Servings: 10
Preparation Time: 45 minutes plus baking

You can substitute with whatever size springform pan that you have in your cupboard without trouble. A large 10- or 12-inch pan will require less cooking time and a few more slices of bread. A smaller 8-inch pan will require a few extra minutes of cooking time in order to set up properly. Allow the torte to cool before slicing.

Fudgy Chocolate Brownies with Walnut Chunks

Nothing finishes a great meal like a bit of dense, dark chocolaty brownie. Team it with chilled, rich ice cream and the party continues.

1   **cup butter (2 sticks)**
8   **ounces semisweet chocolate, chopped**
4   **ounces unsweetened chocolate, chopped**

1   **cup all-purpose flour**
1½   **teaspoons baking powder**
½   **teaspoon salt**
1   **cup granulated sugar**
3   **large eggs**
1   **tablespoon vanilla extract**
1   **cup walnut pieces**
6   **ounces semisweet chocolate, chopped**

Preheat the oven to 350°.

1. Melt the butter, 8 ounces semisweet and 4 ounces unsweetened chocolate in a double boiler over simmering water until smooth. Remove from the heat. Let cool to room temperature.

2. Combine the flour, baking powder and salt in a small bowl.
3. Use and electric mixer to beat together the sugar, eggs, and vanilla until light and fluffy.
4. Add the chocolate mixture to the bowl and beat until smooth.
5. Mix in the dry ingredients.
6. Fold in the walnuts and 6 ounces coarsely chopped semisweet chocolate.
7. Pour the batter into a 13 x 9 x 2-inch baking dish that has been sprayed with vegetable oil spray.
8. Bake for 20 to 25 minutes, or until a toothpick inserted into the center comes out clean.

Servings: 10
Preparation Time: 20 minutes plus baking

This fudgy, dense bar cookie is kin to both a flourless torte and a dense devil's food cake.
Take it over the top by making brownie ice cream bars:

Cut the brownies into squares. Coat the top of one brownie square with softened vanilla ice cream. Top it with a second brownie square. Place on a cooling rack on a baking sheet and immediately place in the freezer. Repeat with all of the brownies.
Melt chocolate in a double boiler over simmering water. Allow to cool. Drizzle the chocolate over all of the brownie sandwiches. Put them back into the freezer.
You have created a brownie ice cream Klondike bar. So yummy!

A Backyard Wedding Party Plan

Party Motivation

You're hosting a very special occasion and you want the menu to mirror the day. Really fussy food is served simply so that you can invite scores of guests.

Party Menu

Chilled Tomato Lime Soup with Avocado Salsa and Seared Scallop Garnish
Grilled Shrimp and Tortellini Skewers with Parmesan Dipping Sauce
Dilled Roasted Salmon with Horseradish Caper Sauce
Beef Tenderloin Tips with Red Wine Hoisin Sauce
Wild Rice, Lentils, and Sautéed Mushrooms
Stewed Vegetables with Basil
Caprese Salad
Fluffy Buttermilk Biscuits
Light As Air Lemon Cake with Lemon Curd Icing **

** Over-the-Top Suggestion

Frosted flower petals garnish this wonderful cake. Choose edible flowers to make it so much more appealing.

Party Strategy

The recipes in this party plan are meant to be multiplied to accomodate your guest list. Food stations are a wonderful way to organize a crowd. Set up several stations so that guests can choose their favorite foods first.

In advance of the party: Order tables, chairs, linens, barware and utensils.

Two days before: Prepare soup, cover and refrigerate.

One day before: Prepare beef tips through step 8. Cover and refrigerate. Prepare rice, cover and refrigerate. Prepare vegetables, place into a chafing dish, cover and refrigerate.

The night before: Prepare cake, cover and refrigerate. Prepare petal garnish. Store separately. Prepare sauce for salmon.

The morning of: Set tables, arrange centerpieces. Chill champagne. Prepare avocado salsa. Prepare skewers and dipping sauce. Store separately, cover and refrigerate. Prepare ingredients for salad. Bake biscuits.

Four hours before: Prepare salmon, cover and refrigerate.

Two hours before: Prepare seared scallop garnish, cover and refrigerate.

One hour before: Bake salmon, cover. Warm tenderloin dish. Warm wild rice. Warm vegetables.

Immediately before: Drain salsa. Assemble salad. Decorate cake with petals.

Shortcuts

Substitute quick cooking rice for the longer simmering wild rice.

Party Backdrop

Set in the backyard, a trellis holds the ceremony. Round tables are set with bowls of fresh cut flowers. Miniature fabric picture frames holds place cards with seating preferences. Garden patterned tablecloths set the tone for an outdoor celebration.

The Table Setting

Set up the food stations.

Station 1 holds a tureen filled with chilled soup. Irish coffee glasses hold the soup with a spoonful of avocado salsa and are topped with a slice of seared scallop. At this station skewered tortellini and shrimp are piled high with a bowl of Parmesan dipping sauce nearby. Set soup spoons, appetizer plates and tons of cocktail napkins (embossed with the name of the bride and groom).

Station 2 offers platters of salmon with a bowl of horseradish dipping sauce nearby. Next to the salmon is a chafing dish filled with stewed veggies. Set out dinner plates, forks and knives.

Station 3 highlights a chafing dish of beef tenderloin tips and a bowl full of wild rice and lentils. Set out dinner plates, forks and steak knives.

Individual baskets of biscuits and platters of Caprese salad sit on each table, so that guests can serve themselves as they are seated.

The last station holds the sweetly decorated cake. The bride and groom make the first cut, and guests are invited to share in the treasure.

CHILLED TOMATO LIME SOUP with AVOCADO SALSA and SEARED SCALLOP GARNISH

The perfect party ice-breaker is a refreshing sip of chilled soup. Add an over-the-top garnish and you have a real show stopper!

2   tablespoons olive oil
1   large yellow onion, diced (about 1 cup)
2   large shallots, minced (about 2 table-
    spoons)
2   28-ounce cans diced tomatoes
2   cups chicken stock
1   tablespoon chopped fresh thyme leaves
½   teaspoon sugar
    Salt and freshly ground pepper

1½ cups cream
⅔   cup sour cream
    Juice of 1 lime (about 2 tablespoons)
2   to 6 drops hot sauce

2   large avocados, diced (about 2 cups)
1   small red onion, diced (about ½ cup)
4   plum tomatoes, seeded and diced (about
    2 cups)
2   tablespoons chopped fresh cilantro
    leaves
    Juice of 1 lime (about 2 tablespoons)
1   tablespoon olive oil

2   tablespoons butter
10 medium sea scallops

1. Heat the olive oil in a large pot over medium high heat.
2. Cook the onions in the oil until soft, about 5 minutes.
3. Add the shallots and cook for 3 minutes more.
4. Stir in the diced tomatoes, chicken broth, thyme, and sugar. Season with salt and pepper. Reduce heat and simmer for 20 minutes.
5. Use an immersion blender or food processor to purée the soup.
6. Stir in the cream, sour cream, and lime juice. Season with as much hot sauce as you like.
7. Cover and chill for at least 2 hours in the freezer or overnight in the refrigerator.
8. Combine the avocado, red onion, plum tomatoes, cilantro, lime juice, and olive oil in a small bowl. Season with salt and pepper. Toss. Cover and refrigerate for 1 hour.
9. Melt the butter in a skillet over medium high heat. Season the scallops with pepper. Cook the scallops in the butter until golden on one side, about 2 to 4 minutes. Turn and cook until golden on the other side, about 2 minutes more. Remove and drain on paper toweling.
10. Serve the soup in an oversized coffee cup, mug, or Irish coffee glass.
11. Drain the salsa. Place a spoon full of salsa into the center of the soup. Top with a scallop.

Servings: 10 or more
Preparation Time: 45 minutes plus refrigeration

A hand held or immersion blender makes short work of puréeing soup ingredients.
A food processor will also do the job. Transfer the soup in batches, pulse and pour into a bowl.
Continue until all of the ingredients have been puréed.
Return the soup to the pot and continue with the recipe.

GRILLED SHRIMP and TORTELLINI SKEWERS with PARMESAN DIPPING SAUCE

These alluring skewers combine the flavors of seafood, pasta and Parmesan. Can it get any better?

1½	**pounds large uncooked shrimp, peeled and deveined (about 24)**
¼	**cup olive oil**
1	**teaspoon Dijon mustard**
2	**tablespoon balsamic vinegar**
2	**tablespoons chopped fresh parsley leaves**
	Salt and freshly ground pepper
1	**pound tri-colored, cheese-filled tortellini**
1	**cup sour cream**
½	**cup Parmesan cheese**
2	**tablespoons tarragon vinegar**
	Juice of 1 lemon (about 2 tablespoons)
2	**tablespoons chopped fresh tarragon leaves**
1	**teaspoon dried red pepper flakes**

1. Place the shrimp in a bowl. Whisk together the olive oil, mustard, balsamic vinegar, and parsley. Season with salt and pepper. Pour this mixture over the shrimp. Cover and refrigerate for 30 minutes.

2. Cook the tortellini according the package directions. Drain and place onto a baking sheet that has been sprayed with vegetable oil spray.

3. Combine the sour cream, Parmesan cheese, tarragon vinegar, lemon juice, fresh tarragon, and red pepper flakes in a small bowl until smooth. Cover and refrigerate. Bring to room temperature when ready to serve.

4. Heat a grill pan over medium high heat. Drain the shrimp from the marinade. Cook the shrimp in the pan, turning once until opaque, about 3 to 5 minutes. Remove from the heat.

5. Thread 1 tortellini on an 8-inch bamboo skewer followed by a grilled shrimp and another tortellini. Continue until all of the shrimp and tortellini have been skewered.

6. Stand the skewers in a vase or tall bowl. Serve with dipping sauce.

Yield: 2 dozen skewers
Preparation Time: 30 minutes

Use a grill pan to quickly sear sea food. Watch the shrimp carefully. Overcooking will produce a tough, chewy shrimp. Discard extra marinade.

DILL ROASTED SALMON with HORSERADISH CAPER SAUCE

The simple preparation of this dish makes it a perfect party entrée. Served warm, room temp or chilled, the flavor is delicious and gently enhanced with the rich sauce.

2	**12-ounce whole salmon fillets**
	Juice of 3 lemons (about ½ cup)
¼	**cup olive oil**
¼	**cup chopped fresh dill**
	Salt and freshly ground pepper
1	**cup sour cream**
½	**cup heavy cream**
2	**to 4 tablespoons prepared horseradish**
	Juice of 1 lemon (about 2 tablespoons)
2	**tablespoons chopped fresh dill**
1	**tablespoon capers, drained**

Preheat the oven to 350°.

1. Place the salmon fillets skin side down on a baking sheet that has been sprayed with vegetable oil spray.
2. Pour the lemon juice on the salmon.
3. Drizzle with olive oil.
4. Sprinkle the fresh dill on top. Season with salt and freshly ground pepper. Bake for 10 to 20 minutes depending on the thickness of the fillet. The salmon should be just rare in the center. Remove from the oven. Cover and refrigerate. Bring to room temperature before serving.
5. Combine the sour cream, heavy cream, 2 tablespoons horseradish, lemon juice, fresh dill, and capers until blended. Season with salt and fresh pepper and additional horse-radish as preferred.
6. Transfer the salmon to a serving platter. Garnish with lemon slices and fresh dill sprigs. Serve the horseradish sauce on the side.

Servings: 10 or more
Preparation Time: 20 minutes

Health professional, trainers, nutritionists, and your next door neighbor boast the benefits of eating seafood rich in beneficial omega-3 oils. Guess what? You need only ask your taste buds and you will know that salmon is a tremendous dish to include in your party menu.

Beef Tenderloin Tips with Red Wine Hoisin Sauce

The addition of Hoisin makes this sauce velvety, tangy and irresistible. Serve the dish over wild rice or homemade egg noodles.

2	tablespoons olive oil
4	pounds beef tenderloin cut into 2 inch cubes
	Salt and freshly ground pepper
2	large yellow onions, diced (about 2 cups)
1	large red bell pepper, diced into 1 inch pieces
1	large green bell pepper, diced into 1 inch pieces
1	pound shiitake mushrooms, stems removed (3 cups)
2	cups red wine
1	28-ounce can diced tomatoes
1	teaspoon dried oregano
1	teaspoon dried basil
1	7.25-ounce jar Hoisin sauce
2	bay leaves
¼	cup cornstarch mixed with ¼ cup cold water

Preheat the oven to 350°.

1. Heat the olive oil over medium high heat in a large roasting pan or Dutch oven.
2. Season the beef cubes with salt and pepper and place (in batches) in the pan to brown.
3. Remove the meat from the pan and place into a large bowl.
4. Add the diced onion, peppers, and mushrooms to the pan. Cook until the vegetables begin to soften.
5. Add the red wine and diced tomatoes to the pan. Stir.
6. Season with dried oregano and basil and additional salt and pepper.
7. Stir in the Hoisin sauce. Place the bay leaves in the sauce. Return the meat and the juices to the pan.
8. Bring to a boil. Cover and place the roasting pan into the oven. Bake for 30 minutes.
9. Thicken the sauce with the cornstarch mixture. Discard the bay leaves.

Serves 10
Preparation Time: 30 minutes plus roasting

Hoisin sauce is a sweet, spicy dark brown sauce that is made from fermented soybeans and red rice, which is a natural coloring agent. It is available in the specialty section of most grocery stores.

WILD RICE, LENTILS, and SAUTÉED MUSHROOMS

This is a great buffet dish as it is equally good served warm or at room temperature. The earthy flavors of the rice and lentils are a excellent substitute for everyday white rice or potatoes.

2   **cups wild rice**
    Salt and freshly ground pepper
1   **12-ounce package dried lentils**
2   **to 4 tablespoons olive oil**
1   **4-ounce package shiitake mushrooms**
    (about 1½ cups)
1   **8-ounce package portobello mushrooms,**
    cut into strips (about 1½ cups)
2   **pounds button mushrooms, sliced**
    (about 4 cups)

1   **bunch (6 to 8) green onions, chopped**
    (about ½ cup)
¼   **cup chopped fresh rosemary leaves**
2   **tablespoons olive oil**

1. Rinse the rice under running water for 2 minutes and drain thoroughly. Place the rice into a pot. Pour in water to cover by about 3 inches. Season with salt. Bring to a boil and cook for 30 minutes or until tender but not mushy. Drain the rice reserving the cooking liquid.

2. Cook the lentils according to the package directions substituting reserved cooking liquid from the rice for a portion of the water.

3. Heat 2 tablespoons olive oil in a skillet over medium high heat.

4. Add the shiitake mushrooms and cook until golden, about 5 minutes. Continue with the portobello mushrooms and button mushrooms adding additional oil as needed. Season with salt and pepper.

5. Combine the wild rice, lentils and mushrooms in a large roasting pan or Dutch oven. Toss with green onion and fresh rosemary. Drizzle with olive oil and season with salt and pepper.

Servings: 10 or more
Preparation Time: 1 hour

Wild rice is not really a rice but instead is a type of aquatic grass.
It is native to Minnesota and has an earthy flavor and crunchy texture.
It pairs nicely with the mild flavor of lentils in this dish.

Stewed Vegetables with Basil

Delectable veggies are just what's needed on a buffet table. These are prepared in advance and have staying power.

2	to 6 tablespoons olive oil
2	large green bell peppers, chopped into ½-inch pieces (about 2 cups)
1	medium red onion, diced (about 1 cup)
2	large zucchini, diced (about 4 cups)
1	pound green beans, cut into 1-inch pieces (about 3 cups)
4	ears fresh corn, corn sliced from cob (about 2 cups)
1	pound fresh lima beans (about 2 cups)
1	28-ounce can crushed tomatoes
2	tablespoons chopped fresh basil leaves
1	tablespoon chopped fresh rosemary leaves
	Salt and freshly ground pepper
8	ounces Romano cheese, grated

1. Heat the olive oil in a large skillet over medium high heat
2. Add the peppers and red onions and cook until soft about 5 minutes.
3. Add the zucchini, green beans, corn, and lima beans. Cook for 5 minutes more.
4. Add the tomatoes and fresh herbs. Season with salt and pepper.
5. Reduce heat and simmer for 15 minutes. Garnish with grated Romano cheese.

Servings: 10
Preparation Time: 30 minutes

For a totally veggie supper, serve this dish over brown rice. Jump it up a notch by adding jalapeño pepper or a dousing of hot pepper sauce.

Caprese Salad

This simple salad is only well done when using the freshest, most ripe tomatoes and the best quality Mozzarella that you can find. Well flavored olive oil and garden fresh basil are a must.

6	**large beefsteak tomatoes cut into ¼-inch slices**
16	**ounces fresh mozzarella, cut into ¼-inch slices**
1	**bunch basil leaves, stems removed**
	Salt and freshly ground pepper
⅓	**cup olive oil**

1. Arrange the salad by alternating 1 slice tomato with 1 slice mozzarella and 1 basil leaf around a platter. Continue alternating until all of the ingredients have been assembled.
2. Sprinkle with salt and pepper.
3. Drizzle with olive oil.

Servings: 10 or more
Preparation Time: 20 minutes

Good quality ingredients are the staple for this fresh salad. Additions include roasted peppers, anchovy fillets and a garnish of minced garlic and lemon zest.

Fluffy Buttermilk Biscuits

Serve these biscuits with flavored butter with a hint of jam for a blast of savory. For a light, fluffy, airy biscuit, work the dough as little as possible. Feel free to add your favorite savory ingredients such as fresh herbs, a touch of cheese or poppy seeds.

4	**cups all-purpose flour**
4	**teaspoons baking powder**
1	**teaspoon baking soda**
1	**teaspoon salt**
1	**teaspoon sugar**
1	**cup butter (2 sticks), cut into pieces**
2	**cups buttermilk**

Preheat the oven to 375°.
1. Place the flour, baking powder, soda, salt, and sugar into the bowl of a food processor. Pulse to combine
2. Place the butter into the bowl. Pulse until the mixture resembles course crumbs.
3. Add the buttermilk and pulse until just combined. The dough will be sticky.
4. Turn the dough out onto a lightly floured surface.
5. Use fingers to pat the dough to 1-inch thickness. Use a 3-inch round biscuit cutter to cut out biscuits. Place biscuits onto a Silpat-lined baking sheet.
6. Bake for 15 to 20 minutes or until the tops are golden.

Yield: 12 biscuits
Preparation Time: 20 minutes plus baking

Light as Air Lemon Cake with Lemon Curd Icing

Perfect for a backyard wedding or baby shower, this delicate cake is as delicious to eat, as it is to see. For a special occasion, decorate with sugared flower petals.

2½   **cups cake flour**
2   **tablespoons baking powder**
½   **teaspoon baking soda**
¼   **teaspoon salt**
1   **cup butter (2 sticks), room temperature**
1½   **cups granulated sugar**
2   **large eggs**
3   **egg yolks**
1   **tablespoon vanilla extract**
      Zest of 1 medium lemon (about 1 tablespoon)
      Juice of 2 lemons (about ¼ cup)
½   **cup cream**

⅔   **cup granulated sugar**
      Zest of 1 medium lemon (about 1 tablespoon)
5   **egg yolks**
      Juice of 4 lemons (about ½ cup)
¼   **teaspoon salt**
½   **cup butter (1 stick), melted**

3   **cups confectioners' sugar**
      Zest of 2 medium lemons (about 2 tablespoons)
4   **tablespoons sour cream**
5   **tablespoons butter, room temperature**
2   **tablespoons Lemon Curd (steps 8-10)**
      Sugared Flowers for garnish (see sidebar, next page)

Preheat the oven to 350°.
1. Combine the cake flour, baking powder, baking soda, and salt in a bowl. Set aside.
2. Use an electric mixer to combine 1 cup butter and 1½ cups sugar until light and fluffy.
3. Add the eggs and egg yolks, one at a time.
4. Mix in the vanilla, lemon zest, and lemon juice.

5. Add the flour mixture and cream in 3 additiosn, alternating ⅓ flour mixture with ⅓ cream until just blended.
6. Pour the batter into 2 9-inch cake pans that have been sprayed with vegetable oil spray and dusted with flour.
7. Bake for 20 to 25 minutes or until a toothpick inserted into the center comes out clean. Cool in pan for 5 minutes. Invert onto cooling racks and cook completely.
8. For lemon curd, place ⅔ cup of granulated sugar and the zest of 1 lemon into the bowl of a food processor. Pulse until very fine.
9. Add 5 egg yolks, ½ cup of lemon juice, and salt. Pulse to combine.
10. Pour the melted butter through the feed tube with the machine running. Pour into a saucepan and cook over medium low heat, stirring constantly until thickened. Do not boil. Cool, cover, and refrigerate the curd for at least 1 hour.
11. Place the confectioners' sugar and zest of 2 lemons into the bowl of a food processor. Pulse until very fine.
12. Add the sour cream, butter, and 2 tablespoons of lemon curd. Pulse until mixed well. Refrigerate for at least 15 minutes.
13. Cut each cake in half using a serrated knife or a length of sewing thread. Place one half onto a serving plate. Spread the cake with lemon curd, leaving a 1-inch border.
14. Repeat with the next 2 layers.
15. Spread the sides and top of the cake with lemon icing.
16. Garnish with Sugared Flowers.

Servings: 10 or more
Preparation Time: 45 minutes plus baking

Make flower garnishes by combining 1 egg white with 1 tablespoon water in a shallow bowl.
Pour granulated sugar into a separate bowl. Dip the flower into the egg white.
Use a clean paint brush to make sure that every petal is coated. Sprinkle the flower with sugar.
Shake off excess. Carefully place the flower onto a baking sheet.
Chill the flowers in the freezer until ready to decorate the cake.

Howling At the Moon Party Plan

Party Motivation

A superbly sculpted no-reason to party—party! The moons and the stars align because she said "Yes" when you popped the question—he reached partnership status a year ahead of the predictions—or, you've just experienced the birth of the first grandchild. Whatever the high—invite your pals to kick back and howl at the moon—a way out there midnight supper—a new benchmark for partying.

Party Menu

Mushroom Scallion Pancakes with Sherry Creamed Chicken
Sweet Potato Pancakes with Lobster Herb Cream Sauce
Ricotta Cakes with Poached Eggs, Hollandaise Sauce, and Caviar
Polenta Cakes with Toasted Corn and Garlicky Shrimp
Croissant Bread Pudding with Pistachio Nuts and Warm Maple Syrup

** Over-the-Top Suggestion

Serve a signature cocktail—Peppered Bloody Mary. In a blender combine 8 ounces premium vodka, ¼ small red onion, 1 cove garlic, the juice of 1 lime, a dash of hot sauce, 3 cups tomato juice, and 2 tablespoons prepared horseradish.

Pour into 4 glasses filled with ice. Garnish with a celery stalk and lime pinwheel.

Party Strategy

The recipes in this menu are designed to be multiplied to accomodate your guest list. Each dish has a station. Prepare all of the ingredients in advance and make each dish to order.

One day in advance: Prepare mushroom scallion pancake batter (shortcut: cook, layer, store, and refrigerate). Prepare sweet potato pancake batter (shortcut: cook, layer, store, and refrigerate). Prepare ricotta pancake batter (shortcut: cook, layer, store, and refrigerate). Prepare polenta pancake batter shortcut: cook, layer, store, and refrigerate).

The evening before: Prepare bread pudding through step 5.

The day of: Prepare sherry creamed chicken, cover, refrigerate. Prepare lobster cream sauce, cover, refrigerate. Prepare garlicky shrimp, cover, refrigerate.

Two hours before: Prepare hollandaise, cover.

One hour before: Bring everything to room temperature.

Immediately before: Poach eggs. Warm dessert.

Shortcuts

Prepare the pancakes in advance and store until immediately before the party. Warm in a low oven or microwave. Keep warm in a chafing dish at each station. Keep moist with damp towels.

Party Backdrop

Offer each pancake dish at it's own station manned by helpers. Great music is on tap. Cabaret tables line the party space with fresh herbs gathered into centerpieces. A basket of party favors include individual ground specialty coffee packets, coffee mugs, and home baked muffins for the morning-after celebration.

The Table Setting

Station 1: Set up an electric skillet and single burner. Pour the batter into the skillet for mushroom pancakes. Keep sherry creamed chicken warm in a pot on the burner. A bowl of freshly chopped parsley is set for garnish.

Station 2: Set up an electric skillet and single burner. Pour the batter into the skillet for sweet potato pancakes. Keep lobster cream sauce warm in a pot on the burner. A bowl of freshly chopped tarragon is set for garnish.

Station 3: Set up an electric skillet, single burner and chafing dish. Pour the batter into the skillet for ricotta pancakes. Keep rich hollandaise sauce warm in a pot on the burner. A chafing dish holds poached eggs. A bowl of chilled caviar is set for garnish.

Station 4: Set up an electric skillet and chafing dish. Pour the batter into the skillet for polenta cakes. Keep garlicky shrimp warm in a chafing dish. A bowl of freshly chopped cilantro is set for garnish.

Station 5: Holds a baking dish of warm bread pudding. A sauceboat filled with warm maple syrup is set nearby. Helpers offer a scoop of vanilla ice cream.

Allow for enough plates, utensils and napkins so that every guest can experience each dish. This party is designed for a celebration that lasts into the wee, wee hours.

MUSHROOM SCALLION PANCAKES
with SHERRY CREAMED CHICKEN

As a starter or a "stop" on a midnight buffet, this dish is decadently rich—absolutely a tummy filler!

2	cups all-purpose flour
1	teaspoon baking powder
1	teaspoon baking soda
½	teaspoon granulated sugar
2	large eggs
1	cup water
½	cup buttermilk
¼	cup olive oil
1	4-ounce package shiitake mushrooms, finely diced (about 1½ cups)
1	bunch (6 to 8) green onions, chopped (about ½ cup)
2	to 4 tablespoons butter
2	6 to 8-ounce skinless boneless chicken breast halves
	Salt and freshly ground pepper
1	tablespoon olive oil
1	medium white onion, diced (about ⅔ cup)
3	tablespoons butter
3	tablespoons all-purpose flour
⅓	cup sherry
3	cups heavy cream
1	bay leaf
	Salt and freshly ground pepper
2	tablespoons chopped fresh parsley

1. Combine the flour, baking powder, baking soda, and sugar in a small bowl.
2. Whisk together the eggs until fluffy. Whisk in the water, buttermilk, and olive oil.
3. Stir in the mushrooms and green onion.
4. Melt 2 tablespoons butter in a skillet over medium heat.
5. Pour the batter, by ladle into the pan creating several 3-inch diameter pancakes. Cook for 2 to 3 minutes or until golden. Turn and cook for 2 minutes more. Transfer the pancakes to paper toweling. Continue with remaining batter using additional butter as needed.

Preheat the oven to 350°.
6. Season the chicken breast and bake until cooked through, about 25 to 30 minutes. Cool for 5 minutes. Chop into ½-inch cubes.
7. Heat 1 tablespoon olive oil in a skillet over medium high heat. Add the diced onions. Cook until just soft, about 5 minutes. Remove from the heat.
8. Melt the butter in a pot over medium high heat. Stir in the flour until smooth and bubbling.
9. Add the sherry, cream, and bay leaf. Cook, stirring constantly until thickened, about 10 minutes. Remove the bay leaf.
10. Stir in the cooked chicken and onions. Season with salt and pepper.
11. Serve 2 to 3 pancakes on a plate. Top with a ladle full of creamed chicken. Garnish with chopped parsley.

Servings: 10
Preparation Time: 60 minutes

These pancakes, like crepes, can be made in advance. Cool and place between pieces of paper toweling. Stack in a plastic bag or air tight container. Store in the refrigerator for several days or in the freezer for several months. Reheat in the microwave on high for 1 minute.

Sweet Potato Pancakes
with Lobster Herb Cream Sauce

Sugary sweet potatoes pair nicely with rich cream sauce in this flavorful and elegant dish.

2	**12 to 16-ounce lobster tails, cooked, shells discarded**
1	**tablespoon butter**
1	**large shallot, minced (about 1 tablespoon)**
¼	**cup white wine**
1	**cup heavy cream**
2	**tablespoons chopped fresh thyme leaves**
2	**tablespoons chopped fresh rosemary leaves**
	Salt and freshly ground pepper
3	**medium sweet potatoes**
2	**large eggs**
1	**cup heavy cream**
1	**cup all-purpose flour**
1	**teaspoon baking powder**
1	**teaspoon baking soda**
½	**teaspoon ground nutmeg**
2	**to 4 tablespoons olive oil**
	Fresh tarragon leaves

Preheat the oven to 350°.

1. Cut the lobster meat into ½-inch thick medallions.
2. Heat 1 tablespoon butter in a skillet over medium high heat.
3. Add the shallots and cook until soft, about 5 minutes.
4. Add the wine and cook until most of the liquid disappears.
5. Add the cream and the fresh herbs. Cook until the cream thickens, about 5 to 10 minutes more. Season with salt and pepper.
6. Reduce the heat to low. Place the lobster into the sauce. Keep warm.
7. Roast potatoes until soft, about 25 to 35 minutes. Cool. Peel the potatoes and place into the bowl of a food processor. Pulse until smooth.
8. Add the eggs and cream. Pulse to combine.
9. Combine the flour, baking powder, baking soda, and nutmeg in a bowl. Stir in the potato mixture until smooth.
10. Heat 2 tablespoons olive oil in a skillet over medium high heat.
11. Pour the batter by ladle into the pan creating several 3-inch diameter pancakes. Cook for 2 to 3 minutes or until golden. Turn and cook for 2 minutes more. Transfer the pancakes to paper toweling. Continue with remaining batter using additional oil as needed.
12. Place 1 to 2 pancakes onto a plate. Top with a ladle full of lobster sauce. Garnish with fresh tarragon leaves.

Servings: 10
Preparation Time: 60 minutes

If lobster is not on the budget, feel free to substitute with cooked shrimp or seas scallops.

Ricotta Cakes with Poached Eggs, Hollandaise Sauce, and Caviar

The secret to this dish is a perfectly poached egg and a silky smooth sauce. Both are easily accomplished are sure to thrill late night guests.

2   cups ricotta cheese
6   large eggs
1   cup all-purpose flour
½   teaspoon salt
2   tablespoons melted butter
2   tablespoons olive oil

6   egg yolks
    Juice of 1 lemon (about 2 tablespoons)
¾   cup butter (1½ sticks), melted
¼   teaspoon cayenne pepper
¼   teaspoon salt
1   tablespoon finely chopped fresh tarragon leaves

10 large eggs, poached
2   ounces caviar
    Chopped chives

1. Whisk together the ricotta, 6 eggs, flour, salt, and 2 tablespoons of melted butter in a large bowl.
2. Heat 2 tablespoons olive in a skillet over medium high heat.
3. Pour the batter, by ladle into the pan creating several 3-inch diameter pancakes. Cook for 2 to 3 minutes or until golden. Turn and cook for 2 minutes more. Transfer the pancakes to paper toweling. Continue with remaining batter using additional oil as needed.
4. Whisk 6 egg yolks and the lemon juice together in the top of a double boiler (not over heat) until the mixture is thick and doubles in volume.
5. Place the top of the double boiler into the bottom containing simmering water over medium heat. Continue whisking. Make sure that the simmering water does not touch the pan holding the egg mixture or they will scramble.
6. Drizzle in the melted butter in very small amounts, whisking constantly. The sauce will thicken and double in volume again.
7. Remove from the heat and whisk in the cayenne, ¼ teaspoon of salt, and fresh tarragon.
8. Place 1 to 2 pancakes onto a plate. Top with a poached egg. Place a spoon full of sauce on top of the egg. Top with a dab of caviar. Garnish with chopped fresh chives.

Servings: 10
Preparation Time: 60 minutes

For perfectly poached eggs, bring a pot of salted water and 1 teaspoon vinegar to a boil. Crack one egg into a cup. Slide the whole egg into the water. Continue with remaining eggs, making sure not to overcrowd the pan. Cook 3 to 4 eggs at a time. When the water returns to a boil, reduce the heat to low and simmer until the eggs are set, watch carefully and remove the eggs when the yolks are still soft, about 2 to 2½ minutes. Remove the eggs from the water and drain on a paper toweling. Season the eggs with salt and pepper.

POLENTA CAKES with TOASTED CORN and GARLICKY SHRIMP

Savory traces of toasted corn feel right at home in a corn cake. Sautéed shrimp in citrus flavored butter sauce make the perfect topper.

2	tablespoons melted butter
2	ears fresh corn, corn sliced from cob (about 1 cup)
¾	cup all-purpose flour
½	cup yellow cornmeal
1	teaspoon salt
1	teaspoon sugar
½	teaspoon baking powder
½	teaspoon baking soda
1	cup buttermilk
1	large egg
2	to 4 tablespoons olive oil
½	cup butter (1 stick)
4	medium cloves garlic, minced (about 2 teaspoons)
1½	pounds large uncooked shrimp, peeled and deveined (about 24)
	Juice of 1 medium orange (about ⅓ cup)
1	tablespoon Dijon mustard
2	tablespoons chopped fresh cilantro leaves
	Salt and freshly ground pepper
	Sour cream

1. Heat the butter in a skillet over medium high heat. Cook the corn in the butter for 3 to 5 minutes, or until the kernels are golden. Remove from the heat.

2. Combine the flour, cornmeal, salt, sugar, baking powder, and baking soda in a bowl.
3. In a large bowl whisk together the buttermilk and egg.
4. Stir in the corn kernels and butter from the pan. Add the flour mixture.
5. Heat 2 tablespoons of olive oil in a skillet over medium high heat.
6. Pour the batter by ladle into the pan creating several 3-inch diameter pancakes. Cook for 2 to 3 minutes or until golden. Turn and cook for 2 minutes more. Transfer the pancakes to paper toweling. Continue with remaining batter using additional oil as needed.
7. Heat ½ cup butter in a skillet over medium high heat.
8. Cook the garlic in the butter until soft.
9. Stir in the shrimp and cook until opaque in the center.
10. Stir in the orange juice, mustard, and fresh cilantro. Season with salt and pepper.
11. Place 1 to 2 pancakes onto a plate. Top with a shrimp and a spoonful of butter sauce. Garnish with a dollop of sour cream.

Servings: 10
Preparation Time: 60 minutes

Spice up polenta cakes with diced jalapeño or minced chipotle chilis. Substitute with blood orange juice for a really upscale treat.

CROISSANT BREAD PUDDING with PISTACHIO NUTS and WARM MAPLE SYRUP

Buttery croissants are a wonderful base for this easy-to-make comfort dessert. Toast the bread first so that it welcomes the rich custard while it bakes.

6   croissants, cut into 1-inch cubes (about 8 cups)
3   cups milk
3   cups heavy cream
1   tablespoon vanilla extract
8   large eggs
1½   cups granulated sugar
8   ounces pistachio nuts, shelled and chopped (about 2 cups)

1   cup maple syrup
     Vanilla ice cream

Preheat the oven to 375°.

1. Place the bread cubes onto a baking sheet. Toast until golden, about 10 minutes.
2. Combine the milk, cream, vanilla, eggs, and sugar in a large bowl.
3. Spray a large baking dish with vegetable oil spray.
4. Place half of the bread cubes into the baking dish. Cover with half of the milk mixture. Sprinkle half of the nuts over top.
5. Place the remaining bread cubes into the dish. Pour the remaining milk mixture over top. Sprinkle with the remaining nuts. Allow to sit for 15 minutes pushing down the bread cubes to absorb the milk.
6. Bake for 25 to 30 minutes or until the top is golden.
7. Serve with warm maple syrup and a scoop of vanilla ice cream.

Servings: 10
Preparation Time: 20 minutes plus baking

Experiment with any type of bread when creating your own bread pudding.
Day old bread works best and toasting helps the process.
For savory bread puddings pumpernickel and rye add a unique flavor.

Acknowledgments

My first book, *At Home in the Kitchen, The Art of Preparing the Foods You Love to Eat* took me four years to write, re-write, edit and rewrite some more. While working on that project, the seeds of *At Home Entertaining* were already being formed. Even so, publishing two books in eighteen months is an impossible task—unless you have the support of an understanding family, the encouragement of creative and talented friends, a group of very determined recipe testers, and one terrific publishing team.

For those missed lunch dates, late nights of typing and days-in-a-row when a T-shirt and jeans (sans makeup or clean hair) was my dress of choice, I say thank you to my patient and loving hubby. He even had the guts to tell me I looked great! For all of the times that he sampled new and unusual foods (I'm talking about yuca, white bean tapenade, and pine nuts on pasta), I say thanks to Chris for expanding his palate to match my deadline. For mastering the art of preparing dinners on his own, especially home made pasta sauces and baked macaroni and cheese, I say thank you to Jon. When I was writing about food—he was the one in the kitchen preparing it. And, for challenging me to do a better job on this book than the last and for not letting me get away with any shortcuts, I say thanks to Treysers—welcome home!

To my gal pals, Sharon Stiles, Doreen Koenig, and Cindy Greenberg, thanks for all of the brainstorming and long talks about food. Hosting parties with style and panache, these three ladies and their devoted husbands cast their net to include a wide range of friends and family, not only sharing their social skills but also benefiting numerous charities and community projects in the process. How lucky am I to always be included on their invitation lists? Thank you for sharing your expertise, your love, and your patience. You guys are the *best*.

My brother Rich and sister Beth have shared so many family parties, special suppers, and just hangin'-out great times. Nieces Lindsay and Meggie-Mo are so what I would want in daughters—such grace and wisdom. Nephews Rich, John, and Patrick are the best that our youth has to offer. Better yet—I think there are some great cooks in the bunch!

Rachael Bender has single handedly made this book a benchmark for party books for young adults. She has tested recipes, edited party plans, and designed website support that is unequalled. More than that, she is my friend and colleague. This book is better because of Rachael. I wish that all of you had a pal like her.

Linda and Mike O'Bryon, Jen and Iva have shared so many family celebrations, that our families are truly blended. Thank you for your counsel, your caring, and your assistance in promoting the book.

Ron and Julie Pitkin make me the best I can be, through suggestions, layout, editing, and marketing. Everyone at Cumberland is a pleasure to work with. They let me live my dream—and I am thankful.

Susan Schwartzman took a chance on an unknown, diligently working to promote my books to everyone who would listen. Beyond that, she is a caring, sensitive professional who lives her life to help others—I am fortunate to work with her.

My most sincere appreciation goes out to the best group of recipe testers. Through an email message, I asked for anyone interested in participating in this project to send a brief reply. Seventy-five people across the country signed on for the task. We tested all of the recipes (over two hundred and fifty) in just four months. That's saying a lot. Their comments were concise, creative, and cohesive. Most of their suggestions have been included in recipe sidebars and in party presentation plans.

Sharron Jackson, a busy mother of three adorable children (and two out-of-this world puppies) single handedly took on the job of sending out the recipes, collecting, and organizing the worksheets. I would not have been able to make the deadline without her good natured and talented assistance. Sharron—thank you.

Rachael Bender of Pompano Beach, Florida is the co-founder of BlueSuitMom.com, Mom Talk Radio and BSM Media—where she is a web designer, editor, radio show producer, and computer guru. In her spare time she loves to cook vegetarian recipes. Rachael and her husband Dave prepared the most recipes. As our standard, if Dave said that he would make the recipe again, it got the "Five Star Dave Award." I am happy to report that there are a bunch of these included in the book.

Louise Proffer, co-owner of several restaurants in Fort Lauderdale, tested the next largest group of recipes on her husband Paul and their friends. One or two of these may sneak onto one of their menus some day!

PJ Forbes is a cookbook consultant in Virginia Beach, Virginia. She was a great resource when testing recipes for my first cookbook, and tested over thirty recipes in this one. When she's not in the kitchen testing or developing recipes she's out helping people produce cookbooks, learn how to market cookbooks, or selling at bazaars.

The rest of the group is diverse, experienced and great food lovers. Thank you to:

Sherry and Jon Hine of Oakland, Florida are co-owners of Legacy Ferns and my very first fondue guests (over twenty-five years ago). They also supplied another generation of tester with their daughter, Brehan of Orlando, Florida, a sales manager for Gucci International.

Margaret Donkerbrook of Arlington, Virginia is Greg's mom and a weekend chef. Lucky Greg!

Doctors Bobbi and Jim Rathmell (she a pediatrician and he an anesthesiologist), together with two children, live in an old farmhouse in Westford, Vermont.

Teri Wysocki hails from Flemington, New Jersey, and is a research scientist for Johnson and Johnson during the day and mother of three, including Jessica Anne, born 4/19/02.

Mary Ellen Lemm (otherwise known as "Mel") from Plano, Texas, who is a paralegal by day and an avid baker and cook by night!

Lucy Weber is a dear friend and an excellent hostess. Her home is always filled with family and friends—most of who stay for days and weeks on end.

Gail Jordan of Raleigh, North Carolina, is a stay-at-home mom and aspiring screenwriter.

Nellie Shelton and Micki Lindemann are great cooks and terrific fundraisers for groups like the Fort Lauderdale Museum of Art and the Museum of Discovery and Science.

Amy Kendall of Nashville, Tennessee, is a biochemist, "supermom," and aspiring chef. Terri Ravnik of Lubbock, Texas a working mom of two delightful boys. Terry Maly of Olathe, Kansas works part-time while collecting recipes and cookbooks full-time. Frances Anne Hernan is the author of *Triumph over Violence, Diary of a Battered Woman* and *The ABCs of Hiring a Nanny.* Slee Arnold, the publisher of the *Triangle Apartment Guide,* lives in Raleigh, North Carolina, is the mother of two boys, and loves to entertain and cook!

Other testers include Shirley Wong and Ann Huie of Falls Church, Virginia, Floyd Konet in Cleveland, Ohio, Erin Bales from Atlanta, Georgia, Linda Adams of Point Manalapan, Florida, and Teresa Loney of Alexandria, Virginia. Also testing were Rose Dreyfus, Kimberly Drinkwine, Susan Holden, Judy Zimmer and Susan Arch of Fort Lauderdale, Florida, Barbara Peet, Diane Gill, Kelley Buckentine, Chaska, Minnesota, Sandra Shu, and Veronica Boyd.

Last, but certainly not least, thanks to Karey Bowens, who led a group of busy moms belonging to Moms AAT Work Group, an American Airlines Employee Resouce Group in Fort Worth, Texas. They tested a bunch of the recipes that needed a little work—and made sure that I kept them simple as well as sumptuous. Thanks to all!

And now—onto the parties!!

Index